Lessons in

SPIRITUAL

ECONOMICS

From the Bhagavad-gita

Part One

Lessons in

SPIRITUAL ECONOMICS

From the Bhagavad-gita

Part One

Understanding and Solving

the Economic Problem

Dhanesvara Das

This book may be ordered from:

www.spiritual-econ.com or www.dhanesvaradas.com

Readers interested in the subject matter of this book are invited to participate in discussion at http://spiritualeconomics.socialgo.com/ or to correspond with the author at: gitagrad@gmail.com. Replies may be delayed.

Please visit::

www.spiritual-econ.com; www.dhanesvaradas.com; www.gitagrad.org

http://spiritual-econ.blogspot.com

http://gitagrad.blogspot.com

www.varnashrama.org.ua (Russian)

Bhagavad-gita As It Is, Sri Isopanisad, and *Srimad-Bhagavatam* text courtesy of The Bhaktivedanta Book Trust International, Inc. www.krishna.com

Lessons in Spiritual Economics from the Bhagavad-gita
  - Part I Understanding and Solving the Economic Problem
© 2009-2010 Dhanesvara Das (Don Rousse). All rights reserved.

ISBN: 1451589719

Dedicated

To my spiritual father and eternal master,
His Divine Grace A. C. Bhaktivedanta Swami Prabhupada
who trained me in the spiritual science and blessed me
with the realization of these concepts, and

to my material father and mother,
Armand and Bertha Rousse,
who gave me this body, a good and loving home,
and a good education,
all of which have helped me to understand
the concepts of Spiritual Economics

Invocation

Let me offer my most humble obeisances
at the lotus feet of my spiritual master,
His Divine Grace A. C. Bhaktivedanta Swami Prabhupada,
who has given me the shelter of his eternal service.
His service is my refuge from the onslaught
of this material world. Let me then offer my obeisances
to the spiritual masters in disciplic succession who have
paved the way for Krishna Consciousness in this world:
Srila Bhaktisiddhanta Saraswati Thakura Prabhupada,
Srila Bhaktivinoda Thakura, and the Six Goswamis
of Vrindavana, each of whom have carried the
message of Love from Sri Krishna Chaitanya Mahaprabhu,
and rendered it suitable for the ears of their contemporaries
and posterity. They have all tasted this relishable fruit and
have passed it along for us to taste as *maha-prasadam*.
We pray for their blessings to make it suitable for our
contemporaries and all those who are willing to
stand in the light of Lord Chaitanya's benediction moon.
Although we are fallen and without qualification we pray also
to be blessed to manifest Sri Krishna's instructions as a
living philosophy in its full splendor, creating a complete
Krishna culture for the benefit of all of the conditioned
souls of this world, now and in the
many years to come.

Table of Contents

Preface

This is not your typical book on economics. Those expecting to find the usual economic jargon such as hedge funds, derivatives, exchange rates, balance of trade, deficit spending, monetary policy, and so on, may be disappointed. But perhaps not. Instead of working with these typically dry and often sterile ideas I approach economics in a way that is more realistic and more alive than these concepts can ever hope to be. I approach economics on the basis of consciousness and relationships based on that consciousness: relationships between people, between people and the earth along with all of her other inhabitants, and between people and God. These are the things that are the most real to us and that give meaning to our lives. The manner in which we handle our economic affairs, which is what most economists concern themselves with, is but a reflection of our consciousness and of the way we see or understand life and our place in it. In that sense economics is the most visible demonstration of our ideas of life. If we desire to change the manner in which we handle our economics we must first understand the conceptions of life underlying our economic behaviors; making changes there and living accordingly, will automatically adjust our economics.

While our economic behaviors do reflect a particular way of life, they may not be, and in many or even most cases are not, the ways in which people think about the world. At first glance that may seem to be a contradictory statement based on what I've said above, but it is not. I present it in that way for the purpose of calling to attention the fact that in our modern world we no longer live according to a specific philosophy of life. Instead we live according to an economic method, or more specifically, a monetary method, while at the same time professing to believe in quite different ideas than are reflected in our economic behavior. Our ways of thinking about the world and our behavior in the world have become dissociated by our economic system. Hardly anyone notices this fact to say nothing about understanding the consequences. Moreover the outcome of such dissociation is significant both in our personal lives and in society as a whole. These differences between thought and action and their attendant consequences will be examined throughout the pages of this book.

My approach to economics is even further removed from typical economic discussions in that I examine economic behavior from a spiritual perspective.

1

All living things in this world are first and foremost spiritual beings and the suit of material energy that they wear has a very specific influence on their consciousness, meaning their perceptions, thinking and behavior. Those influences and behaviors are very visibly displayed in their economic dealings, all of which will be thoroughly explained by reference to the teachings of the *Bhagavad-gita*.

The basis for my analysis is the Gaudiya Vaishnava spiritual tradition as popularized worldwide through the books of my spiritual master and eternal guide His Divine Grace A.C. Bhaktivedanta Swami Prabhupada (Srila Prabhupada). He was the founder and *acharya* of the International Society for Krishna Consciousness (ISKCON), popularly known worldwide as The Hare Krishna Movement. Far from being a newly created religion as some people think, this spiritual tradition reaches back into antiquity more than five thousand years. It is founded on the eternal knowledge revealed to human kind in the Vedas. The Vedas are a vast body of work, requiring a life of study to master. While in earlier times people had sufficient capacity and time for this, modern man most certainly does not. We should not despair however since the most essential and indeed the most elevated elements of the spiritual science are brought to us in four essential works: the *Sri Isopanisad, Bhagavad-gita, Srimad-Bhagavatam* and *Sri Chaitanya-charitamrita*. The introduction of the spiritual science begins with the *Isopanisad* and *Bhagavad-gita* and is continued in the *Srimad-Bhagavatam*.

The title *Bhagavad-gita* translates as "The Song of God." The speaker of the *Gita* is Lord Krishna, who is accepted in the Vedic tradition as the Supreme Lord. If we do not accept Krishna as God then the *Bhagavad-gita* makes no sense. The Vedas acknowledge that there can only be one God, although He is known in different ways to different people. We cannot say that Krishna is a "Hindu God" any more than we can say that the sun while over Germany is a "German sun" and while over America is an "American sun." The sun cannot be so designated and neither can God. If this concept is challenging, the reader may substitute whatever name of God he prefers while reading the text and the meaning will not be disturbed. Or the reader may temporarily put aside such differences and return to his own preferences after having read the book.

Srimad-Bhagavatam translates as "The Beautiful Story of the Personality of Godhead." Its subject matter is *bhagavat-tattva vijnana*, or the science of God, which is considered in minute detail in the 54 volumes of this great work. The *Chaitanya-charitamrta* brings this science to its summit with the teachings of Sri Chaitanya Mahaprabhu, the greatest and most munificent *avatar* of the fifteenth century.

In his books Srila Prabhupada followed the ancient spiritual tradition of elucidating each individual verse with a commentary. In these commentaries he wove the threads of the philosophy of Gaudiya Vaishnavism into a complete philosophical tapestry that beautifully displays a succinct understanding of reality, both material and spiritual. This includes our relationship with God and all of His varieties of energies that are manifest in this phenomenal world in the form of plants, animals, the physical elements, the cosmos, and all other phenomena that lie beyond our imperious gaze of inspection. In this way Srila Prabhupada presented an entirely new worldview, or spiritual paradigm, before his readers. This is a worldview that at once satisfies the intellect as well as the heart. It explains the mysteries of life and creates a singularly unique perspective from which to see the world. This vantage point, unavailable to mankind from other philosophical and religious traditions, permits one to penetrate the labyrinth of confusion that so perplexes today's society, providing insights into solutions for modern problems.

The usefulness of such a spiritual science in dealing with the issues of the modern day has been elaborately described by Sri R. Subramaniam, the Deputy Director of Research in the Lok Sabha, the Secretariat of India's National Parliament. Writing in appreciation of Srila Prabhupada's presentation of the *Srimad-Bhagavatam* he says:

> A strange feature of the modern world is that in spite of vast advances in science and technology and the establishment of a good number of institutions for human welfare, mankind has not found true peace and happiness. Knowledge of material sciences and arts has increased tremendously in recent times, and millions of volumes on each fill the libraries the world over. People and leaders in every country are generally well versed in these arts and sciences, but despite their efforts human society everywhere continues to be in turmoil and distress. The reason is not far to seek. It is that they have not learned the science of God, the most fundamental of every other art and science, and fail to apply it to the facts of life. The need is, therefore, to know and live this science if mankind is not only to survive but flower into a glorious existence. To teach this science of God to people everywhere and to aid them in their progress and development towards the real goal of life, *Srimad-Bhagavatam* is most eminently fitted. In fact, this great ancient work of *Vyasadeva* will fill this need of the modern times, for it is a cultural presentation for the re-spiritualization of the entire human society.

This book, *Spiritual Economics*, is presented as a tool by which to learn how to practically live the science of God. The practice of spiritual economics is the practice of bhakti yoga, which should not be confused as idle meditation with little practical value. As the reader will see, it is a most practical book for solving the problems of life, which are so numerous in today's modern world. It deals with consciousness, the foundation of all human behavior, and it is written for those who are concerned with both the social and economic issues of the day, which include as a subset most of the ecological problems we now face.

I have assumed that the reader is unfamiliar with the Vedic literatures on which this book is based and have therefore taken care to explain the fundamental concepts in some detail; and hopefully in a manner that will also be refreshing for those with previous acquaintance. Since the *Isopanisad* and the *Bhagavad-gita* introduce a worldview that is vastly different from that of the current dominant culture, the complete significance of this work may not be fully and immediately apparent to those who are new to the spiritual science. The reader should not assume that a foundation of thought from other religious traditions such as Judeo-Christian, Buddhist or the so-called New Age, will adequately prepare one for this work. The differences between these worldviews requires study and time to assimilate, after which one will be better equipped to draw conclusions. I recommend that the reader thoroughly study the *Bhagavad-gita As It Is* by A. C. Bhaktivedanta Swami, on which this work is based.

Although this work focuses on economics and introduces a completely new economic theory based upon the principles of consciousness, it is not written for economists. Neither do I anticipate that many economists will find it very meaningful. Some may find it mildly interesting from a theoretical or philosophical perspective, but I have no doubts that most will dismiss it as idyllic sentimentalism of no practical value in the real world. Their world after all, is the "real" one (to their way of thinking at least), the one that deals with the immediacy of the hard facts of life. They may also dismiss this effort for not being sufficiently scholarly. They would be right. I am not credentialed in the field; I have often been forced to use secondary rather than primary sources; and my treatment of many of the issues is not exhaustive from a historical perspective. This book is intended for the layman who is seeking solutions that professional economists do not provide to the existential, economic and environmental problems arising from the current economic paradigm. It is also written for the average person who sees nothing but a dead-end at his job and wonders what his future will be, as well as those who may no longer have a job and simply struggle to survive.

There is one inescapable fact that must not go unnoticed: despite all the posturing and fancy theories, the economic profession as a whole has not solved the problem of providing for the most basic needs of humanity—food, clothing and shelter. Indeed, by the application of their collective efforts things continue to get worse with each passing year. It is a hidden irony that while most professionals work to serve others who are in need, professional economists do not. Carpenters build houses for people who need a place to live, doctors care for those who are ill, cooks whip up delicious meals for the hungry, and mechanics fix the cars of those who don't know a carburetor from a radiator. But do economists ply their trade for those who are in need? To relieve the plight of those who don't have enough money? Hardly it seems. Although the work may sometimes go on in that name, we find exactly the opposite result.

The reason for this is that economists work to preserve the status quo for people who have more money than they can reasonably use and who hire them. Somehow these employers are only interested in increasing their wealth unlimitedly at any-and-everyone else's expense. One must suspect that is the objective because that certainly is the result. I do not fault those in the economics profession personally, however, because they, like the rest of us, require a job and financial support. They simply do what they are paid to do. If they dare to think for themselves or apply discerning intelligence to their work by questioning the workings of their own craft, they may suddenly find themselves unemployed, like Joseph Stiglitz, the former chief economist for the World Bank. He had the audacity to speak the truth to outsiders on various occasions, pointing out that the policies of that leviathan were severely damaging everybody they were purportedly trying to help.

One doesn't need to be a weatherman to know which way the wind blows. Neither does one need the stature of a chief economist to understand the results of economic forces in his own life. In dozens of books and all over the internet one can find a solid explanation of the facts by many amateur and credentialed economic analysts who can clearly understand the situation as it is. A few honest professionals have also come clean on this point and have clearly stated that today's economic methods are actually intended to take from the poor and give to the rich. One such maverick economist, E. F. Schumacher, has taken his profession to task, writing: "The conventional wisdom of what is now taught as economics by-passes the poor, the very people for whom development is really needed...An entirely new system of thought is needed, a system based on attention to people, and not primarily attention to goods...If it [economics] cannot get beyond its vast abstractions, the national income, the rate of growth, capital/output ratio, input-output analysis, labour mobility, capital accumulation; if it cannot get beyond all this and make contact with the human realities of poverty, frustration, alienation, despair, breakdown, crime, escapism, stress, congestion, ugliness, and spiritual death, then let us scrap economics and start fresh. Are there not indeed enough 'signs of the times' to indicate that a new start is needed?"[1] Indeed there are. We offer this book as one such fresh start, a new system of thought that is based on attention, not just to people and their needs on this earth, but to the entirety of all living beings, serving both their spiritual, as well as their material needs.

To give of oneself in the spirit of devotion is an important principle in spiritual life. We actually receive more in giving than the person receiving. Giving *of* ourselves means giving *to* ourselves. I consider this book as an "assignment," the information being given to me for the purpose of teaching it to others. Since Spiritual Economics encourages a gift economy based on devotional service I am making this book available, as far as possible, for free from my websites. In the gift economy everyone offers their services to others without consideration of immediate exchange or direct reciprocation. However, if you feel you have been blessed by what you read here you may want to participate in the gift economy by offering a gift to another person in the mood of "paying it forward." It can, but does not have to be money, and may be your time or expertise in the service of others. If you do pay forward we would be happy to hear the story so that we may use it to encourage the circle of gifting.

Now that this philosophy of spiritual economics has been put into writing it has become my task to demonstrate the practicality of the idea of a spiritual economy that functions on the basis of love (this idea will be more clear after reading volume 2 of this work, "Creating a Culture of Satisfaction to Heal the World"). I am sometimes challenged as a dreamer whose ideas are utopian. Indeed, these ideas are utopian. I will remind the reader that utopian does not mean impossible. It means to live an ideal. And why not have an ideal society when the means to achieve it are right before us? Is there any benefit to be had in creating yet another mundane community based on illusory conceptions of life? For my part I am convinced that the message of the *Bhagavad-gita* is the most practical way to live and through this book I invite as many as possible to join me in creating and living this utopia. The world is in great need of an ideal to show the way out of the hopeless mire of modern economics and the infinite problems it creates. The way to do that is to simply live a life of love according to the instructions of Sri Krishna and the philosophy He presents in the *Bhagavad-gita*. Our efforts to do so take place at our Gitagrad communities, where we are practicing the economics of love, spiritual economics. (Information about our Gitagrad communities is offered in Appendix B). It is my hope that upon reading this book you will be encouraged to join in re-spiritualizing the world by bringing *dharma* into your life, particularly the practice of the *yuga-dharma*, and do your part to establish transcendental communities that lead the way out of the economics of ignorance.

Conventions Used in this Book

I often give emphasis to selected sections of quotes. If the emphasis is contained in the original quote I will note it as such. Otherwise all emphasis should be understood to be mine.

For brevity I have used a convention with citations to the main references of this work: the *Bhagavad-gita* and *Srimad-Bhagavatam*. Citations of only two parts, i.e., (2.4) refer to chapter and verse of the *Bhagavad-gita* specifically. Citations of three parts, i.e., (7.1.14) refer to canto, chapter and verse of the *Srimad-Bhagavatam*. Other citations include the book title.

Appreciations

Many people have helped bring this book into print and I would like to recognize their contributions. First I would like to thank His Holiness Niranjana Swami who invited me to Ukraine and gave his support for my efforts there. This provided the opportunity to speak frequently to receptive audiences, which provided important support and encouragement for this work. Next I would like to thank my interpreters Jaya Mangala Das, Bhakta Maksim Artemenko and Paritosani Citra Devi Dasi, without whose selfless help I could have done nothing in Ukraine. Thanks to: Samba Das, for his editing work, and also Vijitatma Das, Veda Priya Devi Dasi, and Bhaktin Lida for their translation of the Russian edition; and to Bhakta Oleg of Mykolaiv who provided support for my writing. I am very grateful to all of the Krishna devotees throughout Ukraine for their love and support. I am grateful to Chaitanya Chandra Charan Das (Russia) and Chaitanya Chandra Das (India) for reviewing the book, and to Bhakta Nelas of Lithuania for the cover design. And finally, I want to express my deep gratitude to my godbrothers and dear friends Prabhupada Das (Paul Rattray), Sri Nandanandana Das (Stephen Knapp), and Madan Mohan Das (Mark Birenbaum) for their friendship and very helpful, personal support and encouragement during the development of the concepts of spiritual economics.

I must explicitly state that the contents of this work are not to be construed in any way as the official position of ISKCON. I alone am responsible for the content.

Hare Krishna
Gaura Purnima Day, 14 March 2006 (Month of Vishnu, 519 Gaurabda era)
Dnyepropetrovsk, Ukraine

Introduction

In September 2008, the financial markets were in a tailspin. Trillions of dollars in stock value vanished, companies collapsed, and the bastion of free enterprise and capitalism, the United States, began socializing its largest economic institutions. In an unprecedented move, the Federal Government took control of the two U.S. mortgage giants Freddie Mac and Fannie Mae, who had been battling since the previous year to stave off crisis. Congress passed special legislation allowing the Treasury Department to come to their aid with billions of dollars. That month also saw the failure of two of the largest investment banks—Lehman Brothers and Merrill Lynch. Lehman filed the biggest bankruptcy in history, but Merrill Lynch was saved from the same fate by Bank of America's purchase. Then the U.S. government essentially bought an 80 percent stake in the largest insurance company in America, American International Group, Inc. (AIG), for $85 billion. The drama continued as investment banks Goldman Sachs and Morgan Stanley were put under Federal control with the idea that this move would help rescue the ailing U.S. finance system. The Securities and Exchange Commission also did their part by temporarily banning short-selling of 799 financial institution stocks.

As spectacular as it all was, there were a few who could see it coming. Less than a month earlier, a former chief economist of the International Monetary Fund predicted that some "big" investment banks would go belly up.[1] The IMF director general Dominique Strauss-Kahn said: "We have to expect that there may be in the coming weeks and coming months other financial institutions with some problems."[2] That was an understatment. Hundreds of banks, what to speak of millions of mortgage holders defaulted within the next year. The old saying "It ain't over till its over" especially applies in the case of financial crisis.

It was, and continues to be, the worst financial crisis since the Great Depression of the 1930s. By early 2010 it is clear that the pain is far from over—more than four million mortgage foreclosures are expected in the U.S. during the year of 2010. The dominoes continue to fall in countries around the world, with Greece, Ireland, Portugal, Iceland and Latvia being the most egregious examples of monetary policy run amok.

However well our financial experts can accurately predict these crises they don't seem to know quite what to do about them, either before or after the fact.

On September 18th 2008 Senate Majority Leader Harry Reid said the U.S. Congress was unlikely to pass new legislation to overhaul financial regulations that year because "no one knows what to do." He added that neither Federal Reserve Chairman Ben Bernanke nor Treasury Secretary Henry Paulson "know what to do but they are trying to come up with ideas."[3] It seems that Reid was uninformed because the very next day Paulson produced a plan—the mother of all bail outs—$700 billion to allow the government to buy bad loans, taking them off the books of financial firms. Over the weekend the measure was given to lawmakers who were told "give us the money—and NOW!" The White House insisted that there was no time to debate the measure, or consider alternatives that might benefit Main Street and not just Wall Street, and that Congress must authorize it immediately or there was risk of further "unsettling of global financial markets." The price tag for this fix is far into the trillions. But worse yet, after giving away such an unfathomable sum of money the problem hasn't been fixed. Into 2010 bank lending continued to decrease at record rates, and without banks pumping money into the economy it will not get better. America and Europe have begun to experience belt-tightening austerity measures in the social sector, like countries in the southern hemisphere experienced in the 80s and 90s.

"What exactly is the economic problem?" is *the* question; a problem that is not understood cannot be solved. Is the problem the millions of bad mortgage loans, or is it the less-mentioned outstanding $1 *quadrillion* (1,000 trillion) in derivatives trading that also threaten many banks and brokerage firms?[4] Do the problems stem from the fact that safeguards established in the 1930s depression, such as the Glass-Steagall Act, were foolishly rescinded? Is the problem isolated in an individual sector of the financial markets or is it systemic? What about all of that rhetoric of the "invisible hand of the free market" so widely propagated during the rush to a global economy over the past two decades? If the free market works the magic we were led to believe why don't we just let the free market sort out the mess? Let the banks that created the mess fail, and start over again. Is there a recovery or not? What exactly is a jobless recovery? And how can there be an actual recovery when millions of people are destitute? There continue to be problems that are dealt with on a piecemeal basis, but the complete and final solution can only be found once we understand the very root of the problem. What exactly is the economic problem and where does it originate? That is the question answered by this book.

It seems that the busy people trying to find solutions have overlooked the most significant aspect of the problem. They treat the issue as a money problem, or a lack of regulatory oversight, and they offer money and regulatory solutions accordingly. But money alone didn't create the problem and money and regulations cannot solve it.

Where did the problem actually start? Well, modern economics is not a system of nature, like gravity, whose laws are infallible. It is a man-made system, and human beings are fallible, if nothing else. Therefore at the root of a faulty economic problem we find: people. More specifically, many if not most of our economic problems are caused by a people who have a particular consciousness that leads them to cheat, exploit, defraud, and steal in order to enhance their wealth. Good old-fashioned greed, for example, is being credited as one of the primary causes of the current economic crisis. The consciousness of others leads them to competitive economic activity, and yet others to cooperative and egalitarian methods of solving the economic problem. Therefore if we want to fully understand the current economic problem and how to solve it we must first understand people and the nature of consciousness.

To some, that sounds even more complex than solving the financial mess. We've been trying to understand people for millennia and to this day there is no satisfactory gestalt.

Fortunately there is hope. The Vedas, the world's oldest scriptures, offer a very clear understanding. Overlooked or misunderstood by Westerners, they explain human behavior very well. They do so by adding the single most important element that has been missing from most Western models—that we are spiritual beings who have a dual material-spiritual nature; the Vedas further inform us how the material energies of this world affect the consciousness of human beings.

Although we are spiritual beings we have chosen to live in this material world to fulfill our desire to contact the material energy. We want to touch it, taste it, feel it, and see it, in all of its innumerable permutations. That fact figures significantly into the manner in which we handle our economic affairs. It is also the key that will allow us solve our economic problems.

The basic spiritual truths on which we base our economic analysis are found in the *Bhagavad-Gita*. Although it is relatively unknown in the West the *Bhagavad-Gita* is revered as one of the foremost scriptures in the world by more than one billion people. The Gita itself explains that the speaker, Sri Krishna, is none other than God. According to Vedic tradition the Lord Himself visits this world periodically to instruct human beings in the spiritual science, and did so just 5,000 years ago. If we do not accept the speaker of the Gita as God then than all manners of convoluted interpretation are required for it to make sense. Saints in the line of the *Gaudiya Vaishnavas* encourage us to accept the speaker of *Bhagavad-Gita*, Krishna, as God, if only theoretically, in order for us to learn the truths of the Gita, and we follow that recommendation herein.

Still, understanding the *Bhagavad-Gita* is not so easy. Our efforts to do so are hampered by our cultural conditioning. We may read the words of the Gita but the meaning may remain inaccessible to us because we try to understand it in the context of our current culture. We necessarily interpret what we read according to the material conceptions of life by which we are conditioned. Instead the Gita is meant to be understood in its own context. Therefore we need a method that will help us to achieving the proper understanding. My approach herein is to look at words that are familiar to us in a particular cultural context, to strip them of their familiar meaning, and then show their essence in a different way.

Economics is one such word. In this work I discuss what I call "spiritual economics," or economics based on the *Bhagavad-Gita*. The idea that economics is discussed in the Gita often brings quizzical looks since there is nothing in the text for translators to render as the word "economics." Moreover the two words together seem to constitute an oxymoron. But economics and economic activity are definitely found there. For example, everyone can appreciate that all economic activity has a result. In our current culture that result is measured in terms of money and so economics is typically understood as the dealings of money. I would like to point out that this understanding of economics is a relatively recent one since money as a transactional currency did not make its appearance until some time around 8-600 BCE, and then only in some parts of the world. Prior to that time economic activity also had a result, but it was measured differently. Economics therefore is not inherently synonymous with money. While the speaker of the Gita, Sri Krishna, does not say anything specifically about economics or money, He certainly has a lot to say about the results of activity. As it turns out, how we get and what we do with the results of our activity has a very significant relationship to our spiritual growth and development.

Another item of economic interest is demand. Almost everyone is familiar with the economic relationship between supply and demand: the supply will increase or decrease as the demand changes, according to the "law of the marketplace." Sri Krishna also says quite a lot about demand in the pages of the Gita. Many times He refers to the desires and longings of the person in materialistic consciousness. Our desires, which can be thought of as "demands" for material things, also have a very significant relationship to our spiritual growth and development.

Not coincidentally, this same method of "reframing" familiar concepts is employed throughout the Gita itself. The best example is our own existence. People typically think of themselves as the body but Sri Krishna reframes our existence as the spiritual element, or soul within. There are other phenomena that we think of in a particular way according to the dictates of our culture that are similarly reframed by the philosophy of the Gita.

It is these lessons about activity and desires, among others, that I gather together to provide the understanding of spiritual economics. The term "spiritual economics" means two things: first, an understanding of the spiritual nature of the human being and how the influences of the material energy affect his consciousness, which provides a basis for analyzing past and present economic activity; and second, the economic system that is created by the Lord and offered to humankind as a method for dealing with the material necessities of life. By following its precepts we can easily satisfy our material needs. But this is actually a side-benefit, not the objective of the endeavor, which is to bring us closer to God. His methods of economics are not a matter of money and commerce. Rather, they are an exchange of love—love that is demonstrated by the interactions between the Lord and His devotees. It is a method by which we can develop a pure state of consciousness that will allow us to enter into the higher spiritual realms. Actions performed under the banner of spiritual economics are not at all material activity. They are entirely spiritual and constitute the practice of *bhakti yoga*, or the yoga of devotion.

Some Elements of Economics

Generally economics is thought of as the workings of global finance and commerce by highly-trained specialists, but it can also be much less than that, and for most people it is. The word economics comes from the Greek *oeconomia*, which means household. Originally it referred simply to the manner in which people satisfied their most basic needs of food, clothing and shelter. This is what constitutes economics for the average person. How we solve our economic problem of obtaining food, clothing and shelter is the basic economic question and history offers us many examples of ways to do that. The present method of a cash economy is only one of many possible options.

Another simple way of understanding the idea of economics is to consider it in terms of our relationships. In our everyday relationships we generally do not put money (cash transactions) between ourselves and those we love, such as family members and close friends. People generally see close relations as extensions of themselves, and exchanges are typically offered as gifts of love. This is particularly so in what we call the "nuclear family"—parents and children, and perhaps other blood relatives, living under the same roof. However, as our relationships become more distant we introduce money into exchanges. Why? Because our culture doesn't teach us the social mores for sharing with others in the same way that we share with our families.

Western philosophy has raised the individual to the pinnacle of importance in society and has further set him apart from all others, even isolating him, by defining the concept of unlimited private ownership and fixing that concept in law. By legal definition what is "mine" is not "yours," and vice-versa. People become separated and isolated from each other, contributing significantly to a sense of alienation and impersonalism. Individuals are thus set against each other in their interests. This fact alone is responsible for much of the neuroses and strife in today's world. There is no longer any social contract consisting of duty or obligation between the members of society. It is every man, or rather, in today's "progressive" culture, it is all persons for themselves.

Taking is not always a brute business. In many ways it has become a "civilized" affair in which some people take the productive efforts of others by means of creating an unfair advantage. This is considered shrewd business in the capitalist way of thinking. In this valueless concept "successful" people who have achieved wealth through any means are highly respected. In modern society we now value things over people. Wealth and money are important, and our relationships are determined by it. If we can demonstrate good ability to get or control wealth we are offered respect regardless of any other personal shortcomings. Such is the nature of a materialistic society.

By contrast, under the concept of spiritual economics, the functions of the economy are based on social relationships and an informal social contract with corresponding duties. This system is secured not by laws created by men, but by voluntary personal commitment by all sections of the social body to the principles given by God. It is their understanding of the spiritual nature of life, and their dedication to the service of the Lord that serves as the binding contract. Never-ending legislation that is ever-evaded by the conniving is not required.

The Concept of Spiritual Economics

In writing about spiritual economics my purpose is to distinguish it in its character, application and results, from traditional or "material economics." Spiritual economics is understood in light of spiritual knowledge, particularly the definitions and teachings of the *Gaudiya Vaishnava* tradition of India, and based primarily upon *Sri Isopanisad, Bhagavad-Gita As It Is, Srimad-Bhagavatam* and *Sri Chaitanya-charitamrta* as translated and commented upon by Bhaktivedanta Swami.

Spiritual and material economics are to be distinguished by the same differences that separate or characterize the qualities of matter and spirit, to wit: the spiritual element is personal, eternal, fully cognizant and blissful, complete in every respect without lack of any kind and is eternally connected with the Supreme fountainhead of all that be. The material element is impersonal, temporary, existing in a state of ignorance and is without happiness or bliss. It is perceived to be incomplete in itself, due to its being separated from the efficient or supreme cause. Material economics is characterized by the qualities of matter: it is temporary and always changing, founded and maintained in deception and ignorance, and results in misery; Spiritual economics on the other hand, based on a spiritual conception of life, is eternal in nature, it increases and supports our knowledge of spiritual truth and reality, and results in happiness, even bliss, for all of its practitioners.

All living beings are spiritual in nature and are complete with all spiritual qualities. However, when they are born into the material realm and identify with the material coverings of the body and mind, that identification causes them to assume the qualities of the material energy as described above. The living beings attempt to compensate for the resulting quality of incompleteness by possessing increasing amounts of material things. The present economic system is arranged to aid those in material consciousness in their development of a material conception of life. On the other hand, spiritual economics is arranged to aid those in spiritual consciousness in the development of a spiritual conception of life. Material economics promotes a consciousness of lack and the need to "get." Spiritual economics promotes a consciousness of completeness and the joy of giving. It is important to understand that spiritual economics refers to more than an economic system; it reflects a state of consciousness. It is the consciousness of an individual who is fully abiding by the principles of the *Bhagavad-Gita*, and the individual's practice of spiritual economics is the most visible hallmark of such.

Readers Interested in Spiritual Economics

We might ask why those interested in the *Bhagavad-Gita* would be interested in economics, or if indeed economics can be made to be spiritual. To many the expression is a contradiction of terms. Those who study the *Bhagavad-Gita* are generally interested in spiritual pursuits, not economics. Yet there are several reasons why they should be interested. First of all, modern society is arranged in such a way as to force everyone to deal with economics. For most people, taking care of their bodily needs and desires consumes all of their waking energy, leaving little time for anything else. The self-realized sages advise us to live simply and save time for self-realization, but for many, modern life simply doesn't permit that. Most people don't earn enough to take care of life's most basic demands even if they work the majority of their waking hours. There are some who want to give more attention to their personal or spiritual interests but cannot due to their work commitments. Whether we like it or not we live in an economic culture. Are we simply meant to work for a lifetime and then die? While in our current culture many people do, that is not the recommended use of this rare form of human life. What's the solution to this problem? Following the method of economics as suggested by Sri Krishna in the *Bhagavad-Gita*. This method of spiritual economics can solve our economic problems easily, and simultaneously provide a good amount of free time to be used for spiritual and other personal pursuits.

This book will be of interest to several other groups of people, beginning with those who are concerned with the social issues of the day, which are first and foremost the economic ones. The massive protests wherever the World Bank, and IMF meet, are due to the disadvantages these institutions foist upon the weaker elements of society. The economic analysis made in *Spiritual Economics* shows in the most practical way how our economic affairs can be managed to achieve a better world. Another group interested in social issues who would find this book of interest are feminists who conclude that the current state of affairs arises from what has been identified as a patristic culture. Is it true that the male energy is overly aggressive? No. But the male who is overly influenced by the energy of ignorance is. There is such a thing as a male influenced by the energy of goodness, which gives us the shining hero who uses his strength to protect, who does good and punishes evil. The human psychology explained in *Spiritual Economics* reframes the masculine-feminine debate into one of spiritual beings (both male and female) behaving in different ways according to the various influences of the material energy.

Others who can find solutions in this book are environmentalists who struggle for a wholesale, not piecemeal, solution. By saving one forest or one species here and there, the work will never be done in time. Environmental issues are, first and foremost, issues of consciousness, and secondly economic issues. People pollute because their consciousness is polluted. This leads them to use the environment as a dumping ground for "externalizing" the costs of cleaning up after industrial and social practices. The environment is the place where all of our refuse goes when we throw it "away," but as the graffiti philosophers poignantly remind us "there is no *away*." It all stays here on earth, with us. As we too often hear, the environment cannot be cleaned up because it will "cost too much." Why, for example, is the Amazon rain forest being cut down at an alarming rate, and who is going to pay the estimated $33 billion to repair it? Who gets and keeps the money resulting from this activity (economics) is the answer to both of those questions. Solving the economic problem by the method of spiritual economics simultaneously offers a solution to *all* environmental problems.

Additionally *Spiritual Economics* will be interesting to students of psychology, the social sciences and religion, due to the novel and unique manner in which the human psychological-spiritual condition is explained. Other interested readers will include those who analyze the shadowy side of central banks, the machinations of paper money and its controllers, the IMF, etc. and find conspiracies. For those who are willing to go where others are afraid to even look, *Spiritual Economics* reveals the answer to "whodunit" and explains why it is happening the way it is.

The Plan of the Book

Human behavior has puzzled thinkers for centuries. Animals everywhere follow the same instincts of nature—dogs anywhere in the world behave like dogs, as do cats, sparrows or deer. The human being on the other hand is all over the map. He is both saint and sinner, loving and hateful, greedy and generous. Philosophers have speculated endlessly about why man behaves as he does, but the speculation needn't go on any longer. The *Bhagavad-Gita* and *Srimad Bhagavatam* very capably explain the full spectrum of human behaviors. Since our concern here is man's economic activity we begin with first understanding man and his dual material-spiritual nature; we look at the nature of his original spiritual consciousness and how it is affected by contact with the material energy. We learn how the material energy can be categorized as a combination of three qualities of nature: goodness, passion and ignorance. How the human being is conditioned by contact with these energies explains why he can behave either as a divine or demonic personality. Other aspects of human nature, such as lust, envy and greed, figure into his economic behavior, especially in light of the current day and present economic turmoil, and we will examine the origins of these in the second chapter.

In the next three chapters we will examine in detail how the material energies of goodness, passion and ignorance affect man's economic behavior. Formerly, due to the influence of goodness, there were all-inclusive egalitarian societies all over the world where no person is left without. Very few or any of these remain intact today, and deliberately so. The influences of the modern age erode the values on which they are based and we will trace out that process at the end of the chapter on the economics of goodness. Passion characterizes the modern era, a quality that encourages us to be more, do more, and have more. Those passionate influences replace cooperation with competition, the idea that 'may the better man win,' and a winner-take-all mentality. This way of approaching economic activity however, has corresponding negative influences on people, society, and the environment.

From the modern era to the post-modern era our economic practices vary from those of passion to ignorance. It is the influence of ignorance that inspires predatory economic practices that wring profit from suffering, chaos and death, practices that are now observed all over the world. Excessive greed, profiteering at others' expense, exploitation of the earth, the animals and the people, are all symptoms of the influence of the quality of ignorance. The observable trend over the past six centuries has been from goodness, to passion, and to the present influence of increasing ignorance, a trend that has no opposing influences. We trace out that path and how it has been deliberately created despite the continued protestations of the mass of people. If the people don't want it, how then can it happen? Due to the influences of the age, which can be changed if we so will.

The economics of the late twentieth century have been described as predatory capitalism or vulture capitalism. It is a system of exploitation and is founded on atheism. In chapter six we examine the economics of atheism, the illusions on which it is based, and the machinations of the monetary system that are the tools of its expression.

The trend and its influences has an apparent cause which are those whom we might call the "agents of destiny" or the "powers-that-be." In fact they have led society down a path of destruction and have manipulated the economic system over the centuries into a weapon that is now being used to control and exploit anything and everything, causing great harm, even large-scale death, to people and the environment. It would seem as though those who deliberately create destruction and death for economic gain are mad, or even worse, demonic. We want to know: what is the consciousness that gives rise to such deadly and destructive behavior? To understand that we examine the two major types of consciousness in chapter seven—the divine and demonic.

In the final chapter of this first volume we return to the question "what is the economic problem and how can we solve it?" Having examined the nature of consciousness and its influence on economic behavior throughout history we can clearly answer the question. Moreover, we now understand what is needed to fix the economic problems—all of them—and create an economics that is beneficial to all, that cares for the environment, and for all future generations. The answers are all there, given in the time-tested Vedas, the operating manual for the universe. The only thing left to resolve then is *if* we will apply to solution.

An explanation of the spiritual nature of human beings, the influences of the material energy on the behavior of economic man, the historical trends and our present economic course, the factual economic problem, and its solution, together constitute Part One of *Spiritual Economics*: "Understanding and Solving the Economic Problem."

In Part Two of *Spiritual Economics*: "Creating a Culture of Satisfaction to Heal the World," we present the concept of a spiritual economics as prescribed by the *Bhagavad-Gita* and *Srimad-Bhagavatam*. We begin with essential background material explaining the nature of *karma* (action and reaction), its relationship to our economic endeavors, and its implications for the bondage or evolution of the soul. We then examine the nature of, and differences between material and spiritual love, and how they are actual basis for all economic activity. Next we carefully examine the instructions for action in *Bhagavad-Gita* and find in them an explanation for a complete economy of abundance, providing sufficiently for the needs of all living beings, and by which our very ordinary activities can become acts of devotion that carry us to a life of happiness and satisfaction, and ultimately, spiritual emancipation. In the next chapter, in explaining how spiritual economics can be practiced, we introduce the Vedic scientific social system known as *varnashrama dharma*. This social system is a method of organizing society such that everyone's needs—both material and spiritual—are met, so that all people have a place, a function, security, and the satisfaction that arises from proper spiritual engagement and the opportunity to make a significant contribution to society according to one's ability. The *varnashrama dharma* social system is the means of curing the alienation and anomie that so plague modern man.

Since the first two volumes constitute an introduction to the concept of spiritual economics and are directed toward those unfamiliar with the *Bhagavad-gita*, there is need to examine the influences of economic activity in relationship to spiritual practices and progress beyond the treatment given therein. The impact of economic activities on spiritual evolution will therefore be treated in detail for experienced, practicing *vaishnavas* in the Part Three of this work, titled "Advanced Lessons in Spiritual Economics for *Vaishnavas*." This volume will also include a detailed discussion of the concepts of *varnashrama dharma*, and *daiva-varnashrama*.

Living is nothing more than doing one thing instead of another. How then shall we live? Shall we live in a way that ultimately destroys our social fabric, our planet, our own spiritual understanding and finer sentiments, and ultimately our own lives? Or shall we live in a way that heals and supports the planet and all of its inhabitants, eliminating the need or desire for poverty, fear, exploitation, degradation and destruction? To live in the current dominant culture participating in the economics of atheism is to choose the former. To live according to the instructions offered to us in the *Bhagavad-Gita,* following the principles of spiritual economics is to choose the latter. This book is meant to make you think about how you live in this world, and why.

Chapter One

Understanding Economic Man

Brahma first created the nescient engagements like self-deception, the sense of death, anger after frustration, the sense of false ownership, and the illusory bodily conception, or forgetfulness of one's real identity. Srimad Bhagavatam 3.12.2

Economic Behavior = Human Behavior

Considering that economics is a matter of activities engaged in for the satisfaction of our needs and wants, we can dissect the economic question into two basic parts: the first would be human beings, and the second, their activities, specifically their economic activity. Immediately the Vedic perspective diverges from the Western materialistic perspective in that within the Vedic paradigm human beings are understood and accepted as complex multi-dimensional beings, whereas in the traditional economic model people are considered to be hardly more than producing/consuming machines, "homo economicus," whose best interest is realized when these two functions are performed at peak efficiency. In such a case their best interest is considered to be their self-interest, where the concept of "self" is interpreted in a very narrow and literal way. The traditional economic model assumes that people desire an unlimited amount of goods, that the goods they seek are limited in number or availability and that they prioritize their behavior to satisfy those desires. True or not, these assumptions are applied in economic theory. For example, in 1881 Francis Edgeworth attempted to quantify human economic behavior with the simple assumption that "every man is a pleasure machine."[1] Edgeworth thus proposed that economics could quantify both the physical things of this world and also man's economic behavior, and this was attractive to other economists who at the time were eager to give their discipline the perception of being a genuine science. But are people this simplistic? Are people nothing more than producing/consuming machines? No one that you or I know. Since a theory is only as good as the assumptions that underlie it, an explanation of human behavior that fully accounts for all of the varieties and vagaries of our experience will better explain our economic activity and also provide for better economic theory.[2]

Since human behavior undoubtedly involves much more than getting and spending, and since the Vedic worldview provides a much greater understanding of human behavior, I offer that it can also do much better at explaining man's economic behaviors; it possesses sufficient depth to explain a variety of economic strategies, including one of transcendence. We'll first take a look at the many dimensions of the human being within the Vedic perspective, and with those insights, be equipped to understand much more deeply the complexity of human behavior, economic and otherwise.

Who Am I?

To begin with then, let's first consider what human beings are in this world. If we are just like animals who seek to satisfy our most basic urges of eating, mating, defense, and sleeping, then the assumptions upon which the materialistic economic model are established could be considered as valid. But are we nothing more than animals? Are we nothing more than pleasure machines? Are those assumptions valid?

The Vedas say there is much more. The *Srimad Bhagavatam* explains the human condition as a composite existence of several parts—the physical body, the subtle body and the soul (7.7.23):

> There are two kinds of bodies for every individual soul—a gross body made of five gross elements (earth, water, fire, air and ether) and a subtle body made of three subtle elements. Within these bodies, however, is the spirit soul.

The *Bhagavad-gita*, considered the standard introductory text of Vedic spiritual wisdom, explains the nature of the soul:

> That which pervades the entire body, the soul, is indestructible. For the soul there is neither birth nor death. He has not come into being, does not come into being, and will not come into being. He is unborn, eternal, ever-existing, undying and primeval. He does not die when the body dies. As the embodied soul continuously passes, in this body, from boyhood to youth to old age, the soul similarly passes

into another body at death. Just as a person puts on new garments, giving up old ones, the soul similarly accepts new material bodies, giving up the old and useless ones. (2.13, 2.17, 2.20, 2.22)

These verses explain that we are beings of a spiritual nature or energy, in Sanskrit called the *jiva*, or *atma*, understood in Western language as the soul, who temporarily lives in, or occupies, a body made of material energies. We all are familiar with the physical body made of gross material elements, but deeper than that we are encased within an ethereal body, comprised of very subtle material elements. Although these elements are not detectable with scientific instruments, we are all too aware of their existence because they provide our most immediate experience in this world—they are the elements of mind, intelligence, and the conscious concept of self, or the false ego. This subtle body is different from the *jiva* who travels in this material world within a body of both subtle and gross energies. The *jiva*, carried in the subtle body, is given a physical body at the time of conception, and due to its presence the physical body develops. When the *jiva*, again carried in the subtle body leaves the physical body, the event is called death. Actually only the physical body dies. The eternally existing soul, that is, that being or person, who experiences the activities of the body, continues to live.

The *jiva* has its own nature that is diametrically opposed to the material condition, creating a dichotomy in the human being. Where the *jiva* eternally exists and never dies, the material body is mortal. Where the *jiva's* eternal nature is a blissful state of existence, the human condition is subject to pain, suffering and unhappiness. And while the *jiva's* natural condition is a state of complete knowledge, the human condition is subjected to inherent ignorance, only acquiring knowledge through effort.

This condition creates a complex set of circumstances unique to material life. Although I do not want to, I am forced to die. Although I want to be happy it seems an ephemeral quest. And although I need knowledge to function in this world it seems that there is always more to know that will be valuable to me in my endeavors here. The human condition is arranged from the outset to be one of endeavor, but there is often confusion about the aim of that endeavor. Do I satisfy the senses, or the mind, or should I follow the intelligence that wards me away from immediate sense pleasures advising me instead to work now and enjoy later? Do I indulge my senses to their utmost limit, or should I restrain myself and act for the benefit of my eternal soul? But why should I do that if I don't even know what the soul is? How can we know our real self-interest?

Interestingly, the answers to these perennial existential questions will help to explain mankind's various economic behaviors. Let's first look at how we come to find ourselves in such a condition. For that we go back to the beginning—the beginning of time and the universe.

What Am I Doing Here?

In understanding how our present economic situation has come about we turn to the pages of the *Srimad Bhagavatam*, which explains how and why the creation of the material world takes place. The *Bhagavatam* explains how God has immense and innumerable energies, that He alone is the source of all energies, and they can be classified into three broad categories: superior, inferior and marginal. The superior energies are completely spiritual and they eternally exist in a state of perfection in *Vaikuntha*, or the Spiritual world. The superior energies all display consciousness and as such are personal living beings. The material energy, on the other hand is considered inferior because it is not living and displays no consciousness. It is dull and inert, but it is amazingly mutable and may be fashioned in countless combinations and permutations. The marginal energy is also spiritual, being both personal and conscious like the superior energy, but has the unique ability to live in either the spiritual world or the material world (hence the name marginal). We are that marginal energy of the Lord, and although we obviously live in the material realms we can transfer ourselves to the superior spiritual realms if we so desire. This phenomenal material world that we are living in and are familiar with is therefore made from a combination of the inferior and marginal energies.

Thus this material world is created for two reasons: the first is to give the living beings the opportunity to enjoy different varieties of sense pleasures based on contact with the material energy. How this comes about is explained by Srila Prabhupada (2.9.1 purport):

> All of the living entities are desirous of becoming equally as powerful as the Lord, although they are not fit to become so. The living entities are placed under illusion by the will of the Lord because they wanted to become like Him. Therefore the first sinful will of the living being is to become the Lord, and the consequent will of the Lord is that the living entity forgets his factual life and thus dream of a land of utopia where he may become one like the Lord.

That so-called utopia is this material world. In this world of illusion we struggle to achieve a position of complete happiness, but ultimately we must be frustrated because we can never become like God, nor can we find here the happiness and satisfaction we so desire. After becoming thus frustrated we finally desire to understand the nature of reality and the truth of our existence. We desire to free ourselves from the shackles of matter and return to the spiritual world. This is the second purpose of the material creation: to give those living beings that are materially exhausted the opportunity to free themselves from this material creation and go to the spiritual world.

In the matter of creation, Lord Brahma had to provide an appropriate environment for both of these situations. His first act of creation therefore was to arrange for the necessary conditions of material existence for the spiritual being (3.12.2):

> Brahma first created the nescient engagements like self-deception, the sense of death, anger after frustration, the sense of false ownership, and the illusory bodily conception, or forgetfulness of one's real identity.

Srila Prabhupada's comments help to clarify this verse:

> Unless a living entity forgets his real [spiritual] identity, it is impossible for him to live in the material conditions of life. Therefore the first condition of material existence is forgetfulness of one's real identity. And by forgetting one's real identity, one is sure to be afraid of death, although a pure living soul is deathless and birthless. This false identification with material nature is the cause of false ownership of things which are offered by the arrangement of superior control. All material resources are offered to the living entity for his peaceful living and for the discharge of the duties of self-realization in conditioned life. But due to false identification, the conditioned soul becomes entrapped by the sense of false ownership of the property of the Supreme Lord.

We learn that in the creation of Brahma a condition was established by which the beings in this world inherently have a bodily conception of life (i.e., I am this body), a false sense of ownership of the things of this world, and are subject to self-deception, taking things to be different from what they actually are. This false perception of material life is also referred to as *maya,* the illusory energy of the Lord that covers the conditioned living being (ma means not; ya means that; *maya* = not that). This covering of illusion is required for the *jiva* to forget his spiritual nature and experience varieties of material identities and pleasures. Not only does the *jiva* desire self-deception, but he desires to lord it over, control and exploit the material energy. The last sentence of Srila Prabhupada's comment also bears repeating: due to false identification (with the body, mind and senses), the conditioned soul becomes entrapped by the sense of false ownership of the property of the Supreme Lord.

It is here, in the fundamental orientation of the living beings to this world, that we find the bedrock foundation of material economic activity: the living beings of this world want to enjoy, possess and exploit the resources of the material world. Due to identification with the body and its senses they want to enjoy material objects, beginning with their body and the bodies of others, and seek to enjoy all varieties of sense pleasure. They want to enjoy tasting nice foods, to hear pleasing sounds, to touch soft things, to smell attractive smells, and to see beautiful forms. Moreover, another concept of their enjoyment is to consider themselves as the owner of many of these objects of enjoyment, considering that as they possess more they somehow become "more." In this materialistic concept of life they think that they have become greater or better than others if they possess more than others. To enhance their material ego they want to acquire beautiful and valuable things, especially those that others cannot acquire, and they thereby enjoy being the object of others' envy.

Under the illusion that he *is* the material body and mind, the *jiva* becomes irresistibly attracted to the things of this world, and develops unlimited desires to enjoy and lord it over the material creation. Some enjoy engaging the mind in the creation of material things, others engage their senses in manipulating the material energy in various ways, others content themselves to simply enjoy their senses, and yet others want to have power and control. Working and striving by every means to get the things he desires, the soul thinks himself to be the doer of activity, and that the results of his efforts are produced by his endeavors alone. Such endeavors are referred to as "fruitive activity"—activity engaged in specifically to obtain the fruits, or results. This material concept of life drives him forward in pursuit of his objectives. But although thinking that he is controlling the material energy, he is factually becoming increasingly implicated in the complexities of material life.

The Two Tracks of Material Ego

The very act of enjoying the objects of the senses conditions the *jiva* to identification with the body and its senses. That is, he soon forgets his original spiritual nature and mistakenly identifies with the body and senses alone; thus he enters into a condition of spiritual ignorance. Vedic wisdom calls this condition of forgetfulness of our spiritual nature, and adoption of an identity based upon the material aspects of life, the "false ego." False ego has two main components: *ahankara*, I am the doer (*"aham,"* I am; *"kara,"* the doer), and *aham mameti*, I am the possessor (*"aham,"* I am; *"mama iti"* the possessor). This false ego of the conditioned soul thus runs on two tracks: "it is I" (I am the body), and "it is mine" (I am the possessor of things); or "I and mine" (2.9.2):

The illusioned living entity appears in so many forms offered by the external energy of the Lord. While enjoying in the modes of material nature he misconceives, thinking in terms of "I" and "mine."

Srila Prabhupada comments:

The two misconceptions of life, namely "I" and "mine," are manifested in two classes of men. In the lower state the conception of "mine" is very prominent, and in the higher state the misconception of "I" is prominent. In the animal state of life the misconception of "mine" is perceivable even in the category of cats and dogs, who fight with one another with the same misconception of "mine." In the lower stage of human life the same misconception is also prominent in the shape of "It is my body," "It is my house," "It is my family," "It is my caste," "It is my nation," "It is my country," and so on. And in the higher stage of speculative knowledge, the same misconception of "mine" is transformed into "I am," or "It is all I am," etc. There are many classes of men comprehending the same misconception of "I" and "mine,' in different colors.

The living being thus develops a particular ego based upon two aspects: who I think I am, and what I possess. The false ego is thus referred to because it completely excludes any understanding of one's transcendental spiritual existence (real ego), and is based solely on temporary material designations that apply to the body during the course of one short lifetime only. This concept of "I and mine" is further enhanced by, and centers around the sexual attraction between man and woman (5.5.8–9):

The attraction between male and female is the basic principle of material existence. On the basis of this misconception, which ties together the hearts of the male and female, one becomes attracted to his body, home, property, children, relatives and wealth. In this way one increases life's illusions and thinks in terms of "I and mine."

Not only do we identify with our body, but we also identify with the extensions of the body in the form of husband, wife, children, parents, as well as with our community, nationality or country. Our relationships with all of these provide us with the basis for our identity in life, and an orientation from which to understand the world and our place in it. Naturally family life requires so many things for a comfortable existence, and people busy themselves in acquiring these, further increasing their sense of self with the acquisition of land, houses, buildings, furniture, clothing, conveyances, etc. The concept of false ego also includes our position in society, or titles of our work or occupation such as king, president, cabinet minister, mayor, policeman, professor, businessman, clergyman, manager, boss, clerk, worker, baker, carpenter, driver, etc. Our concept of self may be high or low, rich or poor, male or female. It may be based on skin color, black, brown or white. Our bodily relationships with others such as father, mother, son, daughter, sister, aunt, cousin, etc. also form the basis of our false ego, which we further extend to include the concept of national identity, thinking "I am Australian," "I am Ukrainian," "I am Brazilian," and so on. Every possible identity in relationship to this body and its activities is false in the spiritual sense because these are designations that apply to the body alone and for one lifetime only. They have no real meaning to the actual living being, the soul. After the death of this body we are born again into another situation, perhaps completely different. I may have the body of an Irish man in this life, but in the next I may be born as a Cambodian female. When we think about ourselves from this "many-lives" perspective we are forced to question the nature of our real identity apart from all of these changes of "costumes."

Within the concept of "I and mine" we also identify with what we possess. We should bear in mind that it was the conditions imposed upon the creation by Lord Brahma that influences our conceptions of "possession." This consciousness however pervades this entire world, and many books have been written in justification of the idea of private property "rights." A good example comes from social philosopher Henry George, who wrote about private property and ownership in *Progress and Poverty*. There he explains our now common understanding of private property:

> What constitutes the rightful basis of property? What allows someone to justly say, 'This is mine!'? Is it not, primarily, the right of a person to one's own self? To the use of one's own powers? To enjoy the fruits of one's own labor? Each person is a definite, coherent, independent whole. Each particular pair of hands obeys a particular particular brain and is related to a particular body. And this alone justifies individual ownership.

> As each person belongs to himself or herself, so labor belongs to the individual when put in concrete form. For this reason, what someone makes or produces belongs to that person—even against the claim of the whole world. It is that person's property, to use or enjoy, give or exchange, or even destroy. No one else can rightfully claim it. And this right to the exclusive possession and enjoyment wrongs no one else. Thus, there is a clear and indisputable title to everything

produced by human exertion. It descends from the original producer, in whom it is vested by natural law.[3]

Ironically, although he acknowledges the "original producer," George overlooks His claim to this phenomenal world. If the production of something belongs to a person against the claim of the entire world, then no person on this planet may claim anything for themselves, because God first produced everything that we see. However, He produces it specifically for our use, automatically providing for the maintenance of every living being. George's assertion that we can be the rightful owner of something is due to the influence of *maya*. The concept of "mine" factually exists only in our individual and collective imaginations, and is established as a social convention that has varied widely in different times and places. Although George valued the idea of private property he nonetheless held that the earth belonged to everyone, and that some piece of it at least was to be made available to everyone as their birthright. In this one philosopher we thus see two distinctly different conceptions of ownership, and we will give examples of more below.

In our contemporary Western culture we think of ownership and possession as being completely natural, identifying just as strongly with the things we possess. This can readily be seen on the road. People own a car that "expresses" who they are: the elegant Jaguar, rich Mercedes, the "mom-mobile" van, a sporty SUV or convertible, the staid sedan, and of course the ubiquitous pick-up truck. You may have seen the bumper sticker[4]: "Whoever dies with the most toys wins." It's a perfect motto for the materialistic person. We literally become our things. Where we live, dine out, the clubs we go to, our job title and authority, where we go to church, the way we wear our hair, the way we dress, decorate our fingernails, our bodies, our house and its furnishings, the things we collect, such as our art, coins, music, or "Barbie Doll" collections, etc., all become a part of our ego. These and more, are the very things that people use to define themselves, all too often completely forgetting the person within—their very selves. Within the concepts of "I and mine" the individual person can even cease to have importance compared to the things associated with him. In Los Angeles it is sometimes said that it is not who you are that is important, as much as what you wear, what you drive and where you live, these being the litmus test of social acceptability. Unfortunately this mentality is also found far outside the city limits of Los Angeles. May I suggest it pervades the entire world? Is it any wonder then that people suffer the neurosis of alienation, depression, anxiety and other psychological disorders? Preoccupied with the things that we have, and identifying too strongly with them we have become dissociated from our very selves.

One's possessions are thus employed to establish a social hierarchy, as demonstrated by exclusive clubs whose membership is determined by one's social standing, or astronomical entry fees. Other hierarchies are established based on the body alone, either by skin color as in America or South Africa, or by birth, as in the Hindu caste designations. Discriminations and prejudices based on body, wealth, intellect, or physical strength have all been observed through the passage of time, and all of them are based upon envy arising from a material conception of life.

It is not at all unusual then that people struggle to acquire the many adornments of their ego, and struggle further to maintain them. As we have seen in every culture throughout history, people are very willing to lie, cheat, and kill to get what they want, both on a personal as well as collective level. Violent conflicts between kingdoms or countries are frequently fought to increase or defend such possessions. As illusory as all of this is, we are impelled by our desires to enhance our concept of "I and mine," in quality or quantity, or both.

For the materially engrossed person identifying with the body means "I am my body." Such a person has no belief in life after death, and thus thinks that all of his experience will take place in the short span of one lifetime. Needless to say, such a person, thinking that he will one day be gone and enjoy no more, is driven to get, experience and enjoy as much as possible. Americans of my generation may remember the old beer commercial that played on this sentiment: "you only go around once so grab all the gusto you can!" Moreover, besides attempting to maximize the pleasures of his life, it is also likely that such a person will be unconcerned with how they are acquired. Whether by hook or crook is of little consequence, after all, when I'm dead, I'm dead. Finished. Kaput. Sayonara. Why worry? Obviously such an attitude can have significant consequences on a person's moral bearing and dealings with others while alive. Indeed, the motto of some is "do what thou wilt." They care nothing at all for any punishments or rewards because, to them, life ends with the death of the body.

This then is the illusory condition of material life wherein we think that we are our bodies, and that the things that we can acquire and possess while in this body are ours, and that they "belong" to us. Yet both Vedic wisdom and simple dispassionate logic tell us that both of these conceptions are completely false, because one day when we are at death's door we will be forced to give up this body along with its so-called possessions. Can anything *really* belong to us then? Only in a very illusory sense. But take note! The entirety of human, civilization, especially in the West, is based on this illusion!

Such extreme conceptions of "I and mine" as expressed in modern Western culture are not, and have not in the past, been universal. There are indeed many ways in which the concepts of ego and ownership are manifest, and we will examine some of them shortly. First however, we need to further examine the Vedic explanation of human nature and behaviors. This is very important in the discussion of economics, because another of economics' most fundamental assumptions is that human beings behave rationally. Nobel prize-winning economist Amartya Sen remarks that this "rational behavior is not...ultimately different from describing actual behavior."[5] The problem with this statement is that there is an entire panoply of human behaviors, some of which seem to be more rational than others. Which of them is the rational one? All of them or just some? Sen clarifies, that while economists have more than one definition of rationality, one of the "predominant methods" equates rationality with "maximization of self-interest."[6] This assumption, and its interpretation, is often used to justify certain economic behaviors, and we shall have more to say about this in coming chapters. This assumption however, again begs the question, "who is the self?" The Masters of Vedic Wisdom instruct us that our *real* self-interest is not to be found in any variety of material economic activity—it is to understand our true spiritual identity, freeing us forever from the materialistic contemplation that arises from "I and mine." The entirety of this book serves as both an explanation and plan for achieving our *real* self-interest.

Economist Robert Nelson answers the question of rationality a bit differently. He says that economists take it as "an article of faith" (another way of saying "assumption") that the behavior of individuals is not random but follows definite directions. He writes "economists argue that beneath the surface of what often appears to be widespread ignorance, miscalculation, and self-deception, there are in fact deep and powerful forces at work that obey rationally discoverable laws."[7] Although he doesn't clearly say what those laws are (and his language indicates that they are not yet known) we nonetheless agree. But these laws are not unknown nor do they need to be discovered. Long ago the *Bhagavad-gita* clearly explained those forces and the influence they have on the consciousness of living beings. Those influences also help us to understand how it is that a person develops and pursues their various conceptions of "I and mine." What are those "laws?" Do they determine or just predict human behavior? Are there different but equally valid conceptions of "rational" behavior? Perhaps even more importantly, is there some way of affecting people's consciousness that will cause them to behave differently?

Material Energy and Its Influence on Human Consciousness

In this material world the *jiva* is a traveler in a foreign environment. Traveling to foreign places nowadays often requires immunizations against diseases to which a non-native person may be susceptible. The material world is likewise an infectious place for the pure spiritual being. In fact, *everything* in this material world has an infectious nature for the soul, and simply by contacting the material energy the *jiva* becomes infected by its qualities. These influences are known in Sanskrit as *"gunas"* or "ropes." As a person bound with ropes can be helplessly pulled this way or that, in the same way, a person's consciousness is controlled by the *gunas*.

Lord Krishna explains the nature of the *gunas* to Arjuna in the fourteenth chapter of the *Bhagavad-gita*, but before doing so, makes him aware of the tremendous value of this knowledge. He stated: "I shall now declare to you this supreme wisdom, the best of all knowledge, knowing which all the sages have attained to supreme perfection. By becoming fixed in this knowledge, one can attain to the transcendental nature, which is like My own nature. Thus established, one is not born at the time of creation nor disturbed at the time of dissolution." Sacred are these words because this knowledge, when used properly, can be extremely powerful. Just as a key that unlocks a prison cell is very important to the prisoner, all of us prisoners in this material world should similarly value this key of Vedic wisdom, for it opens the passages to spiritual freedom that were previously locked by our ignorance.

The *gunas* are described by Sri Krishna in the *Bhagavad-gita* (Ch. 14):

> Material nature consists of three qualities, or modes—goodness (*sattva-guna*), passion (*rajo-guna*), and ignorance (*tamo-guna*). When the eternal living entity comes in contact with nature he becomes conditioned by these modes. The mode of goodness (*sattva*) is purer than the others, and it is therefore illuminating and gives understanding. It frees one from sinful reactions through the development of knowledge. By working in the mode of goodness one becomes spiritually uplifted, but also becomes conditioned to the concept of material happiness.

> From the mode of passion (*rajas*) unlimited desires and longings are born. Due to this quality one becomes eager to engage in material activities, eager for the fruits, or results, of activities. Passion however conditions one to continually engage in fruitive activity, with the view of gain and increase. When there is an increase in the mode of passion, the symptoms of great attachment, uncontrollable desire, hankering, and intense endeavor develop. However, work done in the mode of passion eventually results in distress to one's self and others.

> The quality of ignorance (*tamas*) causes the delusion of the living beings. The result of contact with ignorance is foolish, violent, or

wrong behavior, laziness and sleep. Actions performed in the mode of ignorance result in foolishness and misunderstanding. Ignorance binds the conditioned soul and conditions him to working against his own best interests. When there is an increase in the mode of ignorance madness, illusion, inertia and darkness are manifested.

From the mode of goodness, understanding, knowledge and happiness develop; from the mode of passion, greed and grief develop; and from the mode of destruction, ignorance, foolishness, and illusion develop. From passion comes creation, everything is maintained by the quality of goodness, and the influence of ignorance brings decay, dissolution and destruction.

Not accepting the spiritual nature of man, and considering him as the body alone, modern social theory proposes that human beings develop their character through social conditioning. However, the *Bhagavad-gita* and *Srimad-Bhagavatam* add significant dimensions to the understanding of human behavior by explaining the influence of the *gunas* on the understanding, knowledge and behavior of man. *Srimad-Bhagavatam* expands on the information available to us from the *Gita* regarding the nature or character that the living entity attains by association with the individual modes of nature:

Mind and sense control, tolerance, discrimination, sticking to one's prescribed duty, truthfulness, mercy, careful study of the past and future, satisfaction in any condition, generosity, renunciation of sense gratification, faith in the spiritual master, being embarrassed at improper action, charity, simplicity, humbleness and satisfaction within oneself and detachment from the material mind and of the senses from matter, are qualities of the mode of goodness.

Material desire, great endeavor, audacity, dissatisfaction even in gain, false pride, praying for material advancement, the distortion of the intelligence due to too much activity, the inability to disentangle the perceiving senses from material objects, an unsteady perplexity of the mind, considering oneself different and better than others, sense gratification, rash eagerness to fight, a fondness for hearing oneself praised, the tendency to ridicule others, advertising one's own prowess and justifying one's actions by one's strength are qualities of the mode of passion.

Intolerant anger, stinginess, speaking on the basis of one's false pride and without scriptural authority, violent hatred, living as a parasite, hypocrisy, chronic lethargy, quarrel, lamentation, delusion, unhappiness, depression, false expectations, fear, laziness and sleeping too much, the failure to attain or disappearance of an awareness of one's higher (spiritual) self, and the inability to concentrate one's attention, constitute the major qualities of the mode of ignorance.

All facets of both the material energy as well as human action are influenced by some combinations of the *gunas*. Sri Krishna explains that everyone living within the material world is influenced by the *gunas*, and in the last several chapters of the *Gita* He further explains their influence on faith, worship, penances, sacrifices, charity, austerities, foodstuffs, time of day and night, knowledge, action, understanding, determination, happiness, work or the performance of action, and the worker.

The Different Qualities of Work and Action

Let's now consider the influence of the qualities of nature on economic activity with several examples, beginning with the performer of work. We learn in the eighteenth chapter of the *Gita* that:

> The worker who is free from all material attachments and false ego, who is enthusiastic and resolute and who works steadfastly, indifferent to success or failure, is a worker in the mode of goodness. But that worker who is attached to the fruits of his labor and who passionately wants to enjoy them, who is greedy, envious and impure and moved by happiness and distress, is a worker in the mode of passion. The worker who is always engaged in work against the injunction of scripture, who is materialistic, obstinate, cheating and expert in insulting others, who is lazy, always morose and procrastinating, is a worker in the mode of ignorance.

This information helps us to better understand the varieties of behavior that we commonly observe in our own experience and that "rational" behavior assumed by classical economic theory. Each of us could probably identify a number of people of each category that we must interact with on a regular basis. Who is the enthusiastic and determined worker? The lazy one doing only what he has to? Who are the ones that are driven by results, prestige and position? Obviously the methods by which these three work are going to be different and have different results. I once attended a management training seminar wherein the students were given an exercise to identify how well they could cooperate for a common goal—such as the overall profitability of the company. Interestingly the most cooperative workers were invariably among the *lowest* ranks of the organization—those who were generally focused on getting the job done. Based upon the information above can you guess what was found at the upper echelons of management, where prestige and position were significant? These persons often achieved their high positions because of a strong desire for status and recognition. Being driven by ego in passion and envious of the success of others, they repeatedly scored the *lowest* in terms of cooperation. Why would the lower ranks be more cooperative? Their activity was free from the negative aspects of passion and ignorance and influenced more by the quality of goodness.

Apart from the worker, work itself is likewise categorized according to the *gunas*. Work performed as an offering to the Lord, without desire for, or consideration of the fruits, is of the quality of goodness. Work performed with a desire to enjoy the results is done in the mode of passion. And work impelled by violence and envy is in the mode of ignorance.

Action is another human trait influenced by the *gunas* and useful in an economic context. Economic activity requires action and results. What does the *Gita* tell us about action?

> Action in accordance with duty, which is performed without attachment, without love or hate, by one who has renounced fruitive results, is called action in the mode of goodness. Action performed with great effort by one seeking to gratify his desires, and which is enacted from a sense of false ego, is called action in the mode of passion. And that action performed in ignorance and delusion without consideration of future bondage or consequences, which inflicts injury and is impractical, is said to be action in the mode of ignorance. (18.23–25)

Again we see a variety of influences according to the various *gunas*. When people work, and perform action in the quality of goodness, their understanding will increase, and they will likely perform their work in the best manner possible, in accordance with duty and without personal attachment. They will also be happy and fulfilled by their work. When people work and perform action with the quality of passion great effort may be expended and they may appear to be doing a lot of work. However, they may also have great attachment to the results, which will invariably lead to conflict with co-workers, duplicitousness, covetousness of others' work, backstabbing, ego-driven ladder-climbing, and so on. Some will undoubtedly achieve their aim of superiority and recognition but create a lot of grief in the process. Those in ignorance want to avoid work, or take credit for work done by others, or perhaps make a show of work only when the boss is nearby, and then slack off after he leaves. They will often falsify the results of their work if possible, to make things look better than they are, or else push the costs of their work onto others who do not share in the results. When work is done in ignorance accidents, waste, shoddy results, re-work and losses are likely to be the result.

The Varieties of Material Happiness

There are several other human qualities important in social and economic activities that are influenced by the *gunas* to which we must give some detail. Primary is happiness. There are different kinds of happiness generated by the *gunas*, and in understanding the modern economic problem it is important that we understand their features, especially happiness in the mode of passion. The happiness of persons under the influence of passion might better be described as pleasure because these persons seek happiness from sense gratification, from the contact of the senses with their sense objects. This idea of happiness is the driving force of consumerism, the desire by many people to "get it all." In America the Sunday newspaper typically contains dozens of advertising brochures to entice people into the stores. In glee people fill their shopping carts to the brim with many unnecessary articles, not because they need them, or even want them, but because they were too good of a deal to pass by.

Although shopping is one of the primary methods of sense gratification, it is not nearly as significant to individuals as romance, sex, and relationship. Sexual attraction, passionate romance and marriage are often viewed as *the* way to find happiness. Indeed, people are very often attracted to each other and unite on the basis of sexual attraction alone. This is the bliss of *rajo-guna*. New romance is certainly blissful, but only for a while. How long does passionate love last? On the average just fifteen to eighteen months. This is the one very serious problem with the happiness of *rajo-guna*. Based on sense gratification it quickly fades. It is wonderful in the beginning, but later it becomes stale, distasteful, repulsive, or even, as the *Gita* puts it, like poison. Once that happiness is lost we find ourselves searching for it again. Remember, things of this world are created in passion, but they are maintained by goodness. In order for marriages to survive couples must bring to their relationship the qualities of *sattva-guna*.

Happiness in the mode of goodness is just the opposite of that of passion. In the beginning, a passionate person may find it distasteful, but gradually it becomes wonderful. Moreover, it awakens one to a higher understanding of the self beyond the body. This is the only lasting happiness available in this world. Such happiness is achieved by doing one's duty, proper living, and so on. In order to pursue happiness in goodness however, we must understand by our intelligence that the result of such activities are in our long-term interest. Unfortunately, this idea is almost lost in our modern "I want it now" society where we can get almost instant gratification through the use of credit. While this may bring us some immediate satisfaction, it also brings lots of debt and endless monthly bills that drain our energy. Nectar in the beginning...but poison in the end.

There is another form of happiness as well—that influenced by the mode of ignorance. It is experienced by sleep, laziness, and illusion. It is blind to self-realization. This type of happiness can be obtained from sleeping for very long periods of time—twelve to sixteen hours, or other forms of laziness. It is a desirable fashion among certain classes of people to do as little as possible, and upon achieving such a state they think themselves happy. Happiness in *tamo-guna* is also derived from intoxication, drugs, and even violence and all other kinds of degraded, licentious behavior. Of course this is the basis of a very large segment of both the normal as well as the underground economy—with up to a trillion dollars spent every year on the consumption of intoxicants, drugs, gambling and illicit sex. Making others suffer can also bring a sort of happiness to those infected with *tamo-guna*; the thrill that aggressive youths find in picking a fight, for example.

Knowledge According to the *Gunas*

Epistemology is the study of knowledge; a branch of philosophy that is concerned with the nature of knowledge, its possibility, scope, and its general basis. It has been the object of study by all Western philosophers, but in all cases they have made a very important omission: consideration of the different types of knowledge based upon the modes of material nature; an exposition that predates their attempts to understand knowledge. Under the influence of the *gunas* there are different types of knowledge which lead to different ways of seeing the world, and by extension, the things we should or should not do, and how to do them.

By knowledge in *sattva-guna* one can also realize the equality of all living beings based on their spiritual nature. Knowledge in goodness allows one to see and value all life equally, regardless of the type of body, be it a frog, a cow, a tree, an insect, or a person from Europe, Africa, or China. The influence of *sattva* provides knowledge of the spiritual basis of life, and the equality of all spirit. These people may be those who are concerned about maintaining the ecological balance, humanitarians, human rights activists, vegetarians, and women who refuse birth control and abortion.

Those in *sattva-guna* also accept an absolute standard of knowledge as was formerly the case for philosophers and people alike. That concept has fallen into disfavor in our modern world. Suggestions of an absolute truth are today met with derision, but that reaction is itself a demonstration of the lack of *sattva* under the influence of *tamas*. That which passes for knowledge today is heavily influenced by passion and ignorance.

Knowledge in *rajo-guna* is based on duality by which everything is understood to be relatively good or bad, desirable or undesirable based on a bodily conception of life. Under its influence people see a different type of living entity in each different body. They are likely to think that a human has a soul whereas a cow, a flower, or a bug does not. They see different bodies relative to themselves and their own needs and desires. They see this world in terms of their enjoyment, in relationship to their personal satisfaction—or in other words, in terms of "I and mine." According to them a cow is an animal for "my milk and food," a tree only as so many board-feet of lumber for "my dwellings," and every insect as a pest to be destroyed before it eats "my crops." Plants, animals, insects, birds have only the value that I assign to them according to my need, and if I do not find value in them alive there may be some value derived from killing them.

Under the influence of knowledge in *rajo-guna* people think for example, that capital punishment is bad, while abortion and birth control are good; capitalism is bad and communism is good; war is bad but euthanasia is good; heroin and crack cocaine are bad, but marijuana and alcohol are good; white skin is good and brown skin is "bad," Mexicans are good but Americans are bad, or Indians are good but Pakistanis are bad, or Palestinians are good but Israelis are bad, and so on. Any of these dualities can be reversed because what is good or bad depends on who is doing the thinking. As such, knowledge in *rajo-guna* is based on relative standards that lead to division and quarrel.

Knowledge in ignorance is based on faith in matter alone. It is materialistic knowledge, by which work is accepted as the basis of everything. Such knowledge in the mode of darkness gives rise to concepts such as: the "Big Bang" theory; the theory of Darwinian evolution; other theories such as sociobiology which declares that genes alone determine a person's every action; the idea that machines can be more intelligent or even more moral than humans, etc. In all of these, matter alone is paramount and plays the most important, indeed, the only role. Such knowledge is of the quality of *tamo-guna*.

Srila Prabhupada's comments on knowledge according to the *gunas* are helpful in our understanding of the subject:

> The 'knowledge' of the common man is always in the mode of darkness or ignorance because every living entity in conditional life is born into the mode of ignorance. One who does not develop knowledge through the authorities or scriptural injunctions has knowledge that is limited to the body. He is not concerned about acting in terms of the directions of scripture. For him God is money, and knowledge means the satisfaction of bodily demands. Such knowledge has no connection with the Absolute Truth. It is more or

less like the knowledge of the ordinary animals: the knowledge of eating, sleeping, defending and mating. Such knowledge is described as the product of the mode of darkness. In other words, knowledge concerning the spirit soul beyond this body is called knowledge in the mode of goodness, knowledge producing many theories and doctrines by dint of mundane logic and mental speculation is the product of the mode of passion, and knowledge concerned only with keeping the body comfortable is said to be in the mode of ignorance.[8]

Understanding and Determination

Reasoning and understanding are fundamental to the rational behavior that economist's assume people have. But what is rational behavior? It may seem that reasoning and understanding are universal traits, but actually there are different ways in which people perceive the world, each perception having its own set of implications for society. Every person's understanding is affected by the particular *gunas* by which they have become conditioned.[9] One kind of understanding impels one to strive always in the wrong direction. They consider wrong to be right and right to be wrong. This understanding is brought about by association with the quality of *tamo-guna*, the mode of ignorance. People with such backward understanding are their own worst enemy—and a problem for society as well. They haven't even the ability for proper understanding. These persons consider irreligion to be religion, and actual religion to be irreligion. They take a saintly person as a common man, and deify a common person as a saint. They take truth to be untruth and accept falsity as truth. Needless to say, persons whose understanding is of the mode of ignorance are very easy to manipulate for either political or economic gain.

Persons influenced predominantly by passion cannot discriminate between action that should be done and action that should not be done. Action that should be done or not done has nothing to do with an understanding of *how* to do things. Certainly many people are engaged in doing things that must proceed in a logical order, and therefore know what to do first, second, third, etc. This is not what is referred to here. The perspective of Vedic wisdom is one of transcendence, and everything is viewed in this light. In this respect, how does one decide what to do and not to do? There must be some reference point. In Vedic culture the reference point is one's eternal spiritual welfare. But that reference point is lost to those in passion whose understanding is bewildered by the bodily concept of life. It is in this sense that they do not know what to do or what not to do for their long-term spiritual well-being and the overall well-being of society. This also applies to their perception of other living beings. By the influence of *rajo-guna* other living things are also understood to be simply the body, and are seen as an object of sense gratification.

Conversely, that understanding by which one knows what ought to be done and what ought not to be done, what is to be feared and what is not to be feared, what is binding and what is liberating, is understanding in the mode of goodness. Such understanding is referenced to spiritual welfare. Srila Prabhupada explains further that: "Performing actions in terms of the directions of the scriptures is called *pravritti*, or executing actions that deserve to be performed. Actions which are not so directed are not to be performed. One who does not know the scriptural directions becomes entangled in the actions and reactions of work [*karma*]. Understanding gained by the use of discriminating intelligence is considered to be in the mode of goodness."

The varied understandings that arise due to the *guna*s have significant influence on what is understood to be rational. Thus there cannot simply be one definition of rational behavior. We will see in coming chapters that, influenced by the *guna*s people have rationally dealt with solving the economic problem in a wide variety of ways.

Determination, used here as a synonym for motivation, is also a very important element of successful economic endeavor and it is also influenced by the *gunas* (18.33): "That determination by which one holds fast to fruitive results in religion, economic development and sense gratification is of the nature of passion." In other words, those in passion are motivated in all activities by the desire for fruitive results—be they in religion, economic development, or sense gratification. Without this element, those in passion lose their determination (motivation) for any endeavor. The ever-present question in considering anything they do is "What's in it for me—personally?" They are not interested so much in the welfare of others (a product of *sattva-guna*). Projecting their own qualities onto the world, they think that others should be similarly motivated, and if they fail to perform it is only due to incompetence or laziness. Attached to fruitive results they are reluctant to support others through welfare based on taxes from their hard work. Moreover they believe that there is no other possibility for motivation than fruitive work, and they tout capitalism, private enterprise, and private ownership as the only practical means of achieving such motivation. To establish the truth of this idea they point to the shallow results obtained by Russian communism, which they say led to its eventual downfall. Indeed, Russian communism was unable to achieve the same results that private enterprise did, because most of the Russian people, who were also steeped in passion and ignorance, required fruitive results or even threat of loss, for motivation and determination. But these motivations were absent from Soviet society. This not to say that there are not other types of motivation.

Those under the spell of *rajo-guna* are bewildered by the determination of those in goodness who are not similarly motivated. They think of them as lazy, incompetent, n'er-do-wells, or un-achievers. In fact though, those in *sattva-guna* have a different determination. They are interested in the welfare of others, including nature, and are motivated to see that everyone is happy, well cared for, and progressing spiritually. They typically work to make the world a better place for all.

The determination of those under the influence of ignorance does not go beyond dreaming, or illusion, they are unable to take any action to fulfill their desires. Such people are morose. They are motivated only by threat of loss, pain, fearfulness and lamentation. They don't have the ability to understand what they can or will gain; that is not as important to them as what they will lose. People too influenced by ignorance thus have no ambition, resourcefulness, or determination for material activities, what to speak of spiritual activities. In order to be productive, people influenced predominantly by ignorance must have the help of those in passion or goodness to direct them in productive work. They haven't the motivation, ability or understanding to know what to do or how to do it.

Faith

An important component of determination is faith. One takes action based on the faith that it will be successful. Without such faith one loses determination. Faith is also of different kinds due to the influences of the *gunas*. Faith based on an understanding of, and directed to, spiritual life is of the quality of goodness. Faith in passion is rooted in fruitive work and its perceived results. And faith that resides in irreligious activities is in the mode of ignorance.

Thus by the myriad influences of the *gunas* we all view this world and act in it in different ways. These influences are the basis of our false ego—who we think we are in this world in our relationship to others. It is therefore a very relative world in which people do not, or (under the influence of *tamo-guna*) cannot, agree either on what is the right or wrong way to do things, nor what should be done. Some people are concerned only about themselves, others concern themselves with the common good of all, and others are concerned only about how to do as little as possible, either for themselves or others. It is the influence of the *gunas* that fuels the debates about what to do or how to do it. Each side feels themselves properly justified; that theirs is the right course, although their ideas have consequences that may be vastly different. It is the influence of the *gunas* that cause some people to be only concerned with profit, others to be concerned with the poor or the environment, and others to be completely unconcerned about anything. It is the influence of the modes of ignorance and passion that are the very root cause of the exploitation of people and the resources of nature.

We Are Conditioned by the Qualities of Matter

We form habits by the ways that we associate with the *gunas*. Year after year we consume the same foods and beverages, do the same activities, associate with the same people, or keep the same hours. By continually associating with the same *gunas* their influences are reinforced, with important consequences— we become conditioned by them.

Becoming conditioned means that we become habituated to a given pattern of thinking, understanding and behavior. As a result a particular stimulus will elicit a predictable response. According to how we associate with the material world and all of its phenomena, we will become so conditioned. Every aspect of this material world has its own quality: a unique mixture of the qualities of goodness, passion, and ignorance. Just as the three primary colors of a television screen combine to generate a possible 72,000 colors, so also the three qualities of matter combine to generate innumerable influences. All of the many aspects of human activity are influenced in different degrees by the modes of nature.

The very idea of conditioning infers a predictable response. The masters of Vedic wisdom have therefore told us that we are not as free as we think ourselves to be. Association with matter influences the soul in such a way that our behavior becomes habitual, automatic or reactionary—even though we each think that we act according to our own free will. The modes, or *gunas*, influence the behavior of people according to their previous association with them over the course of many lives, and they carry this conditioning with them from lifetime to lifetime as various conceptions of life. The *atma*, by force of his unfulfilled desires, is born again and again—unlimitedly. Lifetime after lifetime he is confronted by sense objects for which he feels attraction and repulsion (desire and hate). In this way his heart becomes increasingly contaminated by the dualities of material life. According to his association with the *gunas* he becomes conditioned to a particular way of understanding and thinking. This process has been going on since time immemorial, and because of this the living beings in this world are said to be eternally conditioned. Thus we are already conditioned before we enter into the present life. We bring attitudes and desires with us, and it is our conditioning and our karma that determines the circumstances we are born into. After birth our associations with matter continue to add to the overall effect of the *gunas'* influences and our conditioning.

Drug addiction provides a good example of conditioned behavior. Drug addicts are powerless as a result of their addiction. When such a person actually wants to kick their habit, they are enrolled in a behavior modification program in which they are expected to avoid the places and people associated with the addiction. They are encouraged to find new friends and engage in new activities. In other words they must give up contact with the qualities of nature that they are accustomed to and replace them with positive alternatives. This is not easy or automatic. The very nature of the conditioned state makes such change extremely difficult. The most common addictions are food (over-eating) and cigarette smoking. Anyone who has ever been on a diet or tried to quit smoking knows that such behavioral changes can be very difficult and that they take time to become the normal pattern of behavior. If you want to see behavioral modification in action all you have to do is attend any 10-Step meeting. It may not be clearly understood, but what these people are attempting to do is change their conditioning to become "re-conditioned," so to speak.

Let's take another example. People generally engage in certain types of activity at certain times of the day. The *gunas* have specific influences at particular times of the day. The quality of ignorance, *tamo-guna*, has a major influence during the night hours, waxing and waning from about 8 p.m. to 4 a.m. The influence of *sattva-guna* predominates from about around 4am until noon, and *rajo-guna* from approximately noon to 8 p.m. Those who have cultivated the quality of goodness will retire from activity and will be summoned by sleep during the influence of *tamo-guna*. They often like to go to bed early and get up early as well. But those who have become conditioned by *tamo-guna* are just coming to life around 9 p.m. They think of themselves as "night persons" and are often active all night until *sattva-guna* begins to make its influence felt around 4 a.m. When the mode of goodness begins to show its influence these night-owls will want to retire from activity and go to sleep, while in the early morning those who have cultivated goodness are waking-up to begin their day. *Sattva* and *tamas* are actually polar opposites—what is attractive to the *sattvic* person is disliked by the *tamasic* person, and vice-versa.

As these groups of people continue to behave in their respective ways, their conditioning and expected responses become more consistent and predictable. But all the while, unconscious of these influences, people generally think that they are acting on their own volition. What about the people in passion? Being driven by activity they often stay up late and get up early. With too much to do they are often sleep-deprived. Still, the main influence of *rajo-guna* is during middle of the day when people are moved to action and work. Each of the *gunas* has its predominance and then wanes as another predominates. According to how we have become conditioned by the *gunas* we will similarly be moved to act. The effect of the influence is dependent on both the nature of the combination of the *gunas*, and our particular conditioning.

The *Srimad-Bhagavatam* explains that because our intelligence is polluted by a materialistic conception of life we are subjected to the modes of nature, and thus we become conditioned by material existence. Our conditioning and our enjoying and suffering in material life are, in one sense, false, just like the suffering we may experience in a dream. When we wake up, the suffering of the dream immediately stops. Similarly we are meant to wake up from this material dream which is temporary. Material existence is considered undesirable and unwanted; it continues only due to the ignorance that covers our real knowledge of self. Only while in the human body do we have the opportunity to wake up from the material condition and realize our transcendental spiritual nature. This is the considered by the masters of Vedic wisdom to be the highest achievement of human life.

The *Gunas* and the Grand Epochs

Sri Krishna explains in the *Bhagavad-gita* that He is time, the most powerful of all elements because nobody can check its influence. The time factor is invisible and imperceptible. Nevertheless it carries all living beings just as the masses of clouds are carried away irresistibly and silently by the wind. By its influence the living beings take birth, and by its influence they are all delivered to death's door. Those in the bodily conception of life and who do not understand that time is the influence of the all-powerful Lord are afraid of death: "The influence of the Supreme Personality of Godhead is felt in the time factor, which causes fear of death due to the false ego of the deluded soul who has contacted material nature." (3.26.16)

In order to experience the full panoply of their desires the living beings must change bodies and are given the opportunity to take birth when the external conditions offer the appropriate facility. The Supreme Lord therefore creates the time factor to allow the material energy and the living entity to act within set limits.

The history of the earth according to Vedic tradition differs considerably from the Western worldview offered to us by biologists, anthropologists, and cosmologists. Far from evolving from nothing, as the atheistic scientific worldview would have us believe, the Vedas explain in exacting detail how, why, and by whom this world was created, and how all living beings were established here. The *Puranas*, the ancient histories of mankind, explain tha this world was endowed with intelligent life, and a highly advanced civilization from the very beginning of creation. Due to the influence of the *gunas* however, there is a gradual degradation. Just as the influence of the *gunas* waxes and wanes over the course of the day, they also rotate in their influence over vast periods of time known as *yugas*. Just as our year cycles through the seasons of spring, summer, fall and winter, the entire cosmos perpetually revolves through four great ages—*Satya, Treta, Dvapara* and *Kali*, repeating the same general sequence of events.

The Golden Age, a wonderful time of the distant past, referred to in almost every culture, is described in the Vedas as the *Satya-yuga*. It was the age of goodness, *sattva-guna*, without much influence of the disturbing elements of *rajas* and *tamas*. In this age everyone was noble and principled. The earth was a veritable paradise. During Satya-*yuga* the four legs of religion: truthfulness, mercy, austerity and charity, were fully intact. The people of Satya-*yuga* were for the most part self-satisfied, merciful, friendly to all, peaceful, sober and tolerant. They found pleasure within, seeing all things equally and endeavored diligently for spiritual perfection. The recommended process of self-realization during *Satya-yuga* was the eightfold yoga system, when they had the time, determination and peaceful atmosphere in which to properly meditate.

Gradually by the force of time the mode of passion began to make its influence felt on the consciousness of man and became the dominant *guna* during the silver age, or *Treta-yuga*. In *Treta-yuga* each leg of religion was gradually reduced by one quarter due to the influence of the four pillars of irreligion—lying, violence, dissatisfaction and quarrel. During this age people were devoted to ritual performances and severe austerities. They were not excessively violent or very lusty after sensual pleasure. Their interest lay primarily in religiosity, economic development and regulated sense gratification, and they achieved prosperity by following the prescriptions of the three Vedas.

As time progressed the influence of ignorance began to show its effect during the epoch of *Dvapara-yuga*, characterized by the mixed *gunas* of *rajas* and *tamas*. During *Dvapara-yuga* the religious qualities of austerity, truth, mercy and charity were reduced to one half. People were very noble, devoted themselves to the study of the Vedas, possessed great opulence, supported large families and enjoyed life with vigor. Of the four social classes, the *ksatriyas* and *brahmanas* were most numerous. The end of *Dvapara-yuga* some 5,000 years ago marked the beginning of the current age of *Kali*.

As *Kali-yuga* has progressed the influence of passion has waned as ignorance has increased. *Kali-yuga* is characterized by the unchecked influence of *tamo-guna* and its characteristics of lying, violence, dissatisfaction, quarrel and hypocrisy. Sinful and degraded personalities are born in *Kali-yuga* because this age offers them many opportunities to satisfy their qualities of anger, lust, envy and greed. By the end of this age all good qualities will be lost along with any understanding of religion, what to speak of its practice. Humans will then be barbarians, less than animals, who, lacking other foods will eat each other, and even their own children.

The *Srimad Bhagavatam* (12.3.30–43) long ago predicted in detail the nature of this age:

> When there is a predominance of cheating, lying, sloth, sleepiness, violence, depression, lamentation, bewilderment, fear and poverty, that age is *Kali*, the age of the mode of ignorance. Because of the bad qualities of the age of *Kali*, human beings will become shortsighted, unfortunate, gluttonous, lustful and poverty-stricken. The women, becoming unchaste, will freely wander from one man to the next. Cities will be dominated by thieves, the Vedas will be contaminated by speculative interpretations of atheists, political leaders will virtually consume the citizens, and the so-called priests and intellectuals will be devotees of their bellies and genitals.

> Women will become much smaller in size, and they will eat too much, have more children than they can properly take care of, and lose all shyness. They will always speak harshly and will exhibit qualities of thievery, deceit and unrestrained audacity. Businessmen will engage in petty commerce and earn their money by cheating. Even when there is no emergency, people will consider any degraded occupation quite acceptable. Servants will abandon a master who has lost his wealth, even if that master is a saintly person of exemplary character. Masters will abandon an incapacitated servant, even if that servant has been in the family for generations. Cows will be abandoned or killed when they stop giving milk.

> In *Kali*-yuga men will be wretched and controlled by women. They will reject their fathers, brothers, other relatives and friends and will instead associate with the sisters and brothers of their wives. Thus their conception of friendship will be based exclusively on sexual ties. Uncultured men will accept charity on behalf of the Lord and will earn their livelihood by making a show of austerity and wearing a mendicant's dress. Those who know nothing about religion will mount a high seat and presume to speak on religious principles.

> In the age of *Kali*, people's minds will always be agitated. They will become emaciated by famine and taxation, my dear King, and will always be disturbed by fear of drought. They will lack adequate clothing, food and drink, will be unable to properly rest, have sex or bathe themselves, and will have no ornaments to decorate their bodies. In fact, the people of *Kali*-yuga will gradually come to appear like ghostly, haunted creatures.

In *Kali*-yuga men will develop hatred for each other even over a few coins. Giving up all friendly relations, they will be ready to lose their own lives and kill even their own relatives. Men will no longer protect their elderly parents, their children or their respectable wives. Thoroughly degraded, they will care only to satisfy their own bellies and genitals. In the age of *Kali* people's intelligence will be diverted by atheism, and they will almost never offer sacrifice to the Supreme Personality of Godhead, who is the supreme spiritual master of the universe. Although the great personalities who control the three worlds all bow down to the lotus feet of the Supreme Lord, the petty and miserable human beings of this age will not do so.

The influences of *Kali* are increasingly being felt by the population, and a study of Western culture, which had its advent at the beginning of this age, is a study of the degradation of *Kali*. This can most easily be seen in economic practices.

The *Gunas* and the Different Types of Human Nature

It is, no doubt, a trite understatement to say that people are different. As different as they are however, because those differences are attributable to the *gunas*, people can be broadly categorized in four basic divisions. Actually these four categories, known as *varnas*, are created by the Supreme Lord Himself for the purpose of the progressive development of society. Sri Krishna states in the *Bhagavad-gita* (4.13):

> According to the three modes of material nature and the work associated with them, the four divisions of human society are created by Me.

The modes of nature create four divisions, or *varnas*: those situated primarily in *sattva-guna*, those in *rajo-guna*, those influenced by both *rajas* and *tamo-guna*, and those primarily influenced by *tamo-guna*. Each *varna* has a particular nature and associated abilities. During *Satya-yuga* there was only one *varna*, which was divided into four during *Treta-yuga*. At that time there were persons who were the embodiment of these pure *varnas* who protected the culture by conscientiously performing their duties. Due to the influences of this age however, such ideal persons of pure *varna* and associated characteristics are rarely found. It is helpful nevertheless to understand the influence of the *gunas* on the human consciousness in the pure or ideal state. Afterwards we will look at the realities of *varna* in our modern world.

Persons situated in the quality of goodness have the ability to properly understand things. That is, they can tell right from wrong, good from bad, proper and improper action, what should be done and not done, and truth from falsity. They have natural characteristics of peacefulness, self-control, austerity, purity, tolerance, honesty, knowledge, wisdom and religiousness. Because they are non-acquisitive and non-envious they are naturally leaders in determining what to do and what not to do. They are the rightful intelligentsia of society whose role it is to explain the purposes of life: who we are, where we have come from, and where we are going. In Vedic culture they are called *brahmanas*. They are the rudder of the social flagship. However, because of their *sattvic* nature they are not very active in society. Society therefore requires the help of those who are predominantly influenced by passion.

The influences of *rajo-guna* on the human psyche generate people who are by nature natural leaders: determined, resourceful, courageous, generous, heroic and powerful. Due to the influence of passion they are able to subdue the material energy and bring it under control. They are naturally motivated by working with people and helping others. Being more capable they help to give order and direction to society. They are also skillful diplomats. These types of persons were the *ksatriyas,* the kings and rulers of ancient culture. They were not of the standard of rulers we are familiar with in recent Western history, such as the Roman emperors, the Catholic Popes, or the Russian czars, who definitely neglected, or even deliberately destroyed whatever vestiges of Vedic culture remained. The factual *ksatriyas* were fixed in Vedic principles and lived according to their duties thus prescribed. During *Dvapara-yuga* the bulk of society consisted of such genuine *brahmanas* and *ksatriyas* who were influenced by goodness and passion respectively, but in *Kali-yuga* there are but a few in a hundred. Their numbers are too small to practically organize all human activity, and therefore the help of a third group is required—those predominantly influenced by both passion and ignorance.

The people of this third group, known as *vaisyas* in Sanskrit, have a natural ability for organization and productive activity. They know what to do first, second, third, and so on, and can understood how to bring productive results from any situation. People of this nature can create wealth by producing many valuable things from nature's resources with the help of labor whom they organize. In today's vernacular *vaisyas* would be called businessmen, if businessmen actually followed the ideals of Vedic culture. The workers, known as *sudras* in Vedic culture, require instruction and guidance without which they cannot bring productive results. Nonetheless they can take instruction, and act according to such direction.

These four divisions are observed in every culture. Every culture must and does have intelligentsia, administrators, organizers and laborers, regardless of how close they may come to the ideal mentioned above. These four categories are known as the *varnas* in Vedic literature, and they naturally appear in every society, in every culture. I hasten to point out that this description of the *varnas* should not be confused, either in theory or practice, with the Hindu caste system. The occurrence in society of four types of mentality arise from the influence of the individual's *guna* and *karma*, or nature and abilities, whereas the Hindu caste system is a perverted descendent of the *varna* system, based on birthright alone. Solidifying privilege by birthright is done in ignorance. This idea is as foolish as saying that the son of a doctor, simply by taking birth in the doctor's family, should automatically be considered a qualified doctor without the necessary training or personal qualification. Or an engineer's son should automatically be considered a qualified engineer without suitable training and demonstrated understanding. The very notion is ludicrous. Likewise a *brahmana* must have specific qualifications and abilities in order to properly lead society. The position is not titular, only for a show, but has very real requirements and duties that one must be qualified to execute. The *brahmana* holds particular rank and privilege in Vedic culture because that person's abilities are significant to the overall welfare of society. But to expect the perquisites of the title without qualification, ability, or performing the functions of the position is out-and-out cheating. We might add that the caste system fixed by birth is not supported in Vedic literature, and was not practiced in India until she was subjugated by the British. It was the British who created scheduled castes in order to undermine the culture of India and subjugate her.[10]

Inherent in the system of *varna* is the concept of the duty of each segment of society to the others, with the higher orders, the *vaisyas*, *ksatriyas* and *brahmanas* having increasingly greater responsibility to the other orders. It was the duty of the higher orders to protect the lower ones, and especially to protect the weak and innocent such as *brahmanas*, women, children the elderly and the cows. Indeed, every living creature was considered a citizen in Vedic culture and entitled to the protection of the king. The duties of each *varna* were established by *Manu*, and promulgated in the *Manu Samhita*. Every member of Vedic culture traditionally voluntarily followed their duty, because that was the culture. They were not motivated by desire for gain, or threat of punishment or loss. Because the culture was established in goodness people acted out of a sense of duty—the characteristic of *Sattva-guna*.

Varna Sankara

The above is a description of the *varnas* in an ideal world, and as they existed more or less in their pure form in the ancient Vedic cultures. Think of these *varna*s as precision parts of a social machine, which when properly assembled enabled the entire culture to function as designed—all members working together for the common ideal of achieving the transcendental destination at the end of life's journey. At that time those in goodness, the *brahmanas*, or priests of society, maintained the purity of the culture. Those in passion were not just kings, but due to their spiritual purity were also considered sages, or *rishis*. Consequently they were called *raja-rishis*, or *rajarshis*, meaning saintly king. The *rajarshis* valued and respected Vedic culture and guided by the *brahmanas* insured that all members of society were properly engaged according to their *dharma*, insuring their own, as well as society's welfare. The organizers of society, the *vaisyas*, were not obsessed with accumulation of wealth and self-aggrandizement, but engaged in production as required for the proper maintenance of society according to their duty. And the laborers, or *sudras*, of the social body were submissive, dedicated, and working to their best ability. By such an arrangement everyone in society shared amicably in the material and spiritual benefits.

Ancient Vedic cultures understood the transcendental destination and the value of Vedic principles as necessary elements to help them achieve it. They therefore did their best to maintain the purity of the culture through purity of the individual, and by extension, the purity of the *varna*s. Due to the influences of *Kali* however, the ideal was abandoned as sensual attractions took precedence over maintenance of an ideal culture. Due to repeated intermarriage among the *varna*s over the course of centuries the purity of the *varna*s has almost entirely been lost. The result is called *varna sankara*, or mixed *varna*s, in which the vast majority of people now have some of the tendencies of each *varna*, and nobody really knows who he is in society, nor what role he should play. The parts of that fine-tuned social machine have become worn to the point that they do not work together so well. The priests are not pure, the *ksatriyas* are no longer saintly or otherwise qualified, and the organizers, now called businessmen, do their best to exploit labor and the workers reciprocate in kind. As a result there is chaos and everyone is doing their level best to take as much as they can from the other members of society. Of course, since we are not equals, some are better at taking than others, with the result that some sections of society, including many women, too many children, and often the elderly, are often left in a desperate condition.

The *varna* arrangement of society describes what is called the social body. Like our own body, all of the parts are meant to serve the entire being. The *brahmanas* are considered the head of society, the *ksatriyas* as the arms, the *vaisyas* as the belly, and the *sudras* as the legs. When all parts of the body are engaged in service to the whole, the body can be maintained in a healthy state. This is true for the social body if it acts as one unit. But when one part loses its connection with the whole and seeks its own self-interest, there can only be difficulty for the entire social body. In our modern society this distinction of, and connection between, the various parts of the body has been lost. We each strive for our own self-interest, seemingly independent of the others, as if this were possible. Attempting to find fulfillment in that way is as ludicrous as the various parts of our own body trying to act independently for their "own" welfare. Can the arms be happy independently of the head? Can the head be happy without the help of the stomach for nourishment? Can the stomach be happy without the help of the arms and legs? Or can the stomach simply enjoy everything and neglect to distribute the benefit to all the other parts of the body? No. Neither can the parts of the social body survive without a mutually beneficial relationship, but that is the state of the world today. Each member of society is attempting to take care of themselves alone, with no relationship or obligation to the other sections of society, very few are happy, and all but a very few have insufficient resources for any kind of meaningful life. The idea that we can be independent of others and still be happy in this world is but another of the illusions of modern life.

The personal commitment of the members of Vedic culture to its principles created a social contract that protected and benefited all members of society. The contract was that each member of society would contribute to the benefit of others as their natural abilities allowed. The *brahmanas* would see to the spiritual welfare and direction of society. The *ksatriyas* would provide physical protection from harm as well as ensuring that every member was properly engaged in productive activity. The *vaisyas* organized the productive efforts of society and managed the distribution of goods, while the *sudras* supplied the labor. In the context of a culture devoid of any idea of money, the interdependence of all members was not difficult to recognize. In a smaller personal world it was likely that you knew the person who made your shoes or clothing, or provided your milk. What were you giving in return? Something was expected and an obligation was felt. Importantly, the members of society were able to maintain their personal commitment to this ideal because of the influences of *sattva-guna*, and it continued as long as *sattva-guna* remained. This social arrangement was further supported by each person's commitment to a higher spiritual ideal—the goal of transferring themselves to a higher destination at the end of life—a heavenly reward if not complete spiritual emancipation. It was widely prevalent in years long past, but due to the increasing influences of passion and ignorance, commitment to this ideal could not be maintained. It was perverted into the caste system in Indian culture, and in the West continued in its basic form in medieval society through the Middle Ages.

The *Gunas* and the Natural World

Exploring the influences of the *gunas* farther, let's consider how people see this world. Ecologists claim that one of the foundational aspects of our collapsing ecosystems is that we see others, particularly the non-human world, as fundamentally different from ourselves. Hence we have little or no reason for caring for nature. For example, according to environmentalist Fritjof Capra "logic does not lead us from the fact that we are an integral part of the web of life to certain norms of how we should live. However, if we have deep ecological awareness, or experience, of being part of the web of life, then we will (as opposed to should) be inclined to care for all living nature. Indeed, we can scarcely refrain from responding in this way." Why do only some people have such an environmental consciousness? Because they have some modicum of *sattva-guna*.

Those in passion see each living entity differently. Their consciousness dictates that if the body is different, then the life is different. Persons under the influence of passion (what to speak of ignorance) *cannot* see the oneness of life. For them a fish cannot have the same value as a human being. The fish, pigs, cows, and chickens are all seen simply as objects for man's use. The owls, frogs and birds, all innocent victims of man's sloppy environmental housekeeping and habitat destruction, are not seen on par with people by those too influenced by *rajo-guna*. Neither can they see themselves as just another strand in the web of life, ostensibly equal to the other members of our planetary home. What to speak of animals, they cannot extend a vision of equality to other humans, be they different due to sex, skin color, race, nationality or culture. This understanding of equality is available only to those who have sufficiently cultivated goodness (18.20): "That knowledge by which one undivided spiritual nature is seen in all living entities, though they are divided into innumerable forms, you should understand to be in the mode of goodness." Therefore we can understand social commentator Wendell Berry's conclusion that "people need to understand more than their obligations to one another and to earth; they also need the feelings of such obligations." This simply cannot be realized by the majority of people who are steeped in passion and ignorance. Only by coming to increasing *sattva-guna* can such ideas be grasped.

The destructiveness that we witness in economics, in human relations, in the environment, in politics, or any other place is due to the influences of *tamo-guna*. There is only one way that these can be restored to a healthy condition, and that is by bringing into our activities, thinking and consciousness, the healing and nurturing influences of *sattva-guna*, or *suddha-sattva*—transcendental goodness.

The Vedic perspective provides something else that is entirely missing in modern culture—an absolute standard by which to understand what is beneficial or destructive, what will uplift and what will degrade humanity, and therefore what should be done and what should not be done in the interest of, and benefit for all society. Because its basis for understanding and decision making lies beyond the material condition of life, the Vedic perspective offers an absolute understanding of the differences between good and bad, and right and wrong. The idea of moral relativism, based on the pleasures of the mind and body and relative only to oneself, is based on an illusory bodily conception of life. The *Bhagavata* understanding of life allows us to reestablish the moral compass that has been destroyed by ignorance. This is not a matter of one section of society arbitrarily imposing i's will on others, but a scientific influence that can be observed in practice in any part of the world. The quality of goodness enlightens and uplifts while the quality of ignorance confuses, degrades and destroys. Although there will always be a section of society who are intent on using their free will to degrade themselves, if we want a healthy society, a healthy environment, and a healthy future for our children and grandchildren, society must somehow be brought to the standard of *sattva-guna*. We cannot chart a course there unless we first know where we are now, and that will be understood as we progress through the next few chapters.

We have learned how the *gunas* influence our perceptions of life and in turn how this conditions the consciousness of all people. The manner in which we pursue our economic activity is but a result of that consciousness and conditioning. But there is more to understanding the economic behavior of man, specifically those attributes that are thought, in these modern times at least, to motivate him in his economic dealings—lust, envy and greed.

Chapter Two

Lust, Envy and Greed

O my Lord, those whose hearts are bewildered by the influence of lust, envy, greed, and illusion are interested only in falsity in this world created by Your maya. Attached to various illusions created by maya they wander in this material world perpetually. Srimad-Bhagavatam 9.8.25

In considering the whys and wherefores of the economics of man we should also consider the qualities of lust, envy and greed, which too often in today's world are helpful accomplices for delivering economic results. This is according to one of the 20th century's most able economic captains, John Maynard Keynes. He was of a mind that economics might one day be able to serve the human race, rather than man serving the needs of vested interests. However, although he dreamed of a future time in which everyone would be the beneficiary of economic surplus he nonetheless advocated the use of a lesser morality to achieve that end. In *Economic Possibilities for our Grandchildren* he writes:

> I see us free, therefore, to return to some of the most sure and certain principles of religion and traditional virtue—that avarice is a vice, that the exaction of usury is a misdemeanour, and the love of money is detestable, that those [who] walk most truly in the paths of virtue and sane wisdom [are those] who take least thought for the morrow. We shall once more value ends above means and prefer the good to the useful. We shall honour those who can teach us how to pluck the hour and the day virtuously and well, the delightful people who are capable of taking direct enjoyment in things, the lilies of the field who toil not, neither do they spin.

> But beware! The time for all this is not yet. For at least another hundred years we must pretend to ourselves and to every one that fair is foul and foul is fair; for foul is useful and fair is not. Avarice

52

and usury and precaution must be our gods for a little longer still. For only they can lead us out of the tunnel of economic necessity into daylight.[1]

Lust generally refers to desires of the flesh. This is its definition as a noun. But in this discussion I want to define it as a verb, meaning intense, or extreme desire, which can be directed to objects of any variety such as the lust of consumers to "get it all, *and now!*" In this sense lust is a significant factor fueling the economic engine, particularly for the United States, since consumer activity is the basis for a significant portion of its economy. "Keeping up with the Jones'" is another important aspect of economic activity. The possessions and fortunes of others incite desires in our own heart, thus envy figures importantly in the economic calculus as well. And greed is too often *the* driving force behind much economic activity, especially mergers and acquisitions creating corporate behemoths wherein a handful of companies control the destiny of the entire world. Intense and unlimited desires, the envy of others, and unlimited and unmitigated greed are significant forces shaping modern man's economic conduct. Indeed, lust, envy and greed can be said to be the driving forces behind the practice of what has been dubbed "predatory economics." Therefore, if we are to fully understand economic man in the modern context we must first understand the foundation of these qualities.

Some say that these qualities are the inherent nature of the human being. The Christian and Buddhist traditions for example, accept lust, envy and greed as an unavoidable part of the human condition. But if these qualities actually are inherent in humans why are they not consistently displayed by all humans, across time and throughout populations? And why do they seem to be increasing in our Western culture over the past fifty years? Understanding these influences as they are explained in Vedic literature will help us to understand the economic behavior of modern man.

The Development of Lust

"I want...I want...I want . . ." is the mantra of lust. The list of things that we want seems to be endless. No matter how much we get there are always more things that we want. Our wish list is never fulfilled because our desires continue to expand. The *Bhagavatam* explains why: because we are infected by the modes of nature. The qualities of lust and hankering (desire) are the symptoms of passion and ignorance. By contemplating the objects of the senses we develop a desire to have them; from that desire attachment arises, and from attachment comes lust.

This progression is easy enough to understand. Consider anything that you may have in your possession. Before you acquired it you first thought about having it, and based on your desire you took the necessary action to acquire it. This progression is very subtle of course, and often completely unconscious. We don't stop to examine from where our desires spring; all we know is that we want something. Of course there is practically no limit to the number of desires a person might have, especially given the nature of modern marketing techniques that artificially increase the demands of the senses. How many times have you gone to the store for one item and left with others you had no intention of buying when you walked in the door? Merchandisers know how to increase your desires and they attractively arrange their displays to capture your attention. Once you have seen the item the result is often *fait accompli*. Contemplating the object you develop a desire for it, and another purchase is made.

Children provide very good examples of this phenomenon because they are so transparent in their desires and actions. Take them down the candy aisle and their senses go wild. They want everything they see—their little hands stretching out from the shopping cart with such vigor that it seems that they might well levitate the cherished object right off the shelf. It is often a much harried mom who valiantly tries to get out the door without their little one crying hysterically over the desires that they couldn't fulfill. The *Gita* explains that reaction as well: anger is the result of the frustration of our desires.

Part of our acculturation as we grow into adults is to regulate our desires according to what we can afford or reasonably obtain, balanced against other competing needs and desires, and as importantly, to develop the intelligence to recognize those desires or temptations that we are better off without. Another part of this acculturation is learning to express or conceal our desires in such a way that we think most beneficial to achieving them. Children are clever and often quickly learn how to manipulate their inexperienced or unwitting parents in achieving their desires. While younger children unabashedly reveal their desires, as they mature they learn to be much more subtle or even crafty in expressing them. If crying and temper tantrums work that behavior will be called on whenever required, and as they mature it can develop into a more sophisticated display of emotional distress over unmet desires. Most adults progress beyond temper tantrums to achieve their desires by either subtly or directly expressing them to those capable of fulfilling them. Hints or suggestions, expressions of envy, direct requests, intellectual coercion or even hostile arguments are also employed. Of course the healthiest behavior is to obtain one's desires by one's honest efforts, and good people everywhere do so. But if such desires are very strong and honest means are insufficient, too troublesome, or considered unnecessary to fulfill them, deception, theft, bribery, fraud, and violence can also be used. These may even be the methods of first choice for persons accustomed to such dealings.

At times circumstances may make it socially inappropriate to reveal ones actual desires or intentions. They will then be concealed or expressed in discreet and tactful ways. Vedic texts define this desire to hide one's real mentality as *avahittha*, or concealment. As the Vaishnava *acarya* Srila Bhaktivinoda Thakur expresses in his *Jaiva Dharma* "Leaving this straight path for that of deception, [one] becomes sly, engages in unscrupulous dealings, and tries to hide his crookedness behind a facade of sweet words and postured civility." Oftentimes those sweet words are merely lies. Lies and intrigue are not infrequently employed in obtaining the objects of our desire. Through lies and other obfuscation we may disguise our intentions altogether, or create some elaborate scheme by which to achieve our end without revealing our hand. Efforts in duplicity or falsity however, are a dangerous trap in which the practitioner soon becomes a victim of his own doing. Practicing to deceive by blurring the lines between truth and falsity for others, a person soon *looses the ability* to distinguish between truth and falsity. In other words, by attempting to put others into illusion we ourselves fall under the same illusion. The truth is whatever we want it to be, or so we think, but that does not make it so. By the repeated practice of duplicity we place ourselves further under the control of *maya*. This *maya* helps to form our *ahankara*, or false ego, wherein we hide our real mentality even from our very selves. We become unable to understand our own motivations, and actions.

Our first act of deception is our desire to enjoy the property of God, falsely thinking of ourselves as the rightful enjoyers of the things of this world. Srila Prabhupada explains this in several places throughout his works:

> He is spirit. He has nothing to do with this material world, but he wanted it. Or the real thing is that he wanted to enjoy by becoming the master. He is servant...Sometimes servants desire it that 'Why am I the servant? Why not master?' That is natural. But the natural position is he is subordinate, a servant. If he remains servant of God, then he's happy always. But because he desired to become master, so he cannot become master in the spiritual world, because in the spiritual world the master is God, Krishna. So he is given the chance, 'All right, go to the material world and become master.' So he's struggling for existence, and everyone is trying to become master.[2]

> There is no necessity of tracing out the history of when the living entity desired this. But the fact is that as soon as he desired it, he was put under the control of *atma-maya* by the direction of the Lord. Therefore the living entity in his material condition is dreaming falsely

that this is "mine" and this is "I." The dream is that the conditioned soul thinks of his material body as "I" or falsely thinks that he is the Lord and that everything in connection with that material body is "mine." Thus only in dream does the misconception of "I" and "mine" persist life after life. This continues life after life, as long as the living entity is not purely conscious of his identity as the subordinate part and parcel of the Lord.[3]

The entire process of self-realization is meant to eliminate self-deception, so that we can see the truth as it is, recognize our own position relative to this world and its creator, and let go of our ill-conceived and ill-begotten desires and attachments—the very ropes that bind us to repeated birth and death in this material world. Those who aspire to self-realization become straightforward in their dealings with others. The passage quoted above by Bhaktivinoda Thakur later continues: "True culture, in its pristine state, shorn of all immorality, is found amongst the *Vaisnavas*. Real culture means worthiness to participate in a serious truthful assembly—in other words, simple decency—but the contemporary definition of culture is simply a method of masking mischievous internal motives, which are gradually further perverted into deceit."

Never-Ending Sense Desires

Sensual activity, bringing happiness in the mode of passion, provides immediate gratification and the promise of fulfillment. There is a problem with sensual delight however in that its gratification soon fades, and while it may give us pleasure it does not give us satisfaction. As soon as the immediate happiness fades we seek another experience that promises pleasurable feelings, only to find the satisfaction fade. Again, and again we repeat the behavior. We try different experiences, or different people, endlessly changing the caste of characters, events and places. A new situation may seem to offer a new experience, but it's really just old wine in new bottles. Who bothers to make such an analysis? Few if any, and the process is repeated through countless lifetimes.

The behavior of children once more provides an easy and universal example. Candies taste good, but because their intelligence is not sufficiently developed children don't know when to stop eating them. Children will continue to eat entire bowls filled with candies until they make themselves sick. Eventually we learn when to stop eating candies, but those desires are simply replaced by others some of which can prove addictive for adults. These desires, the list of which is very long, include a variety of sensual activities and other more destructive behaviors. Consider that there are now more than one hundred 12-Step programs, the popular behavioral modification programs designed to help adults to overcome addictions to such things as: gambling, eating addictions and compulsions, consciousness altering drugs, cigarettes, self-mutilators, sex addiction and prostitution, shoplifting, compulsive shopping, and compulsive debt. While the initial experiences may bring some sense of pleasure these behaviors become uncontrollable passions and problems resulting in distress and despair.

The senses are thus bad masters. Regardless of how much one may strive to please them they are never satisfied and always demand more. In order to satisfy their strong desires people may engage in illegal or sinful, even abominable acts, or accept many different types of hardships, austerities, scorn or insults. "Despite being subjected to the necessities of the body, mind and senses and suffering from various types of disease, and other kinds of tribulations, due to his lust to enjoy the world the living entity is carried away by many plans. Although transcendental to this material existence, the living entity, out of ignorance, and under the consciousness of "I and mine," accepts all these material miseries." (4.29.24–25)

The condition of addiction is one where we find ourselves forced to engage our senses with their objects—even against our own will. Aware of the troubles that the senses bring Arjuna asks Sri Krishna how it is that one is forced to obey the dictations of the senses even when they compel him to sinful acts. Sri Krishna replies: "it is lust only Arjuna, the all-devouring sinful enemy of this world. It is born of contact with the mode of passion and later transformed into wrath. The living entity's pure consciousness becomes covered by his eternal enemy in the form of lust, which is never satisfied and which burns like fire. The senses, the mind and the intelligence are the sitting places of this lust. Through them lust covers the real knowledge of the living entity and bewilders him." (3.36–37, 39–40)

To say that the senses, mind and intelligence are the residence of lust is to say that they are polluted or contaminated by lust. Polluted by lust the intelligence is constantly making plans how to achieve the objects of desire; the mind constantly recalls the sensations obtained by engaging the senses with their objects, and the senses themselves hanker for that stimulation. Having been polluted by lust the senses, mind and intelligence become both attached and conditioned to the experience, which act to form a corresponding conception of life in which desires, and the means to achieve them become the very reason for one's existence, justifying whatever means are used to obtain them. In this manner sinful and criminal behavior become accepted or even normal to the person who is the slave of lust.

The *Bhagavatam* provides a fitting metaphor to describe this situation. Picture a chariot being pulled by five horses. The horses represent the senses, the reigns are the mind, the driver is the intelligence, the chariot is the material body, and the passenger is the soul. When the intelligence is good, it controls the mind and senses. Therefore it understands where to go and where not to go, based on the interests of the passenger, the soul. The driver of the chariot of the body thus safely delivers the passenger to the desired destination. But if the horses are out of control or the reigns not properly used or connected to the horses, or if the driver is drunk or asleep, no good result can come of the situation.

First of all the intelligence must be properly established with knowledge of what the body is, who the passenger is, how to control the mind, and what the desired destination of human life is, then, and only then, is the intelligence fit to direct all activities. If the intelligence is untrained, or does not know how to control the mind, it cannot properly direct the action, so the result will be questionable. This describes the condition of modern civilization. There is no longer any understanding of the spiritual nature of man, or our purpose in this world, nor the proper destination of human life. The senses and mind are allowed to run free, completely uncontrolled. The mind and intelligence are used by the senses to aid them in achieving their objects of desire. "The senses are so strong and impetuous, O Arjuna, that they forcibly carry away the mind even of a man of discrimination who is endeavoring to control them." (2.60) Responsible human life thus requires that the mind and senses be strictly controlled. The *Bhagavatam* therefore warns us (7.15.46) "the senses, acting as the horses, and the intelligence, acting as the driver, both being prone to material contamination, inattentively bring the body, which acts as the chariot, to the path of sense gratification. When one is thus attracted again by the rogues of eating, sleeping and mating, the horses and chariot driver are thrown into the blinding dark well of material existence, and one is again put into a dangerous and extremely fearful situation of repeated birth and death."

Mind is the Nexus of Lust Leading to Perpetual Material Life

Not knowing who we are prevents us from resolving the pitiable condition of endless hankering for the objects of desire and lamenting for what has been lost. How can the intelligence function effectively, deciding what is acceptable and what is not, if it is completely unaware of the truths of life? Understanding one's long-term interests depends entirely on one's conception of the self. If the intelligence is not trained to understand that the perceiver of experience is the soul who is different from the body and mind, how can it discriminate on the basis of one's spiritual, or eternal, interests? It cannot. In such a situation the intelligence has no basis for decision making.

Most people think that they are the body, or perhaps the mind. Others may have some idea of the soul, but because of the vagueness of this concept offered in the mainstream religious traditions, they are unsure of what that means. Being conditioned to identifying with the body and the mind, any desire that comes into the consciousness is taken to be "my" desire, and we thus think "'I' want this," "'I' want that." Who does this inner voice that says "'I' want" belong to? There are three possible sources of the inner voice: "I" the soul, "I" the intelligence, and "I" the mind.[4] These elements are so subtle in their nature that one can understand the difference between them only by their function.

The function of the intelligence is to discriminate between that which is desirable or undesirable on the basis of one's long-term interests. The function of the mind is to determine what is desirable or undesirable based on sense gratification, while the actual desire of the soul is to find the ever-fresh source of his satisfaction in his original transcendental state. In order to determine "who" is speaking, introspection is required—we must examine the thought according to these criteria. Training to distinguish between the voices of consciousness is the purpose of the practice of yoga.[5] Does it ask for sense gratification? If so, that is the voice of the mind. Does it encourage one to think about one's long-term welfare? Then that is the voice of intelligence. Of course these voices may conflict with each other. The cartoon of such moral dilemmas depicts an angel on one shoulder and the devil on the other: "do it," "no, don't do it," "yes, do it."...and the battle rages. The devil and angel represent the mind and intelligence respectively. The mind is eager to taste some delectable, even forbidden, fruit, but the intelligence recognizes that there will be a price to pay further down the road, and it is better that one act for long-term happiness.

Since most people do not understand the distinction between the gross and subtle bodies, the distinction between the mind and intelligence, or the presence and nature of the soul, and assume that the inner voice is but a singular "me," they necessarily assume that every desire is "their" desire. Whenever only immediate pleasures are considered the mind has *carte blanche*. But because the uncontrolled mind is one's worst enemy this creates a dangerous situation. Acting according to the dictations of one's enemy can never bring a favorable result. Conditioned by a materialistic conception of life, the mind desires many things that become a source of trouble and repeated births in this material world. The *Bhagavatam* therefore asks (5.6.5): "The mind is the root cause of lust, anger, pride, greed, lamentation, illusion and fear. Combined, these constitute bondage to fruitive activity. Therefore what learned man puts his faith in the mind?" It explains: "The soul's designation, the mind, is the cause of all tribulations in the material world. As long as this fact is unknown to the conditioned living entity, he has to accept the miserable condition of the material body and wander within this universe in different positions. Because the mind is affected by disease, lamentation, illusion, attachment, greed and enmity, it creates bondage and a false sense of intimacy within this material world." (5.11.16)

To further illustrate the role of the mind in creating material bondage as well as happiness and distress Lord Krishna tells us of a story about the *Brahmana* from Avanti:

> This *brahmana* had been an agriculturalist and merchant. He had been extremely greedy, miserly and prone to anger. As a result, his wife, sons, daughters, relatives and servants were all deprived of every kind of enjoyment and gradually gave up their affection for him. In due course of time, thieves, family members and providence took away all of his wealth. Thus finding himself without any property and abandoned by everyone, he developed a deep sense of renunciation. He was grateful that this sense of detachment had arisen in his heart and considered it the factual means for delivering his soul from material bondage.

> In such a state of renunciation the Avanti *brahmana* began to wander about the earth concealing his spiritual position by presenting himself as an old and dirty beggar. Rowdy persons would dishonor him with many insults. Yet while being insulted by low-class men trying to affect his downfall, he remained steady in his spiritual duties. Fixing his resolution in the mode of goodness, he thought:

> "These people are not the cause of my happiness and distress. Neither are the demigods*, my own body, the planets, my past work, or time. Rather, it is the mind alone that causes happiness and distress and perpetuates the rotation of material life. The powerful mind actuates the functions of the material modes, from which evolve the different kinds of material activities in the modes of goodness, passion and ignorance. According to his activities in these modes one develops corresponding statuses of life. I, the infinitesimal spirit soul, have embraced this mind, which is the mirror reflecting the image of the material world. Thus I have become engaged in enjoying objects of desire and am entangled due to contact with the modes of nature.

> "Charity, prescribed duties, observance of major and minor regulative principles, hearing from scripture, pious works and purifying vows all have as their final aim the subduing of the mind. Indeed,

---

* The demigods are the controllers of universal affairs. These agents of the Lord control the functions of the universal elements such as sun, moon, rain, wind, ocean, the movements of the living beings in birth and death, dispensation of karma, etc.

concentration of the mind on the Supreme is the highest yoga. If one's mind is perfectly fixed and pacified, then what need does one have to perform ritualistic charity and other pious rituals? If one's mind remains uncontrolled, lost in ignorance, then of what use are these engagements for him? All the senses have been under the control of the mind since time immemorial, and the mind himself never comes under the sway of any other. He is stronger than the strongest, and his godlike power is fearsome. Therefore, anyone who can bring the mind under control becomes the master of all the senses.

"Failing to conquer this irrepressible enemy, the mind, whose urges are intolerable and who torments the heart, many people are completely bewildered and create useless quarrel with others. Thus they conclude that other people are either their friends, their enemies or parties indifferent to them. Persons who identify with this body, which is simply the product of the material mind, are blinded in their intelligence, thinking in terms of "I and mine." Because of their illusion of "this is I, but that is someone else," they wander in endless darkness."[6]

Sri Krishna concludes the story of the Avanti *brahmana* by confirming the mind as the nexus of our material existence: "No other force besides his own mental confusion makes the soul experience happiness and distress. The perception of friends, neutral parties, and enemies, and the whole experience of material life built around this perception are simply created out of ignorance." Illusion created out of ignorance is thus the genesis of lust.

*   *   *

Envy—The Scourge of Plentiful Prosperity

Envy has very real-world results in terms of economic affairs. Consider that the definition of envy is the desire to have what others possess, even though they have no right to it. When materialistic and envious people see the opulence of others they immediately begin to determine how to get the same or more. In cases of extreme envy, they become spiteful of others' prosperity and seek to impoverish them. There is no better example of the influence of envy and its vicissitude in economics than the history of India.

It was once a country of stupendous wealth. Nicolo Conti described that in the early fifteenth century the banks of the Ganges were lined with one prosperous city after another, each well designed, rich in gardens, and orchards, silver and gold, commerce and industry. Mount Stuart Elphinstone writes "The Hindu kingdoms overthrown by the Moslems, were so wealthy that Moslem historians tire of telling of the immense loot of jewels and gold captured by the invaders."[7] Although extensive trade with India had been going on for millennia, and almost any of her riches could be had by such legitimate means, the lust and envy of the invaders precluded this more reasonable method. Lust over her riches, and the covetousness of "I and mine" over her treasure was their desire.

The wealth of India was repeatedly sacked, but still when Shah Jahan was emperor his treasury included two underground strong rooms, each some 150,000 cubic feet in capacity, that were almost entirely filled with silver and gold. But although the Moguls conquered India, they did not destroy her. The British historian Vincent Smith in his *Akbar* (Oxford, 1919 ed.) acknowledges that India prospered even into the 19th century: "contemporary testimonies permit no doubt that the urban population of the more important cities was well to do." Indeed, travelers described Agra and Fatehpur Sikri as each greater and richer than London. Not only were the cities prosperous but the entire citizenry were as well, as reported by Anquetil-Duperron, who, journeying thru the Maratha districts in 1760 found himself "in the midst of the simplicity and happiness of the golden age...the people were cheerful, vigorous, and in high health." Such prosperity continued into the later years of the Mogul reign, as Maria Graham who visited Pune in the early nineteenth century informs us: "Among the lower classes (castes) it is very common to see a man loaded with gold and silver on his hands, feet, waist, neck, ears and nose." Robert Clive, the chief architect of the British empire in India, upon visiting Murshidabad in 1759, concluded that she "was a country of inexhaustible riches."

India's opulence was due to the fact that the populous adhered to the religious principles of dharma. The higher classes, not being envious, allowed all classes to share in the vast wealth. The populace was active in all varieties of manufacturing, doing an active trade with the Roman Empire even at the beginning of the current era.[8] The Reverend Jabuz Sunderland chronicled: "This wealth, was created by the Hindus' vast and varied industries. Nearly every kind of manufacture or product known to the civilized world—nearly every kind of creation of Man's brain and hand, existing anywhere, and prized either for its utility or beauty—had long, long been produced in India. India was a far greater industrial and manufacturing nation than any in Europe or than any other in Asia. Her textile goods—the fine products of her loom, in cotton, wool, linen, and silk—were famous over the civilized world; so were her exquisite jewelry and her precious stones, cut in every lovely form; so were her pottery, porcelains, ceramics of every kind, quality, color and beautiful shape; so were her fine works in metal – iron, steel, silver and gold. She had great architecture—equal in beauty to any in the world. She had great engineering works. She had great merchants, great business men, great bankers and financiers. Not only was she the greatest ship-building nation, but she had great commerce and trade by land and sea which extended to all known civilized countries. Such was the India which the British found when they came."[9]

In 1750, her relative share of entire world's manufacturing output was 24.5 percent, higher than the combined output of the United Kingdom, France, Germany, Habsburg Empire, Italian states, and Russia. India was also a major producer and exporter of textiles. The city of Kasimbazar in Bengal alone produced over 2 million pounds of raw silk annually during the 1680s, more than eight times that of Europe's foremost silk producer of the time, Sicily. The cotton weavers of Gujarat turned out almost 3 million pieces a year for export alone, dwarfing that of the largest textile enterprise in continental Europe which produced less than 100,000 pieces per year.[10]

However inexhaustible India's wealth might have appeared, it was intolerable to the envious British who made it their policy to eliminate her manufacturing competition and make her an agricultural colony only, bringing the once productive and prosperous Bharata to destitution and dependency. The methods they used to accomplish this ignoble feat are tried and true, and have been repeated all over the globe for hundreds of years since the earliest times of colonization, and even before that on a lesser scale with neighboring countries, cities and even villages. The process continues to this very day on a planetary-wide scale under the seemingly benign, even beneficial, concept of Global Free Trade.

The Result of Lust, Jealousy and Pride

As we have quoted Srila Prabhupada above, when the *jiva* desires to become the lord of this world he is put under the spell of illusion, thus he attempts to imitate the Lord as the enjoyer of this world. To say that the living being wants to lord it over this world does not necessarily mean as the supreme enjoyer, although that may certainly be the case. The factual meaning of being the lord of this world means to be the enjoyer of the material energy. Depending on the qualities of the *gunas* one has become conditioned to, one can take that as far as his consciousness determines. Under the influence of *sattva-guna* one will enjoy that which is naturally obtainable without extensive endeavor. Under the influence of passion one makes a strong endeavor to obtain the objects of his desire. But in ignorance one dispenses with all niceties and simply takes what he wants according to his ability.

Regardless of the scale and scope that one is able to achieve, the desire to exhibit one's superiority over others is characteristic of the materialistic mentality. This desire is called pride. Jealousy, the inability to tolerate the opulence of another, is concomitant with pride. Envy is the resentment of, or even spite toward another, upon seeing their opulence or success. It is derived from the combination of lust, jealousy and pride. These qualities combine in this way: due to lust one is not satisfied with what he has and always wants more—how much more? At the very least he must have more than others, in order to be considered superior to them. Being jealous of those who have more than us, we are unable to tolerate their opulence because of our pride. We are spiteful for what they have achieved, and want what they have.

Envy is the Fuel of Conspicuous Consumption

> Due to ignorance, the materialistic person does not know anything about his real self-interest, the auspicious path in life. He is simply bound to material enjoyment by lusty desires, and all his plans are made for this purpose. For temporary sense gratification, such a person creates a society of envy, and due to this mentality, he plunges into the ocean of suffering. Such a foolish person does not even know about this. (5.5.16)

Persons fully absorbed in the consciousness of "I and mine" are naturally envious and they therefore want to advertise their "superior" status to others. Thus envy drives one to acquire as much as or hopefully more than their rivals so that they feel equal to, if not superior to others in their evaluation of themselves. But there must be some means by which one can measure themselves against others, and thus materialistic persons create a society of envy in which they strive to out-do, out-accumulate, out-use, and out-perform each other. Thus we now see designer labels worn on the *outside* of the latest fashions, and name brands have become the visible means by which one displays their wealth and thus advertises their prestige. It is envy that fuels conspicuous consumption, in which the wealthy extravagantly consume in excess beyond the GDP of two-thirds of the countries of the world, spending for example $300,000 for a Breguet watch, or $48,000 for a Michel Perchin pen.[11]

There is perhaps no better description of the self-absorbed effete materialist than *The Theory of the Leisure Class* written as a satire a century ago by economist and social critic Thorstein Veblen. Veblen describes the mentality of those who think of themselves in terms of the things that they possess, and who, due to their envy of others, must demonstrate their superiority through consumption: "During the earlier stages of economic development, consumption of goods without stint, especially consumption of the better grades of goods—ideally all consumption in excess of the subsistence minimum—pertains normally to the leisure class." Veblen describes the "quasi-peaceable gentleman of leisure" who "consumes of the staff of life far beyond the minimum required for subsistence and physical efficiency." His consumption must be marked not only in quality but in quantity as well. In order to display his status he requires the help of others in disposing of the finer, no, the very best in food, drink, narcotics, shelter, services, ornaments, apparel, weapons and accoutrements, amusements, amulets, and even idols or divinities. Satisfaction though, is not the sole purpose of their consumption. "The canon of reputability is at hand and seizes upon such innovations as are, according to its standard, fit to survive. Since the consumption of these more excellent goods is an evidence of wealth, it becomes honorific; and conversely, the failure to consume in due quantity and quality becomes a mark of inferiority and demerit."

The term "conspicuous consumption" was coined by Veblen in this work, and he demonstrated that it had a very specific purpose—a means of reputability to the gentleman of leisure:

> As wealth accumulates on his hands, his own unaided effort will not avail to sufficiently put his opulence in evidence by this method. The aid of friends and competitors is therefore brought in by resorting to the giving of valuable presents and expensive feasts and entertainments. Presents and feasts had no doubt another origin than that of naive ostentation, but they acquired their utility for this purpose very early, and they have retained that character to the present; so that their utility in this respect has now long been the substantial ground on which these usages rest. Costly entertainments, such as the potlatch or the ball, are peculiarly adapted to serve this purpose. The competitor with whom the entertainer wishes to institute a comparison is, by this method, also made to serve as a means to the end. He consumes vicariously for his host at the same time that he is a witness to the consumption of that excess of good things which his host is unable to dispose of single-handed, and he is also made to witness his host's facility in etiquette. [12]

Lost to any deeper understanding of themselves such persons can no longer understand their existence beyond the brands they use and the labels that they wear, and this is true of people at every income level, not just the leisure class. Precluded from using brand names priced in the stratosphere to note their pedigree, the less affluent use branding as a means of finding an identity both in life and in death. Brand names are thus not just something that make an item stand out on the shelf, but are perceived as offering an entrance into a more desirable world, even replacing religious faith as the source of purpose in life.

A few years back in an article appearing in the Financial Times the advertising agency Young & Rubicam stated that brands are "the new religion," and that people are turning to brands to find meaning in life. The brands that are succeeding they say, are those that portray themselves as being connected with original ideas and strong beliefs on which they appear to refuse to compromise. These brands are also the ones that appear to have the passion and energy necessary to change the world, and in this way they convert people to their way of thinking. [13]

In the Times' article the London design agency Fitch similarly supported the claim of brand name deification by noting that between 1991 and 2001 some 6,000 couples pledged their vows of matrimony at the altar of Walt Disney World, and that instead of going to church on Sundays many people choose instead to pay homage at stores like the home furnishings giant IKEA. The Times' article further tells us that some brands also pave the path to the hereafter and those pearly-gates—being buried in Harley-branded coffins has apparently become a popular final tribute to their deity amongst Harley-Davidson motorcycle aficionados.

Extreme Envy Leads to Self-envy

Just imagine! Lust can increase to such a degree that a person can be envious of their own self—that is, their actual, spiritual self. Not understanding their true spiritual nature, impelled by lust and envy, such persons commit violence to themselves and others, acting in spite of their own future spiritual well being, as explained by Srila Prabhupada (16.18 purport):

> A demoniac person, being always against God's supremacy, does not like to believe in the scriptures. He is envious of both the scriptures and the existence of the Supreme Personality of Godhead. This is caused by his so-called prestige and his accumulation of wealth and strength. He does not know that the present life is a preparation for the next life. Not knowing this, he is actually envious of his own self, as well as of others. He commits violence on other bodies and on his own. He does not care for the supreme control of the Personality of Godhead, because he has no knowledge. Being envious of the scriptures and the Supreme Personality of Godhead, he puts forward false arguments against the existence of God and denies the scriptural authority. He thinks himself independent and powerful in every action. He thinks that since no one can equal him in strength, power or wealth, he can act in any way and no one can stop him. If he has an enemy who might check the advancement of his sensual activities, he makes plans to cut him down by his own power.

Self-envy means to act spitefully towards one's own self, to deny any benefit that might accrue to one's self by introspection, or spiritual practices. Self-envy is the product of the mode of darkness and by this influence one takes that which is wrong to be right, and that which is right to be wrong. Such persons are their own worst enemies.

The Envious Are Intolerant of the Happiness of Others

A person who is lost to his spiritual nature actually endeavors to expand his lust thinking that this increases his enjoyment more and more. This mentality relates to the question posed by Alan Durning in his book *How Much is Enough?* Almost incomprehensible to the average person is the fact that some people want it *all*. The demonic consciousness allows one to think that such enjoyment can and should be increased without limit. Such consciousness however, also prevents one from being satisfied with what they already have, thus increases in lust automatically increase the envy of others. Lust, jealousy and pride combine to generate enviousness of an extreme degree, as noted in the description of the demonic mentality in the Gita: "so much is mine today and it will increase in the future more and more. He is my enemy and I have killed him, and I will kill my other enemy also...I am perfect, powerful and happy." Under the influence of such envy the demonic become unhappy at seeing the happiness of others; they actually become *happier* when they see the unhappiness and suffering of others. Such extreme envy is thus one of the prime motivators behind the predatory economic practices that are disenfranchising and devouring the weak and helpless. We usually think of envy as an emotion or feeling we experience when we see something that others have and we want. What could the poor of the world have, that the wealthy would want? Their money, their happiness and their contentment—*all* of it. We will explore this further in a later chapter.

The commonness of envy and through it the desire to do harm to others was demonstrated by an experiment conducted by Professors Daniel Zizzo of Oxford University and Andrew Oswald of Warwick University.[14] The experiment was a game played which created wealth distribution among participants by means of betting, but some of the participants were given an arbitrary gift, of which everyone was aware, giving them an unfair advantage. After the betting stage of the experiment was completed the participants were allowed to anonymously reduce ("burn") the amount of other participant's winnings, but to do so they would have to pay a price, giving up some of their own cash. Despite this cost, and contrary to the assumptions of economics textbooks, two thirds of the participants spent their own money to hurt other people, ultimately reducing the amount of cash all participants had to take home by more than twenty percent. One of the surprising findings of the experiment was that some 15% of advantaged participants demonstrated an attitude of envy toward the disadvantaged, burning them as much or more than advantaged ones. While the advantaged subjects burned disadvantaged and advantaged subjects alike, the disadvantaged subjects seemed to care only about whether money had been received deservedly or through the unfair advantage, and appeared to use this criterion in deciding who to burn.

Envious persons are naturally attracted to participate in religious systems that encourage the envy of others—meaning classifying others in terms of friends and enemies—invoking the help of God to destroy those whom they envy. The *Srimad-Bhagavatam* explains how envy is even brought into religious systems (6.16.41–42):

> Being full of contradictions, all forms of religion but *bhagavata-dharma* work under conceptions of fruitive results and distinctions of "you and I" and "yours and mine." The followers of *Srimad-Bhagavatam* have no such consciousness. But there are other, low-class religious systems, which are contemplated for the killing of enemies or the gain of power. Such religious systems, being full of passion and envy, are impure and temporary. Because they are full of envy, they are also full of irreligion.

> How can a religious system that produces envy of one's self and of others be beneficial for oneself and for them? What is auspicious about following such a system? What is actually to be gained? By causing pain to one's own self due to self-envy and by causing pain to others, one arouses [God's] anger and practices irreligion.

*   *   *

Greed—Lessons on the Path to Unlimited (and Unearned) Riches

Does greed have anything to do with the workings of the economy? According to Gordon Gekko it does. Gekko, is famous for explaining the virtues of greed: "The point is, ladies and gentleman, that 'greed *is good.*' Greed is right. Greed works. Greed clarifies, cuts through, and captures the essence of the evolutionary spirit. Greed, in all of its forms—greed for life, for money, for love, knowledge—has marked the upward surge of mankind. And greed—you mark my words—will not only save Teldar Paper, but that other malfunctioning corporation called the USA." Taking Gekko's good advice many of our leaders, both economic and political have been using greed as *the* means for saving the day, but it's usually only their day that is saved.

Gekko, of course, is a fictional character of the late 80's movie *Wall Street* but his composite character is based on real people who personified greed: the corporate raiders Ivan Boesky, Michael Milliken and Carl Ichan. They were the captains of junk bonds, insider trading and hostile takeovers, after whom the "decade of greed" was named, having shown us how to get rich by gutting and destroying profitable companies that had the temerity not to be greedy themselves.[15] It was Boesky who made a very real speech on the virtues of greed at the University of California Berkeley in 1986 mentoring the fresh products of American education with the wisdom that "Greed is all right, by the way I think greed is healthy. You can be greedy and still feel good about yourself." The producers of the movie *Wall Street* intended to portray Gekko as a villain, but because of not understanding the increasing greed among the general public he ironically became instead a source of inspiration, and the movie turned out to be one of the most effective recruitment tools the investment banking industry ever had.

Other encouragement in greed came from none other than the U.S. president during most of that decade, "The Gipper" himself, Ronald Reagan. Good leader that he was, Reagan wanted America to be a place where somebody could always become rich, and his tax policies demonstrated that the best persons for becoming rich(er) were the already rich. Of course his tax reform was nothing more than a case of *quid pro quo*. All of these lessons were not lost on America's impressionable youth. The vast majority, a whopping 83 percent, of the children of the counter-culture bred during the turbulent dissent of the 60's, thought that developing a meaningful philosophy of life was more important than being "very well off financially," which then only 44% thought of as important. After the decade of greed the numbers were reversed. By 1990 the share of Americans entering college who believed it was essential to be very well-off financially almost doubled to 74 percent, while those who believed in having a meaningful philosophy of life had dropped to 43 percent.[16] Business Administration capped with an MBA became the hot major on college campuses all over America, while the engineering colleges were turning to foreign students to fill their classrooms.

Unmitigated greed brought Americans the Savings and Loan crisis of the early eighties that cost the public some $150 billion dollars of which $125 billion was directly subsidized by the U.S. government. In that crisis over 1,000 savings and loan institutions failed in "the largest and costliest venture in public misfeasance, malfeasance and larceny of all time."[17] This turpitude took place in large part due to government deregulation of the S&L's allowing them to operate very much like banks but without the strict government oversight that banks are subject to, creating a very attractive environment for the unscrupulous.

Not surprisingly the Federal Home Loan Bank Board cited fraud and insider abuse as the "worst aggravating factors in the wave of S&L failures. The officers of the S&L's would collude with others and make bad loans that could not be repaid, or work with brokerage houses to make loans to certain individuals who would then use the proceeds for example, to purchase Michael Milliken's junk bonds, or take an equity interest in property purchased with the loans. There were many different ways that the banking powers of the S&L's were used, and too often the money went directly into private coffers. Among those implicated in the scandal was Neil Bush, the son of then Vice President George H. W. Bush.

Greed continued to rage on through the 90's, not with hostile takeovers and leveraged buyouts, but through consolidation of banks, oil companies, media companies, you name it. Buying became frenzied, and anything and everything desirable was being bought to render profits alone. Anti-trust legislation that was created to protect the public from monopolies was thrown aside, and companies gobbled each other up creating gargantuan companies whose reach extends all over the globe. Many of these megaliths have revenues that far exceed the GNP of entire countries. The cigarette giant Phillip Morris' revenues for example, exceed that of more than 140 countries (out of 182). And while they have huge revenues, their primary objective is still profit alone. ExxonMobil's profits are increasing at 30-40 percent per year, year after year, despite, or perhaps due to, an energy crisis resulting largely from the war in Iraq. Needless to say, those profits are generated from large and unexpected price increases of more than one hundred percent between 2005 and 2008, despite the fact that there is a sufficient quantity of oil on the market, much of which can be attributed to speculation and profiteering (greed) according to some studies.[18]

The modern corporation is structured in such a way that the sole objective is to make money. Period. As much as possible, and some don't care how they do it. Enron Corporation, formerly the seventh largest company in the United States, is one of those companies who earned such profits in the deregulation and privatization schemes of both water and electricity. They were one of the energy wholesalers that became notorious for exploiting the market during California's energy crisis of 2000 and 2001 and became the object of a separate investigation by The Federal Energy Regulatory Commission (FERC) into that crisis. The investigation included the manipulation of the energy markets by middlemen such as Enron to create exorbitant profits by creating many schemes, including deliberate energy shortages that would result in huge price jumps in the spot market and rolling blackouts. Ken Lay, Enron's CEO, mocked the efforts by the California State government to thwart the practices of the energy wholesalers saying, "In the final analysis, it doesn't matter what you crazy people in California do, because I got smart guys who can always figure out how to make money."[19]

The way Lay's smart guys made money playing the markets was nothing more than a game to them. They created a number of manipulation strategies given names such as "Fat Boy," "Death Star," "Forney Perpetual Loop," "Ricochet," "Ping Pong," "Black Widow," "Big Foot" and more.[20] The Death Star method was explained in this way to Senator Barbara Boxer: "There is a single connection between northern and southern California's power grids. Enron traders purposely overbooked that line, then caused others to need it. Next, by California's *free-market* rules, Enron was allowed to price-gouge at will."[21]

As a result of the actions of electricity wholesalers, utilities companies were buying from a spot market at very high prices but their retail rates were regulated and fixed. Unable to raise their retail rates Southern California Edison (SCE) racked up $20 Billion in debt in just over one year by spring of 2001, and Pacific Gas & Electric was forced into bankruptcy in the same year.

A separate investigation by the California Public Utilities Commission also found evidence of a cartel of companies who closed plants for unnecessary maintenance in order to create artificial shortages and inflate prices, specifically when the state had issued emergency alerts due to seriously low electricity levels. The Utilities Commissioner said that "there are instances that plants, when called to produce, chose not to produce." The plant shutdowns were a key factor in soaring power prices that went from $200 to $1,900 per megawatt hour. The PUC Commissioner further said "I would argue that it's no accident. That in fact it's due to the coordinated behavior of a cartel."[22]

Central to that cartel was Reliant Energy Services, who, almost four years after the crisis had subdued, was indicted by a federal grand jury in San Francisco over a plot to artificially boost power prices by unnecessarily closing their plants. The company shut most of its California power plants when a sudden drop in market prices created likely losses for the company's trading position. They falsely claimed environmental limits and maintenance problems, and withheld additional electricity from the state, prosecutors said.[23]

The FERC study concluded that "many trading strategies employed by Enron and other companies [illegally] violated the anti-gaming provisions."[24] Enron was playing both sides against the middle (the public and government) as they engaged in these practices for the purpose of further multiplying their profits trading in energy derivatives specifically exempted from regulation by the Commodity Futures Trading Commission. The FERC report concluded that market manipulation was only possible because of the complex market design produced by the process of partial deregulation. In other words, the deliberate creation of a cheating system which was allowed to operate at the expense of the public was due to the government's abandonment of its duty.

S. David Freeman, appointed Chair of the California Power Authority in the midst of the crisis said about Enron's involvement: "...electricity is really different from everything else. It cannot be stored, it cannot be seen, and we cannot do without it, which makes opportunities to take advantage of a deregulated market endless. Enron stood for secrecy and a lack of responsibility. There is no place for companies like Enron that own the equivalent of an electronic telephone book and game the system to extract an unnecessary middleman's profits. Never again can we allow private interests to create artificial or even real shortages and to be in control." Good advice but it seems nobody is paying attention because in 2008 the same practices are again being applied to two other commodities that everyone needs—food and fuel, again with skyrocketing prices.

The energy fiasco was finally resolved when companies trading energy in the state were again regulated, and by an increase in the number of power producing facilities. Finally the State of California issued $11 billion worth of bonds to cover the damages. In several cases we experience how deregulation of necessary utilities allows market manipulation and price increases. Did we learn who benefits from such practices? We certainly did, but what does that mean when the officials elected to safeguard the public interest are working on behalf of the profiteers? In the spring of 2001, when officials of the Los Angeles Department of Water and Power met with the National Energy Development Task Force asking for price controls to protect consumers the Task Force refused, and insisted that deregulation must remain in place. Not surprisingly, Vice President Dick Cheney, who has well-known serious conflicts of interest with the public purse, was appointed in January 2001 as the head of that task force.

Glamorous Greed

Early into the new millennium billionaire Donald Trump became the host of a popular "reality" show where young and eager contestants competed for the brass ring of the presidency of one of his many companies. Trump, like Boesky is big on greed, and like Boesky advocates it as a desirable quality for a successful career, encouraging one and all with this unabashed glorification: "The point is that you can't be too greedy"! Greed is no longer one of the seven deadly sins— it is enviable! Presumably envy no longer counts among the big sins as well, but that presumption would be only the opinion of our materialistic friends. Regarding the downside of greed, Andrew Carnegie, one of the great icons of American entrepreneurship, or robber barons depending on one's charity, admitted to the pernicious influence of greed when he said: "To continue much longer, with most of my thoughts wholly upon the way to make more money in the shortest possible time, must degrade me beyond hopes of permanent recovery." Unfortunately his experience is not touted as much as Milliken and Boesky's.

The Path to Never-ending Dissatisfaction

It is perhaps a trite understanding that everyone seems to know, but which cannot be repeated enough—there is no limit to greed. The strong bodily desires and needs of a person disturbed by hunger and thirst are certainly satisfied when he eats. Similarly, anger can be satisfied by chastisement of the offending party. But as for greed, even if a greedy person has conquered the entire world or has enjoyed everything in the world, still he will not be satisfied. The nature of greed is that the more I get the more I want. I measure not by what I have but what I don't have. Is the glass half empty or half full? It is always half empty for the greedy person. He's not looking at what he has but sees only that there is *still* more to get. Where does it come from? Others; and when some take too much others are left with too little.

Greed is based on the delusion of ownership, one of the conditions laid down by Brahma at the beginning of the creation. Many or most of us are able to keep it in check because we have learned to be contented with our lot in life. Others however, when they have the means become obsessed with getting more. Why? Simply because it becomes an addiction, and like all addictions is harmful. The *Isopanisad* tells us that we have a right to as much as we can make productive use of. What is the point of owning, or even possessing that which cannot be properly used? It is none other than to fuel the false ego of "I and mine." This idea of false ownership constitutes one of the many illusions of modern life that we are attempting to live as if it were a reality.

Because the concept of ownership is fundamental to material consciousness and the repetition of birth and death, lessons regarding it are repeatedly brought to our attention in the *Srimad-Bhagavatam*. Of course these include many valuable lessons on the subject of greed as well. Regarding the vain attempt to enjoy the objects of the senses the *Bhagavatam* tells us (11.10.3):

> One who is sleeping may see many objects of sense gratification in a dream, but such pleasurable things are merely creations of the mind and are thus ultimately useless. Similarly, the living entity who is asleep to his spiritual identity also sees many sense objects, but these innumerable objects of temporary gratification are creations of the Lord's illusory potency and have no permanent existence. One who meditates upon them, impelled by the senses, uselessly engages his intelligence.

Such use of one's intelligence is useless because it brings no permanent result. The fact is that permanent, everlasting results are available to the *jiva*. If one has the option of working for permanent benefit, what intelligent person will choose something that brings only temporary results?

The *Bhagavatam* specifically addresses the topic of greed and its impulse on the *jiva* (4.24.66):

> All living entities within this material world are mad after planning for things, and they are always busy with a desire to do this or that. This is due to uncontrollable greed. The greed for material enjoyment always exists in the materially conditioned soul.

While the greed for material enjoyment always exists for the materially conditioned soul, it is not a permanent feature of the *jiva*'s existence. Greed is a symptom of spiritual disease, and that disease can be cured by the proper therapeutic, spiritual treatment.

Sri Krishna, while instructing His disciple Uddhava, gives instructions about the undesirable qualities of greed for wealth (11.23.16–19):

> Generally, the wealth of misers never allows them any happiness. In this life it causes their self-torment, and when they die it sends them to hell. In the earning, attainment, increase, protection, expense, loss and enjoyment of wealth, all men experience great labor, fear, anxiety and delusion.

> Theft, violence, speaking lies, duplicity, lust, anger, perplexity, pride, quarreling, enmity, faithlessness, envy and the dangers caused by women, gambling and intoxication are the fifteen undesirable qualities that contaminate men because of greed for wealth. Although these qualities are undesirable, men falsely ascribe value to them. One desiring to achieve the real benefit of life should therefore remain aloof from the undesirable accumulation of material wealth.

In today's world of artificial wealth people often think that money can solve all of their problems. Thus they make every attempt and use every means, legal as well as illegal, to obtain money. Unfortunately they do not know that money brings with it its own set of problems. Therefore the *Srimad-Bhagavatam* encourages us not to blindly chase after money (8.19.24–25):

> One should be satisfied with whatever he achieves by his previous destiny, for discontent can never bring happiness. A person who is not self-controlled will not be happy even with possessing the entire world. Material existence causes discontent in regard to fulfilling one's lusty desires and achieving more and more money. This is the cause for the continuation of material life, which is full of repeated birth and death. But one who is satisfied by that which is obtained by destiny is fit for liberation from material existence.

*   *   *

An Economics for Every Consciousness

In the first two chapters we examined the composite nature and psychology of human beings from the perspective of the Vedic worldview. With that background we are now in a position to examine how that psychology plays itself out in the activities of mankind, and we will begin by applying our understanding of the *gunas* to economic behaviors. We will look at the influences of each *guna* in turn, giving some examples of how they influence the sense of "I and mine" and corresponding economic practices. We will also examine the transition of economic practices through history charting their course from goodness to passion to ignorance. Then, examining the circumstances in which we currently find ourselves and the influences of the modern day we will be able to clearly recognize the trajectory of modern society, our place on it, and the destructive destination we will arrive at if we do not alter our course.

If we examine the various cultures of the world we will find an amazing variety of ways in which people live. There are still, even today, more than 3,000 indigenous cultures whose members live to some degree according to the traditional ways passed down to them by their ancestors. Often they find themselves in conflict with the concepts held by the encroaching modern Western culture because they have different ways of understanding and living in the world, specifically as regards ownership and possession, and the proper use of the resources provided by nature.

The conception of ownership is the "mine" aspect of false ego. Ownership means different things to different people due to differences in culture, as we have quoted Srila Prabhupada above: "there are many classes of men compre-hending the same misconception of "I" and "mine," in different colors." . Those differences arise from the different combinations of the modes of nature. Those differences in the conception of ownership and what constitutes acceptable economic activity and practices can be summarized as follows:

Under the influence of *sattva-guna* God is recognized as the creator and proprietor of this world. Every member of the group, indeed, every living thing, as a child of God, therefore has a right to the resources of this world. Property is understood as the common heritage of all, it is "ours." In *sattva-guna* the members of society respect and are responsible to each other. Production and distribution are accomplished by cooperative means. Economic activity is done as a matter of duty, according to proper place, time, and based on religious principles. Under the influence of *sattva-guna* we are all deserving children of God and we share the resources provided to us by God.

Under the influence of rajo-*guna* the admonitions of religion are replaced by the laws of man, by which they attempt to make the world as they want it to be, rather than as it actually is. Possession, ownership and exchange are defined in law, ownership becomes the exclusive prerogative of one individual, and transfer of property is established in law as well. Production and distribution are now accomplished through means of competition. The property that is due to me depends on my individual ability to produce. I depend on myself, and you depend on yourself. By my efforts I created what I have therefore I am the rightful enjoyer of it. Passion creates a society of winners and losers by which one demonstrates their superiority over others. You have yours, I have mine. May the better man win.

In ignorance, unlimited and exclusive title to property is established; it is taken by deception, collusion, bribery, theft or force. Indeed, by any means possible. The economics of ignorance destroys the social welfare leaving the majority of people in extreme poverty, in want for their basic necessities of life, helpless, alone and destitute. Both people and property are objects of possession to be exploited, used and abused as far as possible. There is no consideration of spending for maintenance. Especially if something isn't "mine" I am free to abuse it; other's land for example, I use as my waste dump. Property becomes more important than people, and the property of the ruling class even has rights that supersede that of the common people. In *tamo-guna* production is either ignored or accomplished by force and slavery. What is needed is acquired by taking from others, by any and every means, legal or illegal, moral or immoral.

In the 21ˢᵗ Century These Methods Are Mixed

As we progress through our analysis of economics in the various modes of nature the reader will recognize that each of these concepts of economics are simultaneously being practiced at different times and places. They may also be practiced concurrently by a single individual. For example, common ownership and sharing of *sattva-guna* is practiced within a person's immediate family and with close friends; simultaneously they may engage in competitive retail business in the local community, while at the same time, they may also rationalize and support their own country's economic colonialism of other countries and exploitation of foreign resources, environment and people. Such mixed thinking is justified according by the various conceptions of "I and mine"—"my" family, "my" business, and "my" country.

We begin our examination of economics and the *guna*s with the mode of goodness.

Chapter Three

The Economics of Goodness

My dear Lord, everyone in this material world is under the modes of material nature, being influenced by goodness, passion and ignorance. Everyone—from the greatest personality, Lord Brahma, down to the small ant—works under the influence of these modes. Therefore everyone in this material world is influenced by Your energy. The cause for which they work, the place where they work, the time when they work, the matter due to which they work, the goal of life they have considered final, and the process for obtaining this goal—all are manifestations of Your energy. Srimad-Bhagavatam 7.9.20

The quality of goodness is purer than the other modes of nature. It is illuminating, and it lifts one up from the ways of passion and ignorance, giving clarity and understanding. Those situated in goodness experience a genuine sense of happiness in material life. Under the influence of goodness people will do what ought to be done, as a matter of duty, without false ego, yet with great determination and enthusiasm, unwavering in determination regardless of success or failure. Their actions are regulated and performed without attachment, without love or hatred, and without desire for fruitive results.

In the *Bhagavad-gita* Sri Krishna explains that human beings are of two different natures: divine or demonic. The divine qualities are manifestations of the quality of goodness. Persons who possess these qualities cannot separate them from their activities since those in goodness are free from duplicity. As such these qualities must be reflected in the economic behaviors of societies established in goodness. Therefore we expect to see that being charitable and compassionate they will care for every person, protect and nurture the helpless and infirm, and the weak. Being free from envy they are happy to see others prosper, and being naturally renounced they require only what they need to live lightly on the earth, and shun self-aggrandizement. Life (spirit) holds the highest value in *sattva-guna*. This life includes not only human life, but is extended to the animal species as well as the earth herself, and in goodness man lives in harmony with the animals, the earth and with God. Personal (spiritual) development is the objective of this society, and material things are valued to the degree that they are useful to that end. Generally because of developed spiritual practices people are satisfied within and are not driven to find external satisfaction through acquisition of property and things. In that regard wealth is communal or shared among the members, again leaving no one without. Being freed from desires of possessiveness, from covetousness and envy people do not seek to exploit each other, but instead act to nourish and protect each other. In goodness, no one is left behind, ill-cared for, or without the minimum necessities of life. Work is adjusted to that which is necessary, but not more, and time saved is given to leisure, social and civic affairs, worship, spiritual growth, and personal development.

In cultures influenced predominantly by goodness members have an egalitarian perspective toward each other. They literally practice the golden rule. They will identify in others the feelings, emotions and needs that they feel themselves. They are cooperative and non-competitive, nurturing and non-violent in nature. The strength of men is used to protect the weak and helpless against aggressors and wrong-doers, and the nurturing nature of women is employed in the role of maintaining the standards of the culture, defending it from degradation. In these cultures every person is afforded a place in relationship to others; a place defined by the contribution that they can make. Each person depends on others for their skills and abilities. Feeling that dependence they each have a shared sense of responsibility, wherein each individual finds his place. Taken together, this constitutes a social contract that is based on duty, not on legal agreements.

Under the influence of *sattva-guna* we find a personal world organized in a way that each and every individual can fulfill both their material and spiritual needs. Lust, envy, greed and other base qualities are held in check by proper training and social conventions, under the influence of *sattva*.

Everywhere in the *Bhagavad-gita* that *sattva-guna* is mentioned, duty is mentioned as its identifying characteristic, therefore duty is a significant feature of a culture grounded in *sattva-guna*. Within *sattvic* cultures every member has a particular function to perform on the basis of duty. These duties are not whimsically assumed but are given in the codes of religion. They are given in the *Manu-samhita*, or "the laws of Manu," Manu being considered the father of man (as from his name the word "man" is derived). Moreover, the social arrangement of Vedic culture permits these duties to be performed in a very personal manner, to the immediate and direct benefit of others. The social obligations of a society in *sattva-guna* function to provide a very real sense of social security whereby every person feels safe and protected.

From the perspective of our current culture the obligations and duties described might be perceived as being restrictive and limiting the "freedom" that we enjoy. The manner in which our culture is arranged requires no personal obligation to anyone but our own self and perhaps immediate family members. We may also have obligations or duties at our workplace, but they are generally not performed in a personal manner that directly benefits someone. But even if they do the duties of the workplace do not generally extend outside the boundaries of that time or place, our work lives and personal lives being separated and compartmentalized. Such limitations on our duties and obligations give us the relative impression of not being burdened by the needs of others, allowing us the luxury of using our time as we alone desire. From another point of view however, this lack of responsibility to others creates what the *Bhagavatam* terms *nirvishesha* and *shunyavada*, impersonalism and voidism, because although we may have no obligation to others, neither have they any obligation to us. At best this leaves each of us to fend for ourselves in a challenging world, and at worst creates the Hobbesean world of each against all—a lonely and difficult struggle for existence. Personal relationships are in fact strengthened by a bond of mutual dependence, and give each member the security of knowing that they are not alone in this world. The freedom to be "independent" at the same time requires us to be alone, ultimately a very high price.

Economics Influenced by Goodness

One of the most essential qualities of a society functioning predominantly under the influence of goodness was that there was no profit motive *per se*. Instead there was a productive motive, which meant that the ultimate objective of an activity was the immediate thing produced. Things were valued according to their immediate function and utility, not for the profit they might bring. Thus the motive for exploitation of others or of the earth was absent. These things weren't necessarily physical objects like food or furniture, they included services such as education, law, medicine, fighting skills and so on. Moreover, one's efforts, besides producing something of value for society, also gave one the satisfaction of a job well done, be it in martial arts for defense, teaching of students, production of a basket, or sewing of a garment. In this manner work was a source of great satisfaction for all members of society.

In passion, economy functions through competition, and in ignorance through exploitation, but in goodness, cooperation is the main characteristic. Using their individual skills and natural talents everyone is employed to their satisfaction and voluntarily contribute to the group in a joyous and mutually beneficial way. In goodness every member of the community will share in the results of the cooperative enterprise, each to their own satisfaction, with nobody left out.

Those in *sattva-guna* recognize that all of the gifts of this earth are given to humankind by God, and are meant for the benefit and well-being of all. As such the cultures of *sattva-guna* grant every member their sustenance as an entitlement. It should be noted this is not generally linked to their duty. Duty is not performed with the intention of 'earning' a right to sit at the dinner table. The *sattvic* cultures are not fruitive. Rather, they exhibit a reversal of the fruitive mentality. Instead of an attitude to get, earn or take, there is a mood, perhaps even a competition, of giving. In some *sattvic* cultures each person may sustain themselves through the gifts of others, or through some method of redistribution.

The *sattvic* economy also utilizes the natural way of living that is given to mankind by God. By the Lord's arrangement the fundamental needs of the household—food, shelter and clothing—are not difficult to obtain; they can be had directly from the earth at almost every place on the globe. To obtain these necessities of life directly from the earth, and specifically for one's own use is the natural economy, or the natural way of life. The immediate product of one's effort is the desired end, and not a means to some other end. In the production of one's own food, clothing and shelter, one performs that function for its own sake. One is directly interested in the object of their endeavor, and thus they pursue it with greater interest and diligence. The activity itself is thus also a source of satisfaction for a job well done, and brings an honest pride in what is produced.

In artificial ways of living, such as today's world, people do something not for its own sake, but in order to achieve something else. Most employed people are not directly interested in, nor do they benefit directly from their work activity. They go to work and perform some function to get money, and with money they then obtain the objects of their desire. Thus most people have become interested in money only, and have little interest in their activities aside from that end. (This is another source of *nirvishesha-shunyavada*—impersonalism and voidism). The necessity of getting something different than what they create by their effort puts them in a vulnerable and precarious position, and makes them dependent upon whoever controls the intermediate variable. In our society that is money. Its control by others, such as one's boss or the government, gives them an unnatural power over us. The person who has or controls money becomes an authority regardless of how qualified he may or may not be. The result of this is that too often today the inexperienced can command the experienced, and folly commands wisdom. Unqualified people are in positions of authority simply because they control the money; this creates frustration and chaos in the world.

By contrast, a significant feature of the economics of goodness is that, because relationships function on the basis of love and duty, each person who is in command of another must, by necessity, be qualified. A person must earn the right to lead and command by virtue of his abilities, and generally such positions are attained after long periods of training. Experience and wisdom are highly respected and valued, thus in *sattvic* cultures there are generally few unqualified leaders.

In goodness man also cooperates with the animal kingdom nurturing and protecting domesticated animals. Cooperation with the earth is similarly practiced, wherein man nurtures the earth, giving back to her by maintaining the soil through organic means; not just taking, artificially pumping up her capacity to produce while simultaneously depleting her of nutrients.

"I and mine" in *Sattva-guna*

There are many examples of previous cultures characterized by goodness, and one of the best is found in the history of India in the epic *Mahabharata*. Although modern scholars say that India lacks a recorded history they do not properly take into account that which is presented in the Vedic literatures, preferring instead to label it as myth, perhaps because it portrays wonderful qualities and events that we no longer witness in this degraded age of *Kali*. The *vaishnavas* however accept as accurate the historical accounts of the *Puranas*, as well as the *Mahabharata*, which, by its very title "The Great *Bharata*" indicates that it describes the events that took place in *Bharata* (present day India) some 5,000 years ago. In the *Adi-Parva* of *Mahabharata* we are told of the characteristics of earlier times reaching back into the last age, *Dvapara-yuga*, when man lived in harmony with man, with the animals, and with nature (in these passages the "Law" refers to the codes of behavior established by *Manu*):

> Thenceforth living for hundreds and thousands of years, and bent upon the vows of the Law, men were wholly free from worries and diseases. The *ksatriyas* kings governed the entire earth, with her ocean borders, with her mountains, wilderness, and woods. While the *ksatriyas* reigned over this earth in accordance with the Law, all of the social orders found surpassing joy. Casting off such vices as spring from lust and anger, the kings of men protected their subjects, using their staff according to the Law upon those that deserved it. As the *ksatriyas* were law-abiding, and sacrifice was performed according to scriptural injunction, Indra, the god of a thousand eyes and the one-hundred sacrifices, rained sweet rain at the right time and place, swelling the people.

Thus this ocean-girt earth was filled with long-living people. The *ksatriyas* offered up grand sacrifices for which ample stipends were given. The *brahmanas* studied the Vedas with their branches and Upanishads. The *brahmanas* rendered their services to all as sacrifice and not for personal gain, nor did they attempt to unduly persuade anyone to religious causes beyond their ken. The farmers plowed the earth with bullocks: they did not put cows to the yoke, and they let the lean cows live. Men did not milk cows whose calves were still suckling, and merchants did not sell their wares with false weights. People did their lawful chores looking to the Law and devoted to the Law. All the classes devoted themselves to their own tasks, and thus the Law was in no way diminished in that age. The cows and women gave birth in time; trees stood in fruit and bloom in all seasons. And thus the entire earth became filled with many creatures.

But such was the case not only in *Bharata-varsha* (modern day India), for by and large all of the indigenous cultures of the world were of a *sattvic* nature, evidence of which remains with us today. All of these many cultures, even into more modern times, maintained an economic structure that left no individual without sufficient means, usually through the mechanism of shared wealth that, by tradition, was frequently exchanged leaving no person permanently in a superior position to others. There is a nice example of this, also from the *Mahabharata*:

There once lived an exalted sage named Vibhavasu, who was extremely ill-tempered, and his younger brother Supratika, who was a great ascetic. Supratika did not like that the two brothers held their wealth in common, and he constantly recommended dividing it, until Vibhavasu said to his brother Supratika: 'There are many who out of foolishness ever wish to divide their property, but once wealth is divided people become enchanted by their riches and fail to respect one another. When wealth is divided, each man cares only for his own riches, and people thus become separated by holding separate wealth. Then foes in the guise of friends, understanding the situation, begin to create conflict and divide the community against itself.

'Realizing that people are now divided, still others take advantage and prey upon the community. Thus a divided people soon come to utter ruination.

'Therefore, dear brother, the wise do not encourage the division of wealth among those who strictly follow their holy teachers and scriptures and who sincerely wish each other well.'[1]

Historical Examples of *Sattvic* Society and "Economics"

It is the principles of religion that uphold and protect society. Even though this age of *Kali* is immersed in the lower modes of nature, at the beginning of this age and even well into it, the quality of *sattva-guna* was still to be observed almost everywhere. For example...

Not too long ago, in Asia, if you were a member of the Chukchi, one of the tribes of northwest Asia, and you wished to use a boat which was found lying on the beach, you would simply use it, regardless of the theoretical owner, with no question of compensation or even permission. Among the pre-industrial Japanese nothing that was a man's belonged to him exclusively, not even the house in which he lived, since, as in many other cultures, his door was to remain open to all travelers. The Fiji Islanders formerly held a custom called *kerekere* which allowed a man to take another's property with great freedom. In the Fijis, the people shared all belongings with the chief, he was the ostensible owner of everything, but in practice the people owned and used all the property of the chief. However in an emergency the chief could appropriate everything needed to deal with the calamity. For example, if a famine arose, the leader might declare that the products of the fields to be common possession; or if men were needed for planting, canoe-making, or some other public purpose, the chief might conscript the necessary labor. In the event of war, he could exert absolute control over all property, and even all lives. But even in peacetime, the people of one district in need of some commodities could demand them from other districts, albeit with the understanding that they were to repay the gifts either with labor or other things of value. Here we see the ancient doctrine that "what is my neighbor's is also mine," as well as, "I must share with my brother and help him."[2]

Similarly the ancient Samoans would extend communal sharing to relatives even if not to more distant individuals. Anthropologist Margaret Mead tells of them: "From a relative one could demand food, clothing, shelter, and assistance in a feud. Refusal of such a demand would brand one as stingy and lacking in human kindness, the virtue most esteemed by the Samoans. No definite repayment is made at the time the services are given, except in the case of the distribution of food to all those who share in a family enterprise." Generally recognition of the gift received was expected by a return gift at the earliest opportunity. These behaviors were not codified into legal form, maintained by courts and juries. There was no law other than social custom and public opinion.[3]

As recently as the 18th century in Africa the Nuer tribe held that they must assist one another, and if one had a surplus of a good thing he was obliged to share it with his neighbors. Consequently, no Nuer would be found with a surplus. A Nuer was not expected to part with his personal household property, but if a man possessed several spears or hoes or other such objects he would inevitably lose the surplus.[4] And almost into the present day the *Kalihari* bushmen of Africa, a nomadic hunter-gatherer tribe, practiced the egalitarianism for which hunter-gatherers are renowned. All of their needs were supplied *in situ*, and upon the discovery of a food source it was shared by every member of the tribe. So simple were their needs, and abundant the supply that anthropologist Marshall Sahlins describes them as the original affluent society.[5] The Ba-Ila of Africa, make every man's elder relations the beneficiaries of their property. Thus, if the chief grants you some land, it is not wholly yours; your older brother or your uncle or your grandfather or any of your senior kinsmen have the right to it as well, and they may share other kinds of property in the same way. For example, a Ba-Ila who had earned money working for European settlers would be expected to share it with his elder relatives.[6] Among the Bergdama peoples of central Namibia, a man returning from his hunting excursion, or the woman coming back from her search for roots, fruit, or leaves were expected to offer the greater part for the benefit of the community. Among some tribes the headman or other prominent member of the group may act as an intermediary to receive and distribute the supplies.

Ancient Europe also practiced the principle that what belongs to you also belongs to me. In Ireland most of the agricultural land belonged to the tribe collectively and it was redistributed according to need every three or four years. Among the ancient Germans, whose freemen exercised rights in common over the land, the meadows were divided among all the families, but after harvesting the hay, were opened to common use. Even in early Rome the land for the most part was held in common, until the time of the housefather, who, having been placed in temporary occupancy, began to covet the idea of permanent possession. The old Slavic tribes held to a custom called *toloka*, by which every member of society was duty bound to help their neighbor. Toloka was offered as a gift, not a sale, and there was no concept of "repayment" for the kindness of others, understanding that when one had such a need he could also call upon the help of others. The Slavs also did not privately own even furniture or the results of other labor. They possessed all property as a group, did all work as a group, and conceded to every man a right to the food and other articles produced by his brothers.

In the Middle East the old Arab tribes held their flocks and herds in common. And the Essenes of Palestine, the so-called early Christians, held all property of the group in common. According to *Acts of the Apostles*, the unwanted goods of new members were sold and the proceeds distributed according to the need of each.

In the Americas the Aztecs of Mexico maintained a system based upon the communal ownership of productive property, so that a man received his land from the clan. He was not considered the proprietor as much as the current occupant. Periodically, as the needs of the community changed resources were redistributed. Although not an indigenous group, Jesuit priests established a socialist community in Paraguay early in the seventeenth century. They were a moneyless community that shared all labor and its products on a basis of equal work and equal privileges. Their culture thrived for a century and a half, being remembered as a veritable paradise long after its destruction by outside forces.

Another example is that of ancient Egypt, where in theory the people and all they possessed belonged to the divine ruler, the Pharaoh, despite the fact that private property actually did exist. Similarly across the Atlantic Ocean for the Incas, whose ruler, the Inca, was considered a descendent of the sun god. He not only owned everything in theory, but tightly controlled it in practice, regulating the activities of the people as well. Manual labor was afforded a dignified position in Inca society, made so by the participation of the Inca himself. Organization was such that none were overworked, and they even worked joyously. So abundant was their production, that each male citizen even after payment of taxes in the form of three months labor in government service, still had three months of leisure each year. Any resulting abundance or surplus was sequestered against future emergency rather than allowed to accumulate in the hands of individuals.

Sharing of wealth was practiced practically everywhere in North America as well. The Kwakiutl of Vancouver Island in the Northwest had a distinctive institution, the potlatch, whereby they used their riches to serve the ends of vain glory. They practiced acquisitiveness for non-acquisitive purposes, economic activity for anti-economic ends, and efficiently produced material possessions for no other purpose than to give them away. The potlatch was a sort of competition in charity—to see who would have the prestige of giving away the greatest amount. The potlatch served to redistribute the wealth of the community, and in order to reduce the tendency of greed and accumulation whatever remained undistributed was purposely destroyed. Both men and women, therefore, were constantly occupied in accumulating things of value only for the sake of giving them away. The ladies wove mats and baskets, and blankets of cedar-bark, while the men made canoes, and gathered shell-money, etc.[7]

The inhabitants of the Trobriand Islands off of the eastern coast of New Guinea were similar. The islands belong to an archipelago forming roughly a circle, around which an active trade, known as the Kula was carried on. It was a complex system of ceremonial reciprocity between partners that involved two classes of gifts—arm shells and shell necklaces—which traveled in opposite directions around the archipelago. A significant portion of the population and a considerable amount of time were given to activities of the Kula "trade." Although it may be called trade there was no exchange. Nor was there any profit involved, either in money or in kind. Neither did haggling or barter enter into the affair. The arm shells and necklaces were offered as gifts. None of these goods were hoarded or thought of as permanent possessions, and the goods received were enjoyed by giving them away. Kula gift-giving was conducted with a desire to achieve prestige and recognition as a generous giver of great gifts. A man would set out with a canoe full of practical goods and either arm bands or necklaces. He would trade with connections inherited from maternal relatives, and, depending on the item he was trading, he would travel clockwise or counterclockwise around the ring, leaving one item and acquiring the other. The trading maintained social ties which might not otherwise exist and also served as a means for Gimwali trade (simple bartering for needed goods such as pigs, bananas, yams, taro, etc.), which was seen as less worthy and honorable.

Consider the case of an Indian victor, returning home with trophies of war. While he might theoretically have kept everything as his own, in practice he had to share his gains. Robert H. Lowie tells about the practices of the Crows: "A man who exercised his legal prerogative to the extent of actually retaining everything for his own use would certainly be flouted for his greed. To hoard in such a miserly fashion was so repugnant to Crow sentiment that probably no captain ever thus laid himself open to universal reprobation."[8] The Iroquois who lived near the Great Lakes not only lived in communal dwellings, but also shared their possessions: if a man raised some corn or pumpkins, or if a woman cooked, they would all share the food. Guests would also share in the hospitality, and indeed, they would be fed even though the host went without.[9]

A Late 20th Century Example

Bhakti Vikasa Swami joined the Hare Krishna Movement in the mid-70s and has lived in India since 1977, spending many years in West Bengal and Bangladesh.[10] He developed a deep appreciation for the traditional life of rural Indians and has written about it in detail in his *Glimpses of Traditional Indian Life*. Even up to the present day Bengali culture is predominantly *sattvic*, especially in villages, as Bhakti Vikas Swami relates:

> Loneliness is unheard of in Bengal, not because people get lost in the crowd, but because they know how to live as persons. Bengalis like nothing better than to get together and go on and on talking and talking, though their discussions are of little practical value. Boredom is also unknown. Bengalis like to be and do things together. Everyone

gets involved and has his part to play. It's a different kind of pleasure than that derived from an endless variety of external stimuli, the norm of modern society.

Development-minded Westerners often become frustrated at the apparent foolishness of the Bangladeshi, who appears to lack common sense regarding his own best interests. Bangladeshi culture does not promote individual dynamism, competitiveness, or the type of efficiency required for technological advancement. Rather, although not uninterested in economic development, a Bangladeshi is more concerned to preserve the indigenous group culture that fosters the sharing and cooperativeness necessary for a traditional labor-intensive agrarian society.

I was once in a village that had recently been devastated by a cyclone. The residents were cheerfully helping each other rebuild houses from clay. That's how village life works. People are obliged to cooperate throughout the year, and they happily help each other harvesting, irrigating, organizing festivals, or building a wall against a rising river.

Necessity also dictates maintaining good relationships with neighbors. Most people aren't well situated economically, so those who have more are expected to help those with less. It's a culture of sharing and responsibility toward others...Bangladeshis emphasize dependence on others and a sense of group identity. They usually say "our house" and "our country" rather than "my house" or "my country."

Bangladeshis do not like to be judged as individuals, but as members of the group to which they belong. To offend an individual Bangladeshi is to arouse the ire of his group, because he stands for the group and thus also is upheld by it. Group solidarity assures protection of a member if he is attacked in any way. An entire village may seek revenge for the sake of an individual member.

The group lends support when a member is in difficulty, whether moral, social, or economic. Reciprocally, members have obligation to the group, one of which is conformity. In fact, the pressure to maintain fellowship with the group is extremely strong. In this way the group regulates the behavior of its members, keeping them within the bounds of acceptable conduct. What one person does reflects upon his group. A wrong action brings shame, success brings honor, to the group. If someone is behaving improperly, the elders of the family or village will tell him "You will give your family (or village) a bad name." That will be a compelling reason for him to rectify his conduct.[11]

These many examples demonstrate that the influence of *sattva-guna* was once felt all over the world. As long as indigenous cultures were isolated from Western influences, they remained relatively unchanged; some of them well into the 20th century. But as our world shrinks they are being swallowed by the juggernaut of "progress." The magazine *Cultural Survival Quarterly*, dubbed "the conscience of anthropology" by *Newsweek* magazine, reports on the struggle of indigenous peoples everywhere to maintain their way of life free from modern culture and its pernicious influences. In 1989 they reported that a full two-thirds of all violent conflicts in the world involved the efforts of indigenous peoples to maintain their way of life free from the encroachment of Western culture.

In these societies members were clearly dependent on each other. For them, the notion of economic independence was as irrational as social independence, and all notions of economics were subordinated to maintaining a good social standing.

Relationships Are the Foundation of the *Sattvic* Economy

Modern economists who are mesmerized by profits and market economy assume that the mysterious, ubiquitous and magical market and its profits have always been the motivation of human endeavor. This is hardly the case. In the above examples featuring the qualities of *sattva-guna* there was often not even a conception of economics, or the market, or profits, as we now think of them. Economist Karl Polanyi, in his seminal work *The Great Transformation,* explains that

> In spite of the chorus of academic incantations so persistent in the nineteenth century, gain and profit made on exchange never before played an important part in human economy. Though the institution of the market was fairly common since the later Stone Age, its role was no more than incidental to economic life.

In that work Polanyi explains that throughout history there are only three methods of "economic" exchange—redistribution, reciprocity and the market. (I put economic in quotation marks because within the concept of redistribution there may or may not be a motive for gain). Interestingly these reflect the influences of *sattva, rajas* and *tamas* respectively. The market, especially in the manner in which it functions today is increasingly *tamasic*, as will be discussed later.[12]

Redistribution recognizes that the bounty of the earth properly belongs to everyone. In such a system the produce of the members of society are collected at a hierarchical center, reorganized, and then redistributed according to the need of each, without consideration of purchase or who is somehow qualified to receive. This method of exchange was practiced by the Fijians, Kwakiutl, the early Egyptians, the early Christians, and the Bergdama. Polanyi explains that "redistribution tends to enmesh the economic system proper in social relationships. We find, as a rule, the process of redistribution forming part of the prevailing political regime, whether it be that of tribe, city-state, despotism, or feudalism of cattle or land. The production and distribution of goods is organized in the main through collection, storage, and redistribution, the pattern being focused on the chief, the temple, the despot, or the lord."

Redistribution involves what may be called charity on several levels and functions on the basis of duty. First of all the members of the group perform their work and out of duty give the result to be collected. The headman then returns to each according to their requirement, again performing his function on the basis of duty. Frequently the methods of redistribution involved no concept of personal gain, although there are historical examples of redistribution wherein the priests, kings, or other agents of distribution became extremely greedy, keeping for themselves the overwhelming share of the community's production while the peasants starved. Such greedy, selfish, and neglectful behavior of course indicates the influence of *tamo-guna*.

Reciprocity is often a more personal form of exchange, and may range in quality from goodness to passion. If the reciprocation is performed with the attitude of giving, without the expectation of return in equal measure, or if it is given to a person other than whom first gave a gift, it is of the quality of *sattva*. Examples in American culture are the sharing between parents and children. When something is given with the expectation of return, or with the desire for some result, it is of the nature of *rajas*. Thus when reciprocation is expected in roughly even measure, though not necessarily immediately, it is influenced by *rajas*, and is a sort of social contract. The Samoans or more distant familial relations in American culture are examples.

There are a great many historical cultural examples of varieties of both redistribution and reciprocity. In almost all cases the basis for such "economic" activity is not material gain for oneself, which is quite insignificant. Polanyi explains that the social relationships within which the exchanges take place are the most important principle:

> The outstanding discovery of recent anthropological research is that man's economy, as a rule, is submerged in his social relationships. He does not act so as to safeguard his individual interest in the

possession of material goods; he acts so as to safeguard his social standing, his social claims, his social assets. He values material goods only in so far as they serve this end. Neither the process of production nor that of distribution is linked to specific economic interests attached to the possession of goods; but every single step in that process is geared to a number of social interests which eventually ensure that the required step be taken. These interests will be very different in a small hunting or fishing community from those in a vast despotic society, but in either case the economic system will be run on non-economic [non-profit] motives.

...Take the case of a tribal society. The individual's economic interest is rarely paramount for the community keeps all its members from starving unless it is itself borne down by catastrophe, in which case interests are again threatened collectively, not individually. The maintenance of social ties, on the other hand, is crucial. First, because by disregarding the accepted code of honor, or generosity, the individual cuts himself off from the community and becomes an outcast; second, because, in the long run, all social obligations are reciprocal, and their fulfillment serves also the individual's give-and-take interests best. Such a situation must exert a continuous pressure on the individual to eliminate economic self-interest from his consciousness. This attitude is reinforced by the frequency of communal activities such as partaking of food from the common catch or sharing in the results of some far-flung and dangerous tribal expedition. The premium set on generosity is so great, when measured in terms of social prestige, as to make any other behavior than that of utter self-forgetfulness simply not pay. Personal character has little to do with the matter. Man can be as good or evil as social or asocial, jealous or generous, in respect to one another. Not to allow anybody reason for jealousy is, indeed, an accepted principle of ceremonial distribution, just as publicly bestowed praise is the due of the industrious, skillful, or otherwise successful gardener. The human passions, good or bad, are merely directed towards non-economic ends. Ceremonial display serves to spur emulation to the utmost and the custom of communal labor tends to raise both quantitative and qualitative standards to the highest pitch. The performance of all acts of exchange as free gifts that are expected to be reciprocated— though not necessarily by the same individuals—should in itself explain the absence of the notion of gain or even of wealth other than that consisting of objects traditionally enhancing social prestige.[13]

The profit-less "economic" activity he refers to is directly the result of *sattva-guna*—especially when we see deliberate efforts to diminish self-centeredness, envy and jealousy, and so on.

The Range and Evolution of Economic Practices

In this world none of the *gunas* are completely pure, each of them being tainted: material goodness is tainted with some portion of passion and ignorance, passion by goodness and ignorance, and so on. More importantly consciousness is conditioned by a combination of the *gunas* and their corresponding influences. Therefore we should not expect that we are going to find examples of society that are purely in goodness, or passion or ignorance. Rather what we do find is a range of influences and characteristics from each *guna* present in every member of the population who together make up society as a whole. Thus we should expect that expressions of goodness will range from almost pure goodness to the borderline of passion. Likewise passion will range from near goodness to near ignorance; and ignorance from near passion to absolute depravity. We therefore expect to see a wide range of influences and activity in all aspects of human society, both personal as well as in civic and economic affairs.

As explained in the first chapter the influence of the *gunas* varies throughout the different *yugas*, from *sattva* in *Satya-yuga*, to *tamas* in *Kali-yuga* to provide *jivas* of different consciousness with the opportunity to act according to their consciousness. During *Kali* the earth is given over to the degraded and demonic for their purposes, and as such we should not be surprised to see the progressive degradation of society through the course of time. However lamentable the fact might be from one perspective, it is appropriate considering the actual purpose of the material world—for illusioned living beings to enjoy the material energy in all of its varieties and forms. From the transcendental perspective all of it is lamentable, even activities in goodness, because all of the countless *jivas* who make this world their home are misplaced, and cannot find the permanent and unlimited happiness they so desire. From the transcendental perspective this entire world is a prison house for the living beings who desire to live outside the will of the Lord, and according to the masters of Vedic wisdom, whether one is a first-class prisoner or a third-class prisoner makes little difference.

Readers who are not conversant with accounts of Vedic history may be surprised, and even skeptical, to learn of this direction of human evolution, because the Western man especially, has been taught that modern society has evolved from animals, and that the most primitive of men, not long ago mere apes, were as savage as animals themselves, or even more so since they kill their own kind. The propagandists of modern culture tell us that we are presently at the pinnacle of social advancement, and that mankind has never had it so good as he does today, or even, that this is as good as it will ever get. Fortunately, that is not at all the case.

Not only is that not the case, but this "progression" typically presented as Western social evolution is exactly the opposite of the true history of mankind on earth. Vedic history stands in sharp contrast to the modern Western idea that we have evolved from prehistoric, or animal-like ancestors, and instead tells us that in prior ages mankind was far more developed in terms of his knowledge, culture, and civility. The Vedic worldview tells us that as we pass through the pages of time we are *devolving* not *evolving*. Evidence gathered from many quarters supports this truth, especially the evidence of economics. A recent example of this trend was documented by Helena Norberg-Hodge.

Economic Transition in Ladakh

As an example of the transition from goodness to passion we can study the experiences of the Ladakhis through the writings of anthropologist Helena Norberg-Hodge, who was the first foreigner accepted to make her home in Ladakh (Kashmir). She had the privilege of living there over the course of three decades, coming to know life in the traditional villages before the intrusion of Western culture, and she documented what it was like:

> In traditional Ladakh, to link happiness to income or possessions
> would have been unthinkable. A deep-rooted respect for each other's
> fundamental human needs and an acceptance of the natural limitations
> of the environment kept the Ladakhi people free from misplacing
> values of worth. Happiness was simply *experienced*. Though not an
> easy lifestyle by Western standards, people met their basic physical,
> social, spiritual and creative needs within the security of a caring,
> sharing community and an abundant agrarian subsistence economy—
> and experienced evident joy. (emphasis in original)[14]

The symptoms of *sattva* are reflected in this culture—a respect and caring for others as well as the environment, and happiness derived within. Norberg-Hodge has made regular visits to the region over several decades and has documented the subsequent changes as Western-style economic development has taken place. She notes that the advance guard for the contemporary colonization of Ladakh has been a combination of tourists, media, educational models and technology, and also notes that this "development" has "created a void in people's lives, inferiority in their self-perceptions, and a greed for material wealth." The influences are often subtle but nonetheless powerful:

A Western tourist can spend more [money] in a day than what a Ladakhi family might in one year. Seeing this, Ladakhis suddenly feel poor. The new comparison creates a gap that never existed before because in traditional Ladakh, people didn't need money in order to lead rich and fulfilling lives. Ladakhi society was based on mutual aid and cooperation; no one needed money for labor, food, clothing, or shelter...In the traditional economy, Ladakhis knew that they had to depend on other people, and that others in turn depend on them. In the new economic system, local interdependence disintegrates along with traditional levels of tolerance. In place of cooperative systems meeting needs, competition and scarcity become determinants for survival.

Perhaps the most tragic of all the changes I have observed in Ladakh is the vicious circle in which individual insecurity contributes to a weakening of family and community ties, which in turn further shakes individual self-esteem. Consumerism plays a central role in this whole process, since emotional insecurity generates hunger for material status symbols. The need for recognition and acceptance fuels the drive to acquire possessions that will presumably make you somebody...It is heartbreaking to see people buying things to be admired, respected and ultimately loved, when in fact the effect is almost always the opposite...[they are] set apart which furthers the need to be accepted.[15]

As Ladakhi society was penetrated by members of modern society we observe the symptoms of *rajas* entering the society: competition, the desire for acquisition and the impersonal attempts to gain respect through by means of possessions rather than personal qualities and abilities. We also observe the result of passion in terms of social isolation, and insecurity.

Ladakh was relatively late in meeting with the onslaught of passion and ignorance, most areas of the world having succumbed to them long ago. In the next chapter we will look at the introduction of *rajo-guna*, along with its ideas of private property and concentrated wealth based on the agreements of men and all the attendant consequences.

Chapter Four

The Economics of Passion

From the mode of goodness, real knowledge develops; from the mode of passion, greed develops; and from the mode of ignorance develop foolishness, madness and illusion. Bhagavad-gita 14.17

A Culture in Passion

Passion is the hallmark of modern society and as such its characteristics are very familiar to most people. Create, make, do, build, develop, are all watchwords of the mode of passion, or *rajo-guna*. *Rajo-guna* is also characterized by competition, in which winners establish their superiority over the losers. That theme is played out in every aspect of a culture grounded in passion. Competitive sports are popular the world over and every weekend hundreds of thousands, if not millions, root for their team. National pride or shame no longer depends on the actions of its statesmen, but instead rides on the abilities of the players of the football, hockey, or basketball team. In the arena of romance, intense passion is taken to be the indicator of true love. Love is now won in competitive ways, sometimes in front of an audience of millions on such television shows as "The Bachelor."

All members of Western culture are inculcated into competition as soon as tiny tots become socialized. We learn about competition—establishing our superiority over others—in the first years of school and it gradually intensifies as we enter our teenage years. The innocence of childhood is sacrificed at increasingly earlier ages as competitive parents push their children to win over others in sports and to compete against other students for the highest test scores; in that way they earn entrance into the finest schools. Of course this childhood training is not lost upon graduation from school. The graduates, having long since been conditioned to competitive play and education, become competitors in the field of business and in career pursuits. For those in passion the idea of gain figures prominently in religion as well, where worship and proper invest-ment (tithing) are frequently promoted by ministers as the best and proper means to material prosperity. Prayer itself does not go far beyond the entreaty for material wants and desires. Such petition is not limited to the church by any means. Supplication of any powerful person is employed, be he God Himself, or any number of lesser gods, who determine the course of the more ordinary things in this world.

It is not unexpected then that for people in passion, competition would be the distinguishing factor, both in business, and as the underpinning of the economy such as the monetary system. The competitive struggle for gain (win-ning) against loss (losing) is what capitalism is all about, and it is the economic system of choice for passionate cultures. Look at the business section of the paper any day, and you will read about production, growth, earnings and losses, endeavor for gain, competition to win over rivals, acquisition, and so on. The dream of passion is the possibility of unlimited gain through individual effort, supported by an environment where no person's initiative is checked and any man can pull himself up by his own bootstraps. At the same time it's every-man-for-himself and may the better man win. Loss is also thus a significant feature of economics in passion.

Another feature of *rajo-guna* that figures prominently in the activities of modern culture is how people see the world. The *Gita* tells us that a person under the influence of passion sees a different living being to be present in every different body and thus sees with decidedly *un-equal* vision. Persons with different skin color will be seen as inherently different and unequal. Those in passion will afford a different measure of respect to different persons, either higher or lower according to their personal characteristics of beauty, wealth, fame, etc. Thus we see that a person's status in society, the respect afforded them, even the doors that are opened for them, are influenced by such things as their ancestral pedigree, family wealth, personal connections and so forth.

This manner of discrimination along social and economic lines is not limited to capitalistic countries. In the older societies that have a rigid caste system or other social hierarchies, the influence of passion also shows up in economic discrimination and disparity. Because of a differential outlook in terms of bodily features and social position, discrimination is made as to who is fit or unfit, equal or unequal. Those who stand as peers in the privileged class will reap rewards, but those of lower status are generally denied such privileges, rewards, opportunities, or even sufficient means to live a proper and decent life.

Passion is bounded by goodness and ignorance, and shows itself across an entire spectrum of activity according to the influences of those *gunas*. Passion influenced by goodness is naturally concerned with the building of families, the arts, commerce, infrastructure—entire cultures—for the benefit and welfare of all members. The culture is inclusive, egalitarian, and aspires to high, even lofty, ideals. The primary objective of passion influenced by goodness is the creation and development of a wonderful world for all of its members. A primary goal is not simply employment or even proper employment, but work done with dignity and pride, to a high degree of perfection. Money may used as a means to assist these efforts, but profits are of secondary consideration, and may even be viewed with a wary eye.

When the influence of goodness wanes and ignorance increases the focus becomes increasingly narrowed to "special" groups of individuals related by blood, marriage or other socially important ties. Insider and outsider status is created and discrimination begins to take place. Development is now for fewer and fewer of the culture or group, and even within the insiders group a competitive environment exists in which members vie for dominance over the others, and a strong "pecking order" develops. Unabated achieving and ranking, with accompanying lust, envy and greed pushes the interest for personal and exclusive gain. Where does that gain typically come from? Most often and most easily, it comes at the expense of the weak and "inferior" classes—the outsiders—who have few options and must settle for the lot that is dealt to them. The influence of *tamo-guna* added to *rajo-guna* results is a society of haves and have-nots, and as *tamo-guna* increases so too does the disparity.

As *tamo-guna* continues to increase and the influence of *sattva-guna* declines, so too does the proper maintenance of any and every thing, including families, children, education, infrastructure, society, culture, etc, because the emphasis is on the here and now; the future can take care of itself. The weak are neglected first—their needs, their health, their roads, their sewage. As those at the top take more, the ranks of the weak and neglected grow. Lacking proper maintenance, decay and dissolution of infrastructure, of people, and of society, set in. Weakened by selfish interests the culture succumbs to either attack from without, rebellion from within, or both, resulting in chaos, destruction and collapse. This has been the pattern of every civilization in Western history, and according to some the present one is also following that trend and is now in its dwindling phase. However, ours is exceptional in that instead of it being contained in a limited geographical area, the modern culture encompasses the entire globe. If and when it crumbles, it will bring the entirety of humanity to ruin all at the same time.

Will it come to that? It has already begun. The present dissolution of Zimbabwe is a good example. Other African countries are not too far behind. America's economy faltering in 2008, with worse projections for coming years, is also on the brink. The "popular wisdom" displayed on the internet and in books such as *America: End of an Empire*, and *Nemesis: The Last Days of the American Republic* tell us that we cannot go on the way we have been. Change or die is their message. The future is still yet to be fully determined, and it is not too late to make the necessary changes to create a different and better future, if only we will. It is the intention of this book to show the way to that change.

The overarching trend of civilization over the course of *Kali-yuga* is from goodness to ignorance. This is reflected quite clearly in economic practices, which are a very visible demonstration of the consciousness of people. I would also like to point out that the methods and trends differ considerably at different strata of society, as we shall demonstrate below. Oftentimes the people were strongly at odds with the methods and practices of their "leaders" and were violently forced to comply. We will look at how goodness and ignorance influence economics in the mode of passion in this chapter. I do not want to give the impression that this is simply one smooth and neat progression, everywhere the same. It most certainly was/is not. Every part of the world has had its own progression, but the overall trend has been the same, particularly as travel has increased and culture has been homogenized.

Shifting from Goodness to Passion

It may strike some as ironic that the religious beliefs of the Protestants encouraged the demise of the economics of goodness. That should not surprise us however, since religions too, interpreted by men, reflect the influences that the *gunas* have on them. It was the Protestant Christian ethic in particular that at least enabled, if not fomented, the dissolution of the economics of goodness and opened the door to the economics of passion. This enabling is explained by Max Weber in his essay on *The Protestant Ethic and the Spirit of Capitalism*.[1] This story begins in the Middle Ages when most productive work was managed through the system of craft guilds. The guilds themselves operated according to a code of conduct that purposely limited competition by uniting members of the same occupation, or essentially uniting competition. They were in essence cartels that managed trade in such a manner that all members could have a reasonable life, and to accomplish this end they inculcated in their members certain civic virtues. Through a long established tradition they encouraged a subsistence policy that discouraged members from raising profit above honor and social responsibility. In this way they sought to maintain society in a manner beneficial to all. Weber writes that in the guilds there was frequently a control of the general ethical standard similar to that exercised by the ascetic protestant sects. But, he says, there was an unavoidable and significant difference between the effects of the guilds and that of the sects upon economic practices:

> The sects, on the other hand, united men through the selection and the breeding of ethically qualified fellow believers. Their membership was not based upon apprenticeship or upon the family relations of technically qualified members of an occupation. The sect controlled and regulated the members' conduct exclusively in the sense of formal righteousness and methodical asceticism. *It was devoid of the purpose of a material subsistence policy which handicapped an expansion of the rational striving for profit.* The capitalist success of a guild member undermined the spirit of the guild—as happened in England and France—and hence capitalist success was shunned [within the guild]. But the capitalist success of a sect brother, if legally attained, was proof of his worth and of his state of grace, and it raised the prestige and the propaganda chances of the sect. Such success was therefore welcome. The organization of free labor in guilds, in their Occidental medieval form, has certainly—very much against their intention—not only been a handicap [for their continued success] but also a precondition for the capitalist organization of labor, which was, perhaps, indispensable.

> But the guild, of course, could not give birth to the modern bourgeois capitalist ethos. Only the methodical way of life of the ascetic sects could legitimate and put a halo around the economic "individualist" impulses of the modem capitalist ethos.[2]

The significant difference to note is that the guilds were content to limit economic activity to its proper sphere of providing for sustenance, so that profit should not become a goal in its own right. This attitude reflects the consciousness of *sattva-guna*—living in harmony with nature's economy, which provides for the sustenance of all creatures. The Christian worldview declares that God put men on the earth to be abundant and happy. He gave them dominion over all things for this purpose. Historically the interpretation of the Christian worldview has been that the destiny of man is to be the Lord of nature—that he is to subdue and conquer her. In their view God wants man to work hard and enjoy all of the rewards that this world can offer; worldly success and increased profits are taken as a sign of God's favor. It can be understood that Christianity thus interpreted is a religion for those in passion, because these are the characteristic of *rajo-guna* as explained in the *Srimad-Bhagavatam* (11.25.3, 17):

Material desire, great endeavor, dissatisfaction even in gain [desiring even more], praying for material advancement, the distortion of the intelligence due to too much activity, the inability to withdraw the perceiving senses from material objects, sense gratification, and justifying one's actions by one's strength are qualities associated with the mode of passion.

In Weber's statements we encounter again the darling word of economists—"rational"—and here we can witness how its meaning varies according to the consciousness and *guna* of the players. Weber admits that what is considered rational can differ considerably, although in his opinion it was rational to increase one's profit and gain and he considers the Protestant ethic as the "rational" choice. However under the influence of *sattva-guna* the guild's rational choice was to promote cooperation and limit competition, which they did to the extent that a member dare not under-price his goods, or put them "on sale" as we now say, to increase his sales at the expense of his fellows.

By the time Weber visited America he observed that many of the qualities of the Protestant ethic had become freed from any religious connection. Thrift, hard work and frugality were no longer followed to curry either God or man's favor, but by observation of their contribution to success were thought to be a practical formula for material life. Historian R. H. Tawney examining the connection between capitalism and Protestantism saw their influences as mutual, explaining that the Protestant ethic, with its insistence on hard work, thrift, etc., had contributed to the rise of capitalism, but at the same time Protestantism itself was also influenced by an increasingly capitalistic society.[3] He saw that Protestantism adopted the risk-taking, profit-making ethic of capitalism; however he went even further to indict Christian preachers for being laissez-faire and *not* bringing their ethics into the sphere of economics and business:

If preachers have not yet overtly identified themselves with the view of the natural man, expressed by an eighteenth-century writer in the words, "trade is one thing and religion is another," they imply a not very different conclusion by their silence as to the possibility of collusions between them. The characteristic doctrine was one, in fact, which left little room for religious teaching as to economic morality, because it anticipated the theory, later epitomized by Adam Smith in his famous reference to the invisible hand, which saw in economic self-interest the operation of a providential plan...The existing order, except in so far as the short-sighted enactments of Governments interfered with it, was the natural order, and the order established by nature was the order established by God...Naturally, again, such an attitude precluded a critical examination of institutions, and left as the sphere of Christian charity only those parts of life which could be reserved for philanthropy, precisely because they fell outside that larger area of normal human relations, in which the promptings of self-interest provided an all-sufficient motive and rule of conduct.[4]

The decades of the late 19th and early 20th centuries were a time of philosophical upheaval brought on by the combination of ideas from Darwin's *Origins of Man,* and Adam Smith's *Wealth of Nations*. Smith's "invisible hand" of the market was combined with Darwin's concept of "survival of the fittest" to justify a new "natural order" in economic affairs, one in which all forces and results were now considered the impersonal result of chance and even the forward progress of the continued natural evolution of mankind. Smith's fictional "invisible hand" was the prescription that admonished governments to stay out of the market's affairs and allow it to work its magic. This is but another of life's illusions that modern man has tried to bring to the level of reality, with tragically disappointing results for millions of people. It is in fact the continued progression from passion to ignorance, and the results support that conclusion. This audacious and patently false fiction—that the pursuit of one's own self-interest would magically result in the best interests of all—has been used as a propaganda campaign to justify the methods of the clever and able, as they exploit the politically weak and less able. The concept continues to have currency even to the present day as "economic Darwinism" is put forward as serious economic philosophy by some to justify current predatory economic practices. This philosophy is also used as justification to exploit nature. Survival of the fittest is extended to the economic realm, and combined with the concept of man's dominion over nature as commanded in Genesis. Man is the fittest and is therefore justified in whatever he does. This, along with increasingly powerful technology, gives the captains of business and industry a green light to fully exploit nature, giving no consideration to the idea of nurturing or caring for her benevolence. Whatever she offers is simply taken, with little regard for any damage caused, or thought that there might be a debt to repay to her. In the early stages of industrialization she was able to absorb the deficit. Two centuries later however she is overwhelmed, defeated by the immense forces and scale of mankind's technology. We will come back to the environmental issue below as we discuss the progression of the economics of passion to the economics of ignorance. First we will trace some of the history of the economics of passion influenced by *sattva-guna*.

Economics of Passion Influenced by Goodness

Although the Protestant philosophy helped to pave the way to a life of *rajo-guna*, for some sects it continued to be strongly attached to some aspects of *sattva-guna*. In Weber's same essay he explains how "Protestant asceticism [became] the foundation of modern vocational civilization—a sort of 'spiritualist' construction of the modern economy." This essay was written after Weber visited the United States in the early 20th century during which he observed first-hand the influence church membership held, not only in business, but in social and political circles as well. Indeed, in earlier periods in America religious beliefs were completely integrated with every aspect of life. During the colonial period (prior to 1776) in the central areas of New England for example, full citizenship status in the church was one of the *preconditions* for achieving full citizenship in the state—it was the religious congregation that determined one's citizenship status. At that time one didn't simply "join" a particular church as we might today. Membership was gained only after one had repeatedly proved his religious qualification through personal conduct, in the broadest meaning of the word, and further passed an investigation into, and a determination of his moral worth. Such candidates even then were only admitted after being elected by vote. Proven moral conduct was also especially significant in determining with whom one should do business.

The literature of the Quakers and Baptists, up to and throughout the 17th century instructs that "the children of the world distrust one another in business but they have confidence in the religiously determined righteousness of the pious."[5] Therefore credit was given to and money deposited only with those who were deemed pious after thorough scrutiny. These measures eventually led to the success of the Protestants because "there, and there alone, they are given honest and fixed prices."[6] The Baptists claimed to have made fixed prices a principle, while the Methodists imposed even broader restrictions upon their followers, who were forbidden:

1. to make words when buying and selling (bargaining or haggling)
2. to trade commodities before the custom tariff has been paid on them
3. to charge rates of interest higher than the law of the country permits
4. to "gather treasures on earth" (meaning to transform investment capital into "funded wealth," and living off of money, not work; i.e., becoming a capitalist).
5. to borrow without being sure of one's ability to pay back the debt
6. luxuries of all sorts [7]

It is well known of Protestants that they were both admonished and reputed to be thoroughly honest, thrifty and frugal. An individual was also religiously compelled to follow a secular vocation with zeal and hard work, because lack of worldly success was thought to be due to either laziness or divine disfavor:

> ...premiums were placed upon "proving" oneself before God in the sense of attaining salvation—which is found in *all* Puritan denominations—and "proving" oneself before men in the sense of socially holding one's own within the Puritan sects. Both aspects were mutually supplemental, and operated in the same direction: they helped to deliver the spirit of modem capitalism, its specific *ethos*: the ethos of the modern *bourgeois middle* classes.[8] (all emphasis in original)

The striving for material success, as well as the spirit of modern capitalism as Weber defines it, are both characteristic of *rajo-guna*. The strict adherence to principles of honesty, consideration not to harm others, and adherence to legal statutes indicate the influence of *sattva-guna*. The Protestant sects strove for success and reward as long as it was earned according to *their* ethical standards, and their ethical standards created perhaps one of the best examples of the economics of passion influenced by goodness.

This example offers evidence that human society does not exist simply in a pure state of goodness, passion, or ignorance. Although one may be prominent, the influences of the others are always present to some degree. As we traverse the path of *Kali* the quality of goodness wanes while ignorance increases, and life on earth continues to reflect the changing influences.

Moving Toward Ignorance

Under the influence of *sattva-guna* material wealth was shared, but under *rajo-guna,* personal profit and gain come into play, along with the concept of individual private ownership. Indeed, the entire concept of "I and mine" changes dramatically. The change of consciousness from *sattva* to *rajas* brought with it dramatic changes in relationships between people and the manner in which they handled their economic affairs. This shift did not occur spontaneously on the part of the people, but was imposed on them by the ruling classes with the use of force (*tamo-guna*).

In one sense the idea of controlling the people did not change, but the locus of power was shifted. The ruling classes of the early modem times determined to create a culture of dependence with themselves replacing the popes as the dispensers of favor; those favors now being decided by money. It was necessary therefore to make the populace dependent on money alone and for that their sustenance from the land and mutual dependence had to be abolished. The desired social transformation would turn the independent commoner into a dependent of *disinterested* others (industrialists or government). It would make them compete with each other to obtain such favors as the right to *survive*—paid employment being the only means of sustenance available. To achieve this, the former social customs of shared ownership, mutual aid, and the commons had to be destroyed. It mattered not what was lost in the process. More important was that society be transformed into the concept that the ruling classes wanted. It was a concept that was to chiefly benefit the ruling class at the expense of everyone else.

Destruction of The Commons

In earlier times when cultures were established in goodness, land was recognized as the only means of sustenance to which everyone had a rightful claim, not by proprietorship, but by use. "The commons," as it was generally called, provided sustenance for "the commoners," or peasant class—those who lived in a subsistence economy. A subsistence economy is one in which people make, or trade, for what they need instead of purchasing their needs with money. There were four significant social developments that were required for that long-standing arrangement to be changed. One was industrialization and markets for the goods produced, the second was a pool of laborers who would give themselves to factory work, the third was a paper money economy that could provide people with sustenance seemingly independent of the land, and the fourth was the development of the modern state.

Industrialization, applying other than human or animal power to machines, and increasing the scale of operations beyond cottage industry, required a work force that would not directly benefit from their work activity. This would require some incentive, which was the role of money. But why would the peasant subsistence farmers, who could happily maintain themselves in rural village life without extreme endeavor be motivated to take up an onerous and monotonous job tending a noisy machine, working long hours in a dirty, hot, or cold, sometimes dusty and otherwise rank factory atmosphere? If a person could live a life of independence on the land, even if meager, why would they choose to become dependent on the mercy of others in the city? They wouldn't, and didn't. Something had to be done.

These changes in the social structure were accomplished, as they typically are in *Kali-yuga*, by force. From the 16th century and continuing into the 20th century, land has been confiscated by state authorities, forcing people into a dependent lifestyle. In England from the 16th through 19th centuries a series of "enclosure laws" were enacted to eliminate the use of village lands and the commons. Of course the commoners resisted the loss of their prerogatives with petitions, threats, foot dragging, the theft of new landmarks and surveys, covert thefts and even arson. By law, the commoners had previously been entitled to the produce of the soil. Their cattle also had a right to the grass.[9] The soil itself, the land, was not owned by the commoners, but the use of it was. That use, what the law called *profit a prendre*, was a common right that ensured the survival of peasants whose social relations were structured by access to land, common agriculture and shared use-rights, and they did not want to surrender any of these rights. This contest of wills was decided by force over the course of three centuries, as 19th century social revolutionary and commentator Peter Kropotkin explains:

> In France, the village communities began to be deprived of their independence, and their lands began to be plundered, as early as the sixteenth century. However, it was only in the next century, when the mass of the peasants was brought, by exactions and wars, to the state of subjection and misery which is vividly depicted by all historians, that the plundering of their lands became easy and attained scandalous proportions. 'Everyone has taken of them according to his powers... imaginary debts have been claimed, in order to seize upon their lands'; so we read in an edict promulgated by Louis the Fourteenth in 1667. Of course the State's remedy for such evils was to render the communes still more subservient to the State, and to plunder them itself...As to the appropriation of communal lands, it grew worse and worse, and in the next century the nobles and the clergy had already taken possession of immense tracts of land one-half of the cultivated area, according to certain estimates—mostly to let it go out of [agri]culture.

> ...What took place in France took place everywhere in Western and Middle Europe. Even the chief dates of the great assaults upon the peasant lands are the same. In Germany, Austria and Belgium the village community was destroyed by the State. Instances of commoners themselves dividing their lands were rare, while everywhere the States coerced them to enforce the division, or simply favoured the private appropriation of their lands.

> The communal lands continued to be preyed upon, and the peasants were driven from the land. But it was especially since the middle of the eighteenth century that, in England as everywhere else, it became part of a systematic policy to simply weed out all traces of communal ownership...The very object of the Enclosure Acts, as shown by Mr. Seebohm, was to remove this system, and it was so well removed by the nearly four thousand Acts passed between 1760 and 1844 that only faint traces of it remain now. The land of the village communities

was taken by the lords, and the appropriation was sanctioned by Parliament in each separate case.

In short, to speak of the natural death of the village communities in virtue of economical laws is as grim a joke as to speak of the natural death of soldiers slaughtered on a battlefield. The fact was simply this: The village communities had lived for over a thousand years; and where and when the peasants were not ruined by wars and exactions they steadily improved their methods of culture. But as the value of land was increasing, in consequence of the growth of industries, and the nobility had acquired, under the State organization, a power which it never had had under the feudal system, it took possession of the best parts of the communal lands, and did its best to destroy the communal institutions.[10]

We note in the above that the newly formed political organization called "the State" gave the nobility powers that it never had under the feudal system, allowing the lords to simply usurp the land of the peasants without consideration. The development of the money economy and the State allowed the lords to free themselves from the mutually dependent relationship they had had with the vassals and serfs. The enclosure laws were specifically intended to eliminate their means of sustenance making the peasants dependent on wages to provide a labor pool for developing industrial and commercial agricultural concerns. Many of the advisors to the Board of Agriculture in England recommended the creation of complete wage dependence, arguing that wage dependence would create "discipline" amongst the somewhat independent commoners. Being mostly self-sufficient the commoners were independent enough to avoid being exploited, much to the ire of the large landholders. It was therefore argued that the threat or reality of unemployment of the commoner cum laborer would benefit the farmers who were required to reach mutually agreeable terms with them. Wage work would give the landholders an unfair advantage and the ability to force their terms upon labor. The proposals went even further to state that once the commoners had been made dependent they were to be prevented from ever again becoming independent of wages. For example, it was proposed that cottage gardens must be sufficiently small to prevent independence and always require wage work. The intention of the Board of Agriculture was to create a working class culture by eliminating the commoner, permitting only agricultural proletariats.[11]

In his book *Commoners: Common Right, Enclosure and Social Change in England, 1700-1820* author J.M. Neeson challenges the view that England had no peasantry or that it had disappeared before industrialization. It documents

18th century debate on the enclosure laws from original sources, and shows that parliamentary enclosure changed social relations, created both antagonisms and a pervasive sense of loss on the popular culture. All 18th century commentators recognized the relationship between the decline of the common right and the nature of social relations in England. Both sides of the published debate agreed that enclosures would end independence, the only argument was whether to welcome or disapprove of the change.

The process of enclosure saw laws enacted to the advantage of the ruling classes as if to legitimize their usurpation of the resources of the politically weak "common man." Although these acts were ostensibly legal, they were written to serve the interests of one section of society over another, creating a culture of winners and losers expressive of the mindset of those mired in *rajo-guna*, and the use of force to obtain the result adds the element of *tamo-guna*. Whether such laws were for the protection and benefit of the majority or the minority determines the relative influence of goodness or ignorance. The influence of *sattva-guna* allows one to see the unity of all beings, to have empathy for others, and to treat others as one would treat oneself. As the influences of *rajo-guna* and *tamo-guna* increase the conception of "I and mine" increasingly narrows, ultimately bringing one to the deluded position where he thinks himself all-important.

Let us recall that the *Srimad-Bhagavatam* states that living as a parasite is one result of the quality of *tamo-guna*. Insomuch as the ruling classes do not care for the citizens—spiritually as well as materially—they are guilty of living as parasites, consuming the produce of the citizens without performing their prescribed duties. To say that the ruling classes (*brahmanas* and *ksatriyas* in the Vedic tradition, bishops and kings in the medieval period) must see to the spiritual development of the citizens is not to say that they dictate what to believe. Rather, it is their duty to see that the citizens are properly educated in spiritual knowledge, and follow universal, non-sectarian religious principles, such as given in *Bhagavad-gita*. Who one chooses to worship, be it Jesus, Mohammed, Allah, Krishna or whoever, is left to the individual person to decide according to the merits of their own consciousness.

In the history cited above, and continuing on into the present day, the shift in social organization brought with it a change in the social contract, and with it political forces became arrayed against the common man. No longer were a people protected by their betters against common external threats and enemies. Class distinctions were now based on wealth and the control of wealth, with the owners of wealth occupying, influencing and engaging governmental forces on their behalf, organized against the common man. With enclosure the rulers of society had devised a method that would free them from all responsibility to those who labor on their land or in their factories. In feudal society the lord was responsible to see to the maintenance (however meager it might have been) and protection of those in his charge. They were a source of expense to him, and he wanted to be free of it. They determined to reorganize society in a manner that would bring them all of the benefits with none of the expense. They reorganized the kingdom into the state, and for that they wanted to create a situation in which everyone was dependent on them through an impersonal mechanism such as a wage job. The developments of the nation state, exclusive title to property, industry, and a paper money economy gave them the means to do so. One of those ruling dynasty's was, and continues to be, the Rothschilds, who controlled the Bank of England at that time. Through the bank they promulgated this concept to American bankers in a document which read in part:

> ...chattel slavery is likely to be abolished by the war power [referring to the American Civil War]...This, I and my European friends are in favor of, for slavery is but the owning of labor, and carries with it the care of labor, while the European plan, led on by England, is that capital shall control labor by controlling wages.[12]

Gustavus Myers, writing about slavery in America, corroborates that the idea was to exploit the worker as far as possible, and more than slavery alone would permit:

> ...chattel slavery could not compete in efficiency with white labor...more money could be made from the white laborer, for whom no responsibility of shelter, clothing, food and attendance had to be assumed than from the Negro slave, whose sickness, disability or death entailed direct financial loss...The perfect slave thinks he's free.[13]

Social psychologist Eric Fromm explains how this change in the social structure led to the loss of control over one's own destiny by impersonal forces:

> The breakdown of the traditional principle of human solidarity led to new forms of exploitation. In feudal society the lord was supposed to have the divine right to demand services and things from those subject to his domination, but at the same time he was bound by custom and was obligated to be responsible for his subjects, to protect them, and to provide them with at least the minimum—the traditional standard of living. Feudal exploitation took place in a system of mutual human obligations, and thus was governed by certain restrictions. Exploitation as it developed [under the money economy] was essentially different. The worker, or rather his labor, was a commodity to be bought

by the owner of capital, not essentially different from any other commodity on the market, and it was used to its fullest capacity by the buyer. Since it had been bought for its proper price on the labor market, there was no sense of reciprocity, or of any obligation on the part of the owner of capital, beyond that of paying the wages. If hundreds of thousands of workers were without work and on the point of starvation, that was their bad luck, the result of their inferior talents, or simply a social and natural law, which could not be changed. Exploitation was not personal any more, but it had become anonymous, as it were. It was the law of the market that condemned a man to work for starvation wages, rather than the intention or greed of any one individual. Nobody was responsible or guilty, nobody could change conditions either. One was dealing with the iron laws of society, or so it seemed.[14]

The Russian aristocrat and social reformer Lev Tolstoy also recognized that the end result was to be the same, albeit by deceptive means that would allow the enslaved to think they are free. He wrote "Money is but a new form of slavery, distinguishable from the old simply by the fact that it is impersonal—there is no human relation between master and slave." Being the relationship is impersonal the slave is left in a truly helpless circumstance. To whom shall he complain when his chains weigh too heavily on him? Who shall he revolt against? Due to impersonal circumstances he cannot find his enemy and his protests are rendered ineffective in procuring his relief. His situation appears not to be anyone's fault in particular. It is simply "the way things are." That's life. There is nobody to blame and everyone should simply accept the lot that is dealt to them in life. But Tolstoy adroitly penetrates the obfuscation and identifies the source of the problem—the ruling class—writing: "I sit on a man's back, choking him, and making him carry me, and yet assure myself and others that I am very sorry for him and wish to ease his lot by any means possible, except getting off his back."[15]

Driven from the land the common man now needed to find shelter in some manner. Under the new organization of society that shelter was arranged for him as his own private property. Formerly the aristocrats held exclusive title to the land, including the commons, and were thus forced to provide for those under their care. Under the new system exclusive land rights were to be shared with the common folk who would be permitted to also own land. Land thus became a commodity, but access to it would of course be limited to those who had the money to buy it. If the common people were given only minimum wages for their work they would be unable to accumulate the capital to buy land. Commonly throughout the world the common man has not achieved widespread land ownership and the ruling classes have continued to hold the vast majority of the land. In Ireland in the late 19th century for example, 616 landowners owned 80 percent of the country and 1.5 percent of the Russians owned 25 percent of that vast country. Even today in Brazil less than 3 percent of the population own two-thirds of the country's arable land and two-thirds of England is owned by a mere 0.3 percent of the population.

For the wage earners the privilege merely to live would require that they continually pay a significant portion of their hard earned income as rent to moneyed class. Those landlords would continue to accumulate capital under such an arrangement with which they would build more housing to rent to future generations. After some time it simply becomes a way of life, "the natural order" of things.

"I and mine" in *Rajo-guna*

Our modern Western conceptions of ownership come to us from Roman thought which held that everything must to have an owner. The Romans did not recognize the ownership of God as did other earlier cultures; they thought that everything should have a human owner, and a very select human owner at that. Roman law eventually came to decree that it was possible for a "free" man (i.e., a Roman citizen) to own and possess unlimited quantities of anything which he found the means to acquire, including animals, land and other human beings as slaves. Roman ideas of private property were codified into law, and it is the Roman's *juris prudence* that is often regarded as their greatest contribution to Western culture.[16] The exclusive ownership and control of land in particular is one of the foundational aspects of modern culture, and its introduction into society marks the passage from *sattva-guna* to *rajo-guna*, increasingly narrowing the sense of "I and mine."

Exclusive title to land as private property did not evolve naturally but was also imposed on society during the changes of the middle ages, despite the unwillingness of people to accept it. In the earlier organization of society a social contract existed that gave every member of the group at least the minimum for survival through the communal character of shared property, and a right to the commons. But these social relationships were antagonistic to the type of society that the rulers wanted to establish. They had determined that each person was to become apparently independent of others, to depend on money alone and their individual abilities to obtain it. This of course would give them the greatest leverage in exploiting the workers, which was their chief aim. To establish this idea it was necessary to destroy the commoners mutual dependence on each other, and the rulers attempted to do so by the method of divide and conquer. But their efforts to divide the people met with frustration as the people continued to follow their long-standing traditions of mutual dependence on each other. From Kropotkin we learn that:

> the peasants still maintained their communal institutions, and until the year 1787 the village folkmotes, composed of all householders, used to come together in the shadow of the bell-tower or a tree, to allot and re-allot what they had retained of their fields, to assess the taxes, and to elect their executive, just as the Russian mir does at the present time. This is what Babeau's researches have proved to demonstrate.

> The Government found the folkmotes "too noisy" and too disobedient. In 1787, elected councils composed of a mayor and three to six syndics, chosen from among the wealthier peasants, were introduced instead. Two years later the Revolutionary Assemblee Constituante, which was on this point at one with the old regime, fully confirmed this law (on the 14th of December, 1789), and the bourgeois du village had now their turn for the plunder of communal lands, which continued all through the Revolutionary period. Only on the 16th of August, 1792, the Convention, under the pressure of the peasants' insurrections, decided to return the enclosed lands to the communes, but it ordered at the same time that they should be divided in equal parts among the wealthier peasants only—a measure which provoked new insurrections and was abrogated the next year, in 1793, when the order came to divide the communal lands among all commoners, rich and poor alike, "active" and "inactive."

> These two laws, however, ran so much against the conceptions of the peasants that they were not obeyed, and wherever the peasants had retaken possession of part of their lands they kept them undivided. But then came the long years of wars, and the communal lands were simply confiscated by the State (in 1794) as a mortgage for State loans, put up for sale, and plundered as such; then returned again to the communes and confiscated again (in 1813); and only in 1816 what remained of them, i.e. about 15,000,000 acres of the least productive land, was restored to the village communities. Still this was not yet the end of the troubles of the communes. Every new regime saw in the communal lands a means for gratifying its supporters, and three laws (the first in 1837 and the last under Napoleon the Third) were passed to induce the village communities to divide their estates. Three times these laws had to be repealed, in consequence of the opposition they met with in the villages.[17]

We note that every time the land was divided the peasants put them back into communal ownership, undivided. It took centuries of effort to destroy their mutual dependence to the point that they could adopt an individual conception of "I and mine." These efforts were combined with a campaign of propaganda (see Divide and Conquer below) to enshrine the rugged individual as the champion of determination, heroism, and all things good. The self-made man is made out to be superior to all others. The same propaganda is used to instill an envy of others and to ridicule the less able as parasites who suck the wealth that others created. The propaganda continues to this day, and the people of the West have finally accepted individualism as the natural order of things. Americans especially can no longer conceive of any other social organization and suggestions to unite property outside of the family are immediately ridiculed with cries of "socialism" or "communism," forgetting that the hallowed family unit is actually one such form of communism, and that everyone belongs to one larger family as "the children of God." People have been brought to heel, faithfully following what they have been taught: to depend on oneself alone, what you create is yours alone. It is the government's responsibility to help those in need, keeping the state in between the relationships of people. These efforts are very effective, to the point that people today have not an inkling of how they are indoctrinated and controlled.

Destruction of the Commonwealth Continues

This same technique is used to this day, centuries later, to divest people of their traditions of mutual dependence and shared resources. The following example comes from the peoples of Alaska: the Inupiat, Yup'ik, Aleut, Athabascan, Tlingit, Haida, and Tsimshian, collectively known to us as Eskimos. The story is detailed in *Village Journey—The Report of the Alaska Native Review Commission* by Thomas R. Berger.[18] The Eskimos have been living in the Arctic Tundra for centuries. Their forebears were already there when Columbus first "discovered" the "Americas." They have been able to maintain their place in the world because of the traditions carefully passed from one generation to the next. Their way of life has been relatively simple: they share the land on which they live, as well as the life-sustaining resources that they obtain by gathering, hunting and fishing. This territory was "sold" by Russia to the United States in 1867, and these tens-of-thousands of acres have since been considered the property of the United States Government, although the natives have been allowed to continue to live on these lands of their forefathers.

In 1972 the United States Government sought to change their way of life, ostensibly to help these people, although the people themselves did not ask for or want the so-called help. Something else must have been the motivation. Matters were settled the way they had been centuries earlier in Europe. A government thousands of miles away passed The Alaska Native Claims Settlement Act (ANCSA). Under ANCSA law Alaskan Natives were to receive $962.5 million in cash and title of ownership to forty-four million acres of their ancestral lands. Bear in mind the vast majority of this "land" is covered by snow the majority of the year in one of the harshest winter climates in the world. The people there are mostly subsistence hunters and fishermen. The land and the waters around it are their principal concern. This land itself is the source of their life. For all practical purposes, the land is their life. In their own words:

> Our subsistence way of life is especially important to us. Among other needs it is our greatest. We are desperate to keep it (Paul John, Tununak).

> We Yup'iks do not wish to lose the land. We would like to use the land as our ancestors did. We would like to use it without any problems. (Mike Angaiak, Tununak).

In Alaska subsistence living requires free access to land and the waters. Moreover it requires that the land and waters are free from intrusion and ownership in order for nature's bounty to proliferate. Subsistence has been a way of life that—far from being marginal—fulfills these people's spiritual and economic needs. But it was a life that the ruling powers wanted to destroy.

Alaska Natives were given the impression that the ANCSA "settlement" would protect their lands so they could pass them on to future generations. But by ANCSA, Congress extinguished aboriginal title of (common) ownership throughout *the entire state* of Alaska, and subjected the land, which before had been the common property of all and owned by God, to private ownership of individuals. Now it was subject to the concepts of "I and mine," divisible and subject to sale. Previously these natives were secure on God's land. Dividing it and subjecting it to private ownership through ANCSA they were now faced with the very real possibility that they could lose their land, and along with it, their way of life.

ANCSA brought the fictitious concept of incorporation to this frozen world and divided the land into areas of incorporation. It further disenfranchised future generations by distributing corporate shares only to adults over 21 years of age. The supposed purpose of the village corporations was to make profits and pursue economic purposes. But the villagers have always been chiefly concerned with subsistence activities, not monetary ones—they had no interest in private profit. This placed the corporations, run by city "professionals" at cross purposes with their village shareholders. Further the law decreed that after ten years the land could be subject to taxation, even though it generates no revenues. Where were these people going to get money to pay taxes? Obviously only from a job in some distant city. Moreover, if the village corporation fails, for whatever reason, creditors could attach the ancestral land of these villagers. Additionally, after twenty years (1991), shares in the corporation were allowed to be sold, and therefore after this date outsiders could take over the village corporation and its assets, including the land, driving the original natives off of it.

For most village corporations, the story is a sad one. Undercapitalized, without corporate experience, with virtually no business prospects, these fledgling corporations were at the mercy of the lawyers, advisers, and consultants who flocked to the villages like scavengers. The money was quickly spent, mostly on lawyers for the settlement of land claims until the land itself was at risk, and with it their way of life.

ANCSA introduced serious changes to native life that grew with the passage of time. It affected family relations, traditional patterns of leadership and decision making, customs of sharing, and subsistence activities—the entire native way of life. The village has lost its political and social autonomy. In short, its culture was destroyed. Unable to see a future for themselves, as the young adults came of age they began to leave for the cities to earn money. With the loss of the next generation to the money culture, the elders could understand that their way of life was also coming to an end. Where would these people go but the cities? Which, of course, was the original purpose. Under the ruling order established in the Middle Ages nobody is simply entitled to live, but all must earn their place in the money economy.

Economics of Passion Influenced by *Tamo-guna*

The influence of *tamo-guna* brings covetousness, envy, force and violence, anger and hatred, duplicity and cheating, theft, false pride, stinginess, hypocrisy, destruction, and so on. By the influence of passion people see with an unequal vision, considering themselves superior to others. As the influence of *tamo-guna* increases so does envy. Those so infected cannot stand to see others prosper. They get to the point where they can exploit and neglect without a twinge of conscience. The economics of passion influenced by ignorance is thus characterized by the attempt to increase one's gains by means of cunning, deception, cheating, exploitation, force and violence without consideration of the consequences to others.

Because the trend of society is now rushing pell-mell toward ignorance in almost every sphere, the function and utility of economics is as well. There are almost an unlimited number of cases that could be cited that are indicative of either passion bordering on ignorance, or ignorance bordering on passion, the distinction being subtle. The assessment must be based on the relative component of the characteristics of each *guna* as described in the *Bhagavad-gita* and *Srimad-Bhagavatam*. I will give several examples to illustrate the economics of passion influenced by ignorance. Each of these examples reveals the intent to increase gain through force, violence, or exploitation: 1) the violent destruction or elimination of competition in order to secure markets and extract the wealth, 2) exploitation of the worker with the help of government, 3) dividing and conquering the common man, 4) creating unequal trade, with an example of how the British extracted the wealth of India, and 5) the Christian concept of man's dominion over nature.

Stifling the Competition

One of the major, and often overlooked, problems with a money economy is the necessity to produce something that one cannot use in the real sense—money. The modern economy puts money in between people and the objects of their desire. We cannot eat or wear money, but the arrangement of a money economy requires money in order to have food to eat, or clothes to wear. This emphasis on something completely artificial in order to sustain life creates problems in society that otherwise do not exist. A paper money economy was artificially created and necessitated, so that unnecessary wealth could be stored and accumulated in vast amounts. Bhaktivedanta Swami has called it the "unlawful accumulation of wealth."[19] Stemming from a false consciousness of "I and mine," those who desired to increase their sense of self through increasing their possessions enjoy this artificial money mechanism. Cleverly, its creators also retained to themselves the exclusive privilege of its creation giving them unlimited power and control over others.

The use of the money economy instead of the subsistence economy, in which people simply labor to produce what they need, creates many more problems by introducing a very unnatural competition, which in turn brings about strife, struggle, suffering and wars. In fact, it can be said without too much exaggeration that almost all of the wars of Western culture have been wars to obtain advantages in, and control, over trade.[20] The reason that the competition is unnatural is due to the excess wealth that can be accumulated and stored using an artificial measure of wealth (paper money). Excessive desire for profits (over and above what can be used in a reasonable period of time) leads to desires for increased market share, which can be gained by restricting the activities of competitors. This is what gangsters are famous for. But not only gangsters recognize the value of a monopoly. As one of America's foremost robber barons John D. Rockerfeller puts it, "competition is a sin!"

Monopoly control of industries was the objective of J. P. Morgan, J. D. Rockefeller, and other business tycoons of the late nineteenth century. However, by that time those in the inner sanctums of Wall Street understood that the most efficient way to gain an unchallenged monopoly was political—under the name of the public good and the public interest. This strategy was detailed in 1906 by Frederick C. Howe in his *Confessions of a Monopolist*. There Howe wrote:

> The rules of big business are reducible to a simple maxim: Get a monopoly; let society work for you and make a business of politics. To control industries it is necessary to control Congress and the regulators and thus make society go to work for you, the monopolist. A legislative grant, franchise, subsidy or tax exemption is worth more than a Kimberly or Comstock lode, since it does not require any labor, either mental or physical, for its exploitation.

That maxim has been applied everywhere since, regardless of the costs necessary to establish it.

We should note that there is no such artificial competition in a subsistence economy. If you trade your apples for Victor's wheat there is a natural limit to the transaction since you only have so many apples and can only eat and store a limited amount of wheat. But although need has definite limits greed does not. Since money is used as a store of wealth and it is imperishable, you can accumulate vastly greater quantities of it than you can wheat. Add to this the ego-enhancing nature of accumulating wealth and then excess profits become highly desirable. People are thus encouraged to earn more than they can use in a reasonable amount of time, and store that wealth to further enhance their ego, or their control over others. The hallmarks of passion and ignorance are seen in these efforts: material desire, great endeavor, dissatisfaction with simple gains and desiring more, false pride, envy of others, justifying one's actions by one's strength, stinginess, intense competition in which some win and others lose, personal distinction, considering oneself different from or better than others.

Economist J.W. Smith explains that the rules of what he calls *plunder-by-trade* are arranged to bring profits from the periphery of an empire to the center. Trade is therefore restricted in such a way to benefit the powerful as much as possible, at the expense of others. This approach to economic affairs began in the Middle Ages at the same time that the feudal system was being dismantled. Karl Polanyi has pointed out how stifling the competition has been an economic policy beginning in years long past:

> Up to and during the course of the fifteenth century the towns were the sole centers of commerce and industry to such an extent that

none of it was allowed to escape into the open country....The struggle against rural trading and against rural handicrafts lasted at least seven or eight hundred years...The severity of these measures increased with the growth of 'democratic government'...All through the fourteenth century regular armed expeditions were sent out against all the villages in the neighborhood and looms and fulling-vats were broken or carried away. The problem of the towns collectively was to control their own markets, that is, be able to reduce the cost of items purchased from the countryside and to minimize the role of stranger merchants. Two techniques were used. On the one hand, towns sought to obtain not only legal rights to tax market operations but also the right to regulate the trading operation (who should trade, when it should take place, what should be traded). Furthermore, they sought to restrict the possibilities of the countryside engaging in trade other than via their town. Over time, these various mechanisms shifted their terms of trade in favor of the townsmen, in favor thus of the urban commercial classes against both the landowning and peasant classes.[21]

Dr. Smith explains further:

The loss of the city's markets for both raw material and manufactured products due to the comparative advantage of the countryside meant impoverishment and possibly even starvation for those in the city who produced that cloth. The same loss of monopoly through increased technological knowledge of the countryside and its natural comparative advantage held true for other products and other cities. The wealth-producing process had to be protected. The comparative advantages of the outlying villages were eliminated by force to maintain dependency upon the city and lay claim to both the natural wealth of the countryside and the wealth produced by technology.

When one city took over the countryside markets of another city, the dispossessed would again face starvation. Thus the wars between the City-states of the Middle Ages were wars over control of trade. City-states evolved into countries that also went to war over control of trade. Powerful countries evolved into empires which controlled resources and trade far beyond their borders.[22]

Exploitation of Labor

The envy of *tamo-guna* is not exclusively directed towards others who have more than we have, as is generally thought. But, being a state of consciousness, it is extended everywhere the glance is cast. When employed in the class divisions of business and labor, each side sees their interests as divided and they attempt to exploit each other. Adam Smith details this conflict, and the advantages management holds over labor in ability, resources and law:

> The workmen desire to get as much, the masters to give as little as possible. The former are disposed to combine in order to raise, the latter in order to lower, the wages of labour. It is not, however, difficult to foresee which of the two parties must, upon all ordinary occasions, have the advantage in the dispute, and force the other into a compliance with their terms. The masters, being fewer in number, can combine much more easily; and the law, besides, authorises, or at least does not prohibit their combinations, while it prohibits those of the workmen. We have no acts of parliament against combining to lower the price of work; but many against combining to raise it. In all such disputes the masters can hold out much longer. A landlord, a farmer, a master, manufacturer, or merchant, though they did not employ a single workman could generally live a year or two upon the stocks which they have already acquired. Many workmen could not subsist a week, few could subsist a month, and scarce any a year without employment. In the long-run the workman may be as necessary to his master as his master is to him; but the necessity is not so immediate.

> We rarely hear, it has been said, of the combinations of masters; though frequently of those of workmen. But whoever imagines, upon this account, that masters rarely combine, is as ignorant of the world as of the subject. Masters are always and every where in a sort of tacit, but constant and uniform combination, not to raise the wages of labour above their actual rate. To violate this combination is every where a most unpopular action, and a sort of reproach by a master to his neighbours and equals. We seldom, indeed, hear of this combination, because it is the usual, and one may say, the natural state of things which nobody ever hears of. Masters too sometimes enter into particular combinations to sink the wages of labour even below this rate. These are always conducted with the utmost silence and secrecy, till the moment of execution, and when the workmen

yield, as they sometimes do, without resistance, though severely felt by them, they are never heard of by other people.[23]

We learn here from Smith how the masters have arranged the laws in their favor at the expense of labor, and how the masters collude for the sake of controlling wages to their lowest possible level. Such acts, indicative of *tamo-guna*, result predictably in conflict. But it is not, as Smith, Marx and so many others are convinced, that the conflict between labor and management is inevitable in all circumstances. The conflict results from greed and envy brought about by the influence of *raja* and *tamo-guna*. Under the influence of *sattva-guna* an entirely different situation will result as was noted above regarding the craft guilds of medieval society. Under those circumstances management and labor assisted each other and cooperated for the overall good, without perennial conflict. Absent the influence of *sattva-guna* however, conflicts of interest result in an ever-tenuous working relationships, disturbed whenever one party finds an opportunity to further exploit the other.

Divide and Conquer

One method of increasing market share is to increase the market by eliminating the competition altogether. This was another motive in destroying the commons—to prevent people from providing for themselves. Forced to take wage work they would purchase their necessities with the money they earn. Not only was the commons destroyed, but the tendency of the commoners to support and rely on one another was as well. The fear of course was that the workers would organize themselves and establish collective bargaining with employers. The state apparatus was intent on dismantling any union or collaboration of individuals. As noted above, this idea was established by championing the self-made man, the rugged individual, as a model to emulate. Again Kropotkin provides the necessary history:

> For the next three centuries the States, both on the Continent and in these islands, systematically weeded out all institutions in which the mutual-aid tendency had formerly found its expression. The village communities were bereft of their folkmotes, their courts and independent administration; their lands were confiscated. The guilds were spoliated of their possessions and liberties, and placed under the control, the fancy, and the bribery of the State's official. The cities were divested of their sovereignty, and the very springs of their inner life—the folkmote, the elected justices and administration, the sovereign parish and the sovereign guild—were annihilated; *the State's functionary took possession of every link of what formerly*

was an organic whole. Under that fatal policy and the wars it engendered, whole regions, once populous and wealthy, were laid bare; rich cities became insignificant boroughs; the very roads which connected them with other cities became impracticable. Industry, art, and knowledge fell into decay. Political education, science, and law were rendered subservient to the idea of State centralization. *It was taught in the Universities and from the pulpit that the institutions in which men formerly used to embody their needs of mutual support could not be tolerated in a properly organized State*; that the State alone could represent the bonds of union between its subjects; that federalism and "particularism" were the enemies of progress, and the State was the only proper initiator of further development. By the end of the last century the kings on the Continent, the Parliament in these isles, and the revolutionary Convention in France, *although they were at war with each other, agreed in asserting that no separate unions between citizens must exist within the State*; that hard labour and death were the only suitable punishments to workers who dared to enter into "coalitions." "No state within the State!" The State alone, and the State's Church, must take care of matters of general interest, while *the subjects must represent loose aggregations of individuals, connected by no particular bonds, bound to appeal to the Government each time that they feel a common need.* Up to the middle of the century this was the theory and practice in Europe.[24]

The effort of the rulers was to establish complete control over the lives of the people, and to insert their bureaucratic agents in between the people. By dividing their land, their interests, and their efforts, the rulers sought to exploit the citizens as much as possible. We can understand that this was their intention because it certainly was the result, irregardless of where one lived. By the end of the nineteenth century, the unlivable wage that was paid to the workers in London was no different than that paid in New York, or in St. Petersburg. The various powers had determined that the way of life was going to change to what is now called the "modern" way of life. It more properly deserves to be called money slavery, since everyone, without exception, is a slave to obtaining money simply to survive. In order to further hide the truth, we are indoctrinated into life as if it's different aspects were neatly divided and compartmentalized into separate spheres of activity—political, economic, social, religious and so on. Life is no longer an integrated whole (the impersonalism that characterizes *Kali-yuga*). We have the impression that we are governed by a certain political arrangement called democracy, or a constitutional republic, and so on. Nothing could be farther from the truth. We are in fact governed by money, or more specifically, by those who control money, as attested to by Rothschild.

Creating Unequal Trade

The other critical factor in social developments at this time was the creation and expansion of the manufacturing of commodities. The output of machines was vastly greater than what local markets could typically absorb, and therefore new markets had to be found in order to make the factory produce the greatest possible profit. When markets were saturated at home naturally they were sought in other nations. But more than that, by controlling trade in a strategic manner wealth could be extracted from trading partners. This is Smith's plunder-by-trade, and it is explained by Adam Smith in *Wealth of Nations*:

> A small quantity of manufactured produce purchases a great quantity of rude [raw, unfinished goods] produce. A trading and manufacturing country, therefore, naturally purchases with a small part of its manufactured produce a great part of the rude produce of other countries; while, on the contrary, a country without trade and manufactures is generally obliged to purchase, at the expense of a great part of its rude produce, a very small part of the manufactured produce. The one exports what can subsist and accommodate but a very few, and imports the subsistence and accommodation of a great number. The other exports the accommodation and subsistence of a great number, and imports that of a very few only. The inhabitants of the one must always enjoy a much greater quantity of subsistence than what their own lands, in the actual state of their cultivation, could afford. The inhabitants of the other must always enjoy a much smaller quantity...Few countries...produce much more rude produce than what is sufficient for the subsistence of their own inhabitants. To send abroad any great quantity of it, therefore, would be to send abroad a part of the necessary subsistence of the people. It is otherwise with the exportation of manufactures. The maintenance of the people employed in them is kept at home, and only the surplus part of their work is exported.[25]

This process of importing raw materials and exporting finished goods allows imperial nations to extract the wealth of their colonies and trading partners, enriching the former and impoverishing the latter. When the value of their currencies differ this results in an exponential net transfer of wealth, as explained by Dr. Smith.(in this example substituting the words "cotton cloth" for "widgets" will prepare the reader for the next section):

> Consider how long the underpaid nation must work to buy one unit of wealth from the high-paid nation and then *consider how many units of wealth the high-paid nation can purchase from the underpaid nation with the wages of their equally-productive labor working that same number of hours.*
>
> Capital accumulation advantage increases or decreases exponentially with the differential in pay for equally-productive labor. The equally-productive worker in the poorly-paid nation produces a unique widget, is paid $1 an hour, and is producing one widget an hour. The equally-productive worker in the well-paid nation produces another unique widget, is paid $10 an hour, and also produces one widget per hour. Each equally-productive nation likes, and purchases, the other's widgets. All true costs are labor costs so we ignore monopoly capital costs, which go to the developed world and only increases the advantage anyway, and calculate the cost of those widgets at the labor cost of production, $1 an hour and $10 an hour. The $1 an hour country must work 10 hours to buy one of the widgets of the $10 an hour country but, with the money earned in the same 10 hours, the $10 an hour country can buy 100 of the widgets of the $1 an hour nation. In a homogenized market (a mixture of high-paid and underpaid equally-productive labor) there is a 10-times differential in wealth gained. *At that 10-times wage differential in a non-homogenized market there is an exponential 100-times differential in capital accumulation or buying powe...*All wealth is processed from natural resources by labor utilizing industrial capital, most of those resources are in the weak, impoverished world, and that natural wealth is transferred to the powerful *imperial-centers-of-capital* through low commodity prices and unequal pay for equal work, as per this formula. (all emphasis in original)

Given this understanding it isn't surprising that the imperialistic nations established the value of currencies of their colonies not on par with the homeland, allowing them to take advantage of this principle and transfer the wealth of the world to themselves. The result was impoverishment of the colonies. Regarding India's experience Prime Minister Jawaharlal Nehru noted: "If you trace British influence and control in each region of India, and then compare that with poverty in the region, they correlate. The longer the British have been in a region, the poorer it is."[26] Continuing the exploitation up to the present time, a deliberate devaluation of currencies is often a precondition for loans from the World Bank and an integral part of the IMF's structural adjustment programs.

Stealing and Destroying the Wealth of India

In *Economic Democracy* Smith explains how the impoverishment of India is a classic example of plunder-by-trade backed by military might. As we noted in an earlier chapter, India, prior to the advent of British rule was a well-organized, and wealthy country. When the British arrived they "found a thriving industry and a prosperous agriculture. It was, in the optimistic words of one Englishman, 'a wonderful land, whose richness and abundance neither war, nor pestilence, nor oppression could destroy.'" Production in India was very decentralized and many thousands of independent artisans produced handicrafts. In Bengal woven cloth was the specialty. It was common to find hand-weaving done by a person who would sing or chant prayers in time with the clickety-clack rhythm of the machine. Although he was a very skilled and expert craftsman, and the cloth that he produced was the best in the world, Indian cloth could still be sold for far less than that produced in Europe.

Before the British fully understood Adam Smith's principles they purchased much of their cloth from India. However, there was little exchange between the two countries due to a lack of interest in India for English goods, and the British had to make up imbalance in trade with payments of gold, a drain on her reserved wealth. However, after India was colonized and the British controlled her trade this arrangement came to an abrupt halt. Indian textiles were forbidden on the British markets. Instead the British imported from India only the raw materials for production of cloth in England, producing it with mechanized weaving technology. Britain's machine made cloth was still inferior to that which the Indians themselves could produce, but to create a market for it Indian produced cloth was heavily taxed. As a result of manipulating production and the market Britain quickly came to dominate the Indian cloth market, destroying domestic production. Historian Lewis Mumford explains how the British eviscerated the Indian economy:

> In the name of progress, the limited but balanced economy of the Hindu village, with its local potter, its local spinners and weavers, its local smith, was overthrown for the sake of providing a market for the potteries of the Five Towns and the textiles of Manchester and the superfluous hardware of Birmingham. The result was impoverished villages in India, hideous and destitute towns in England, and a great wastage in tonnage and man-power in plying the oceans between.[27]

By 1947, when the sun finally set on the British Empire in India, Eastern Bengal had been reduced to an agricultural hinterland. In the words of an English merchant, 'Various and innumerable are the methods of oppressing the poor weavers...such as by fines, imprisonment, floggings, forcing bonds from them, etc.' By means of every conceivable form of roguery, the [British East India] company's merchants acquired the weaver's cloth for a fraction of its value.[28]

This example of stifling the competition of India is far from being an isolated case. What applies to British colonialism applies to all colonialism, and according to J. W. Smith, India and China were actually the least damaged of all colonial regions. The same process, carried to extremes, continues to this day at an accelerated pace under the name of Globalization and Free Trade, which will be discussed in the next chapter as the economics of ignorance.

Christian Dominion as "I and mine" of *Rajo-guna*

Having earlier traced our path into *rajas* following the influence of Christianity we should not overlook Christianity's influence in abetting the consciousness and effects of *rajo-guna* and *tamo-guna* into the twentieth century and beyond. The bible states that God has given man dominion over nature, which has historically been interpreted to mean that nature is at man's disposal, literally. The idea has long been presented in Christian circles that God made this world specifically for mankind to enjoy. The idea of man as the rightful enjoyer of nature, not in modesty, but as far as his appetite permits, was expressed by Thomas Traherne, a seventeenth century clergyman who gushes at the idea of possessing the world:

> It is of the nobility of man's soul that he is insatiable: for he hath a benefactor so prone to give [God], that he [God] delighteth in us for asking. Do not your inclinations tell you that the world is yours? Do you not covet all? Do you not long to have it; to enjoy it; to overcome it? To what end do men gather riches, but to multiply more? Do they not, like Pyrrhus the King of Empire, add house to house and lands to lands, that they may get it all?

Historian Lynn White, reflecting on such attitudes, is credited with making a lasting indictment of Christianity as *the* culprit of the ecological crisis. He challenges that the ideology of Christianity—that man is given dominion over the earth and all of its life—has been used as a provocation, even encouragement, for exploiting nature to the fullest degree. [29]

White asks and answers: "What did Christianity tell people about their relations with the environment?" That "no item in the physical creation had any purpose except to serve man's purposes." He says that Christianity, in absolute contrast to ancient paganism and Asia's religions, not only established a dualism of man and nature but also insisted that it is God's will that man exploit nature for his proper ends. By destroying pagan animism, Christianity made it possible to exploit nature in a mood of indifference to the feelings of natural objects.

Moreover White suggests that Christianity has nothing to contribute to solving the environmental crisis. Social commentator Wendell Berry agreeing observed: "the culpability of Christianity in the destruction of the natural world and uselessness of Christianity in any effort to correct that destruction are now established clichés of the conservation movement." The environmentalists are looking beyond Christianity for another worldview that has protection, and not dominion, as its central principle. In White's opinion "what we do about ecology depends on our ideas of the man-nature relationship. More science and more technology are not going to get us out of the present ecologic crisis until we find a new religion, or rethink our old one."

White's thesis damning Christianity, and the unlikely success of Christianity's rearguard action on the issue, is forcefully reinforced by ecologist Keith Helmuth:

> Revising our understanding of dominion and rehabilitating a theology of Creation is not likely to alter the fact that the ethos of domination permeates Western culture. The technology and economics which are poisoning and disabling the Earth have come straight out of our Biblically-dominated culture. There is no escaping this accountability...A growing range of cultural studies has shown that the categories of thought through which we organize our understanding of the world, and the structures of language through which we express that understanding, have been shaped by the ethos of domination. The urge to dominate is undoubtedly a pre-Biblical behavior. But the Biblical injunction to march under the banner of a progressively widening dominion, has amplified this tendency into such cultural prominence as to have become a virtual worldview, a generally unconscious assumption about the natural order of things and relationships.[30]

The reader should be able to recognize by now that the Christian worldview as portrayed by White and Helmuth is one predominated by the mode of passion influenced strongly by the mode of ignorance. That being the case White is quite correct to assert that such a worldview will never provide solutions for the ecological crisis.

In response to White's essay Christian thinkers have entered into an extended debate about the role of Christianity in creating and sustaining a destructive attitude toward exploitation of nature, and have generated three alternative approaches. The first is the Stewardship model that requires Christians to exercise dominion with care and prudence. This alternative, although still mired by the *rajasic* conception of "I and mine" has some elements of *sattva*, and would have been a better approach had it been applied centuries ago. But given the severity of the problems it is not much more than a band-aid attempt to heal a gaping wound.

Within liberal Christianity, two other models are offered to reform Christianity's exploitative influences: eco-feminism and creation spirituality. Eco-feminism advocates that our deliverance can be found in modification of the masculine, patriarchal institutions that have dominated not only the environment but women as well. This sexist approach does not properly analyze the problem; it equates destructive tendencies with masculine energy. In fact, exploitation and destruction arises from masculine energy under the influence of the mode of ignorance. Modern women are likewise overly influenced by *tamo-guna*, and transference of power to females under its influence is not an appropriate nor adequate solution. Under the influence of *tamo-guna* women and men alike cannot understand what is to be done and what is not to be done. Instead both male and female energies must be raised to the platform of *sattva-guna* which nurtures and sustains all—people and environment alike. Creation spirituality and its counterpart, eco-theology, lack an adequate conceptual frame from which to understand the nature of the problem and thus provide the necessary solution.

Even though the external characteristics of Christianity have largely faded from modern society, an underlying consciousness of exploitation survives. It is not a problem that is going to be dealt with by Christians making their philosophy politically correct. Exploitation, not just of nature, but of everything and everyone is the current state of the Western world today. It is the de facto worldview of the entire globe. To remedy a solution it is not enough to simply recognize the need for change, or to call for others to change, a new way of thinking is required. As White said we "are not going to get us out of the present ecologic crisis until we find a new religion, or rethink our old one."

The actual root of the ecological crisis is the consciousness of modern man mired in *rajo-guna* and *tamo-guna*, and in that state ecological exploitation and destruction will continue. Everything in this world, and even the world itself, rests on consciousness. The only factual remedy for the problems of the world is the upliftment of the consciousness of mankind from the lower modes of nature to that of *sattva* and *suddha-sattva*, or transcendence. If only a small fraction of the population moves in this direction, even three to five percent, it will be sufficient to bring about a cure.

While his correlation of the church's interpretation of Christianity and environmental problems may be correct, does this mean that Christian theology on the whole is thus guilty as charged? Looking at the history of the Christian faith we must answer, no. One example to the contrary is sufficient to demonstrate that Christianity can be understood and practiced in a different and positive light, by those of a different consciousness. Among others, one example is Francis of Assisi, who communed with nature as if he were with the Supreme Being. Francis, it seems, saw the divine personality present in all of creation, and expressed a commensurate reverence to nature. It is not the doctrines of Christianity per se that are at fault but the manner in which the Roman and Protestant churches chose to understand them. Unfortunately they adhered to a more *rajasic* and *tamasic*, self-serving, interpretation, instead of Francis' more *sattvic* vision and understanding, which would also be more appealing to others situated in *sattva-guna*.

The Result of Economics in Passion

Most of us are familiar with the economics of passion because we live in cultures where passion is the dominant mode. Especially in the so-called developed world. In many of the "developing countries" the *sattvic* villages are becoming deserted as people flock to the *rajasic* cities. That's where the money is. The influences of passion are tempting. The shops are full of attractively displayed products and many people are well-dressed and attractive, and as the *Gita* teaches us: while contemplating the objects of the senses one develops attachment for them. There is a sense of euphoria that comes from passion, a seductiveness that entices all people. Hopeful of being freed from a life of ordinariness and often drudgery, and enticed by the prospect of becoming a more attractive person by the display of stylish accoutrements, city dwellers spend their hard earned money on the latest electronic gadgets and fashions. Getting money for all of this consumerism becomes the driving force of the American, and increasingly other, economies.

There has not yet been a single culture in the history of Western civilization that has been able to withstand the seductiveness of passion. Nor have there been any who have had sufficient *sattva* to avoid their inevitable demise. For all of the material gain there is a social loss that is too subtle to be recognized by most as it is happening. Norberg-Hodge as an observer to the Ladakhi culture could see it as it was in the process of happening. So has Jeremy Seabrook. In his book *What Went Wrong? Why Hasn't Having More Made People Happier?* he describes the increasing despair of the working class people of England, despite their material progress. He offers a number of personal cameos that demonstrate the pain and resentment that existed in working-class communities despite their material gains:

> Abundance is seen as something absolute, like life itself, self-evidently desirable; and as such, is a sacred taboo. But what if it has been achieved in a way that is corrupting and damaging to our human associations and relationships? Under the pretext of being released from a rigid and oppressive system of work we have also been robbed of our skills and the satisfaction in what we did...

> Most of us now do not want for basic comforts; and this has been achieved, not for the most part by exercising our skills, but by forfeiting them. Many of us resent the work we do now. We grudge the use of our time, and are often indifferent to the things we make or the services we provide. We feel bored and functionless. We see work as something else; it is an unhappy intrusion into the real business of our lives. We measure ourselves not by what we do, but by what we can acquire. Our function is no longer a primary determinant of our identity...

> The chance to abolish poverty, one of the great scourges of mankind, should have given rise to a spontaneous and sustained cry of joy; but instead, there is nothing but discord and violence, ruined human relationships, the contamination, not only of work, but of neighborhood, kinship and comradeliness, division between generations, distrust within families. The price is too high: humanity is not liberated, but subordinated by this capitalist plenty, which is sold to us as though it were life itself. It is joyless and destructive: it cannot be without significance that when you talk to the old about their poverty, the great consolation in all that suffering was the quality of human relationships; now that things have been so well perfected, the only thing wrong seems to be people.[31]

The point is that no amount of material progress alone is sufficient to satisfy the soul. When people are poverty stricken and struggling simply to survive they have the impression that if they have material comforts that they will then be happy. The simple fact is that they were not happy when they were in poverty, nor are they happy after they attained some degree of affluence. Seabrook's lament does not arise from the increasing prosperity as he perceives it, but is a direct result of the influence of *rajo-guna*—grief is the result of the mode of passion; happiness derived from contact of the senses with their objects, appears to be like nectar at first, but as the Gita teaches us, it is poison at the end.

The losses that he laments and the happiness, satisfaction and fulfillment he longs for are all qualities of *sattva-guna*. The transition that has so affected the people and culture of England is that of economics of passion neglecting goodness. *If* we were the body then material comforts should yield happiness, but since we are in fact spiritual beings, *jivas*, other considerations are at play as Tawney also observed, commenting that "both the existing economic order, and too many of the projects advanced for reconstructing it, break down through the neglect of the truism that, since even quite common men have souls, no increase in material wealth will compensate them for arrangements which insult their self-respect and impair their freedom."[32]

Chapter Five

The Economics of Ignorance

For human society, constantly thinking of how to earn money and apply it for sense gratification brings about the destruction of everyone's interests. Srimad-Bhagavatam 4.22.33

Economics Influenced Predominantly by Ignorance

Whereas competition in the mode of passion is characterized by a level playing field, under the influence of ignorance everything is done to tip the field significantly, or even completely, to one's own side. The desire for gain becomes incessant and relentless. Any means, especially foul, are used to accumulate wealth. All of the qualities of ignorance find a valuable role: lying, cheating, stealing, deception, harshness, exploitation, coercion, and violence. Gain at others' expense (win-lose) is preferable to mutual gain (win-win), and "may-the-better-man-win" becomes "winner-take-all." Personal gain progresses to the point of malignant narcissism until there is nobody else to think about beyond oneself.

Under the influence of ignorance exploitation is the rule not the exception, and economic advantage is taken wherever it can be found: from competitors, from suppliers, from buyers, and from workers. Costs are "externalized" to those who have no benefit from the transaction, with the environment and future generations being the favorite stooges.

Cultures that are predominantly influenced by the quality of ignorance are harsh, cruel, exploitative, violent, combative, employ methods of cheating, hypocrisy, double-dealing, covetousness, hoarding, fraud, and slavery. Thinking only of oneself or extended self such as family members and colluding friends, those influenced by ignorance even take delight in seeing others suffer. Acts of

129

conquest, looting, and destruction of one's enemy are typical, as are acts of genocide.

By the influence of ignorance, outright largesse, bribery of, and kickbacks to government officials are the means for businesses to obtain exclusive markets. The government in turn passes laws to protect the profits of their contributors from taxation or even economic calamity and failure. Lucrative contracts and gifts of money or favors are awarded to political cronies. So-called heads of state rob the government coffers and the citizenry, secreting the money to their off-shore accounts. The armies of state are used to install regimes friendly to international commerce (such as land and resource grabbing foreign firms) and to defeat "local insurgents" (those who are trying to protect their land, water, and right to a decent livelihood). In ignorance it will all have the appearance of propriety and the legitimacy of laws passed by "the representatives of the people" but that is only a guise, for behind the masks are rogues and thieves stealing from the very people they are supposed to protect. Black markets, drugs, and underground economies have major influences on the global economy. By the influence of ignorance the social contract breaks down and it's every man, no, every person, for themselves. The innocent, weak, and infirm, are unprotected, and the unwanted old people are euthanized. Women and children are ruthlessly exploited, even made to be sexual and servile slaves.

Societies such as those characterized by these demonic traits lead the world to ruin. Nazism and fascism represent societies functioning under the demonic influence of ignorance. Nor are they a recent development—this is the entire history of Western culture dating back to the 4th millennia BCE and continuing into the modern day. Marauding invaders, present at the dawn of Western 'civilization' include the Assyrians, Hittites, Greeks, Romans, the Ottomans, Mongols, Visigoths, Germanic tribes, the Roman Church, etc. Still later the colonial powers brought destruction to indigenous peoples all around the world. Violence is the base of such economic expediency and this modus operandi continues even to this day—the demonic plunder from behind the mask of corporations, freely roaming the globe for every opportunity of profit at the expense of others.

"I and mine" in *Tamo-guna*

Under the influence of *tamo-guna* we have entered into a "winner-take-all" society, and the winners are indeed taking as much as they possibly can, 'winning' through fraud, extortion, slavery, violence and any of the other tools from *Kali's* toolbox of horror. People are no longer shocked and dismayed by political graft and corruption; it is the norm. It is now *expected* that government and industry leaders are going to take as much from the public as they can, with little or no oversight, accounting, or legal recourse. Most people simply throw up their hands in despair and dismay, and if they vote, they vote for the lesser of two evils. If the people get anything at all, well and good.

"I and mine" under the influence of *tamo-guna* means that any and everything should be owned and as much as possible. Privatization of anything that can turn a profit has become the objective of government policy and the international economic community. Anything that was formerly held to be the commons or public property, created as a result of taxes at work, formerly deemed for the public good, is being sold into private hands for private profit to those who can pay the required franchise fee. The most notorious recent examples include the electromagnetic bandwidth of television or radio, electrical generating plants, municipal water systems and highways in America. In the former Soviet Union this included all of the "state owned" enterprises that were sold to private parties for insignificant fractions of their actual value.

Under the influence of *tamo-guna* there are no limits to private ownership— land, water, and even life itself, are being claimed for exclusive privilege. Patent ownership of genes, foods, plants, animals, and life-forms, including pathogens is progressing at a break-neck pace in order to claim monopoly rights for 20 years. Now known as "bio-piracy," corporations frequently attempt to patent existing life forms. For example, W. R. Grace & Co. tried to patent the neem tree which has been growing in India since time immemorial, Ricetec, Inc. of Texas applied for patents on basmati rice, while the University of Florida was using genetic manipulation to create their own patent of Thailand's jasmine rice.

More than 20 human pathogens are already privately owned, including Hepatitis C, the owner of which collects millions of dollars in royalties from laboratories around the world interested in studying it. Genetically modified organisms, especially foodstuffs, have created furor around the world. The European community's fight to keep America's GMO corn or soybeans off the continent has failed, while at the same time a great percentage of Mexico's many varieties of indigenous corn are becoming contaminated with GMO pollen. This means that in the future the "owner" of that GMO variety will sue the indigenous, subsistence farmers for royalties.

Under the influence of *tamo-guna* where profits are valued above everything else it is easy to predict that the time will come when some laboratory creates a deadly pathogen, patents it, disseminates it throughout a population and then charges exorbitant fees for studying it to find a much needed cure, ala Ken Lay's smart guys. Tests for a certain marker for breast cancer already cost $3,000 instead of the $1,000 they could cost because the "owner" of that gene takes the difference in royalties. Only the wealthy have the right to survive under the influence of *tamo-guna*.

Capitalism — the Economic Method of *Tamo-guna*

Each of the *gunas* has its characteristic economic method. Under the influence of goodness gifting is the preferred economic method. Under the influence of passion equal exchange is the method of choice. But under the influence of ignorance, those who can profit at the expense others are considered to be the best and most intelligent persons. There is no better description of capitalism. We therefore issue an indictment against capitalism as being the preferred economic system for those who are under the spell of ignorance and illusion. Being of the quality of ignorance, capitalism can only lead to the results of ignorance—suffering, ignorance, illusion, death and destruction—which is exactly what capitalism has brought since its inception. Of course in the modern day capitalism is lauded everywhere as the very best economic system ever created, which clearly identifies those making such claims as also being under the influence of the material mode of ignorance.

But, the capitalists and all others conditioned to value this method, protest: "I risk my capital and therefore I am entitled to the profits!" In reply to this argument the *Isopanisad* states that the Lord Himself is *isavasya*, the ultimate controller or owner of *everything*—everything in this world is His property alone. As the maintainer of everyone He has created this world and has arranged for the maintenance of every living being who takes birth:

> Everything animate or inanimate that is within the universe is controlled and owned by the Lord. One should therefore accept only those things necessary for himself, which are set aside as his quota, and one should not accept other things, knowing well to whom they belong. (*Isopanisad*, mantra 1)

Only under the spell of illusion do we claim anything as our own. Nothing is ours to claim as our personal property beyond the minimum necessary to maintain a healthy life. Therefore, the capitalist cannot claim "his" so-called capital as his own, and neither does he therefore risk anything of his own. Any accumulated capital must have already been unlawfully taken from others. As such all claims of exclusive entitlement to profit are null and void, and the proceeds of the enterprise should equally be distributed among those who labored together to produce the result.

The *Bhagavad-gita* (18.25) gives further proof of this argument. There it is explained that actions performed under illusion (of ownership), in disregard of scriptural injunctions (such as from *Isopanisad* above), and without concern for the future bondage of people or for violence or distress caused to others is said to be in the mode of ignorance. This is an apt description of capitalism. The *Srimad-Bhagavatam* (11.25.4) adds that stinginess, and living as a parasite are the symptoms of *tamo-guna*. In this regard Veblen's leisure class, the capitalists immediately come to mind.

There are many who recognize that the modern expression of capitalism is deeply flawed and who put forth suggestions of how it may be amended, particularly in the creation of a sound-money system that is not a fiat, but is backed by commodities of some sort, be it gold, or grain, or another. While their intentions are good they do not recognize that the root cause of the problem is not the money per se, but the consciousness of those who are influenced by the mode of ignorance. In order for a sound money system to continue to be sound, people absolutely must have some measure of *sattva-guna*, otherwise as people become degraded they will intentionally debase the currency and economic calamity will follow. This is exactly the history of all money-based systems throughout the history of Western civilization. The longest period of sound money—over a thousand years—was that of the Byzantine Empire, and that culture was the longest lasting as well. When they finally succumbed to *tamo-guna* and debased their currency, their civilization collapsed within two hundred years time.

With the help and influence of *sattva-guna* it is possible for capitalism to function in a more just and reasonable manner, allowing the development of a significantly sized middle class, perhaps as exemplified by American society in the 1950s, but this is a rare occurrence and by far the exception in the history of capitalism. This experience, isolated in time and place, is a long-forgotten past unknown to most of the people of the world in their experience of capitalism. By far the rule has been extreme exploitation, both in the past and the present, in which workers are paid an insignificant sum insufficient to provide them with a decent life. Nonetheless those who desire to reestablish what is referred to as the "good" capitalism should understand that this goal can only be accomplished by bringing society as a whole to the much higher standard of *sattva-guna*, especially the leaders and the elite. Only under such circumstances can sound money be maintained. The challenging question is how do we get there from here?

During the late 40s and early 50s there was some measure of *sattva-guna* (restored after the world was chastened by the ravages of WWII) but it has since waned practically to nil, being overcome by the influence of *tamas* which is now the standard of life everywhere. Illicit sex, meat eating, intoxication and gambling, the four pillars of *tamo-guna*, are found on every street corner throughout the world. We even acculturate our children to think of these as "normal," with Las Vegas becoming a family tourist destination, for example. But the fact is that however much our lives may be compartmentalized in separate spheres for work, play, church, and so on, we are nonetheless integrated beings, and what is done in one sphere impacts all of the others. It is sheer foolishness to think that we can degrade things over "here" without degrading them over "there." When almost 100 percent of the people unnecessarily kill animals to eat them, those acts of violence impact the way we think about economics and it becomes "normal" to have violent economics. When 20 percent or more of the population are alcoholic and almost everyone drinks socially, deliberately inviting the illusory effects of alcohol, it becomes "normal" for us to conceive of, and actually savor illusory economic concepts. When it becomes a norm for married partners to each have another lover, that cheating propensity also invades our economic behavior and cheating becomes the standard economic practice as well. Is it any wonder therefore that when the moral standard of society becomes degraded the economic system becomes degraded as well? It shouldn't surprise us in the least. Indeed, it is impossible for it to be otherwise since our economic behavior only reflects our consciousness.

So degraded has our thinking and consciousness become that everyone is doing their best to cheat the system, from the top to the bottom of society, with the result that capitalism has required more and more degraded expressions to reflect the one-sided, exploitative manner in which it is practiced. Thus we now regularly hear such terms as the suicide economy, tapeworm and Machiavellian economics, predatory capitalism, vulture capitalism, savage capitalism, casino capitalism, criminal capitalism, finally achieving new lows with disaster capitalism—unabashedly based on suffering and death—which has become the standard economic practice for the twenty-first century at the state level (as we will explain below). Each of these expressions has surely been earned. Although some aspire for a "good" capitalism of the old days, there simply isn't enough *sattva-guna* throughout the population for it to function. Further, people who elevate their consciousness to the level of goodness will "suddenly" become aware that capitalism fails miserably to consider the welfare of everyone. As such, they will reject it as being unsuitable for an enlightened society.

This is not some speculative philosophy, or my biased opinion. The nature of the *gunas* is a living philosophy that can be put to the test. They are very real. Everyone in any part of the world can easily study this and see that it is indeed a sound philosophy by which human nature can be understood. Once understanding it we can mold ourselves as we desire—if we have the inclination and the will.

Such a sweeping indictment of capitalism makes it impossible not to follow with a rejoinder regarding communism, and we will, below. First however let us become further acquainted with the economics of ignorance.

Because common men follow what great men do, the economics of ignorance is rampant throughout society—from the halls of power to the streets and alleyways—the abuses and injustices have filled hundreds, maybe thousands, of books. The greatest difficulty in writing this chapter was in deciding which of the hundreds of scams, schemes and frauds to use as examples. Because of the numbers of people that are affected, the main story takes place at the global level, but before getting to it I want to present a cameo of what life can be like at the local level, where most people live, when *tamo-guna* becomes pervasive.

Increasing "I and mine" by Theft at the "Local Level"

When ignorance is not counter-balanced by *sattva* and *rajas* the results are devastating to society as it descends into lawlessness, chaos, anarchy where the law of the jungle—survival of the fittest—rules. The most desperate stories always seem to come from the African countries whether from ethnic wars, millions of fleeing refugees, famine, or the devastation of AIDS. An American writer who lived in South Africa relates the crime and corruption as it was in the late 1990s:

> The acting head of the Licensing Department for the Johannesburg area, Gerrie Gerneke, issued a report in July 1997 confirming that the department was in the control of criminal syndicates. He said that half of all cars stolen in the Johannesburg area are "legalized" with new official documents within 30 days of being stolen. He said that cooperation between criminal gangs and union members has made it impossible for senior staff members or security staff to take any action. After Gerneke's report to the government was made, two anonymous letters accused him of being a racist. As a result of these anonymous complaints, Gerneke was suspended for five months. A year later Gerneke says the government has not acted on any of his recommendations to deal with corruption. When a car theft ring was recently exposed, five of the sixteen individuals arrested were policemen. The chief investigator said, "We found that policemen were receiving stolen cars and then selling them to their clients."

> In 1997 corruption reached such a level that [then President Nelson] Mandela appointed a "Special Investigating Unit" to look into the matter. According to Judge Willem Heath, head of the unit, there are currently more than 90,000 cases under investigation. If Heath and his crew manage to resolve one case of corruption per day, including weekends and holidays, it will take about 247 years to clear the current backlog. This doesn't include any new cases that will arise. Heath thinks the cases involve a sum of around 6 billion rand.

Approximately 2,300 police officers were charged with corruption in 1997—just about one every three hours. Almost 500 police officers have appeared in court on charges of working with criminal gangs. In the Johannesburg area alone 700 police officers are facing trials for committing crimes ranging from murder to burglary. And everyone assumes this is only the tip of the iceberg.

Over the last two years, there have been dozens of major highway robberies. In broad daylight gangs of a dozen men armed with AK-47s and other military weapons attack security trucks carrying large amounts of cash. These robberies have netted millions for the gangs. Government officials blame security companies, banks, and anyone else they can think of. But some arrests have finally been made, and the ringleaders who were arrested were officials in the so-called "armed wing" of the ANC, Umkhonto weSizwe. One gang leader had been Youth League secretary for the Johannesburg area. A close associate of his, also a gang leader, was arrested but "escaped" from jail. Both were recent guests at the birthday party of Peter Mokaba, Deputy Minister of Environmental Affairs and Tourism.

In 1997 alone, there were 465 bank robberies. In all about $40 million was taken.

Crime seems to be the only thing that works in South Africa—the risk of being arrested, tried and convicted is minuscule. In 1997, only 14.6 percent of murders led to arrest and conviction. Of 52,110 rapes there were only 2,532 convictions—about 6.7 percent. For the 330,093 burglaries there were 15,710 convictions, about 4.8 percent.

This is life in South Africa today.[1]

South Africa will not be an isolated case if the world-wide calamity continues; increasing crime has been reported in America as the economic crisis there continues. Grand theft of banks, cars and armored vehicles is one thing, but the theft of one of the world's greatest countries is another thing altogether.

Increasing "I and mine" by Theft of a Nation

That other great empire of the 20th century, the Soviet Union, was looted upon its demise mostly by the members of the former ruling party, the kitty handsomely embellished with billions in grants from America. Although President Yeltsin shelled his own parliament building and ignored the Russian supreme court he was lauded in the American press as a great statesman who was bringing democracy(?!) to the Russian people. What he was doing was looting the country but because he cut the Western elite in on the action this theft was ignored, even applauded. The immense wealth of the Soviet state, ostensibly the property of the people under the doctrine of communism, was simply stolen from them and sold for a song to a very small number of private individuals using foreign money loaned to the country for stabilization purposes. The result is that no more than several dozen people seized ownership of the majority of Russia's natural and productive wealth, and in the process further impoverished the population.

Within seven or eight years more than 80 percent of Russia's farms had been bankrupted, and seventy *thousand* factories were closed, out of some 225,000 in total, to reduce the competition to the remainder that were privatized. In the Soviet Union a factory was the town—the entire town. Everything—employment, the schools, markets, and culture—were centered on the factory, and there was typically only one. When the factory closed there was no surrounding economy for people to shift to. Generally the only options were to survive from the kitchen-garden at their dacha, or to flee to somewhere where money could be found. That typically meant either Moscow, where some four-fifths of the money of the entire country is located, or emigrating to another country. Millions fled for the possibility of a decent life elsewhere: between 1992 and 2006 the population declined by 6.6 million people.[2]

Amazingly with no assistance to explain what to do, or what to expect, people who were perhaps happy that the Communist nightmare was finally over, were faced with the capitalist nightmare. They were expected to suddenly shift, overnight, from a protective government (however minimal) to taking care of themselves under the capitalist system. The problem was that there were no jobs. Even worse, under "guidance" from the West the ruble collapsed and whatever savings people might have had became utterly worthless. Unemployment was rampant and millions immediately descended into a poverty that they had never expected. Prior to Yeltsin's reforms two million out of a population of some 150 million were living in poverty (less than $4 a day). By the middle 90s 74 million people were in poverty, and the condition of 37 million of those was described as "desperate" by the World Bank.[3] In the same period the suicide rate almost doubled, alcoholism became epidemic—by some estimates as much as 40 percent of the population—and homelessness, almost unknown under communism soared, including somewhere between 750,000 and 3.5 million children.[4]

Increasing "I and mine" by Stealing from the Shareholders

Collapse of giant firms who had deceived the investing public with fraudulent accounting practices shocked us as we entered into the new millennium. In one of the world's biggest financial debacles, the Enron Corporation, once the seventh largest corporation in America, went down in a spectacular heap, taking with it the promise of a comfortable retirement for many of its shareholders, including the company's employees who were forced to invest their 401K retirement accounts in the company's stock. Before it collapsed however, it was looted by the company's executives who received more than $744 million in payments and bonuses in its last year alone.[5] The company's former CEO Kenneth Lay received at least $152.6 million in cash and potential stock, and another 100 or so executives received some $600 million in cash and stock options from the company in its last year.[6] At bankruptcy however, Enron workers lost $800 million from their pension funds, 5,000 employees lost their jobs, and after filing for bankruptcy Enron lost $68 billion in (stock) market value.

Increasing "I and mine" by Stealing from the People

The idea that one's sustenance is an entitlement—their due given by God—is completely out the window under the influence of *tamo-guna*. Everyone grabs whatever, and as much as they can, resulting in an extremely imbalanced and distorted world. One percent of the people of the world now own 40 percent of the world's wealth, while at the same time, the poorest 50 percent of the people have to share a mere 1 percent of the wealth.[7] But at the top, wealth is even more concentrated. Consistently over decades in America, the top 1/2 of 1 percent hold from 25 to 30 percent of all wealth.[8] Looking just a little further, 85 percent of the wealth is held by the richest 10 percent, while the vast majority of the people—90 percent—hold a mere 15 percent of the wealth.[9] And what do the rich do with all of that wealth? Spend it thoughtlessly to impress others in the society of envy. The world-wide sales of luxury goods, that is as an ostentatious and unnecessary display of wealth, now exceeds the gross national product of two-thirds of the world's countries.[10]

Of course accumulating more wealth is entirely unnecessary in any practical sense. The wealthy already have much more than they can possibly use. How can one spend a billion dollars, what to speak of tens of billions? The only possible use of more is to feed an inflated ego laboring under the illusion of "I and mine." And where do they get all that money from? When a famous Chicago gangster was asked why he robbed banks, he retorted "because that's where the money is!" A fortune of billions is similarly gathered by taking from "where the money is"—not from banks, but from the people.

For example, in America between 1977 and 1987, during Reagan's decade of greed, the average after-tax family income of the lowest 10 percent fell from $3,528 to $3,157, a 10.5 percent drop in ten years, while during the same period, average income of the top 10 percent increased from $70,459 to $89,783 up 24.4 percent. The trend has been the same with wealth. Between 1983 and 2004, the average wealth of the top 1 percent of households grew by 78 percent, while the bottom 40 percent of the population lost 59 percent of their wealth. And those trends continue into the 21st century. Census data shows that median household income fell $1,700, or 3.8 percent in the five years from 1999 to 2004, a period when average productivity rose 3 percent per year. That varies from place to place however. In Illinois for example, the median income of families declined 12 percent between 1999 and 2005, while in Michigan hard hit by layoffs in the auto industry median income dropped 19 percent in the same period.[11] All the while costs of living continue to increase. Housing, healthcare, education and childcare costs rose 46 percent between 1991 and 2002, squeezing workers at both ends.[12] In 2005 a full-time minimum-wage worker in America earned only $10,500 for an entire year. The CEO of Wal-Mart however, was paid $3,500 *an hour*, the CEO of Halliburton was paid about $8,300 *an hour*, and the CEO of Exxon-Mobil was paid some $13,700 *an hour*—more than 2,600 times what the minimum wage earner makes. Or to put it another way a minimum wage earner would work for 2,600 *years* to make what that CEO made in one.

Although $5.50 per hour is not a living wage in America, it's still too much to pay when labor can be had for next to nothing around the world. During the 90s with the help of "free trade" and "downsizing" of America's corporations, productive work was sent overseas, to Bangladesh for example, where a 19 year-old worker is paid a mere 8 cents (US $0.08) to sew ten caps in an hour (her 12-14 year old helpers are paid just 5 cents an hour). The labor cost is one-half of one cent for a hat that sells for more than $10 at American universities. Can they not afford to pay this girl even double that wage? Of course they can. But they don't. The likelihood is that she has taken that job from somebody in Mexico who would have been paid 40 cents an hour, who, in turn, took it earlier from an American minimum wage worker.

At another Bangladeshi sweatshop seamstresses sewed shirts for the Disney Corporation. They were paid about 12 cents per hour, and worked 15 hours a day, 7 days a week. They were denied basic necessities such as maternity leave, and beaten if they fell behind quota or complained about the horrendous working conditions. They were paid 15 cents to sew a shirt Disney sold for $18. To earn as much as Disney CEO Michael Eisner makes in *one hour*, which was $63,000 (his base salary is $133 million a year, but with stock option he took home $570 million in 1998) the Bangladeshi women would have to work about 6 lifetimes–260 years.[13] When the women bravely took a stand, Disney pulled its operation out of the factory, and left all the women unemployed. Eisner's attitude sums up and "justifies" Disney's, as well as other corporations' employment practices: "We have no obligation to make history. We have no obligation to make art. We have no obligation to make a statement. To make money is our only objective."[14]

Can people live on 8 cents or even 12 cents an hour, even in Bangladesh? No, it's impossible. With every member of the household working the entire family can still hardly survive. And many don't. The World Health Organization tells us that worldwide ten million children a year die from causes related to poverty—30,000 *every day*—because they haven't clean water to bathe with or drink, nourishing food to eat, proper clothing or health care. As much as one-third of the global work force—one billion people—are now unemployed, and thus have no lawful means of income, which is not to say that they don't have income. Everybody requires money under the economics of ignorance, and if it's not obtained legitimately, it must be had in any way possible. Driven to desperate circumstances these unfortunates are forced to deal in other of *Kali's* methods: theft, violence, drugs, prostitution, murder and so on, in order to merely survive.

Increasing "I and mine" by Slavery

Not only is money stolen but people are also, used against their will to generate money for others by labor or sex. The U.S. Central Intelligence Agency estimates that some 50,000 people, many of whom are minors, are trafficked into or through the United States annually as sex slaves, domestics, garment workers, and agricultural slaves. Generating some $10 billion a year in America alone, the United Nations estimates that trafficking in persons is one of the top three sources of revenue for organized crime behind drugs and weapons. The Central Intelligence Agency declared that in 2004 it detected sixteen thousand undocumented Mexicans and Central Americans subjected to sex and labor slavery in the United States. In 1986 it was estimated that 20,000 children in the Philippines were involved in the sex trade, and that number had increased to over a hundred thousand by the year 2000. According to a survey by *India Today Magazine* there are between 400,000 and 500,000 child prostitutes in India. UNICEF reported that in 1994–5 there were an estimated 200,000 child prostitutes in Thailand, 40,000 in Vietnam, 30,000 in Sri Lanka, and more than 250,000 in Brazil.[15]

While human trafficking is a huge international operation, millions of others are trafficked annually within their own countries. According to an ABC news report there are 25 distinct Russian organized-crime groups operating in the U.S., with 250 pending investigations targeting Russian gangs in 27 states.[16] And the Russians are not the only ones. Among others an international trafficking ring in San Jose, California and Toronto, Canada, trafficked women from Southeast Asia for prostitution. The women were prostituted under debt bondage to pay off a $40,000 debt for their passage.[17]

Escape for abductees is often impossible. Fear maintains their victim status. Minors live in fear of sadistic acts by "customers," fear of being beaten and abused if they fail to bring in their quota (ranging from $500 to $1,800 a day/ night), fear of losing their coping mechanisms (drugs and alcohol), and fear of losing a place to live and food to eat. These children are also ashamed and fear their families will find out what they have been doing. They fear the police and fear being returned home. They have no place to go. Cardinal Renato Martino, former longtime Vatican envoy to the United Nations and current head of the Holy See's office, concerned with migrant and itinerant peoples, told a news conference at Pope Benedict XVI's annual message dealing with the problems of migrants "It's worse than the slavery of those who were taken from Africa and brought to other countries."[18]

Men are also forced into slavery all around the world. In Brazil young men are enslaved to make the charcoal for making steel, getting black lung disease and a life of suffering after only six or eight months of such labor, while in Florida slaves from Mexico pick your breakfast oranges. In most such places armed guards prevent anyone from making a run for freedom. Kevin Bales, author of *Disposable People: New Slavery in the Global Economy*, estimates that from 27 million, to as many as 200 million people, are enslaved today making every conceivable consumer item and commodity. Slaves work as housemaids in every major city of the world.

John Bowe offers more horror stories in his *Nobodies: Modern American Slave Labor and the Dark Side of the New Global Economy*. Indian men brought to Oklahoma to weld oil-refinery tanks for example. They sign contracts mortgaging their futures thinking that they will be making American wages, become established in America, and even send some money back home. When they arrive they are told that the contracts are not legally binding, and they are not even given the minimum wage of America. Deep in debt for their passage they are forced to pay it down, while at the same time being charged exorbitant rates for room and board in conditions primitive even by Indian standards. There is no escape for these fellows because the supervisors hold their passports.

We must not think that these things are happening because of a breakdown of the economic system. No. This *is* the economic system under the influence of *tamo-guna*. These things don't happen by chance. They are deliberately planned by the elite and supported by governmental policies, with the aid of major corporations, banking and other international financial institutions, often in cooperation with organized crime.

Although heartbreaking, disillusioning, and thoroughly disgusting for most normal, ordinary, decent and good people, we must understand that such abuses are the *reactions* to previous actions, which is not to say that justice should not be done. All people should always be given proper protection. Such activities are not surprising, however, for those who have studied the wisdom of the

Bhagavad-gita. The *Gita* explains that actions performed under the influence of the mode of ignorance degrade the consciousness, leading to further degraded actions in a downward spiral. Life is an integrated whole, not separately compartmentalized parts. Performing actions in *tamo-guna* such as eating the flesh of animals, the killing of unwanted children conceived as a result of illicit sexual activity, gambling and taking intoxicants degrades not only the consciousness of the individual, but drags down the entire society. With increasing *tamo-guna* people actually lose the ability to understand the difference between right and wrong, what they should or should not do, and they act against their own best interest. The result can only be degradation, dissolution and destruction accompanied by great and widespread suffering. Being a product of the mode of ignorance the economics of ignorance must absolutely bring tragic results. Under the strict laws of material nature there is no way to escape the reaction of such sinful activities. Suffering must follow actions performed in passion and ignorance, just as the back end of the car must follow the front.

Increasing "I and mine" Through War

Economics Professor and investigator Michel Chossudovsky does much to explain the death dealing economics of ignorance in *America's "War on Terrorism,"* which was written "to refute the official narrative and reveal—using detailed evidence and documentation (not speculation based on opinion alone)—the true nature of America's 'war on terrorism.'" His opinion is that it is actually a pretext for a permanent "New World Order"—wars of conquest for the purpose of serving the moneyed interests: Wall Street, the US military-industrial complex, Big Oil, corporate and other interests who profit in death and destruction. These interests, working in collusion, are perpetrating a hugely massive scheme that harms the public interest in the name of protecting it, and according to Chossudovsky, placing the world "at the crossroads of the most serious crisis in modern history."[19]

On the evening of that fateful day, September 11th 2001, at 9:30 p.m., just twelve hours after the twin towers in New York City had been attacked, a War Cabinet was formed from a select number of top intelligence and military advisors. The meeting was concluded by 11:00 p.m. when the 'War on Terrorism' was officially launched. The decision was announced to wage war against the Taliban and Al Qaeda in retribution for the 9/11 attacks. News headlines the next day asserted with certainty former CIA Director James Woolsey's identification of "state sponsorship" of the attacks. America's lapdog press sounded the call and roused the shocked citizens, still reeling from the previous day's events, for military retaliation. The still-stunned Americans, and apparently the press too, weren't thinking clearly enough to ask how in the short space of one day, with no obvious in-depth investigation, that the Taliban and Al Qaeda had been identified as the guilty parties. Yet, although our efficient military apparatus, with all its spies and muti-billion dollar budget, were unable to thwart the attack in advance, within a matter of hours they had identified the perpetrators and broadcast their photos around the world. They then went on to attack the Taliban in Afghanistan, on the plea of George Bush that he would "make no distinction between the terrorists who committed these acts and those governments who harbor them," conveniently overlooking the fact that most of those identified as the perpetrators were in fact not from Afghanistan, but were instead Saudi Arabians.

Chossudovsky clearly demonstrates that the Taliban government was not responsible for the attacks, and the United States' government knew it. However they needed a guise for an attack on Afghanistan. As General Tommy Franks describes it, Americans would have to experience a "terrorist, massive, casualty-producing event" to arouse enough public anger for the Bush administration to justify their actions. Although large scale theater war is never planned and executed in a matter of weeks, four weeks later on October 7, the bombing of Afghanistan began and American troops invaded in partnership with the United Islamic Front for the Salvation of Afghanistan. This war, like all others, was months in the making, waiting for the trigger event to allow it to happen.

The Taliban was ousted from control of Afghanistan in 2001 for various reasons, one of which was their effort to free their country from opium production—which had nearly succeeded. That was turned around however as a result of the United States' efforts. One curious result of the Afghan war was the *reinstatement* of opium production. UN anti-drug chief, Antonio Maria Costa, estimated the 2006 production at a record 6100 tons (enough for 610 tons of heroin)—92 percent of total world supply, and opium production is flourishing again under Northern Alliance-occupation forces rule. Drugs and their trafficking are a quintessential example of the economics of ignorance. In fact drugs are the third biggest global commodity in cash terms after oil and the arms trade, generating some $500 billion annually according to the UN. Chossudovsky explains that narcotics are a major source of wealth not only for organized crime, but also for the "US intelligence apparatus" (recall National Security Council aide Oliver North's involvement with the Iran-Contra drugs and arms trade) representing powerful "spheres of finance and banking."[20]

Intelligence agencies and legal business syndicates often cooperate closely with criminal enterprises, and at times they are indistinguishable. Western and international banks and their offshore affiliates in tax havens are key components of the process. They redirect billions of dollars from the drug trade into stocks, bonds, and other speculative investments, as well as into legal enterprises such as real estate and manufacturing.[21]

Through exhausting research Chossudovsky exposes the war on terrorism as a fraud used to create the "myth of an 'outside enemy' and the threat of 'Islamic terrorists' [that became] the cornerstone (and core justification) of the Bush administration's military doctrine." He offers evidence that al Qaeda itself "was a creation of the CIA going back to the Soviet-Afghan war," and that in the 1990s Washington "consciously supported Osama bin Laden, while at the same time placing him on the FBI's 'most wanted list' as the World's foremost terrorist." This charade has allowed Washington to wage permanent aggressive wars beginning with Afghanistan and Iraq, ignore international law, and repeal civil liberties and constitutional government through repressive laws such as the Patriot Act and the Military Commissions Act. The key objective has been, and continues to be, Washington's quest to control the oil supplies of the Middle East where two-thirds of known reserves are located, because as Henry Kissinger teaches, those who control the oil control the countries of the world, and those who control the food control the people. In other words, the "War on Terror" is a euphemism for the economics of ignorance.

We can understand why war is considered the most desirable route to a prosperous future by examining the ideas of one of George Bush's neo-conservative (neocon) advisors Michael Ledeen, who is very enthusiastic about war and the benefits it brings—to some. Ledeen is an associate at the right-wing "think tank" The American Enterprise Institute, where he works with the former chairman of the Defense Policy Board, Richard Perle. The titles of his books such as *Universal Fascism* and *Machiavelli on Modern Leadership: Why Machiavelli's Iron Rules Are as Timely and Important Today as Five Centuries Ago* give an idea of his mentality. He has said: "In order to achieve the most noble accomplishments, the leader may have to 'enter into evil.' This is the chilling insight that has made Machiavelli feared, admired and challenging...we are rotten...It's true that we can achieve greatness if, and only if, we are properly led."[22] And his idea of leadership is revealed in *Machiavelli on Modern Leadership*: "Creative destruction is our middle name, both within our society and abroad...they must attack us in order to survive, just as we must destroy them to advance our historic mission." Our historic mission? He doesn't say what that is, but we may surmise that it is the creation of a New World Order, a term expressed by many heads of state after the economic debacle of 2008. The New World Order is a two-class society of the privileged and the destitute created by destroying the existing social order and violently imposing the new one. The New World Order is the unabashed exploitation of the vast majority for the benefit of the few, created and maintained by violence and death.

As Chossudovsky tells it "war and globalization go hand in hand." As Ledeen puts it in his book, "change, above all, violent change, is the essence of human history." He believes that violence should be used in the spread of his idea of "freedom" around the world (freedom for who? we ask): "Total war not only destroys the enemy's military forces, but also brings the enemy society to an extremely personal point of decision, so that they are willing to accept a reversal of the cultural trends. The sparing of civilian lives cannot be the total war's first priority...the purpose of total war is to permanently force your will onto other people."[23]

Increasing "I and mine" Through Global Enslavement

"A game as old as empire" is how the former "economic hit man" John Perkins describes what goes on under the economics of ignorance. The "game," of course, is the method by which the empire is built. Formerly through messy and often prolonged wars of conquest, today the battle is neatly fought with pens and pencils, balance sheets and economic projections, together conjuring illusions of future prosperity and grandeur, all secured by legal contracts and yes, enforced when necessary by military strength. Today's empire building is nothing more than loan-sharking writ large, and it threatens to enslave the entire planet.

In his *Confessions of an Economic Hitman* Perkins describes how sharply dressed men make financial slaves of entire countries and their people for today's empire. They identify a third-world country that has coveted resources, such as oil. The advance team of specialists visits and explains to a President or Prime Minister what wonderful prosperity could be brought to their country if only they were modernized enough to be able to exploit the bounty nature had endowed them with. They then prepare grandiose economic projections based on huge infrastructure projects that will bring the country into the modern age and prosperity with it: airports, deep-water ports, electrical generation and transmission, industrial parks, and wide, paved highways. This development and the need for resources will of course bring jobs, and those jobs in turn will fuel the prosperous economy. Everyone will benefit. Next a gargantuan loan is arranged from the World Bank or private financial corporations to finance all of the work. Then it's only a matter of few years and prosperity will run "right off the charts!" That's the sales pitch and how it's supposed to happen—in theory.

In practice it works like this. Most of the money from that loan never gets to the borrowing country. Instead, never leaving the shores of America it goes to large United States' construction firms such as Haliburton, Bechtel, Brown and Root, who build the projects. The money is simply transferred from one U.S. bank to another. Local labor is hired, but it is contracted out to private placement companies that pay only the very bare minimum. The other needed resources are often brought from other countries, leaving the country taking the loan with very little internal economic growth. The development that occurs—the ports and other infrastructure—actually only benefit the very rich ruling elite who are collaborators in the process. The poor who shoulder the great burden of the debt receive absolutely no benefit whatsoever from the development because they are not connected with the power grids, they don't have the skills to get the jobs in the industrial parks, they don't have the cars to drive on the highways, or own ships to use in the ports. Following King Solomon's maxim that the poor shall serve the rich and the borrower is slave to the lender, conditions are purposely arranged to overextend the borrower such that the loan cannot possibly be repaid.

No sooner than the ink on the contract has dried the trap is set. One or two years down the road when it becomes obvious that the promised progress has not materialized, Perkins explains that the "economic hit-men then go back and say listen, you can't pay your debts so give us a pound of flesh, sell oil to our oil companies real cheap, or vote with us on the next critical UN vote, or send troops in support of ours to some place in the world, like Iraq...Sometimes we fail, it doesn't happen very often, but when it does then what we call the 'jackals' go in. The jackals overthrow governments as we tried to do with Caesar Chavez in 2002 in Venezuela, or they assassinate the leaders of these governments such as Hyme Roldos in Ecuador and Omar Tarihos in Panama. On the few occasions the jackals also fail, then, and only then, does the military go in. That's what happened in Iraq."[24]

The ruling elite are often made party to the deal with bribes the size of a fortune in the form of a "commission." Asif Ali Zardari, also known as "Mr. 10 Percent," is an example recently brought to mainstream attention by the assassination of his wife, the late Benazir Bhutto. Apparently that was his take on all government contracts, stealing directly from the Pakistanis they were supposed to be the guardians of. By such graft the family siphoned some $1.3 billion out of the country during Bhutto's two terms in power.[25] Such arrangements are the norm rather than the exception. Billions of dollars have been spirited into offshore accounts in practically every country successfully invaded by the economic hit men. Anyone can understand that such bribes are not paid simply out of kindness or some goodwill. These hundreds of millions are offered as an incentive because the offering parties' intend to take so much more. The presidents are offered such sums to overcome the resistance created by pangs of conscience they might experience by selling-out their country and their people, who will suffer all manners of deprivations to pay back the loan. The bribe also provides a safety net, funds to bribe others, and the purchase of protection if or when the fed-up citizens depose and attempt to kill him.

The much vaunted prosperity was simply a ruse, and it never arrives because the purpose was to appropriate wealth from the periphery to the center of the empire.[26] Because the loans have been arranged such that they can never be repaid, compounding interest only increases the debt. There simply is no way out. If the country defaults on debt payments then they are cut off from all international funding (one of the conditions that all countries enter into before receiving a loan). The international racketeering between the global financial institutions and multinational corporations has come a long way since Perkins worked with them in the 70s. Just as he left the business in 1981 the art of economic enslavement was being perfected to a superb degree.

The World Bank, IMF and Povertization

Everyone is familiar with the supra-national body called the World Trade Organization (WTO) that works together with the World Bank and International Monetary Fund (IMF) to promote "free trade" and the global economy, but few actually understand the role these Washington-based institutions play in bringing suffering, poverty and death to the world. In the tradition of *Kali* they are key players in serving up the economics of ignorance behind the mask of do-gooders offering aid and assistance. The World Bank was established at the Bretton Woods Conference in 1944 as a lending institution composed of member governments to help rebuild post-war economies. The IMF was created to restructure and organize the market systems of member nations by promoting international economic cooperation and trade, and by encouraging stable currencies. The business of the World Bank is ostensibly to make loans for development projects, while the supposed business of the IMF is to lend to governments to ease deficits and make their economies more stable. That's the reasoning fed to the public. What happens in practice is another thing altogether.

The criticism can be found on all sides, but perhaps the most telling is always from the inside. Davison Budhoo was a senior economist with the IMF for more than 12 years. He publicly resigned as an act of conscience via a book-length open letter to Michel Camdessus, managing director of the IMF, titled *Enough is Enough*,[27] in which he thoroughly criticized the IMF's policies as "genocidal." After leaving the Fund he created the Bretton Woods Reform Organization to campaign *against* the IMF-World Bank structural adjustment programs.

Modern countries cannot exist today without borrowing money. But like any borrower, in order to obtain loans from the IMF-World Bank certain conditions must be met. Budhoo explains that these conditions, called structural adjustment programs (SAPs), are designed to reduce consumption in developing countries and to redirect resources to manufacturing exports for the repayment of debt. This has caused overproduction of primary products and a precipitous fall in their prices. It has also led to the devastation of traditional agriculture and to the emergence of hordes of landless farmers in virtually every country in which the

World Bank and IMF operate. Food security has declined dramatically in all Third World regions, but in Africa in particular. Growing dependence on food imports, which is the lot of sub-Saharan Africa, places these countries in an extremely vulnerable position. They simply do not have the foreign exchange to import enough food, given the fall in export prices and the need to repay debt. SAPs also require drastic cuts in social expenditures, especially in health and education, and force governments to remove subsidies to the poor on basic food-stuffs and services such as rice and maize, water and electricity. Tax systems are made more repressive, and real wage rates are allowed to fall sharply.[28]

The basic structural adjustment requirements of the IMF-World Bank include:

- Drastic cuts in social expenditures, especially in health and education.
- Removal of subsidies to the poor on basic foodstuffs and services such as rice and maize, water and electricity.
- Tax systems are made more repressive, and real wage rates are allowed to fall sharply.
- Required devaluation of the currency which brings inflation and increases the price of all imported foodstuffs.
- The removal of price controls which allows the prices to skyrocket, making it even more difficult for the poor to meet their needs.
- Interest rates are raised causing bankruptcies in domestically owned small businesses and further unemployment.
- Trade restrictions are removed making it difficult for domestic industries to compete, thus they are forced to close, bringing more unemployment.
- Foreign exchange restrictions (on currency) are lifted allowing the wealthy elite who benefit from all of these actions to export funds overseas (capital flight) thus further challenging the economy due to less currency in circulation and creating problems in the balance of payments.
- All government owned enterprises that can produce a profit are privatized, often after reducing wages or increasing prices.

All of this is done under the assumption that such measures are going to somehow improve economic conditions in the country. But even on the basis of objectives established by the IMF-World Bank themselves, SAPs have not been successful. Subsequent programs have failed even more dismally in relation to IMF-World Bank self-imposed objectives, as demonstrated by the United Nations Development Program (UNDP) and UN Economic Commission for Africa.

Budhoo recalled how, at one IMF board of directors meeting, then-President Ronald Reagan declared that the sole duty of the IMF was to convert all countries to freewheeling Western market economies. Reagan's declaration signaled that the IMF no longer had to operate under the guise of "development," or alleviating poverty or any other humanist philosophy. We note that this is not Adam Smith's hidden hand of the free market, but the iron fist of an imperial power. As *New York Times* columnist and author of *The Lexus and the Olive Branch*, Thomas Friedman put it: "For globalization to work, America can't be afraid to act like the almighty superpower that it is. The hidden hand of the market will never work without a hidden fist. McDonald's cannot flourish without McDonald-Douglas, the designer of the F-15, and the hidden fist that keeps the world safe for Silicon Valley's technology is called the United States Army, Air Force, Navy and Marine Corps."[29]

Budhoo called the core staff of the IMF "successors of colonial civil servants." Pointedly observing that South Africa is administered by the European Department, not the African Department, an observation confirmed by an official of the Institute for African Alternatives who revealed that the IMF completely controls the economic activities of countries who have borrowed from them as one of the preconditions for loans: "Under structural adjustment, the IMF and the World Bank do not merely supervise individual sectors of the economy as in the past...they now manage each country entirely...They have to approve annual national budgets...monetary, trade and fiscal policies...before countries can negotiate with other foreign lending agencies."[30] Budhoo concludes "these programs have created economic, social and cultural devastation whenever and wherever they are introduced."

Chossudovsky echoes Budhoo's criticism of the structural adjustment programs. The professor has been researching the effects of so-called globalization for decades, detailing its dark and deadly machinations and results in *The Globalization of Poverty and the New World Order.* The structural adjustment programs he says are "conducive to a form of 'economic genocide' which is carried out through the conscious and deliberate manipulation of market forces. When compared to previous periods of colonial history, its social impact is devastating."[31]

In *The Globalization of Poverty* he goes on to explain that "the internationalization of macro-economic policy transforms countries into open economic territories and national economies into "reserves" of cheap labor and natural resources."[32] And "at the heart of the global economic system lies an unequal structure of trade, production and credit which defines the role and position of developing countries in the global economy."[33] This is old wine in new bottles. The macro-economic policies enacted by the World Bank and IMF create exactly the same relationships and conditions of unequal trade used to extract the wealth of colonies that we learned from Adam Smith and Dr. J. W. Smith in the previous chapter. Nothing has changed except the appearance and scale, bringing the same devastating result to ever greater numbers of people. Rather than helping anyone the supposed aid instead is actually poisoned bait on a hook, the result of which is the opposite of what it promises. Chossudovsky:

> The economic stabilization package destroys the possibility of an 'endogenous national economic development process' controlled by national policy makers. The IMF-World Bank reforms brutally dismantle the social sectors of developing countries, undoing the efforts and struggles of the post-colonial period and reversing 'with a stroke of the pen' the fulfillment of past progress. Throughout the developing world, there is a consistent and coherent pattern: the IMF-World Bank reform package constitutes a coherent program of economic and social collapse...these measures go far beyond the phasing out of import-substituting industries. They destroy the entire fabric of the domestic economy.[34]

King Solomon was right, wasn't he? Deceitfully ironic the motto of the World Bank is "A World Without Poverty."

The "Chicago Boys" and the Globalization of Poverty

There was another war that started on September 11th, twenty-eight years before that now infamous date in 2001. It was the date that a military coup headed by General Augusto Pinochet overthrew the elected government of President Savador Allende in Chile. At that time Chossudovsky was teaching at the Institute of Economics of the Catholic University of Chile, which was as he puts it "a nest of Chicago trained economists, disciples of Milton Friedman, also known as 'the Chicago Boys.'" Initially Chossudovsky was surprised to find the Chicago Boys rejoicing at the success of the coup, but he quickly understood why—barely a week later several of his colleagues were appointed to key positions in the new military government. Their glee was due to the fact that they were now going to have an unfettered opportunity to employ Freidman's economic theories in a living laboratory—on the people of Chile.

Several weeks later the new dictator ordered a 264 percent hike in the price of bread. Other commodities also followed suit, and although food prices were going through the roof, wages had been frozen to ensure "economic stability and stave off inflationary pressures." From one day to the next the entire country descended into abysmal poverty. In less than one year the price of bread increased thirty-six times and 85 percent of the population had been driven below the poverty line. Chossudovsky writes:

> These events affected me profoundly in my work as an economist. Through the tampering of prices, wages and interest rates, people's lives had been destroyed; an entire national economy had been destabilized. I started to understand that macro-economic reform was neither "neutral"—as claimed by the academic mainstream—nor separate from the broader process of social and political transformation. In my earlier writings on the Chilean military Junta, I looked upon the so-called 'free market' as a well-organized instrument of 'economic repression.'[35]

A few years later it was dejà vu all over again and Chossudovsky was a guest professor during another coup, this time in Argentina while he was at the National University of Cordoba. He describes it as a carbon-copy of the CIA-led coup in Chile. "Behind the massacres and human rights violations, 'free market' reforms had also been prescribed—this time under the supervision of Argentina's New York creditors."[36]

At this time, in the mid-70s, the IMF's economic package, the "structural adjustment program" had not yet been launched; the experiences of Chile and Argentina having been but the early experiments of the Chicago Boys. They were just beginning to get a handle on how to introduce Friedman's stark and repressive economic measures. But when it was finally understood, the process was repeated almost everywhere. In the early 90s Chossudovsky visited many countries to study the economic transformations taking place in the name of the "free market." In India, Bangladesh, Vietnam, Kenya, Nigeria, Egypt, Morocco, Brazil and the other Latin American countries, and the Philippines, he "observed the same pattern of economic manipulation and political interference by the Washington-based institutions [IMF and World Bank]."

Chossudovsky details the methods used by the IMF-World Bank that brought poverty literally around the globe: Rwanda, Uganda, Congo, Sub-Sahara Africa, Ethiopia, India, Bangladesh, Vietnam, Korea, Brazil, Peru, Bolivia, Russia, Yugoslavia, and Albania. These methods served to further enrich the already rich and destroy whatever middle class might have existed, condemning billions to poverty. By the end of the century the same IMF economic medicine had been applied in more than 150 countries, resulting in what Chossudovsky calls the "globalization of poverty." He writes that "The imposition of macro-economic and trade reforms under the supervision of the IMF, World Bank and WTO purports to 'peacefully' re-colonize countries through the deliberate manipulation of market forces. While not explicitly requiring the use of force, the ruthless enforcement of the economic reforms nonetheless constitutes a form of warfare. More generally, the dangers of war must be understood. War and globalization are not separate issues." And he continues: "The ideology of the "free" market upholds a novel and brutal form of state intervention predicated on the deliberate tampering of market forces. Derogating the rights of citizens, 'free trade' under the World Trade Organization grants 'entrenched rights' to the world's largest banks and global corporations...The New World Order is based on the 'false consensus' of Washington and Wall Street, which ordains the 'free market system' as the only possible choice on the fated road to a 'global prosperity.' All political parties including Greens, Social Democrats and former Communists now share this consensus."[37]

We must not think that this "treatment" is reserved for the developing countries alone. It has extended its grip to all major regions of the World, including even the "developed countries" in Western Europe and North America, although povertization there is being "sold" in a different manner. America has been hollowed out in the past 25 years as her manufacturing industries have been relocated to Southeast Asia, leaving former factory workers who could once provide a decent home for their families with a declining standard of living supported by much lower-paying job in the service sector. There is nothing that would indicate that this trend is going to change. Indeed, Americans are being prepared to expect further declines. They are warned that the looming recession (2008) is going to be the worst in 50 years, with at least one analyst expecting dozens of banks to fail by 2010. Others warn that a "rising wealth gap" will somehow, even more than usual, lead to disproportionate pain for middle and lower-income people (whatever happened to Reagan's trickledown theory? Isn't that increased wealth on the other side of the gap supposed to create more jobs? That apparently was only possible in the 80s). In early 2008 Federal Reserve Chairman Ben Bernanke told Congress that the economy is deteriorating, and Sen. Christopher Dodd, D-Conn. warned that "our economy is clearly in trouble." The translation of this economic-speak means "we told you so." Meanwhile in Britain Mervyn King, the Governor of the Bank of England, issued a stark warning that tough times are ahead and the period of "easy prosperity" has come to an end. Families there have been warned to expect a decline in their standard of living. What this all means is that the "average" people of the developed world are about to find themselves in increasingly difficult straits, but the wealthy will continue to do just fine.

How Economic Globalization Works

Another insider turned critic is Joseph Stiglitz, formerly the Chief Economist of the World Bank and winner of the 2001 Nobel Prize in Economics. He was asked to resign his position in 1999 for criticizing the bank's policies, having the audacity to point out that every country the IMF/World Bank got involved in ended up with an economy in ruins, their government in shambles, and the populace rioting. He explains how the IMF and World Bank operate:

> The IMF likes to go about its business without outsiders asking too many questions. In theory, the fund supports democratic institutions in the nations it assists. In practice, it undermines the democratic process by imposing policies. Officially, of course, the IMF doesn't "impose" anything. It "negotiates" the conditions for receiving aid. But all the power in the negotiations is on one side—the IMF's—and the fund rarely allows sufficient time for broad consensus-building or even widespread consultations with either parliaments or civil society. Sometimes the IMF dispenses with the pretense of openness altogether and negotiates secret covenants.[38]

And in his book *Globalization and Its Discontents*, he is particularly critical of the IMF:

> The IMF is pursuing not just the objectives set out in its original mandate...it is also pursuing the interests of the financial community.[39] A half century after its founding, it is clear that the IMF has failed in its mission. It has not accomplished what it is supposed to do—provide funds for countries facing an economic downturn, to enable the country to restore itself to full employment. IMF funds and programs not only fail to stabilize situations, in many cases they actually make matters worse—especially for the poor.[40]

The actual tactics of the IMF and the World Bank have been verified by noted investigative journalist Greg Palast, who had access to a sizeable stash of secret documents passed to him by disaffected World Bank and International Monetary Fund workers. He also interviewed Stiglitz after his departure from the bank. From the interview and his research of the trove of insider documents, this, he says, is how economic globalization actually works:[41]

- A nation applies to the IMF for a bank loan.
- The loan is contingent on the nation's rulers signing secret agreements by which they will sell off the nation's key assets to whatever corporation the IMF selects (the water systems, the railways, the telephone companies, the nationalized oil companies, gas stations, etc.). For example, according to a secret agreement between the leaders of Argentina and Jim Wolfensen, the president of the World Bank, a pipeline that runs between Argentina and Chile was sold off

to a company called Enron. According to that same secret agreement the water system of Buenos Aires was sold for a song to a company called Enron.

- The rulers must sign a secret agreement, averaging one-hundred and eleven items, whereby they will run the economy according to the dictates of the IMF; if they don't follow those steps they are cut off from all international borrowing.
- The IMF/WB pays a "commission" (usually a sizeable personal fortune) to the ruler's Swiss bank accounts when they sign the secret agreements stripping the nation of its assets.
- The secret agreements result in nothing short of slavery for the entire population since the IMF conditions include such murderous facets as laying off huge numbers of workers and creating a general state of financial austerity.
- The IMF often requires "austerity measures" called Structural Adjustments that require a borrowing country to reduce benefits in health, education, and welfare to its citizens. The Structural Adjustment Program in Tanzania required that school fees be introduced. A great many students simply stopped going to school because they could not afford to pay them.

Increasing "I and mine" by Shock and Suffering

The Chicago Boys dealing out the bitter economic medicine in Chile and Argentina mentioned above, were students of Milton Friedman at the University of Chicago. True to the methods given by their mentor they introduced severe and repressive economic measures on country after country. Friedman had the notion of developing a "pure" capitalism, free from all interference by government restrictions, trade barriers, collective bargaining and minimum wages. He held, and taught to generations of economists, what could be described as an idealized vision of radical free-market economics. His ideas were idealized in that he believed that "the market" had its own intelligence that could automatically solve every economic problem if it were left alone. These ideas were radical in 60s political context in which policy makers were enthralled by Keynes' ideas and prescriptions in which government played a major role in managing the economy through control of credit, borrowing and releasing money into circulation via social spending, etc. In Friedman's view the Keynesians who encouraged direct government involvement in the economic decision making were not the solution, but the cause of the problems. His radical ideas were the very antithesis of Keynes' and can be summarized in three words—deregulation, privatization and cutbacks. In his *Capitalism and Freedom* he put forth his concepts of laissez-faire:

1. all laws and regulations standing in the way of profit should be rescinded.
2. governments should sell off (privatize) all assets that could be run at a profit, such as the post office, health care, education, etc.
3. governments should not spend money on social programs.
4. taxes should be low; rich and poor should be taxed at the same rate
5. corporations should be free to sell anywhere in the world
6. capital should be free to roam the globe in search of any opportunity
7. governments should not protect local markets or ownership
8. all prices, including labor, should be determined by the market
9. government should not interfere in wages—no minimum wages

Friedman doctrine was that the reforms should be massive—cutting government spending for example by 25-50 percent across the board, and announced suddenly and implemented quickly, so the effect *deliberately created* shock and disorientation. He himself called his methods a "shock treatment." The biggest challenge for Friedman was how to push through such radical reforms. Everywhere on the planet decades of social planning, legislation, and policies were in place that would, as far as he was concerned, interfere with the freedom of the market. And as long as the Keynesians held sway Friedman was destined to remain a theorist. He wanted the market to become unharnessed and free to work its magic. But how?

Friedman believed that the only way to free the future from the chains of the past, the "tyranny of the status quo" as the title of one of his books puts it, was through crisis: "only a crisis—actual or perceived—produces real change. When that crisis occurs, the actions that are taken depend on the ideas that are lying around. That, I believe, is our basic function: to develop alternatives to existing policies, to keep them alive and available until the politically impossible becomes politically inevitable."[42]

Moreover it wasn't necessary to simply sit on one's hands and wait for a crisis, but it could be deliberately and willfully created, and while people were in shock, dazed and trying to collect their wits, the economic reforms could be imposed with little to no resistance. Friedman estimated that rulers had to act within six to nine months of crisis, otherwise the window would close and resistance to radical change would be too high.

The first opportunity of crisis that Friedman sought was created by the CIA in Chile on September 11th 1973 with the coup of General Pinochet. Amazingly "coincidentally" Friedman's troops were already on hand, and as the bullets were flying outside, the Chicago Boys feverishly printed their detailed economic doctrines so they could be on the desks of the new junta the first day they took their jobs as the new "leaders." Within a few more days the economic shock began with the price of bread going up 36 times while at the same time wages were frozen. Within a year unemployment was 20 percent, and inflation was from 500 percent to as much as 1,000 percent for basic necessities, indicating that the Chicago experiment was a bust. But rather than call it quits, they called in Friedman himself who advised that they hadn't gone far enough and that the shock needed to be increased! In speeches and interviews he repeatedly called for "shock treatment" as the "only true medicine. Absolutely. There is no other long-term solution." Friedman assured the dictator that if his advice were followed "that subsequent recovery would be rapid," he "could end inflation in months," unemployment would be brief, and he would be able to take credit for an "economic miracle."

That miracle never arrived. In 1975 public spending was cut by 27 percent in one stroke, and by 1980 federal spending was only 50 percent of what it had been before the coup, with huge losses to health care and education. Pinochet privatized more than 500 state-owned companies and banks, often for a song, tore down trade barriers that protected local businesses resulting in the loss of more than 170,000 jobs by 1983, by which time manufacturing was reduced to levels of the early 40s. This is the excellence of the hidden hand of the free market? Well perhaps. The question to be asked is *cui bono* – who benefits? The answer to that is very clear.

It wasn't the general public, 45 percent of whom within fifteen years was below official poverty levels, spending a whopping 74 percent of their income for bread alone, eliminating any money for "luxuries" such as milk. But for the elite of the country the work of the Chicago Boys was an unmitigated success. In that same time period their annual income was up by 83 percent. Using our standard of judging a thing by its results, the evidence suggests that these results were quite intentional, all the rhetoric of the magic of the free market aside. As early as 1980 it was even possible to reveal it as such in the open press. That year an article in *The Economist* described Pinochet's work as a "counter-revolution" that returned to the elite the gains that had been won from them under Keynesian policies.[43] Perhaps that was the idea all along.

The Shock Doctrine and Disaster Capitalism

Quickly following in Chile's wake, more or less similar methods continued to be applied in country after country—Uruguay, Argentina, and less violently in Brazil, which was already under the control of a U.S.-supported junta. Was there a procedure besides Friedman's being followed? Was it just economic shock or was there more to it? Was all of this human calamity necessary in order to achieve economic stability? In her stirring and detailed book *The Shock Doctrine—The Rise of Disaster Capitalism* Naomi Klein demonstrates that intentional shock has become a doctrine that was, and continues to be, used as a means for the elite rulers, with government as their agents and violence as their means, to assert their will over dazed and confused people, rob them of decency and a living wage, and facilitate the private ownership of anything that could be made to produce a profit. In keeping with the deception of *Kali* these methods are employed under the rhetoric of "democracy."

Klein backs up that premise with example after example. Building on Friedman's notions of shock treatment, she demonstrates that the stage is set with violence—as a result of natural disaster as in the Indonesian tsunami, or the hurricane that struck New Orleans, or through a coup such as in Chile, Argentina, and Peru, or war such as in the former Yugoslavia, Britain's Falklands War, China's Tiananmen Square massacre, or Yeltsin's shelling of Russia's Parliament. The second shock then comes in the form of economic dislocations. The currency is devalued, destroying purchasing power and creating immediate impoverishment, while at the same time price controls are lifted allowing the now "free market" to send the price of commodities, particularly food, through the roof. At the same time wages are frozen preventing people from being able to do anything to improve their own situation. Naturally people respond to these shocks with resistance and gather together to express their calamity and resentment, often taking the shape of widespread unrest, mass protests and strikes. That is when the third shock is then applied—mass and very public arrests, people disappearing for as long as a decade, often being tortured, and bodies showing up in garbage heaps, being washed up in the surf or floating down rivers, often missing fingers and teeth. In Chile for example, some 3,000 people disappeared or were murdered, and at least 80,000 were arrested and imprisoned. Kidnapping not only focused on the leaders of the strikers, but anyone who opposed or threatened the economic reforms. Everyone quickly gets the idea that *this* is the new world order and anyone who dares to oppose it will suffer greatly. Those arrested went to torture centers that used the methods of the CIA's *Kubark* torture manual: early morning arrest, placing a hood over the head, drugging, forced nudity, isolation, sensory deprivation and electroshock— methods made famous around the world by the stories and photos from the Abu Ghraib prison in Iraq.[44]

All of this shock is intentionally planned to violently impose the will of the ruling elite on people who would otherwise strongly resist.

A Fabricated Crisis Is As Good As a Real One

The personality of *Kali*♣ would be proud of the deceptive inventiveness of policy makers in the international financial institutions. If a real crisis is not immediately handy the impression of a crisis can be created and work just as well. An influential Washington economist and consultant to the IMF and World Bank, John Williamson, raised the idea in 1993:

> One will have to ask whether it could conceivably make sense to think of deliberately provoking a crisis so as to remove the political logjam to reform...Is it possible to conceive of a pseudo-crisis that could serve the same positive function without the cost of a real crisis?

Mr. Williamson was apparently behind the times and hadn't been in close touch with his colleagues at the IMF. Budhoo informs us that when he was with the IMF, fund employees engaged in elaborate statistical malpractices to exaggerate numbers in IMF reports to give the impression of severe problems that didn't exist. For example, the IMF more than doubled the statistics of labor costs in Trinadad and Tobago in 1985 to make them look highly unproductive. He also stated that the fund "invented literally out of the blue" huge unpaid government debts. These fictions triggered very real problems when Trinidad became viewed as a bad risk and its financing was cut off, sending it begging to the IMF for "help." The IMF agreed on the condition that the whole gamut of structural adjustments was accepted. The process Budhoo says was the "deliberate blocking of an economic lifeline to the country through subterfuge... Trinidad and Tobago [were] destroyed economically first and converted thereafter." [45]

Klein relates how subterfuge was used to create the appearance of crisis to get the government of Canada to reduce taxes by reducing social benefits in health, education, and unemployment. These social programs, which were supported by a large majority of Canadians, could only have been reduced if there was the impression of an impending catastrophe. A "deficit crisis" was created where none actually existed. Canada's debt was rated A++ by Moody's Investor Services, but the press constantly presented the national finances as catastrophic, predicting that within "the next year, maybe two years Canada's credit will have run out." The ruse worked; government reacted to the false alarms cutting spending on social services and the cuts have remained despite

---

♣ Not to be confused with the goddess *Kali*. The personality of *Kali* represents the qualities of the age of *Kali*-yuga.

the fact that Canada has since seen surplus budgets. Investigative journalist Linda McQuaig later exposed that the perception of the "crisis" had been accomplished by think tanks funded by the largest banks and corporations in Canada.[46]

In order to get the full impact of the devastation wrought by the unconscionable acts perpetrated by the economics of ignorance one must read Klein's *Shock Doctrine*. She spells out in minute detail the deliberate planning and execution of destruction and death wielded through economic machinations over the course of the past three decades. It is a devastating work that forces open our eyes to realize and accept that the world is not the way it is simply by chance, but by deliberate demonic acts. The Shock Doctrine is the new method by which today's economic hit men do their work. Under the influence of ignorance and with a demonic mentality, the ruling elite appear bent on destroying any general prosperity for the people throughout the world and creating a two-tier social structure of wealthy and slaves. This can be understood by the results:

- The income gap between rich and poor in the Third World doubled in the course of the 1980s, according to a United Nations 1992 Human Development Report, mainly because of inherent inequities built into SAPs.
- Today, the richest fifth of the world (including most of Europe and North America) receives 150 times more in income than the poorest fifth.
- 1.2 billion people in the Third World now live in absolute poverty—almost twice the number of the 1980s.
- 1.6 billion people in the Third World are without potable water.
- Well over two billion are unemployed or underemployed.
- At least six million children under five years of age have died each year since 1982 in Africa, Asia and Latin America because of the anti-people, even genocidal, focus of IMF and World Bank SAPs.
- Even though debtor countries paid more than $1.3 trillion to the IMF between 1982 and 1990, they were 61 percent more in debt by the 1990s than they were in 1982. According to the 1988 UNICEF annual report, debt and interest payments by Southern countries totaled more than three times the amount of aid received from the World Bank and IMF.

Budhoo considered the IMF's programs to be a form of mass torture which was willingly applied while a callous and blind eye was turned as "screaming-in-pain governments and peoples [are] forced to bend on their knees before us, broken and terrified and disintegrating, and begging for a sliver of reasonableness and decency on our part. But we laugh cruelly in their face, and the torture goes on unabated."

It finally got to him. Reaching his limit Budhoo began his catharsis with this statement in his *Open Letter of Resignation to the Managing Director of the International Monetary Fund*:

> Today I resigned from the staff of the International Monetary Fund after over 12 years, and after 1000 days of official fund work in the field, hawking your medicine and your bag of tricks to governments and to peoples in Latin America and the Caribbean and Africa. To me, resignation is a priceless liberation, for with it I have taken the first big step to that place where I may hope to wash my hands of what in my mind's eye is the blood of millions of poor and starving peoples. Mr. Camdessus, the blood is so much, you know, it runs in rivers. It dries up too; it cakes all over me; sometimes I feel that there is not enough soap in the whole world to cleanse me from the things that I did do in your name and in the name of your predecessors, and under your official seal.[47]

Communists and Capitalists-Brothers in Principle

To say that capitalism is the economic method of choice for those under the influence of passion and ignorance is not to say that communism is or was anything better or even different. In fact, it is quite the same thing, economically speaking, to a large degree because communism was created by the capitalists to further their control. Distinguished English historian Nesta Webster in *The Surrender of An Empire*, writes:

> Had the Bolsheviks been, as they are frequently represented, a mere gang of revolutionaries out to destroy property, first in Russia, and then in every other country, they would naturally have found themselves up against organized resistance by the owners of property all over the world, and the Moscow blaze would have been rapidly extinguished. It was only owing to the powerful influences behind them that this minority party was able to seize the reins of power and, having seized them, to retain their hold of them up to the present day.

While he was a scholar at the prestigious Hoover Institute, scholar Antony Sutton investigated the connection between the owners of property, the capitalists, and the communists. During his time at the Institute he wrote the major study *Western Technology and Soviet Economic Development* in three volumes, detailing how the West played a major role in developing Soviet Union from its very beginnings up until 1970. He wrote another two volumes that penetrated the relationship of Wall Street and the Bolsheviks, two more books detailing American aid to the Soviets, and an additional two books examining Wall Street financiers and their influences over government and politicians. In the Preface to *Wall Street and the Bolshevik Revolution* he writes: "Since the early 1920s, numerous pamphlets and articles, even a few books, have sought to forge a link between 'international bankers' and 'Bolshevik revolutionaries.' Rarely have these attempts been supported by hard evidence, and never have such attempts been argued within the framework of a scientific methodology." However some fifty years after the October Revolution the United States government declassified related documents and Sutton found evidence he sought in the State Department Decimal File, particularly the 861.00 section. "When the evidence in these official papers is merged with nonofficial evidence from biographies, personal papers, and conventional histories, a truly fascinating story emerges. We find there was a link between *some* New York international bankers and *many* revolutionaries, including Bolsheviks. These banking gentlemen...had a financial stake in, and were rooting for, the success of the Bolshevik Revolution."[48](emphasis in original).

What was that stake and who were the men behind it? Russian General Arsene De Goulevitch wrote in *Czarism and the Revolution* "the main purveyors of funds for the revolution, however, were neither crackpot Russian millionaires nor armed bandits or Lenin. The 'real' money primarily came from certain British and American circles which for a long time past had lent their support to the Russian revolutionary cause." DeGoulevitch further said that the revolution was "engineered by the English, more precisely by Sir George Buchanan and Lord (Alfred) Milner (of the Round Table)...In private conversations I have been told that over 21 million rubles were spent by Lord Milner in financing the Russian Revolution."[49]

William Boyce Thompson, a director of the Federal Reserve Bank of New York, a large stockholder in the Rockefeller-controlled Chase Bank, and a financial associate of the Guggenheims and the Morgans, contributed $1 million to the Bolshevik Revolution for propaganda purposes.[50] Another $5 million in gold and safe passage through wartime Germany was obtained from sources there. And banking magnate Jacob Schiff contributed some $20,000,000 for the final triumph of Bolshevism in Russia according to his grandson John.[51] That money was deposited in a Warburg bank, and later transferred to the Nya Banken in Stockholm where it was picked up by Lenin. Trotsky traveling from New York on an American passport later joined him in Petrograd.

Schiff was not just for the Bolsheviks but was in fact intent on subverting Imperial Russia. The Jewish Communal Register of New York City, 1917–18, confirmed that Schiff's firm Kuhn-Loeb & Co. "floated the large Japanese war loans of 1904–5, thus making possible the Japanese victory over Russia..." The report also states that "Mr. Schiff financed the enemies of autocratic Russia and used his financial influence to keep Russia from the money market of the United States."[52]

In addition the U.S. State Department published a three-volume report on the establishment of Communism in Russia, *Papers Relating to the Foreign Relations of the United States,* 1918, which recounts from intelligence reports and intercepted correspondence how German banks, under the influence of banking magnate Max Warburg, originated a system for the dispersion of large payments to Lenin, Trotsky, and others in their attempts to overthrow the Czar. The syndicate was set up with "...very close and absolutely secret relations established between Finnish and American banks," as well as banking houses in Stockholm and Copenhagen, who were intermediaries between high-finance in the West and revolutionaries inside Russia.[53]

Obviously if these men were financing it they had no fear of international Communism, the so-called mortal foe of the capitalists. It is only logical to assume that if they are willing and even eager to cooperate with it, it must be because they control it. Indeed, Lenin understood that somehow or other he wasn't in control. He wrote: "The state does not function as we desired. How does it function? The car does not obey. A man is at the wheel and seems to lead it, but the car does not drive in the desired direction. It moves as another force wishes."

Who is controlling it then? Professor Sutton writes:

> The gigantic Russian market was to be converted into a captive market and a technical colony to be exploited by a few high-powered American financiers and the corporations under their control. What the Interstate Commerce Commission and the Federal Trade Commission under the thumb of American industry could achieve for that industry at home, a planned socialist government could achieve for it abroad—given suitable support and inducements from Wall Street and Washington, D.C.

> Finally, lest this explanation seem too radical, remember that it was Trotsky who appointed tsarist generals to consolidate the Red Army; that it was Trotsky who appealed for American officers to control revolutionary Russia and intervene in behalf of the Soviets; that it was Trotsky who squashed first the libertarian element in the Russian

Revolution and then the workers and peasants...In other words, we are suggesting that the Bolshevik Revolution was an alliance of statists: statist revolutionaries and statist financiers aligned against the genuine revolutionary libertarian elements in Russia.

... The question now in the reader's mind must be, were these bankers also secret Bolsheviks? No, of course not. The financiers were without ideology. It would be a gross misinterpretation to assume that assistance for the Bolshevists was ideologically motivated, in any narrow sense. The financiers were *power-motivated* and therefore assisted *any* political vehicle that would give them an entree to power: Trotsky, Lenin, the tsar, Kolchak, Denikin—all received aid, more or less. All, that is, but those who wanted a truly free individualist society.

This, therefore, is an explanation that fits the evidence. This handful of bankers and promoters was not Bolshevik, or Communist, or socialist, or Democrat, or even American. Above all else these men wanted markets, preferably captive international markets—and a monopoly of the captive world market as the ultimate goal. They wanted markets that could be exploited monopolistically without fear of competition from Russians, Germans, or anyone else—including American businessmen outside the charmed circle. This closed group was apolitical and amoral. In 1917, it had a single-minded objective— a captive market in Russia, all presented under, and intellectually protected by, the shelter of a league to enforce the peace.[54] (all emphasis in original)

The Soviet Union was the businessman's dream come true: monopolies on an entire empire dealing through only one agent—the government. Immediately (by 1919) business began to flow: $10 million for food products, $4.5 million for printing presses, $3 million for machinery, $3 for clothing and another $3 million for boots and several other contracts worth $1.5 million.[55]

The major payoff for previous political and financial support however, came in 1923 when the Soviets formed their first international bank, Ruskombank, to facilitate trade between Russia and Europe and Russia the USA, i.e. to allow British and American firms to sell their goods in the vast Russian market. J. P. Morgan associate Olof Aschberg became the nominal head, and its main source of capital was 3 million pounds sterling from the British government, by far the largest initial investment in the bank. A vice president of J. P. Morgan's Guaranty Trust, Max May became a director of Ruskombank, and the Ruskombank promptly appointed Guaranty Trust Company its U.S. agent. Rockefeller's Chase

National Bank (later Chase Manhattan Bank) helped establish the American-Russian Chamber of Commerce in 1922, and its first president was Reeve Schley, a Chase vice-president. In 1925 Chase National developed the program for financing Soviet raw material exports to the United States, and Chase National and Equitable Trust Co. were also the major forces in Soviet credit dealings.[56]

Industrialization

The Soviet's chief economic priority during Lenin's New Economic Policy (NEP) was the industrialization of the country, but after years of war the Soviets were in no condition to do that themselves, nor was that the intention. They offered more than 350 foreign concessions under the NEP during the 1920s. These concessions enabled foreign entrepreneurs to establish business operations in the Soviet Union without gaining property rights. The industrial capacity of the Soviet Union was, to a great extent, built by American companies and the Wall Street financiers. Although many of those concessions were withdrawn by the end of the 1920s, somehow this was not a deterrent. By 1931 Western corporations had immense contracts for the development and manufacturing of Russian resources that included engineering services and plant construction for: rubber, automobile manufacturing, smelting furnaces, hydroelectric generation, irrigation, fertilizer, electrical components for automobiles, paper mills, steel mills, copper and other non-ferrous metals industries, tractors, petroleum, gasoline production, oil-drilling technologies, electricity, electrical generators and related equipment, coal production and machinery, aniline production, gasoline engines, aviation, architecture, gas and coking plants, coal mining, chlorine, acetic acid, construction of an electrolytic copper plant, and an aluminum plant that consumed one-half of the world's bauxite.[57]

Additionally Standard Oil of New Jersey bought 50 percent of the huge Caucasus oil fields, and in 1927, built a large refinery. Standard Oil, with their subsidiary, Vacuum Oil Co., made a deal to sell Soviet oil to European countries. The Soviets also signed an agreement with the Ford Motor Company in 1929 to purchase $30 million worth of automobiles and parts over four years, and Ford agreed to give technical assistance until 1938 to construct an integrated automobile-manufacturing plant at Nizhni-Novgorod (Gorki). The MZMA plant in Moscow, which manufactures small automobiles, was also built by Ford Motor Company. In 1932, Du Pont began construction of an immense nitric acid plant with a capacity of 1,000 tons per day (nitric acid is a component in the manufacture of explosives).

Western firms supplied designs and specifications, process technology, engineering capability, equipment, and startup and training programs. These contracts were package deals that were highly profitable. This support of Soviet technology continued throughout the 20th century.[58]

The international bankers continually made efforts to maintain or increase their business with the Soviet Union. They encouraged the American government to recognize the Soviet Union as a nation in 1933, as other nations were doing, to save "them" from financial ruin. They were also busy with other plans to insure their business dealings. Just a year later in 1934, by executive order President Roosevelt established the Export-Import Bank of Washington. Known as Eximbank, it underwrites (guarantees) loans for international business, and was created specifically to promote and finance trade with the Soviet Union. In 1972 the U.S. government issued $1 billion in licenses to export equipment and technical assistance for the Kama truck plant. Planned as the largest truck plant in the world, it covers 36 square miles and produces more heavy trucks, including military trucks, than the output of all U.S. heavy truck manufacturers combined. The Eximbank provided $153 million in loan guarantees for Kama River Plant, and $180 million for Occidental's string of chemical plants at half the prime lending rate.

At the Bretton Woods Conference in 1948 the World Bank, International Monetary Fund, and the General Agreement on Trade and Tariffs (GATT) were created. At the heart of GATT is the "Most Favored Nation" status that allows a country to trade with a minimum of tariffs and trade restrictions. The Nixon Administration prepared to extend to the Soviets Most Favored Nation tariff status, as part of the Nixon-Kissinger *détente,* shortly after the May 1972 Summit Conference in Moscow. David Rockefeller, board chairman of Chase Manhattan Bank, claimed the move could help slow the arms race: "The desire of the Soviets to use Western trade, credits and technology to bolster their own economy hopefully could be accompanied by their giving lower priority to military programs," he reasoned.[59]

The reader may ask why these apparently normal business dealings should be called to our attention. The point is that these business contracts helped to build the industrial might of the Soviet Union, whom many if not most Americans, have always considered their sworn enemies. They were told that the Communists wanted to destroy their way of life, and were continually threatened by Soviet nuclear missiles throughout the second half of the 20th century. When they hear about the immense American help given to the Soviets during this same period they can hardly believe it, especially since a great deal of that assistance has military applications, and was directly employed against American soldiers during the Vietnamese war. The point I have labored to make clear is that it has been Western capitalists that established the Soviet Union as a colony from which to extract profits. Under the influence of *tamo-guna,* profit is profit regardless of the cost of lives to acquire and maintain it.

This follows Frederick Howe's maxim to a "T"—a super monopoly over not just a country, but an empire, and the government itself was their agent. By the middle of the 20th century they had also established the same arrangement in America. Consider the following relationships between the American government and the executives of some major companies: The head of Eximbank when the Kama River Plant was given loan guarantees was William J. Casey, a former associate of Armand Hammer (a major Western industrialist in Russia) who later became Director of the Central Intelligence Agency. Financing was arranged by Chase Manhattan Bank, who's then Chairman was David Rockefeller. Chase is also the former employer of Paul Volcker, who became Chairman of the Federal Reserve Bank. The U.S.-Soviet trade accords including Kama and other projects were signed by George Shultz, a long- known as a proponent of more aid and trade to the Soviets, who later to become Secretary of State in the Reagan Administration. Shultz is also the former President of Bechtel Corporation, a major international engineering firm. All a nice, cozy, incestuous family taking care of business, and fully guaranteed by United States' taxpayers. These same close and inter-changing relationships continues today between government and the financial industry.

Collectivization

In addition to being one of the Soviet Union's most vital economic resources, grain also served as a nexus between cities and villages where more than 80 percent of the population lived. The NEP intended to create such a level of peasant prosperity that it would create an internal market for manufactured goods from the industrial sector, but simultaneously the Soviets wanted to ensure a net profit for industry and further industrial expansion by charging higher prices for industrial goods than for grain.

This plan was fraught with ideological problems however, because the very idea of a developed peasantry was oxymoronic to the Soviets who expected the peasantry to disappear with the advance of a modern industrial society. Making matters worse the communists viewed the peasantry with a cultural contempt, assigning them an inferior class status.

As plans for industrialization increased, so did the need for grain exports. Distribution and supply networks faltered in 1927 due to drought and the fact that peasants preferred to store grain waiting for higher prices in the winter and next spring. Stalin was not content to wait and demanded a tribute in the shape of forced extractions of grain as well as "surplus" money resources. The countryside then became "the new front" and grain procurements represented a "fortress to be captured at any cost." The communists prepared for a new type of war, but one with domestic objectives and domestic enemies. The solution, according to Stalin, was "to strike at speculators and kulak resellers" as well as at all those in the lower-level apparatus "who connive at, or abet, speculation."[60] According to Russian scholars:

> The dilemma confronting the Soviet regime was not new to Russian economic development. The alternatives appeared completely dichotomous: either the regime could allow the peasantry to prosper, and through balanced growth and social stability the needed revenues for industrialization would gradually accrue, or, risking social discontent, it could "squeeze" the peasantry through heavy taxation, maintain low agricultural prices, expand grain exports, and with the rapid accumulation of capital thus obtained push forward with a forced program of industrialization. In either case, the peasantry was perceived mainly as an economic resource, in effect little more than an internal colony. And the factors that determined the approach were more often political than economic.

> The first option was less attractive to a regime with revolutionary designs for restructuring Russian society. The issue of the pace or tempo of industrialization became a major and contentious problem for the regime. During the first years of NEP, L. D. Trotsky and the Left Opposition pushed aggressively for higher industrial growth rates. In the mid-1920s, E. A. Preobrazhensky, a theoretician for the Left Opposition, urged that the terms of trade be turned more steeply against the peasantry, that a "tribute" be exacted in order to speed up capital accumulation and industrialization. With neither irony nor shame, he dubbed this process "primitive socialist accumulation," echoing and subverting Marx's detested "primitive capitalist accumulation" in the interests of Soviet power.[61]

In November 1927, Joseph Stalin launched his "revolution from above," idealistically setting two impossible goals for Soviet domestic policy: rapid industrialization (a 330 percent expansion in heavy industry) and collectivization of agriculture. His aims were to erase all traces of the capitalism that had entered under Lenin's New Economic Policy and to transform the Soviet Union as quickly as possible, without regard to cost, into an industrialized and completely socialist state. The First Five-Year Plan also called for transforming Soviet agriculture from small-hold individual farms into a system of large state collective farms believing that collectivization would improve agricultural output and would produce sufficient grain to feed the growing urban labor force. Collectivization was also expected to liberate (force) many peasants from their land to make them employees of the state, either on the collective farms or for industrial work in the cities.

The reaction to this drastic cultural change was almost identical to that of the peasants of Europe during the 15-17th centuries. The peasants opposed collectivization and responded with acts of sabotage, burning of crops and slaughtering of draught animals. They also destroyed property and attacked officials and members of the collectives. Isaac Mazepa, former prime minister (1919-20) of the Ukrainian National Republic (UNR), boasted that the political right had succeeded in 1930-32 in widely sabotaging the agricultural works:

> At first there were disturbances in the kolkhosi [collective farms] or else the Communist officials and their agents were killed, but later a system of passive resistance was favored which aimed at the systematic frustration of the Bolsheviks' plans for the sowing and gathering of the harvest...The catastrophe of 1932 was the hardest blow that Soviet Ukraine had to face since the famine of 1921-22. The autumn and spring sowing campaigns both failed. Whole tracts were left unsown, in addition when the crop was being gathered...in many areas, especially in the south, 20, 40 and even 50 per cent was left in the fields, and was either not collected at all or was ruined in the threshing.

The Soviet government responded dramatically and harshly by cutting off food rations and other necessities such as salt to areas where there was opposition to collectivization, especially in the Ukrainian region. Hundreds of thousands of those who opposed collectivization were executed or sent to forced-labor camps. Peasant families were forcibly resettled in Siberia and Kazakhstan in exile settlements and tens of thousands died along the way.

In 1932 Stalin further raised Ukraine's grain quotas by 44 percent, which was a de facto death sentence. Under Soviet law all grain first went to meet the government's quota before any could be given to the members of the farm. With the aid of regular troops and secret police the Soviets waged a merciless war against those who refused to give up their grain. Even seed grain was forcibly confiscated. Any man, woman, or child caught taking even a handful of grain from a collective farm could be, and often was, executed or deported. So difficult were the times that those who did not appear to be starving were suspected of hoarding grain. Six to seven million perished in what Ukrainians call "Holodomor"—the "Famine-Genocide."

Estimates of the dead across the Soviet empire from starvation or disease directly caused by collectivization number in the high millions. According to official Soviet figures some 24 million peasants disappeared from rural areas with only an extra 12.6 million moving to State jobs. The implication is that the total death toll for Stalin's collectivization program was on the order of twelve million people. The heaviest losses occurred in Ukraine, which had been the most productive agricultural area of the Soviet Union. Determined to crush any remaining nationalism, the famine was accompanied by a purge of the Ukrainian intelligentsia and even the Ukrainian Communist party. The famine broke the peasants' will to resist collectivization and left the entire population politically, socially, and psychologically traumatized.

Ukrainian historian Valentyn Moroz in detailing how the famine was significantly related to changing the traditional culture wrote: "The Ukrainian village had long been recognized as the bastion of national traditions. The Bolsheviks sought to strike a fatal blow at the village structure because it was the life spring of the vital national spirit."[62] One of Stalin's lieutenants demonstrated the Communists attitude that the famine in Ukraine was a great success. It showed the peasants "who is the master here. It cost millions of lives, but the collective farm system is here to stay."[63] (He sounds eerily similar to Michael Ledeen doesn't he?)

In a speech to the House of Commons on November 5, 1919, Winston Churchill said: "Lenin was sent into Russia...in the same way that you might send a vial containing a culture of typhoid or of cholera to be poured into the water supply of a great city, and it worked with amazing accuracy. No sooner did Lenin arrive than he began beckoning a finger here and a finger there to obscure persons in sheltered retreats in New York, Glasgow, in Berne, and other countries, and he gathered together the leading spirits of a formidable sect, the most formidable sect in the world...With these spirits around him he set to work with demoniacal ability to tear to pieces every institution on which the Russian State depended."

The economics of ignorance extracts power and profits at any cost, and the cost of consolidating business in Russia and forcing people to use their productive energy in the service of a master is measured in millions of lives. Between 1930 and 1950 more than 20 million Russians died in forced labor camps, and Khrushchev personally supervised the massacre of more than 10,000 Ukrainians at Vinnitsa. There is no certainty of the exact number of deaths but the number is at least 20 million, including victims of the forced collectivization, the hunger, large purges, expulsions, banishments, executions, and mass death at Gulags. Alexander Solzhenitsyn puts the number at 66 million.

There is little difference whether one is forced to work for a capitalist master or a communist one. Both the capitalists and the communists have created an economics of ignorance through cruelty, force, violence, and death. In both cases the labor of millions is usurped by a small minority who accrue wealth to their own advantage, and there is no significant difference between the two.

We may ask how the International Communist experiment, an exercise in exploitation (*tamo-guna*), ended without a violent revolution that should be expected by the influence of *tamo-guna*. The answer in my humble opinion is that the 70-year experiment between the capitalist model and the communist one demonstrated that far more can be squeezed out of people if they think they are free, and are given unrestricted sense gratification. They will work like asses to be able to purchase insignificant, unnecessary trinkets to increase their own petty sense of "I and mine," and in the process enrich the masters of capital. Why bother then to engage in a destructive war if you already control a place and people? History shows that most of the wars in the past two thousand years have been fought to decide who gets to exploit a place and people.[64] If you already control them why is a war necessary? Nonetheless much ado had to be made to explain the "ideological shift" to millions of Soviet citizens who had bought into the communist ideology and who were now feeling abandoned by their leaders. And, if all the Communist rhetoric was actually true then why wasn't the capital of the Soviet state, ostensibly the property of "the people," delivered to them when the empire was privatized? Because all along it had been accruing benefit to only a small segment of "the people" and with slight adjustments those in control were given the privilege to continue their ownership when communism fell. There is in fact no "state" to labor for, all states are a fiction. In the case of the Soviets "the state" was the rulers of Communist Party who were acting in the name of the State. External appearances to the contrary, very little actually changed.

The people in the former Soviet Union are now playing a game of catch-up attempting to acquire all of the many tantalizing goodies imported from around the world. There are thousands of shops that were nowhere to be seen in communist times, along with easy credit, with nothing down and a 0 percent rate of interest, tempting shoppers to "buy now." And it works. People fill the shops and, like the rest of the world, are quickly becoming more "American-like." But there is a price to pay. As I travel there I ask people if they are working harder now under capitalism than they were under communism; invariably they say they are.

Many, in dismay, recognize the game for what it is. They understood that earlier they were being exploited under communism and that they are now being exploited under capitalism. There actually isn't a dime's worth of difference between the two—both clearly show themselves to be the same economics of ignorance.

Chapter Six

The Economics of Atheism

"...without God and immortal life? All things are lawful then, they can do what they like?" Dostoevsky – The Brothers Karamazov
"Do what thou wilt" Motto of the Illuminati

Promise Me a Paradise

Materialists of all stripes, including the gamut of the worldly philosophers (economists) have been speculating for centuries to realize the moment of "Eureka —I've found it!"—the discovery of the formula for a blissful life of material existence. Well, wait no more. Nobel prize-winning economist Herbert Simon has found the source of our future bliss in the classical theory of economics, of all places, based on the assumption that the pursuit of our individual self-interest will bring us all to a condition of "omniscient rationality!" Omniscience is of course a quality formerly attributed only to God, but it appears that it will somehow now become widespread through the workings of blind economic forces and self-interest alone, leaving one to wonder why the tens of millions of self-interested opportunists that have gone before us have not yet found the said promised land and bequeathed it to us. That rational economic model is, he concludes, a world that is "strikingly simple beautiful."[1] Such vaunted and idyllic dreams are so naturally appealing that they mislead many down the yellow brick road to more illusions. Following the same misguided wishful-thinking another economist, Robert Nelson, concluded that "self-interest thus is not a crass and selfish motive but, paradoxically, a necessary quality of human behavior if men and women are to enter onto a path toward a greater future rationality *and, in its perfection, a future heavenly peace and harmony on earth...To put mankind on the path of economic growth is...to follow a route that leads eventually to the spiritual fulfillment of mankind.*"[2]

A paradox indeed! Were it true, the almost endless, and certainly ubiquitous, self-interest rampant in the world today after Reagan's decade of greed, Clinton's roaring 90's, and the simultaneous grabbing of the Soviet Union's assets by the greediest, should have had us all in nirvana a decade or two ago—or even a millennia or more ago. Self-interest is nothing new. The idea, or even the hope, that economic growth can lead to the spiritual fulfillment of mankind leads to serious questions as to what Nelson's concept of spiritual actually is. But he leaves no doubt that it is a so-called heaven on earth. His ideas are certainly not the same as that explained in the Vedas, by whose definition mundane economic activity alone leads us further down the abyss of ignorance. The spiritual qualities explained in the *Bhagavad-gita* and *Srimad Bhagavatam* can never be achieved by any material means, and to think that genuine spiritual happiness can be achieved by some material means is only to demonstrate one's ignorance of spirit. It is but another of the great illusions of modern materialistic society. Every sober person would do well to not be led astray by such false promises. Simon, Nelson and people of their ilk want the kingdom of God, but without God.

Nelson continues this vain search for heaven on earth in a subsequent book titled *Economics As Religion*.[3] No kidding. What does this priest of economic salvation preach? That through economic progress "sin can be eliminated from the world." And what is that sin? Economic irrationality. He says that "to be irrational is to be possessed by the modern equivalent of evil." Irrational means not acting "economically," which means not to act in such a way as to preserve or increase one's wealth, which also means that money must be valued above all other things. Money and wealth are thus Nelson's Gods. He argues that "if what is rational is what yields economic progress, and if economic progress will eventually abolish human sinfulness, then it follows directly that to behave rationally must be to obey the highest moral commandment of mankind."[4] In other words, morality lies not in what authority you follow, nor how you deal with others. It lies in creating money and wealth—Gods whose positions are paramount above all other considerations. Furthermore, the self-righteous Nelson tells us that there is only one understanding of rationality—his—and that organizations such as the Peace Corps and the various international development agencies are the new missionaries whose job it is to take this message of salvation around the world.

He goes on to argue that:

> ...the elimination of economic scarcity will bring the arrival of heaven on earth, all people in every nation will be saved in the same way and will someday share the same heaven. If religion is concerned above

all with the path of salvation and the ultimate prospects of mankind, all human beings will be followers in the same worldwide theology whose message is contained in the economic preachings [sic] of the twentieth-century welfare state.[5]

The fact is that Mr. Nelson's religion is atheism, his heaven is a world of unrestricted sense enjoyment and the vehicle with which he promises to deliver us to that heavenly kingdom's pearly gates is none other than the economics of atheism. These are pathetically poor substitutes for the actual realization of true transcendence and the unlimited bliss of realizing our genuine eternal spiritual nature—concepts and realizations that will remain forever out of the reach of people with such a mentality. Moreover, Nelson's propositions can never bring lasting happiness to anybody, regardless of how he might imagine it to be so. There is no amount of material pleasure that can permanently fulfill us, the spiritual being. *Unending* amounts of material sense pleasure cannot make a person happy. If it could then why are the already egregiously wealthy not satisfied and happy? Why do they continue to prey on the poor and destitute? What is that amount that is required to finally satisfy someone? As we have already discussed, there isn't one. Indeed, unrestricted and increasing amounts of sense enjoyment do nothing but fuel the flames of more desires which burn like fire and give no peace. Lost in the inferno of lust these lost souls continue to create scheme after scheme to get it all.

The Illusions and False Assumptions of Modern Economics

How we understand and relate to each other is always influenced by our understanding of who we are, what this world is, and our purpose here. These existential questions are answered by every bona fide religion because God has not simply wound this world up like a clock and cast it adrift to function on its own as the deists claim. He has given us instructions for how to live in this world and promulgates them in religious teachings, specifically the Vedic literatures. He regularly sends His representatives—the *acharyas*, gurus and saints—to guide us back to the proper path. He even comes here Himself to show us how to live by His own example. The priests and intelligentsia of every society are the agents whose responsibility it is to bring those instructions to us, and thereby steer the social flagship. But this understanding of the arrangement of the Supreme has become lost in this Age of *Kali*, and the many serious problems that the world now faces result from thinking that these existential questions are relative and may be interpreted according to any individual's whim. This false assumption has led to a host of other false assumptions about this world, many of which are found in the concepts of modern economics which are so influential in the way the world works today. Examining these assumptions in light of Vedic wisdom provides us with a way of clearly understanding the obstacles that are standing in the way of an economics that is beneficial for everyone.

We identified some of the false assumptions above. Here we will consider in detail those that form the foundation of the economics of atheism (modern economics), which has had such catastrophic consequences for the vast majority of the people of the world. These foundational assumptions include: 1) the idea that there is no God, 2) that we can personally own any amount of private property, 3) that we create the results of our actions which are thus ours to have and enjoy, 4) the idea that the pursuit of one's own selfish-interest magically results in the best interests of all—the so-called Invisible Hand of the market, 5) that corporations and other notional institutions are real, necessary and beneficial, and 6) that paper money has value, along with the entire host of assumptions and problems associated with it.

The Foundation of Atheistic Civilization

The English word atheism comes from Greek *atheos*, meaning godless. In Greek the prefix *a-* indicates without, and the word *theos* means God. This is identical to the meaning of atheism found in the Vedas. According to Vedic literature anything that has no connection with God is considered atheistic. Furthermore the concept of atheism is connected with the concept of *maya*. Early in the story of the creation, Brahma, desiring to search out the cause of his lone existence, performed great austerity and meditation. Pleased by his efforts the Supreme Lord revealed Himself to Brahma and explained that He only is the basis of all existence, and He also explained the distinction between reality and illusion (2.9.33–34):

> Brahma, it is I, the Personality of Godhead, who existed before the creation, when there was nothing but Myself. Nor was there the material nature, the cause of this creation. That which you see now is also I, the Personality of Godhead, and after annihilation what remains will also be I, the Personality of Godhead. O Brahma, whatever appears to be of any value, if it is without relation to Me, has no reality—know it as My illusory energy, that reflection which appears to be in darkness.

Srila Prabhupada explains the connection between atheism and *maya* in his comments on these verses: "We should note very carefully that the Personality of Godhead is addressing Lord Brahma and specifying with great emphasis Himself, pointing out that it is He, the Personality of Godhead, who existed before the creation, it is He only who maintains the creation, and it is He only who remains after the annihilation of the creation. Brahma is also a creation of the Supreme Lord...any stage of the cosmic manifestation—its appearance, its sustenance, its growth, its interactions of different energies, its deterioration and its disappearance—has its basic relation with the existence of the Personality of Godhead. As such, whenever there is forgetfulness of this prime relation with the Lord, and whenever things are accepted as real without being related to the Lord, that conception is called a product of the illusory energy of the Lord. Because nothing can exist without the Lord, it should be known that the illusory energy is also an energy of the Lord." This illusory energy we have identified earlier as *maya*. Under the spell of this illusory energy we see everything in relationship to ourselves, accepting it for our own use, pleasure or enjoyment, forgetting its relationship with God altogether. Thus without having a connection to God all conceptions and activities are atheistic and influenced by *maya*, or illusion. The *Srimad-Bhagavatam* aims at destroying this illusion by establishing the connection of everything in this world with God. The eradication of this illusion is undertaken in the very beginning of this great work. The second of the 18,000 verses states (1.1.2):

> Completely rejecting all religious activities which are materially motivated, this *Bhagavata Purana* propounds the highest truth, which is understandable by those who are fully pure in heart. The highest truth is reality distinguished from illusion for the welfare of all. Such truth uproots the threefold miseries.✲

If *maya*, or illusion, is that which is thought to be separate from God, then all of the underlying assumptions of modern economic thought are illusory. What allows these illusions to exist is that we have accepted them together as a society and attempted to make them function as if they were reality. But they are not and can never be reality. The result of this widespread psychosis of "make-believe" is that billions of people are suffering in want and need, living miserable lives, and too often going to an early grave. As long as we cling to these illusory concepts and attempt to exploit them for our material enjoyment the widespread social and economic problems we now face must remain. In other words, it is the false assumptions of modern society that generate the problems. That remains true regardless of how the details of economic formulae are tweaked. The problems cannot fully and ultimately be solved for everyone's benefit until these false assumptions are given up and we choose to live according to reality. With no apologies to Margaret Thatcher, there is no alternative to this if the people of the world are to live happily.

✲ The threefold miseries are those caused by the body and mind, by other living beings, and by the forces of nature.

Unlimited Personal Private Ownership

We examined the illusion of ownership briefly above, but here we want to look at it as one of the foundational assumptions of modern economic thought. In modern culture the unlimited personal acquisition of wealth is both lawful and morally acceptable. Almost everyone thinks of it as natural, normal, and even beyond question. As such our economic system is built around this idea. Everyone has "their own" possessions that are separate from those of others. We also think that everyone has the God-given right to increase these possessions more and more. The workings of the money economy dictate that this increase must come from others. In some cases there is an equitable exchange, but not always. Many times people are made to pay dearly for the necessities of life resulting in great disparities of wealth. On one hand billions of people live in great need, while on the other billionaires cannot even comprehend how much money they have, what to speak of use it for any personally productive purpose. Not only is unlimited ownership an anathema to civilized culture, but the very conception that the living being can own anything in this world is one of the main illusions of *maya*. A spiritually progressive culture educates its citizens as to the danger of this impulse and provides ways and means for them to minimize the tendency.

The word owner implies a controller. If you own a house or an automobile for example, you control it. You possess the keys and it is for your exclusive use. But how did you obtain ownership of it? You either created it, or you traded something of value (generally money) with the creator or previous owner. The first owner was the manufacturer who assembled its thousands of parts into a functional whole. But where did he get the raw materials for those parts? Naturally they could only have come from the earth. Who owns the earth and its resources? This question is one of the most, perhaps *the* most, significant question of economic theory, because the answer forms the basis of how we conduct the remainder of our economic affairs.

We may claim that nobody owns the earth because nobody created the earth and her resources are therefore ours for the taking. This is the position of atheists who exploit the earth for their own personal advantage. Others may claim that God created the world, but He created it for our use, and therefore her resources are ours for the taking. Even though belief in God may be expressed, the end result of these two positions is the same—people attempt to unlimitedly exploit the resources of nature, taking more than their fair share, without further consideration. There is a third position—understanding that God created the world for the benefit of all of his children—all the living beings who are here by His arrangement who are thus entitled to their due. This is the position we find in the Vedic literature which is explained with the following example.

Suppose a person is walking down the street and finds a wallet with $500 in it. There are different ways in which he can respond. He might say, it's not mine, and walk on leaving the wallet on the street. Or he might pick it up and say "hey, this is my lucky day!" taking the money for himself. Or he might understand that somebody lost this wallet and money, look for any identifying information in the wallet and attempt to return the wallet and money to the rightful owner.

The first person's detachment displays an artificial sense of renunciation. Although he does not steal the money, neither does he properly acknowledge its value, nor its owner. The second person, who takes the money, is obviously a thief. But the third person recognizing the value of what he has found, by attempting to return it to the proper owner, acts properly.

We can see the entire world in this way. Understanding that the person who creates something is its natural owner, we can understand that the person who created this world is its owner. That person is universally accepted as God. He is the owner and controller of everything as stated in Text 1 of the *Isopanisad* "Everything animate or inanimate that is within the universe is controlled and owned by the Lord. One should therefore accept only those things necessary for himself, which are set aside as his quota, and one should not accept other things, knowing well to whom they belong." This instruction, when followed, assures that everyone has what they need to live a decent life, because as the *Isopanisad* also tells us, God has arranged for the maintenance of all living beings. However, if someone takes more than their rightful allotment, others will be deprived of their necessities.

We may claim ownership for some time, but our ownership is extremely limited. One hundred years ago everything that was in this world was "owned" by somebody else. Where is their claim to ownership now? Null and void. As they died "ownership" passed to some other person, and when they die "ownership" again passes to another. In another hundred years everything we now "own" will be owned by somebody else, and what will become of our claim of ownership? Null and void. Therefore as admonished by the *Isopanisad* and *Bhagavad-gita* nothing of this world can truly be ours. First of all everything is already owned by God, and secondly anything we have is "ours" only for a short period of time. Our claim to ownership is therefore illusory. And since nothing actually belongs to us, then all of our attempts at exchange under this illusion, including the dealings of the vast global marketplace of which we hear so much about, amounts to nothing more than a den of thieves who are working cooperatively to exchange the booty to their own satisfaction.

Personal individual ownership seems natural because our *ahankara*, our false ego, is hinged on the concepts of "I and mine," and the "mine" part of the false ego is naturally attracted to the idea of possession. Thinking that we own any amount, whether the pauper's penny or the capitalist's billion dollars, betrays the same mentality. Many writers have commented on the vast inequalities resulting from unlimited personal private ownership and have argued for limitations as to what a man may claim as his. But by the Vedic standard any consciousness of ownership is to be avoided as one would avoid a disease. From the spiritual perspective it is not the amount that is significant, but the false consciousness of ownership that keeps the *atma* trapped in this material world of repeated birth and death.

The materialistic economic philosophies in the world are in direct opposition to the instructions of *Isopanisad*, regardless of the banner they fly: capitalist, communist, or socialist. The capitalist claims extensive resources as his own, or that of his corporation, which means they are under the control of the person who owns the majority of the corporation's shares. The communists claim that the resources belong to the state, which actually means they are under the control of the person who is the representative of the state. Both of these systems aim at usurping the property of the Lord to place it in the control of a few. Although they are typically thought of as being in philosophical opposition they are identical in their effort to usurp the property of the Lord and place it into the hands of a favored minority. The socialists claim that everyone is the owner. This is closer to the truth but it also misses the point, because they also fail to recognize that the resources belong to God. Likewise, most people today assert their claim over whatever resources, land, buildings, consumer goods, and animals they can acquire. Since all of us are acculturated with this understanding, it seems to be the most natural thing in the world. But if we stop to ponder the question for just a minute or two, we can understand that nothing in this world can belong to any of us in the true sense of the word. We come into this world with nothing and leave with nothing. In between any claim we might make to anything as "ours" is simply our illusion—the influence of *maya*.

We are entitled that that which is necessary to maintain our lives in a decent manner, as the *Isopanisad* (text 2) encourages, adding that this way of living is fully sustainable: "One may aspire to live for hundreds of years if he continuously goes on working in that way, for that sort of work will not bind him to the law of *karma*. There is no alternative to this way for man." To say that there is no alternative means that there is no sustainable alternative. No successful, happy and lasting alternative. If we follow the Vedas, seeing everything in relationship to the Lord and acknowledge that He has given us what we require to live, we can adjust to what, from the materialist's perspective, appear to be limitations. This is accomplished by rising above a limited material vision and living on the plane of transcendence. Srila Prabhupada explains this plan of the Lord:

To be poor in this world is a curse for ordinary people, those under the concept of material life, whereas the spiritually enriched have nothing to do with the poverty or wealth of this world. The living entities are not meant to be poverty-stricken, because they are part and parcel of the Supreme Lord, the supreme proprietor. Every living entity has the birthright to enjoy God's property, just as the son inherits the property of the father. That is the law. But under the spell of illusion we have forgotten our relationship with the supreme father; therefore we are suffering.[6]

The spiritually enriched know their proper relationship with this world as well as the science of achieving spiritual satisfaction and liberation from the material conceptions of life. Thus they do not crave unnecessary amounts of material goods. They are happy to use what they need, to possess it as long as they can make productive use of it, and afterward pass it along to someone else.

Individual ownership is the cornerstone of the economics of atheism. Accepting the concept of personal private ownership leads to a world divided with everyone's interest separated from that of all others. It then becomes every man for himself, which is a lonely, lonely place. Attempts to live this illusion as reality entangle us in an enigmatic web of insolvable problems.

We Do Not Create the Results of Our Activities

We briefly considered another one of the illusory foundational concepts of modern economics—ownership of the results of our activities—in the discussion of "I and mine" above. Let's explore the idea further here and expose it as a false assumption that supports atheistic economics.

Everyone works for some result, and because they have worked for that result they lay claim to it as theirs. But Sri Krishna informs us that we are not the cause of the result of our activities, and as such we cannot consider ourselves as the rightful owners of what we produce (2.47):

> You are entitled to perform your prescribed duty but you are not entitled to the fruits of action. *Never consider yourself to be the cause of the results of your activities*, and never be attached to not doing your duty.

Krishna also explains why we have no claim over what we produce (3.27):

> The spirit soul bewildered by the influence of false ego thinks himself the doer of activities that are in actuality carried out by the three modes of material nature.

Contrary to what we think, the results of our actions are made manifest by the actions of the modes of nature, or *daivi maya*, and not by our actions alone. An example will help to make this clear. Many people with good talent, ability, and work ethic engage in business, however most are not successful and a great majority fail within the first several years despite their earnest desire and hard work. Why? There must be something besides our actions alone that explains the success of one person and the failure of another. That something is our *karma* which gives or restricts the results according to our activities in previous lifetimes. *Karma* may be thought of as a kind of personal bank balance that accounts for both good and bad actions and from which we "withdraw" enjoyment or suffering. The dispensation of these results is managed by the *devatas*, or demigods, the controllers of the universal affairs. Although we may desire some result and work hard to attain it, if it is not within our *karma* it will not be attained. If it is within our *karma* and is attained, then we should understand that the result is given by the material energy, or *gunas*, and is not a product of our efforts alone.

Since it is the material energy that gives us the result of our actions we have no claim to them as ours. If out of ignorance we lay claim to them we create further *karma*. Krishna refers to such persons as misers. A miser is a person who does not know the proper value of something and therefore misuses it, the most common example being money. Money has utility when it is circulated and put to use, but misers store up money instead, and are very reluctant to use it even if they are in need. Another kind of miser does not know the value of action, which when performed in the proper consciousness will bring the wonderful result of spiritual emancipation. But the miserly person performing actions in the consciousness of "I and mine," with attachment to the results, instead generates further bondage to this material world under the law of *karma*.

Claiming the results of action as our own is another illusory yet foundational principle of modern economics. How the results of action are created will be explained in more detail in the chapter on *Karma* (Volume 2).

The Fallacy of Selfish Serving

In *An Inquiry into the Nature and Causes of the Wealth of Nations* Adam Smith's arguments are for selfish concerns, that is, how one side may increase their wealth, often at the expense of others, or at least without regard for the welfare of others. In Book IV he deals with international trade. There he writes about what has become known as "comparative advantage"—that each location due to natural endowments will have an advantage in producing a particular item more efficiently and at less cost. These goods, Smith contends, should be allowed to find their market, and should not be restricted from a domestic market despite the fact that they may be foreign produced. His arguments form the basis of what has been relentlessly pushed in the last two decades as "free trade."

Smith attempts to convince the reader that the allowance of such unrestricted trade enables all of the desirables and needs of society to be provided much more completely than could be accomplished by any planning commission. His argument is meant to disparage a command economy wherein men of limited capability attempt to control vast markets and the innumerable variety of goods therein by restricting or encouraging certain aspects of trade. Smith eschews protectionism of taxes and tariffs that are typically imposed in order to nurture domestic developing industries.

How and where should capital be employed to bring the most effective good? He answers this question saying: "every individual, it is evident, can, in his local situation, judge much better than any statesman or lawgiver can do for him. The statesman, who should attempt to direct private people in what manner they ought to employ their capitals, would not only load himself with a most unnecessary attention, but assume an authority which could safely be trusted, not only to no single person, but to no council or senate whatever, and which would no-where be so dangerous as in the hands of a man who had folly and presumption enough to fancy himself fit to exercise it."[7]

As each of these individuals work for their own self-interest and seize the opportunities before them which they alone may recognize, the overall interests of society are served. It is as if they are "led by an invisible hand to promote an end which was no part of his intention. Nor is it always the worse for the society that it was no part of it. By pursuing his own interest he frequently promotes that of the society." This sole reference to the phrase "invisible hand" in Wealth of Nations marked its entrance into the economic lexicon. What Smith actually intended by this concept is explained more simply by another capitalist maxim: "find a need and fill it."[8] Millions of men capturing the opportunities they find before them provide the best and most efficient way to serve the myriad needs of society.

Smith's argument in regard to the fulfillment of the needs of the marketplace is valid. The dismal results of the command economies of the former Soviet Union have amply demonstrated the inability of the planned economy to do what millions of independent eyes, ears, and desires did much better in free market economies; the empty shelves of the few stores in the Soviet Union compared with the almost unlimited variety and number of goods in numerous Western stores tallying the score.

Perhaps predictably due to the influence of *rajo-guna* and *tamo-guna*, Smith's arguments have been misinterpreted and misapplied to justify the selfish behavior and neglect of vast numbers of society. People too often hear what they want to hear. Commonly Smith's maxim is translated as the belief that an invisible hand automatically turns selfish greed into public benefit, as if to justify selfishness and greed.

Perhaps the language he chooses betrays an instinctual lust for profit, and many are thus encouraged to read him in that way, but the concept of the invisible hand as he presents it can as easily be understood in a way that does not imply that greed is good. The idea of the invisible hand is that men acting independently and without interference can fulfill their wants and needs. Men everywhere experience needs which they understand as common. If they have a need others also have the same need, because human beings after all are similar in every culture. Fulfilling that need provides them with their livelihood and simultaneously serves the needs of others. This is what is meant when Smith says "by pursuing his own interest he frequently promotes that of the society."

This is not the manner in which Smith's doctrine is typically promoted. Instead current economic theory holds that pure self-interest leads to the greater good for all through the 'invisible hand of the market'. This interpretation implicitly justifies all of the many ills of modern business practices: illegal and ruthless competition, economic policies that externalize costs to workers, the public, the environment, or future generations, huge gaps between haves and have-nots, poverty, hunger, and violence—all of the qualities of the economics of ignorance. It is not Adam Smith's argument that I take issue with, but this type of interpretation.

The argument that pure self-interest leads to the greater good for all through the invisible hand of the market is too often thought of as some sort of Zen maxim that must be correct but exactly how that happens is beyond our understanding. That interpretation may be useful for those who want to justify their wanton behavior, but to say that an action results in the greater good of all, is not to make a nebulous argument. Goodness has very specific qualities as we have already explained: mercy, generosity, charity, being embarrassed at improper action, seeing the equality of all living beings, and so on. If the greater good is actually being served then we must see that result in practice. Since we do not, but instead see the opposite, then judging by the result tells us that this interpretation of Smith is wrong. Moreover this interpretation is narcissistic, and by the calculation of the *Bhagavad-gita*, demonic.

The proper interpretation of an invisible hand is the hand of God who regulates the functions of the universe and sees to the maintenance of all living beings. *Nityo nityanam chetanas chetananam*—there is one eternal being who is the maintainer of all others.[9] Although we cannot perceive directly how God is taking care of everyone, by His wonderful arrangement this is taking place.

Acknowledging God and His invisible hand can bring us closer to a state of harmony and help solve the economic problems, but the illusory invisible hand of the market can only create and further contribute to the extreme economic problems that face the world today.

Corporations Are Real, Necessary and Beneficial

The corporation has been a tool for the profit of some by the efforts of others since its inception and remains so to this day. Special privileges were granted by the King of England to form the East India Company and the Hudson Bay Company so that the shareholders, primarily the King, could enjoy the profits generated by these ventures. Corporations continue to enjoy privileges not available to an individual person for the same reasons. Chief among these privileges are favorable tax structures, or no taxes at all; the anonymity provided to both the owners, and managers who act not in their own name, but in the name of the corporation; and separation of the owners and workers by means of a management structure, preventing the workers from taking action directly and personally against the owners in cases of disagreements over working conditions, pay scales, and so on. Corporations are an extension of the social engineering that began in the 15th century in the transition toward the economics of ignorance.

Corporations are an illusion of modern society because they have no existence in fact. They are a fiction agreed to by those who hold power; the rest of us merrily go along with the established order as we do with the other fictions, accepting them as a given fact of life. But they are not a fact of life. We think of them as reality because we have been acculturated to do this from the time we were children, and they simply become a part of things that "are." Some "out-of-the-box" thinkers such as futurist Buckminster Fuller have understood the game for what it is. In his essay *The Grunch of Giants*, he explains: "Corporations are neither physical nor metaphysical phenomena. They are socioeconomic ploys—legally enacted game-playing—agreed upon only between overwhelmingly powerful socioeconomic individuals and by them imposed upon human society and all of its unwitting members."

Given the nature and purpose of the corporation it is one of the pillars of the economics of atheism. If the idea of atheism is to forget God, to allow us to think of ourselves as God, that is, to be a law unto ourselves, then the creation of corporations can be seen as an effort of people to act as if they were God. They think: God creates and destroys. So can we. God grants life and brings death. So can we. God creates eternal beings with qualities that transcend normal reality, and so can we? In the creation of corporations we do. The creation of a corporation can even be seen as a material attempt to create a spiritual being.

Compare them: the spirit soul is a non-material, eternal entity, and the corporation is a non-material, eternal entity (they have no expiration). The soul should live in a state of bliss with no effort expended to achieve that state, while the corporation delivers unearned profits with no effort expended by the owner so that he can have material bliss (as in Robert Nelson's idea of heaven). If the *atma* is eternal and transcendental to all material considerations, the corporation is also a supernal entity beyond many laws that apply to most ordinary people. Corporations can also be seen as an effort to become the Supersoul by being in many places at once and having many people act in "their interest" simultaneously. Just as God creates and gives us a body, the word corporation implies a body, since it is derived from the Latin *corpus*, which means body, or *corporâtus*, to make into a body.

Artificial Persons Rise Above Real Persons

Early in the history of corporations in the United States (nineteenth century and earlier) corporations were highly regulated and it was not uncommon for corporate charters to be revoked when they adversely impacted the common welfare. It was illegal for corporations to participate in the political process—corporations couldn't vote, and neither were they allowed to try to influence votes. It was illegal for corporations to lie about their products, and their books and processes were required to be open to government inspectors. Both the States and the Federal Government were able to investigate if workers were harmed or hazardous conditions created.

The tycoons of business found these conditions too confining. They wanted to be free to act as they pleased, and sought the ways and means of doing so. The answer came with the victory of the north over the south at the end of the civil war. Then in 1868 the Fourteenth Amendment to the Constitution was enacted to provide full constitutional protection of law to the now-emancipated former slaves. By this and the Thirteenth Amendment all human beings were to be recognized as real persons, independent citizens, and not the property or chattel of another person.

At that time the railroads were the greatest corporations and they sought to take advantage of these amendments and repeatedly sued various states, counties, and towns in which they argued that corporations were artificially created persons and entitled to the same privileges and protection of law that natural persons enjoyed. For example, they claimed that they were being treated as different "classes of persons" because different railroad properties were being taxed in different ways in different places, and that this constituted illegal discrimination under the Fourteenth Amendment. Need we point out that this argument has no basis in fact? What exactly is an "artificial person?" Has anybody ever seen one? There is no such thing in reality and the effort to impose this idea on us is nothing more than an effort to hoodwink us into accepting illusion as reality. To their credit they have been very successful.

They continued their legal assault for some twenty years reaching a zenith in 1877 when four cases were brought to the Supreme Court attempting to achieve corporate personhood. In each of these cases, the Court ruled that the railroad's arguments pertained to interstate commerce which was not applicable to the Fourteenth Amendment; therefore the courts would not rule that corporations were persons.

But in 1886, with a sleight of hand so characteristic of *Kali*, that victory was achieved in another tax issue: the Santa Clara County versus The Union Pacific Railroad. The victory came not by the decision of the judges, but simply by the notation of a court clerk J. C. Bancroft Davis, who happened to be the former president of a small railroad. Davis wrote into his headnote, which is a commentary that clerks write about each case, that the Chief Justice had said that all the Justices agreed that corporations are persons. He wrote this although he knew that the justices had not ruled on that specific issue in the case.[10] This headnote had no legal standing but was accepted as such by later judges under the color of law.

But corporations are not ordinary persons. They don't die, they possess the non-human ability to be in many places at the same time, they increasingly have the ability to avoid liability, given their economic clout they can define the laws under which they live, they don't pay taxes as ordinary people do, and they have shown themselves to have little sense of moral responsibility, with many being recidivist criminals.

Let me back that up with several examples. As far as influencing the laws that pertain to them, over the past 30 years the automobile industry has endeavored to block legislation that would impose criminal penalties on pre-meditated and willful violations of the federal auto safety laws. The result is that only civil fines are imposed and few, if any, executives, making decisions that affect the lives of people are indicted and convicted for their morally irresponsible actions.

As far as not paying taxes, consider that incorporating in Delaware, which is the legal home of more than 50% of all U.S. publicly-traded companies and 58% of the Fortune 500, has the following advantages:

> There is no state corporate income tax in Delaware on goods or services provided by Delaware corporations operating outside of Delaware. There is no state corporate tax on interest or other investment income in Delaware, when earned by a Delaware holding company. Delaware has no ad-value or value-added tax (VAT). There is no State of Delaware inheritance tax on stock of Delaware

corporations operating outside of Delaware held by non-residents of Delaware. Delaware also has a separate court system for corporate law that doesn't involve juries. The advantage of this is that companies don't have to worry about juries [ordinary people] deciding corporate cases. Instead, a judge who is familiar with corporate law oversees the case. And Delaware corporations also have a special "Director Shield" that permits corporations to shelter their directors from personal liability in connection with their actions as board members.

Corporations are Recidivist Criminals.

Because of this personal legal shield, the anonymity of the corporate structure, their immense financial and political power, and the resources to defend themselves in courts of law and in the court of public opinion, the executives of big corporations thumb their noses at the law with impunity. And as we demonstrated in the last chapter they often have the government paving the way for their activities around the world. If the company is found guilty of wrongdoing, fines may be imposed, but rarely will the decision maker be faced with jail. When shielded from penal consequences, people with a criminal consciousness are far more likely to repeatedly engage in criminal behavior in order to derive some gain. After all, there is nothing to stop them!

On the average some 60 percent of the leading corporations are habitual criminals, as shown by an in-depth investigation of sixty-eight of the largest American companies in mid-20th century. Having an average life of 45 years, there were a total of 980 decisions against them with a maximum of fifty for one, and an average of fourteen convictions per corporation. In all there were 307 adverse decisions on restraining trade, 97 on misrepresentation, 222 on infringement of law, 158 on unfair labor practices, 66 on rebate fraud and 130 on other cases.[11]

The situation has not improved in time. In the 1990s, of the one hundred largest corporate criminals in terms of convictions and fines paid ($150,000 or more) in the United States alone: thirty-eight engaged in environmental crimes, twenty in antitrust activity (price-fixing, stifling competition), thirteen in fraud (excessive charges, generally on government contracts), seven in campaign finance violations, six in food and drug violations, and four in financial crimes. During the decade many pled guilty to more than one crime.[12]

In the wake of the sub-prime mortgage-lending fiasco that is said to be the cause of the current economic woes of America, although the FBI has arrested more than 1500 mortgage brokers, developers and real estate agents on charges of fraud, only two on Wall Street were charged [13]

Taking Off the Corporate Mask

With a good deal of justification the corporation has become the favorite whipping boy for those calling for economic justice over the past two decades. Following David Korten's compelling critique of unrestrained corporate cultural dominance in *When Corporations Rule the World*, dozens of other books have brought similar charges, and there is now a movement to rescind the legal status of corporate personhood. This is a step in the right direction. The next step is to understand that there is no corporation, but only real people acting semi-anonymously in the name of a corporation. We hear about how "Monsanto" creates and pushes genetically modified foods on an unwilling populace, or how the "IMF" impoverishes people with their SAPs, how "Company B" (military jargon) commits atrocities on a conquered people, or how "Shell Oil Company" pollutes the environment in Africa. But none of these "companies" do these things. It is only people who make the decisions, it is people who carry out those decisions, and it's only individual people who carry out the atrocities. There is no IMF, there are only people who act in the name of IMF. There is no Monsanto, but only people who act in the name of Monsanto. There is no Shell Oil, United States Army, IBM, Microsoft, General Electric, etc., etc., etc., but only individual people who act in the name of those fictions. There is also no corporate crime. Any crime done by "corporations" can only be done by individual people acting in the name of the corporation.

There once was a time when there were no corporations, and life was in many ways much better for that fact. In that time people lived more simply generally serving their own purposes directly. Can we return to such a world? Of course we can—if enough people are willing to let go of the illusion and live in reality. People can act in their own name and for their own purposes if they are given the opportunity to do so. And if we want to heal the world, that is what people everywhere must do—stop playing "make believe" and live in reality.

Economics' Black Box

In science there is a concept called the "black box." This name is given to any function or process that is mysteriously unknown or unknowable, and every field of science has many such black boxes. A good example of a black box that most of us can understand is a computer. We may know how to use it, but what goes on inside when we push the keys is a complete mystery.

The field of economics also has a black box that almost nobody seems to understand, but to which everyone pays very close attention. That black box is also another of modern economics' illusions. Of course this black box is considered a reality, and because people treat it as such it has very real effects on their behavior. The black box of economics is paper money.

All persons now living were born into a world that uses paper money. So common is the experience that we normalize it as a de facto part of our existence. It is common and constant and seems as real as the air and sun. But very few people ever trouble themselves to learn where money comes from and how it works. German economist Silvio Gessel wrote in his 1911 book, *The Natural Economic Order*: "the indifference of the general public, of science, of the press, of business men, to monetary theory is so great that it would be difficult to collect among the millions of the German population a dozen persons for a serious discussion of the subject." The same applies everywhere even today. Most people simply do their best to get what they can within the limits of their moral understanding of life.

However familiar money may be to us, and however legitimized it may be in our minds, the fact is that it works against the interests of almost everyone on the planet to the advantage of the already very wealthy few. For the average person it is a scourge that enslaves him more completely than iron shackles ever could and without his even being aware of the fact.

Paper money is perhaps the main tool of the purveyors of evil and is fit for *Kali-yuga*—posing as something benign when it is actually quite insidious. It has many destructive effects which we will give some detail to below. A complete explanation of the origin, manipulation and machinations of paper money is beyond the scope of this book however. That discussion has filled many volumes some of which are referenced in Appendix D for the interested reader. In this discussion we will confine ourselves to the illusory nature of this "wealth" and its destructive effects on people individually and collectively.

The Value of Paper Money is an Illusion

You may protest this heading since the money that is in your wallet is indeed real and since it can purchase goods that have value, the money itself must have value. What you have in your possession are some pieces of paper with ink on them in various artful and official looking designs. What you call money has no intrinsic worth, and any value it has is only what you and others place in it. Paper money works, and will remain only as long as everyone agrees to its value. The fact is that people are interested in paper money because it promises them the possibility of obtaining what they actually want some time in the future. Notice in that sentence the words "promises" and "possibility." These two words also indicate that what you want may *not* be obtained by money because the value of paper money may change at any time or become worthless altogether. Paper money offers no absolute guarantee that you will later be able to get what you want at the price you expected. The fluctuation of the value of currencies is a daily discussion in economic pages of newspapers, and for some countries the change of its relative value it is more extreme than for others.

When I was a child a loaf of bread cost 25 cents. Today the same loaf of bread costs $4.00. A loaf of bread always has constant value—feeding hungry stomachs—so the value of the bread has not changed in all of those fifty years; instead it is the value of the dollar that has changed. In more recent times compare the value of the dollar to the euro. When the euro was created in 1999 the euro was worth $0.86 U.S., and a few months later it fell to $0.77. By 2008 the situation had reversed and one dollar can only purchase 0.6 euros. But this more than 50% drop in the value of the dollar pales in comparison to Zimbabwe for example, where the official inflation rate in January 2008 stood at 100,580%! (one hundred thousand, five hundred eighty percent) and the value of that currency changes by the minute. Under such circumstances a ten kilometer taxi ride costs 90 billion dollars, and additional school fees for children in 2008 are one hundred billion Zimbabwean dollars![14]

There have been many, many episodes in history when the value of money has been entirely lost to the great dismay of its holders, and there are lessons from all over the world. This story from American, Douglas Herman's experiences in Brazil during the 1980s is representative:

> At the time I arrived, you received three Cruzados Novo for each American dollar. This new "novo cruzado" was stamped with a triangle designating its new value—or devaluation—over the old 1,000 cruzado note. In 1989, the Brazilian government decided to drop three zeros and change the name of the currency henceforth to Cruzado Novo. Since then the currency has been changed yet again to the Real. Frequently, on my walks, I would see large paper bills, 50,000 or 100,000 "old" Cruzeiros, in the gutter, but after awhile I never picked up any more money. I found it wasn't even worth a fraction of a cent.[15]

The change in the value of a currency is dependent on government policy, because it is the government's printing more and more money, or debasing the currency, that is the cause of inflation. Since the value of paper money is so ephemeral, it cannot be considered a proper store of wealth. Other things, such as wheat never change in value because their value is the same everywhere in the world at all times.

The Aura of Mystique

It may well be that the confusion Gessel wrote about exists because it has been deliberately created. Friedrich List, a contemporary of Adam Smith, accused Smith of deliberate obfuscation. He said of Smith's *Wealth of Nations*:

"Americans have to understand that his system, considered as a whole, is so confused and distracted, as if the principal aim of his books were not to enlighten nations, but to confuse them for the benefit of his own country."[16] The charge has been made by Dr. J. W. Smith that this is indeed the case, and that Smith's philosophy is being promoted in the name of free trade while the protectionist philosophy of Friedrich List is practiced by the "first-world countries." Some establishment economists are forthright enough to spell it out clearly. The venerated economist John Kenneth Galbraith informs us that "the study of money, above all other fields in economics, is the one in which complexity is used to disguise truth or to evade truth, not to reveal it."[17]

Recently retired Chairman of America's Federal Reserve Bank, Alan Greenspan, confessed that it was his deliberate intention to obscure the truth. In an interview on the television show "60 Minutes" regarding his statements about the economy and his actions as the Chairman of the Federal Reserve Bank, Greenspan admitted with a chuckle: "I would engage in some form of syntax destruction, which sounded as though I were answering the question, but, in fact, had not." Listening to a quote of himself saying "Modest pre-emptive actions can obviate the need of more drastic actions at a later date, and that could destabilize the economy," he commented, "Very profound." Indeed. As well as unintelligible, and as he admits, meaningless.

There have been a few attempts to go behind the shroud of mystery surrounding money. One timid effort in this regard was William Grieder's 1987 book *Secrets of the Temple: How the Federal Reserve Runs the Country.* There Greider uses Nelson's ideas of economics as religion as a literary device for explaining the mystique:

> To modern minds it seemed bizarre to think of the Federal Reserve as a religious institution. Yet the conspiracy theorists, in their own demented way, were on to something real and significant. The Fed did also function in the realm of religion. Its mysterious powers of money creation, inherited from priestly forebears, shielded a complex bundle of social and psychological meanings. With its own form of secret incantation, the Federal Reserve presided over awesome social ritual, transactions so powerful and frightening they seemed to lie beyond common understanding...Above all, money was a function of faith. It required implicit and universal social consent that was indeed mysterious. To create money and use it, each one must believe, and everyone must believe. Only then did worthless pieces of paper take on value.

Why the obfuscation? Because most people would be livid with rage to know how the debt-money system operates. As Mr. Henry Ford put it: "It is well enough that the people of the nation do not understand our banking and monetary system, for if they did, I believe there would be a revolution before tomorrow morning."[18] Why? Because it is nothing less than a very sophisticated cheating system designed to enslave everyone, and as people find out how the money system actually works it does make them angry. It has the stamp of *Kali* all over it.

How the Money System Works

A very brief (and very incomplete) summary of the creation of money will help. The following is taken from a lecture given by Edward Griffin author of *The Creature from Jekyll Island,* a book that documents in detail the creation of the Federal Reserve Bank (the central bank) of the United States and explains our money system. This illustration pertains to the United States in particular but the money and banking system operates the same way in every country in the world, with the exception of Iran, North Korea, Sudan, Cuba and Libya, which, interestingly, just happen to be a part of George W. Bush's "Axis of Evil."[19] Griffin tells us:

> I want to assure you that in spite of the simple language everything I'm going to tell you is absolutely 100% technically accurate. The other thing I want to warn you about is don't try and make sense out of this because it can't be done; this does not make sense and you'll blow a fuse trying to make it make sense. Just remember that it is a scam and if you keep that fact in mind then you'll have no trouble comprehending what's going on.

> Here's how it works. It starts with the government side of the partnership; it starts in Congress which is spending money like crazy. It spends far more money than it takes in. How can it do that? Basically this is what happens. Let's say Congress needs an extra billion dollars today so it goes to the treasury and says 'we want a billion dollars' and the treasury official says 'you guys have got to be kidding, we don't have any money here, everything that we've taken in taxes you fellows have spent by March.' Then they get the idea that they'll borrow the money. So they stop at the printing office but they don't print money at the printing office, they print certificates of different sorts. They're very fancy things with borders on the edge with an eagle across the top and a seal at the bottom and it says 'US

Government Bond' or 'Note' or 'Bill' depending on the length of the maturity of it. It should really say 'IOU' because that's what it is.

They go further down the street to the Federal Reserve "Bank." The Fed has been waiting for them—that's one of the reasons it was created. By the time they get inside the Federal Reserve building the officer is pulling out his checkbook and he writes a check to the US Treasury for one billion dollars, or whatever the amount they need. He signs the check and gives it to the treasury official.

We need to stop here for a minute and ask a question. Where did they get a billion dollars to give to the treasury? Who put that money into the account at the Federal Reserve System? The amazing answer is there is no money in the account at the Federal Reserve System. In fact, technically, there isn't even an account, there is only a checkbook. That's all. That billion dollars springs into being at precisely the instant the officer signs that check and that is called 'monetizing the debt,' that's the phrase they throw at you. That means they simply wrote a check for which they had no funds. If you and I were to do that we would go to jail, but they can do it because Congress wants them to do it. They are in this thing together. In fact, this is the payoff, this is the benefit to the government—it gets instant access to any amount of money at any time without having to go to the taxpayer directly and justify it or ask for it. Otherwise, they would have to come to the taxpayer and say we're going to raise your taxes another $3,000 this year and of course if they did that, they would be voted out of office. There in a nutshell is the reason the government likes this method—easy instant access to any amount of money of any kind without the taxpayer being directly involved.

But what about the banking side? This is where it really gets interesting. Let's go back to that billion dollar check. The treasury official deposits the check into the government's checking account and all of a sudden the computers start to click and it shows that the government has a billion dollar deposit meaning that it can now write a billion dollars in checks against that deposit which it starts to do real fast. For the sake of our analysis, let's just follow $100 out of that billion in a check that for some reason they write to the fellow that delivers the mail to our door. The postal worker gets a check for $100 and he looks at this thing and he can't imagine in his wildest dreams that that money didn't exist two days ago anywhere in the universe. As long as he can spend it, he wouldn't even care if you told him. He deposits it now into his personal checking account. Now we're finally out of the Federal Reserve and out of the government's check and into the private banking system.

We're finally now able to show that part of the partnership which is the banking cartel. A $100 deposit has now been made in the local bank and the banker sees that and runs over to the loan window and opens it up and says "attention, everybody, we have money to loan, someone just deposited $100." Everyone is overjoyed at that because that's one of the reasons they come to the bank, they come to borrow money. It's a sign of national health if you're in debt, so they're happy to know that the bank has money to loan. They heard the banker and they say $100 that's not very much and he says not to worry we can loan up to $900 based on that $100 deposit. How can that be done? It gets complicated the way they do it so I'll tell you in very simple terms. The Federal Reserve System requires that the banks hold no less than 10% of their deposits in reserve. The bank loans out $900 and holds 10% in reserve, that's $100.

It's only a $100 deposit but it creates $900 more in loans. Where did the $900 come from? The answer is the same—there was no money before the loan, but this $900 springs into existence precisely at the point at which the loan is made. When the money is created out of nothing for the government it is spent by the government, and the government pays interest on it. On the banking side it's created out of nothing, loaned by the banks to you and to me, and we have to pay them interest on it. Think about this for a minute. This money was created out of nothing and yet they collect interest on it which means that they collect interest on nothing. Not too shabby! What a concept! I wish I had a magic checkbook like that where I could just write checks all day long even though I didn't have to have any money, loan it to you folks and you would be silly enough to pay me interest on it. That's how it works...

Another interesting thing about this is that the bank loans you money which it created out of nothing—it cost nothing to make it—but they want something from you. They want you to sign on the dotted line and pledge your house, your car, your inventory, your assets, so that in case for any reason you cannot continue to make your payments they get all of your assets. They're not going to lose anything on this.

Whether it's expansion or contraction, inflation or deflation the banks are covered and we go right along with it because we haven't figured it out, we don't know that this is a scam. Of course we have no choice either right now because it's all enforced by law. We have no choice so it's probably better that we don't understand it because then we won't complain about it either.[20]

The fact that money is created from nothing by banks has been confirmed many times by people in a position to know. Graham Towers, Governor of the Bank of Canada from 1935 to 1955, acknowledged: "Banks create money. The manufacturing process to make money consists of making an entry in a book. That is all...Each and every time a Bank makes a loan...new Bank credit is created—brand new money."[21]

Robert B. Anderson, Secretary of the Treasury under Eisenhower, said in an interview reported in the August 31, 1959 issue of *U.S. News and World Report*: "[W]hen a bank makes a loan, it simply adds to the borrower's deposit account in the bank by the amount of the loan. The money is not taken from anyone else's deposit; it was not previously paid into the bank by anyone. It's new money, created by the bank for the use of the borrower."

And Sir Josiah Stamp, president of the Bank of England and the second richest man in Britain in the 1920s declared in an address at the University of Texas in 1927: "The modern banking system manufactures money out of nothing. The process is perhaps the most astounding piece of sleight of hand that was ever invented. Banking was conceived in inequity and born in sin...Bankers own the earth. Take it away from them but leave them the power to create money, and, with a flick of a pen, they will create enough money to buy it back again.... Take this great power away from them and all great fortunes like mine will disappear, and then this would be a better and happier world to live in...But, if you want to continue to be the slaves of bankers and pay the cost of your own slavery, then let bankers continue to create money and control credit."

The Federal Reserve Bank was created by an act of Congress in 1913. Woodrow Wilson who was president at that time later regretted his role in bringing the bank about. Regarding this, he later said: "I am a most unhappy man. I have unwittingly ruined my country. A great industrial Nation is controlled by its system of credit. Our system of credit is concentrated. The growth of the Nation and all our activities are in the hands of a few men. We have come to be one of the worst ruled, one of the most completely controlled and dominated Governments in the world — no longer a Government of free opinion, no longer a Government by conviction and vote of the majority, but a Government by the opinion and duress of small groups of dominant men."[22]

It is important to point out that the Federal Reserve Bank is not a government organization but is a private corporation owned by member banks which are in turn owned by private individuals.[23] Thus there is a small coterie of people who have the privilege of creating money which they loan at interest to the governments of the world. Among them are the Rothschild family, whose patriarch Mayer Amschel Rothschild (1744–1812) is quoted as having said "Give me control of a nation's money and I care not who makes her laws." No less a figure than Presidential Candidate and Congressman Ron Paul made it a pledge of his campaign to abolish the Federal Reserve Bank. He stated: "We must have sound money, and not a giant counterfeiting machine called the Federal Reserve that causes recessions and inflation."

Paper money is a game in which the money masters win and the people of the world lose, yet we continually go on playing it despite its disadvantages. Why? Because of our own envy and greed. We are controlled by our own bad qualities that permit the elite to manipulate us. This is explained by none other than that master manipulator Adolph Hitler: "The great masses of the people in the very bottom of their hearts tend to be corrupted, rather than purposely or consciously evil...therefore...they more easily fall a victim to a big lie than to a little one, since they themselves lie in little things, but would be ashamed of lies that were too big."

If we can rise above our lower nature it would be possible to throw off the yoke of monetary slavery and become established in freedom. The *Bhagavad-gita* advocates becoming free from the base qualities of lust, envy, and greed. As hopeless as the situation may seem it is not at all impossible.

Is Paper Money a Necessary Feature of an Economy?

The above discussion should call into question the practices, if not the necessity of, paper money. Can a better system not be developed? Of course it can, and there are many people who think long and hard about how to do just that. Alternatives proposed include government sponsored methods such as: government issued fiat paper currency not based on debt, government issued paper currency that is backed by a commodity such as gold or grain, and government issued precious metal currency. But private currencies issued by individuals to serve their own communities have become increasingly popular in more recent years. There are a variety of these virtual and local currencies that are created by the people and for the people such as LETS (Local Employment and Trading System) developed by Canadian Michael Linton in use in more than a thousand communities around the world, Ithaca HOURS used in that New York community, and Time Dollars in which everyone earns the same rate for their work no matter whether they are a lawyer or a dishwasher, and many more.[24] We offer a spiritual alternative in volume two of this book. Many of these are very good ideas, are well thought out, and would work much better and more equitably than the current system. The local currency works as well as the government currency and for the exact same reason—everybody that participates agrees to accept it as a medium of exchange.

However all of these alternatives, with the exception of our concept of Spiritual Economics, continue to use and depend on at least some of the illusions of modern life. Additionally, all of those that would create a more equitable economy also require a modicum of *sattva-guna* in order to function effectively. And to make it a widespread economy many thousands of people would have to come to the standard of *sattva-guna*. We can solve that problem. More on that later.

The Problems with Money

The very effective tool of the economics of atheism is the debt-money system; a completely artificial system providing little advantage to the common man, yet having many disadvantages for both individuals and society. The insidious and pernicious nature of money was recognized by the Greek philosopher Sophocles in 450 BCE, not long after money as a medium of exchange first made its advent. He said: "money lays waste to cities. It sets men roaming from home. It seduces and corrupts honest men and turns virtue into baseness; It teaches villany and impiety." This opinion has been shared throughout the ages by many others, among them American Horace Greely who offered the same grim assessment: "While boasting of our noble deeds, we are careful to conceal the ugly fact that by an iniquitous money system we have nationalized a system of oppression in which, though more refined, is not less cruel than the old system to chattel slavery."

Now that we understand a bit about how paper money is created let's take a look at the problems that it introduces into our lives, personally and collectively.

Money imposes a debt burden on all people of the world

Modern money is called debt money because it is borrowed into existence. There is a very important feature of this money system that is often overlooked, and that is that although the money that is loaned is created by the loan, the interest that will be paid on that loan is not. This has significant implications for the economy, and important consequences for society. The first point is that there is not now, nor will there ever be, enough money in existence to fully pay off the debt created. A simple example helps to explain this. Let's say that the first $100 is the total amount of money created by a loan and that no other money is created. The terms of the loan are that the loan is to be repaid at 7 percent interest after one year. At the end of the year the loan is due and $107 must be returned. Where will that extra $7 come from? If it is not created by a loan it does not exist and cannot be repaid! This system is thus a "Ponzi scheme" that absolutely requires more and more loans in order to continue.[25] Such activity is illegal for ordinary people, but because the government has entered into collusion with the bankers, this one is protected by law. Since more borrowing is always required to continue this money system it is also rightfully called debt slavery. People must work longer hours or take two or three jobs in order to simply survive. Books are being written about the working poor and how the middle class is being robbed of their hard-earned money in innumerable ways.

Another important aspect of this system is that banks continually siphon money out of the economy through interest payments. If for any reason banks stop making new loans but continue to receive payment on old loans as agreed, the money supply increasingly dries up. Without sufficient money the economy begins to falter, and as the problem gets worse it is technically called a recession or depression. In such times some people lose their jobs, they can't make their payments on time, and the banks will claim the collateral that they pledged for their loans, their car or house, for example. This so-called business cycle does not happen by the vagaries of the market but is controlled by the expansion and contraction of the money supply.

A very telling aspect of our cultural conditioning is that we do not buy or sell without the official currency, despite the fact that people still have wants and needs and are willing to work. During the Great Depression of the 1930s for example, the Federal Reserve and member banks contracted credit (the money supply) which was the actual cause of the depression.[26] Without money men loitered in the street for want of work and goods wanted for buyers. But there are many ways to run an economy that do not depend on money whatsoever, and we looked at some of them in earlier chapters. . Can people get out of this box of cultural conditioning and act without the government leading them by the hand? For at least 20 years people have.

Money Distorts the Natural Social Order

The *varnashrama* social system is a natural social order based on inherent qualities of leadership. The higher social orders—*brahmana*, *ksatriya*, and *vaisya*—must all be endowed by *guna* and *karma*, natural qualities and ability, in addition they must also have a voluntary dedication to spiritual principles and goals, and a sincere interest in the welfare of others, both materially and spiritually. Proper training is also required. This social order functions successfully without ongoing political bickering to enact an ever-increasing number of laws, because all members voluntarily follow religious principles established by the Lord, found in the *dharma-shastras* such as *Manu-samhita, Kautiliya Arthashastra*, etc.

This proper social order, ordained by the Supreme Lord, has been perverted under the influence of the money culture in which mere possession of money commands the actions of others, to the great detriment of the entire world. Too often it is the greediest, lowest-class people who are interested only in money who rise to positions of authority, as though money itself were a qualification for leadership. It is not. Money allows the unrighteous to command the righteous, to bring others into consented slavery whereby people work for slave wages that cannot possibly provide for their needs.

The result is a society in which money buys people for any reason or any purpose. Money buys political influence subverting all political principles; money buys scientists and "scientific" conclusions; money buys entry into and graduation from schools; and money buys hundreds or even thousands of people working to discover selectively-beneficial technologies of dubious value, technologies that benefit a few at the expense of the many, such as terminator seeds and genetically modified foods.

Money Divides Us and Isolates Us from Each Other

As an artificial form of wealth, money has a tendency to divide people. It causes us to think in terms of "I and mine." Compare money to natural wealth such as food. Food tends to perish quickly and there is a natural tendency to share with others what might otherwise spoil. Money is typically thought to be a better store of wealth specifically because it does not (generally) perish. But at the same time it divides us. I have my money and you have yours, and our interests are thus divided. Recall please the earlier anecdote from Vibhavasu and his younger brother Supratika, and the earlier story of the Eskimos who lost their land due to a gift of almost a billion dollars from the United States government.

Money Gives the Impression That I can be Independent of Others

If I have money I may think that I am independent of others, but that's another illusion, because materially all of us are dependent on many thousands of other people. If the clerk doesn't go to work and the store is not open what can you buy? If the electrical engineer does not maintain the power house and fuel the boilers what will happen when you flip the wall switch? If the many thousands of people do not do their job to bring gasoline to your local fill-up station what good is your car? Practically everything we do in life is dependent on others, but if I have money I can easily think that I can do as I please and that I do not need anybody else. Money removes our ability to see our dependence on each other by separating producer and consumer by hundreds or thousands of miles.

The spiritual reality is that all of us are always dependent upon God. He controls this world, everything in it, and how long we are here. It is He who sees that everyone gets their due. Financial prosperity has a tendency to make us forget this fact, but in times of adversity we quickly learn to appeal to a higher order to rectify the situation.

Money Often Creates a Consciousness of Lack

Being required for survival yet being separate from the *atma,* money creates a consciousness of incompleteness and feelings of lack and need. In order to get what I need to live in the modern world I require money, something separate from myself. As such people are constantly thinking about how to get money thinking that it will make them feel more complete. Thinking like this a person develops a consciousness of "getting," which turns into selfishness, stinginess, and a hard-hearted, callous disregard for others. But the spiritual reality is that we are all maintained by the Supreme Lord.

Srila Prabhupada explains how the completeness we all yearn for can be realized in his commentary to the invocation of the *Isopanisad*:

> The Complete Whole, the Personality of Godhead, has immense potencies, all of which are as complete as He is. Thus this phenomenal world is also complete in itself. The twenty-four elements of which this material universe is a temporary manifestation are arranged to produce everything necessary for the maintenance and subsistence of this universe. No other unit in the universe need make an extraneous effort to try to maintain the universe...All facilities are given to the small complete units (namely the living beings) to enable them to realize the Complete Whole. All forms of incompleteness are experienced due to incomplete knowledge of the Complete Whole...Because we do not know that there is a complete arrangement in nature for our maintenance, we make efforts to utilize the resources of nature to create a so-called complete life of sense enjoyment.

> Because the living entity cannot enjoy the life of the senses without being dovetailed with the Complete Whole, the misleading life of sense enjoyment is illusion. The hand of a body is a complete unit only as long as it is attached to the complete body. When the hand is severed from the body, it may appear like a hand, but it actually has none of the potencies of a hand. Similarly, living beings are part and

parcel of the Complete Whole, and if they are severed from the Complete Whole, the illusory representation of completeness cannot fully satisfy them.

The completeness of human life can be realized only when one engages in the service of the Complete Whole. All services in this world—whether social, political, communal, international or even interplanetary—will remain incomplete until they are dovetailed with the Complete Whole. When everything is dovetailed with the Complete Whole, the attached parts and parcels also become complete in themselves.

Money Encourages the Cheating Propensity

As an artificial store of wealth money encourages gambling and speculation—one of the four pillars of sinful life which leads to the bondage of the soul. Gambling is characteristic of *tamo-guna*, the mode of ignorance, because it is an effort to get something for nothing. It can also become an addiction that leads to other forms of crime or destructive behavior, and further leading into the depths of *maya*.

Since we can obtain everything we want and need with money, people everywhere endeavor to get all that they can in the shortest possible time. One of the easiest ways to obtain money is by gambling. On a personal level gambling is carried out in casinos, racetracks, and at the corner store. Since it's an easy business to conduct, and since the house always makes money, this type of enterprise is increasingly run at different levels of government. Most common in the United States are the ³tate lotteries where very small wagers can be made and at times huge fortunes can be won. But gambling is not at all limited to casinos, racetracks and lotteries—it has become legitimized and even made glamorous in the form of stock market "investing." The great majority of stock market "investing" is actually sophisticated gambling. Let me give a brief analysis and some examples.

Investing implies the idea of ownership. For most people their major investment is their house. They invest their money there mainly because they need a place to live, but also because the nature of a house is that it always has value. Some people however also speculate in home ownership, and in the real estate bubble of 2002–2007 thousands or perhaps millions of people were investing in homes because the prices were appreciating so rapidly. Many would buy houses and "flip" them a few years later reaping enormous sums of money. The real estate bubble in America and England burst in 2007 however, and prices went into freefall, depreciating as much as 25 percent in a year. At the same time the adjustable rate mortgages with which many of those houses were purchased ratcheted up and millions found themselves unable to make their payments. Being foreclosed, thousands suddenly found themselves homeless and living in their cars, even in upscale communities such as Santa Barbara, California. That speculative fever and its aftermath is cited as cause of the financial calamites befalling America in 2008.

Stocks are very different from houses. Very few people invest money in stocks as a safe place to store their excess money. Instead they buy stock with the hope and expectation that its value will increase and provide them with unearned wealth. All manners of "investments" have been devised to allow speculators to make money on a moving market regardless of whether it rises or falls. By selling short for example, a speculator can make money when the value of a stock decreases. Short selling involves "borrowing" the stock from another stockholder and selling it at the present, presumably higher price. When the stock later falls in value it is purchased on the market and "repaid" to the original owner. All manners of such transactions have been created that allow speculators to greatly leverage their positions for the possibility of making great profits, but at the risk of great loss as well.

Future contracts are another such speculative venture. Originally they were designed as a risk management technique to protect against future price fluctuations. A farmer for example could buy a futures contract for corn at a fixed price for a delivery say three months in the future when his crop would be harvested. Should the current price of corn be lower he will earn the price agreed to, protecting the investment he made in agriculture.

Future contracts have become transmogrified from risk management to the hottest thing for the "smart money" speculators, and these markets are now threatening the world economy. Futures contracts form part of what is now called derivatives trading. Derivatives are financial instruments that have no intrinsic value themselves, but derive their value from something else. They hedge the risk of owning things that are subject to unexpected price fluctuations, e.g. foreign currencies, food commodities such as rice and wheat, stocks and bonds. There are two main types: futures, or contracts for future delivery at a specified price, and options that give one party the opportunity to buy from or sell to the other side at a prearranged price.

The speculation has become frenzied. Before 1973 the ratio of investment to speculative capital was 9:1, but since 1973, these proportions have reversed, and we have entered the era of casino capitalism. "The point everyone misses," wrote economist Robert Chapman a decade ago, "is that buying derivatives is not investing. It is gambling, insurance and high stakes bookmaking. Derivatives create nothing."[27] So huge have the leverage and derivative instruments become that their value now far exceeds the total economic value of the planet. In 2003 the value of all derivative trading was $85 trillion, while the size of the world economy was only $49 trillion. Early in 2008, while the total GDP of the planet reached only $60 trillion, the Bank for International Settlements reported that derivatives trading, including those based on debt, currencies, commodities, stocks and interest rates expanded to an amazing $596 trillion. This amount does not include Credit Default Swaps, which when included brings the total amount to well over $1 quadrillion. Economic writer Ellen Brown explains credit default swaps:

> Credit default swaps (CDS) are the most widely traded form of credit derivative. CDS started as a sort of insurance policy between two parties on whether or not a company will default on its bonds. In a typical default swap, the "protection buyer" gets a large payoff from the "protection seller" if the company defaults within a certain period of time, while the "protection seller" collects periodic payments from the "protection buyer" for assuming the risk of default. CDS thus resemble insurance policies, but there is no requirement to actually hold any asset or suffer any loss, so CDS are widely used just to increase profits by gambling on market changes. In one blogger's example, a hedge fund could sit back and collect $320,000 a year in premiums just for selling "protection" on a risky BBB junk bond. The premiums are "free" money—free until the bond actually goes into default, when the hedge fund could be on the hook for $100 million in claims.[28]

And there's the catch: what if the hedge fund doesn't have the $100 million? The fund's corporate shell or limited partnership is put into bankruptcy; but both parties are claiming the derivative as an asset on their books, which they now have to write down. Players who have "hedged their bets" by betting both ways cannot collect on their winning bets; and that means they cannot afford to pay their losing bets, causing other players to also default on their bets. The dominos go down in a cascade of cross-defaults that infects the whole banking industry and jeopardizes the global pyramid scheme.

Warren Buffet, sometimes called the world's greatest investor, said in the 2002 report to his shareholders at Berkshire Hathaway: "We view them as time bombs both for the parties that deal in them and the economic system...In our view...derivatives are financial weapons of mass destruction, carrying dangers that, while now latent, are potentially lethal." Indeed, destruction is one of the characteristics of *tamo-guna*.

Buffet is not alone. In a page one story in the *Financial Times*, the President of Germany, Horst Kohler, a former head of the International Monetary Fund lashed out at bankers, calling them monsters. Kohler said global financial markets have become a "monster" that must be "put back in place" because of their "massive destruction of assets." He called for tougher and more efficient regulation of the securities markets. In 2005 one of his colleagues, German Vice-Chancellor Franz Muntefering, attacked hedge funds as a "swarms of locusts" whose profit maximization strategies "posed a danger to democracy."

The risks are tremendous. For example, in 1995 the century old Barings Bank was bankrupted by its 28 year-old trader Nick Leeson who lost $1.4 billion by gambling that the Nikkei 225 index of leading Japanese company shares would not move substantially from its normal trading range. That false assumption was shattered by the Kobe earthquake on the 17th January 1995. In 1994 Metallgesellshaft lost $1.5 billion on oil futures, and ten years later China Aviation admitted to losing $550 million in speculative trading. In September 2006 the US-based Amaranth Advisors hedge fund suffered $6 billion in losses trading natural gas futures. Derivatives trader Stan Jonas tells us that banks no longer make money the old fashioned way; gambling is now their stock-in-trade: "I once had to explain to my father that a bank didn't really make its money taking deposits and lending out money to poor folk so they could build houses. I explained that the bank actually traded for a living."[29]

The potential profits and losses are so huge that efforts are made to manipulate markets to control prices as was done in the California energy crisis. Now we see this speculation driving up prices in food causing the average world price for rice to rise by 217 percent, wheat by 136 percent, corn by 125 percent and soybeans by 107 percent between early 2006 and June 2008, and the quadrupling of staple food prices in the stores, despite the fact that the supply of food has not substantially changed. "We have enough food on this planet today to feed everyone," the head of the U.N. Environment Program, Achim Steiner, told The Associated Press in a telephone interview, as he blamed market speculation on the growing global catastrophe. Despite the fact that the food is there, many cannot afford the dramatically escalating food prices which have resulted in riots in more than a dozen places around the globe early in 2008.

An April 2008 article in the *British New Statesman* magazine titled *The Trading Frenzy That Sent Prices Soaring* attributes the calamity to speculation: "The reason for food 'shortages' is speculation in commodity futures following the collapse of the financial derivatives markets. Desperate for quick returns, dealers are taking trillions of dollars out of equities and mortgage bonds and plowing them into food and raw materials." It goes on to add "Under conditions of growing debt defaults arising from the US sub-prime [housing] crisis, speculators and hedge fund groups have increasingly switched their investments from high-risk 'bundled' securities into so-called 'stores of value,' which include gold and oil at one end of the spectrum and 'soft commodities' [foodstuffs] at the other...Just like the boom in house prices, commodity price inflation feeds on itself. The more prices rise, and big profits are made, the more others invest, hoping for big returns. Look at the financial web sites: everyone and their mother is piling into commodities."

The Münchner Investment Club of Germany certainly is. Their investment in wheat alone brought profits of 93 percent for the 2,500 members of the club in the first six months of 2008. Asked if its members give any thought to the catastrophic consequences for undeveloped countries of their speculative investment policy, manager Andreas Grünewald stated "Most of our members are rather passive and orientated to profit." He goes on to say "Raw materials are the mega-trend of the decade," and his company intends to intensify its involvement in both water and agricultural stocks.

The chickens are coming home to roost, and the news is now breaking faster than I can write about it to include it in this book. In September of 2008 it appears as though those financial weapons of mass destruction are primed to go off. To prevent that, the United States government is in effect socializing the largest investment banks and underwriting the losses to the tune of $1 trillion or even more, and the head of the IMF tells us that more is yet to come. Derivatives and CDS are widely discussed as *the* cause underlying the problems with the investment banks. Will they bring down the entire Ponzi-scheme financial system? We will have to wait and see.

Gambling is a moral curse for the soul. It often leads to calamitous difficulties in life and material bondage afterward.

Money Enables the Manipulation of Markets

Those who have enough money (and there are many) can easily manipulate markets and shear the unsuspecting. This is exactly what we discussed above. Here is an example of how markets can be manipulated in derivatives trading:

> The speculator takes out huge forward contracts to sell pounds for French francs at 9.50 to the pound in one month's time: say forward contracts totaling 10-billion pounds. For these he must pay a fee to a bank. Then he waits until the month is nearly up. Then suddenly he starts buying pounds again in very large volumes and throws them against the exchange rate through selling them. So big is his first sale of pounds that the currency falls, say 3 percent against the franc. At this point other, smaller players see the pound going down and join the trend he has started, driving it down another 3 percent. Overnight he borrows another vast chunk of pounds and sells into francs again,

and meanwhile the word is going around the market that none other than the master speculator is in action, so everyone joins the trend and the pound drops another ten percent. And on the day when the forward contract falls due for him to sell pounds for francs at 9.50 the pound in the spot market is down at 5 francs. He takes up his huge forward contract and makes a huge profit. Meanwhile there is a sterling crisis, etc.[30]

Money Enables Thought Control and Indoctrination

Those who control the money of the world control what the world thinks. Harry Rositzke, a retired chief at the Central Intelligence Agency, described how the CIA influenced what people think: "Covert propaganda operations in the third world were, in effect, a fight for the media...Foreign editors and columnists were recruited, newspapers and magazines subsidized, press services supported. Propagandists ranged from paid agents to friendly collaborators, from liberal and socialist anti-Communists to simple right-wingers. Facts, themes, editorial outlines, model essays were sent out to third world stations to be reworked for local consumption."[31] We would be quite naive to think that this is not going on everywhere, especially in our own country. Of course, this is all accomplished with money.

The wealthy can control what people think by controlling the content of the media; they do this by buying the media, and not just one. In the mid-1980s, broadcasting networks were not allowed to control local media that reached over a fourth of the households, nor could it own more than 12 stations in total. The Telecommunications Act of 1996 raised the limit to 35 percent which paved the way for almost 200 television station mergers and acquisitions that followed. Since that time the number of corporations owning most newspapers, magazines, book publishers, recorded music, movie studios, television and radio stations have shrunk from 50 to five global firms, operating with many of the characteristics of a cartel—Time-Warner, Disney, News Corp., Viacom and Bertelsmann AG based in Germany.

A mere eight advertising and public relations agencies have an overwhelming influence on what is seen in the media in America because they control 80 percent of all media spending. Using their clout, advertising is increasingly mixed into program content, with the intention of subliminally influencing viewers. Robert McChesney, a leading media scholar, critic, and a prominent researcher and writer on US media history, warns that we're "rapidly moving to a whole new paradigm for media and commercialism, where traditional borders are disintegrating and conventional standards are being replaced with something significantly different." It marries content with commercialism so pervasively they're indistinguishable, and it shows up everywhere all the time—television, radio, movies, publications, music, popular culture, schools, universities, public vehicles, commercial ones, public broadcasting and radio, art, subways, restrooms, and any and all other ways advertisers can reach people whether or not we approve. McChesney calls it "the greatest concerted attempt at psychological manipulation in all of human history."[32]

Money is also used to control what people think by controlling the limits of debate. What gets funded and what doesn't in academia, often determines the "current" wisdom, however much it might be at odds with both common sense and the facts themselves. Professor of Linguistics and social critic Noam Chomsky explains why this method of control is not widely understood:

> The smart way to keep people passive and obedient is to strictly limit the spectrum of acceptable opinion, but allow very lively debate within that spectrum—even encourage the more critical and dissident views. That gives people the sense that there's free thinking going on, while all the time the presuppositions of the system are being reinforced by the limits put on the range of the debate.[33]

In their seminal work *Manufacturing Consent*, Chomsky and co-author Edward Herman explained the "propaganda model" that consists of five filters used to control the message the public gets—media ownership, advertising, sourcing, flak and anticommunist ideology. These are used to "filter the news to print, marginalize dissent (and assure) government and dominant private interests." The "filters" remove what's to be censored and leaves in "only the cleansed (acceptable) residue fit to print" or broadcast.[34]

What people believe is not just influenced by the media. Science is busy influencing people too. E. O. Wilson, the father of a theory called sociobiology which says that sexual and other human behaviors are determined only by our genes, tells us that "human beings are absurdly easy to indoctrinate. They seek it." Further he says that they are characterized by blind faith: "Man would rather believe than know."[35] He and other biologists are busy helping people believe many things that are just plain false, but are able to do so because they receive financial support for their efforts.

Biologist Richard Lewontin describes how science is successfully being used to legitimate an entirely *fictitious* story—that of human sexual preference. He writes in *Biology as Ideology*:

> The entire discussion of the evolutionary basis of human sexual preference is a made-up story, from beginning to end. Yet it is a story that appears in textbooks, in courses in high schools and universities,

and in popular books and journals. It bears the legitimacy given to it by famous professors and by national and international media. It has the authority of science. In an important sense, it is science because science consists not simply of a collection of true facts about the world, but is the body of assertions and theories about the world made by people who are called scientists. It consists, in large part, of what scientists say about the world *whatever the true state of the world might be*.

Science is more than an institution devoted to the manipulation of the physical world. It also has a function in the formation of consciousness about the political and social world. Science in that sense is part of the general process of education, and the *assertions of scientists are the basis for a great deal of the enterprise of forming consciousness*. Education in general and *scientific education in particular, is meant not only to make us competent to manipulate the world but also to form our social attitudes.*[36]

I am willing to bet that you didn't know that one of the functions of a "scientific" education was to convince your children that sexual preference, a disingenuous way of saying homosexual inclination, is written in their genes, and therefore such inclination must be accepted as "normal." This goes on because these "scientists" are being paid to indoctrinate young people into such misguided thinking.

The Rights of Money Trump the Rights of Living Persons

David Korten has also critiqued the overwhelming political influence of money: "Political democracy vests rights in the living person, one person, one vote. By contrast, the market recognizes only money, not people – one dollar, one vote. It gives no voice to the penniless, and when not balanced by constraining political forces, can become an instrument of oppression by which the wealthy monopolize society's resources, leaving the less fortunate without land, jobs, technology or other means of livelihood. Only when wealth is equally distributed can the market be considered democratic in any meaningful sense...Many mega-corporations command more economic power than do the majority of states [countries] and dominate the political processes of nearly all states [countries]."[37]

Money is Foremost in the Consciousness in a Money Culture

In a money economy getting money becomes the focus of everyone's efforts, almost always at the expense of proper engagement and duty. The duty referred to here is prescribed according to one's psycho-physical nature, or *varna*, in Vedic literatures such as the *Manu Samhita*. The concept of acting according to one's duty is entirely lost in a money economy since the only way people can survive is to get money. Despite the fact that following another's duty is described as dangerous, people often do whatever they can that makes the most money without regard for working according to their nature. Is it any wonder that 80 percent of people do not like their work?

Money Can Solve All the Problems of Life

Money promotes the idea, especially to the poor, that all problems of life can be solved simply with money. Many perceive that their problems arise because they haven't enough money, and they think that if they had a significant sum of money all of their problems would be solved. The problems we all experience in life have, in fact, nothing to do with money. They arise from our own *karma* and are given to us to learn to apply the spiritual lessons we have learned. Problems can be used for our transformation in spiritual growth. The idea money can solve all problems is another illusion stemming from a money economy.f

Everything has a Price but Nothing Has Value

When money becomes the measure of all things everything has a price, everything can be sold, and there no longer remains any way to understand the proper value of things. When everything is thought of in terms of money, all other values disappear. Values are priceless. They cannot be measured. They are those guidelines of human behavior that cannot be violated for any reason. They are the basis of culture, yet they must also have a basis. That basis is the spiritual principle of a culture. What are the values in a materialistic culture? There are none, and this fact is becoming increasingly obvious to anyone who cares to look.

Money Wastes Time and Effort

Today there are millions of cashiers, clerks, bookkeepers and accountants, lawyers, bank tellers and managers, loan agents, insurance agents, securities brokers and traders, fraud detectives, armed couriers, police agencies and many others involved in counting, accounting, protecting, printing, trading, manipulating, and gambling with the vast sums of the world's money. If they didn't have to make, count and protect money these people would be free to engage in positive, productive work that would result in tangible physical wealth that people want and need. Such economic systems exist in *sattvic* cultures.

It Fosters a Consciousness of Scarcity and Neediness

Because money is difficult for the working man to obtain and because people often live beyond their means they are constantly in need of more money. Without money a person develops the feeling of lack, and the need to get, which can become the foremost thought in a person's consciousness. They can then become so conditioned and remain in this consciousness for a very long time (lifetimes). Many people recognizing their "poverty consciousness" attempt to reform themselves with positive affirmations that life is filled with abundance. God's economy is certainly one of abundance but not the artificial man-made economy that is controlled by a small segment of the population for their own purposes. Those seeking a world of abundance would do better to create it within the natural economy arranged by God.

Atyahara

A significant practice for a spiritually progressive culture is giving up *atyahara*, or gathering more wealth or goods than required, because such gathering can become a stumbling block in spiritual life. Jesus encouraged his followers not to store up wealth, and gave the birds and animals as examples that God is looking after all of His creation. The Vedas enjoin *nityo nityanam cetanas cetananam—* the one Supreme eternal being is providing for all of the others. Understanding that principal we are encouraged to act on it in practice, and so doing learn to take shelter of the Lord.

However, in a money economy and materialistic culture, the accumulation of wealth in the form of money is not only seen as a method of security, but as a means to social position and prestige. In modern society the collection of money is encouraged, and runs directly counter to the principles of the Vedas. Thus people learn to take shelter of money, instead of learning how to take shelter of God. The result is that in times of crisis people think that money can save them.

The following is a true anecdote. A very wealthy man's son was critically injured in an automobile accident. The man went to the bank and filled a suitcase with money. Marching into the operating room where his son was being attended to by a team of physicians the man displayed the money for the surgeons. "Here is $6 million for you. Save him."

The doctors were not successful however and the boy died. His father was shocked and aghast. "How could they fail?" he wondered. "They had all the money they needed!" But money cannot check death. It is one of the fallible soldiers that we take shelter of in life only to find that at the moment of death it can do nothing. At the time of death there is only one person who can do anything to help us—the person who controls life and death. If we practice taking shelter of Him during life we will be able to take shelter of Him at death as well. The natural economic system arranged by the Lord reminds us of our dependence on Him, which is why we are encouraged to use it.

Unexamined Assumptions Tell Us Where the Fault Lies

It is telling that in the ten college textbooks of 600 or more pages that I examined, the concept of ownership was not once mentioned. Nor are any of the other assumptions that we are examining here. These concepts are obviously so accepted as givens by modern economists that they do not merit even the slightest discussion in the pages of economic textbooks. Where do these ideas then enter our culture? They are codified in law. Ownership has a legal definition. The transfer of ownership and the result of productive energy are contractual agreements between individual parties and are also codified in law. The creation, production and use of money are also established legally. International trade is made possible because all parties have subscribed to the same understanding, legal definitions and agreements. It is these legal agreements that have opened the entire world to the economics of atheism.

The fact that the modern world has made these concepts "legal" does not stop them from being illusory. The *Bhagavad-gita* and *Srimad-Bhagavatam* address illusions in the very beginning because their purpose is to help us become fixed in reality. The highest truth is reality distinguished from illusion for the welfare of all. Such truth uproots the threefold miseries.

These six illusions form the foundation of the economics of atheism, modern economic theory, and our attempts to make these illusions reality are the root cause of the majority of the economic problems of the world. No amount of tinkering with the dials of economic theory is going to adjust things so that such delusional economics finally "works" for everyone. It can't and it won't. It is all created to benefit only a few at the expense of the many, and to allow people to think that they are the rightful owners and enjoyers of this world usurping the position of the rightful owner and enjoyer, God.

Chapter Seven

Divine and Demonic Consciousness

With the increase of sattva-guna the strength of the godly increases. When rajo-guna increases, the demoniac become strong. And with the rise of tamo-guna the strength of the most wicked increases. Srimad-Bhagavatam 11.25.19

So disturbing are the actions described in the many books regarding the global economy that I found it troubling to read them for very long—a reaction not untypical of many other people. Most who hear the anecdotes of the economics of ignorance naturally feel revulsion and disgust. The despicable behaviors are so far from the thinking and actions of human beings with a sense of morality that they find such accusations incredulous, even unbelievable. The sad fact is however that these things are going on, and have been going on for centuries. We wonder how is it that some people can be so extremely greedy when they already have more than they can conceivably use. Is it really possible that they can be so envious of others to actually *like* to see them suffer? Why is it that some like Stiglitz can see and criticize the obvious results of their actions, but others, like his boss who asked for his resignation, are not to be disturbed by the same thing? How is it that Perkins or Budhoo are so bothered by their conscience that they can no longer participate in creating the suffering, slavery, and deaths of others, while the many others who take their place or work alongside of them have no problem? How is it that people like Keynes tell us that we must pretend that "fair is foul and foul is fair," and how is it that people like Ledeen are not

211

only enthusiastic to violently impose their will onto others, condemning them to suffering, but are enthusiastic to do more? Are these people not evil, even demonic?

Some people consider the idea of evil personalities as superstitious, the ignorant thinking of the past, long since abandoned by the modern "thinking" man. Rather than abandoning our discrimination in favor of a neat solution that "evil" is something of a foolish past we would do better to understand the truth, not by the rhetoric used to support or defend the actions, but by *phalena paricyate*—judging by the results. The results of too many actions, from the personal to the global level, are horrible. To relegate the idea of evil to the dark days of the past, is to risk not understanding our problems completely, and thus not grasping their solution. That is, to not understand evil is to risk a great deal. Carl Jung, among others who have studied the human personality, warns us that "The wolf in sheep's clothing now goes about whispering in our ear that evil is nothing but a misunderstanding of good and an effective instrument of progress. We think that the world of darkness has thus been abolished for good and all, but nobody realizes what a poisoning this is of man's soul."[1] Throwing out that poison, let's see what possible light that world of darkness can shed on understanding such murderous behavior.

The Love of All That is Dead

Whereas good is defined as being life-supporting and enhancing, evil is defined as that energy that is directed against life, or to put it another way, the predilection for death. The German Psychologist Erich Fromm was one of the first to make a thorough study of the evil personality, induced to do so by the actions of Adolph Hitler and his Third Reich. He describes three orientations directed against life which in their malignant and gravest forms converge to create "the syndrome of decay." This represents the "quintessence of evil," and is, "at the same time, the most severe pathology and the root of the most vicious destructiveness and inhumanity." In our investigation of evil and the demonic we will consider two of these orientations: necrophilia and narcissism.[2]

Necrophilia is often thought of as being a desire to have sex with the dead, or a morbid desire to be in the presence of the dead body. While these may be specific manifestations of this psychosis, the word itself is of a more general nature which means a "love of all things dead." In pure psychological terms the person with such an orientation is attracted to, and fascinated by, that which is not alive. It can be observed in individuals to various degrees. Hitler and his aide Eichmann are used as examples of extreme necrophiliacs by Fromm, but this consciousness—far from being reserved to that infamous past—has actually infested the entire world to one degree or another. Necrophilia has become the orientation of our entire society due to the fact that the vast majority of people share this same attraction for dead things. So much is this the case that to a large degree a death-dealing culture seems normal to us—everything being just as it should be. To say that we are conditioned souls explains how we have become accustomed to a culture of death.

Some may find these statements shocking or just plain wrong—"I do NOT love all things dead" they might object. But let us take a deeper look at our world before we jump to hasty conclusions based on our biased self-perception, and instead look at the result of our actions, both individual and collective. If evil is love of death and not life, evil is thus an attraction to *dead matter*. To say that we "love all things dead" is simply another way of saying that we live in a materialistic society. Matter in fact is dead. And it is widely acknowledged that modern society is very, even extremely, materialistic. It is spirit that has life. Let's look at our culture from this perspective.

Our attraction to and fascination with matter has resulted in the modern industrial economy which produces in factories all the things we love to consume such as our mp3 players and audio disks, DVD movies, flat-screen televisions, computers, boats, cars, skis, golf clubs, washing machines and appliances, furniture, clothing, and all of the other myriad consumer items. Don't get me wrong—I am not saying that we don't need such things, or that they don't make our lives more comfortable. Living in a material world requires us to have and use material items. The point is not that we shouldn't have them; rather, it is the emphasis that we give to them as well as how we produce them. In all those many factories raw materials go in and come out improved, but the living human workers come out depleted after working 12, 15, and 18 hour days. They turn into almost death-like zombies often doing repetitive tasks that cannot be made to be done by a machine, and are able to function in such circumstances only with liberal applications of consciousness-altering substances such as caffeine, alcohol, and drugs. Why do we torture ourselves like this? Because we participate in a world that requires us to have an artificial creation simply to live—money—even though money in and of itself is useless. And to save money we look for "bargains" forgetful of the fact that they are likely produced by slave labor around the world and carry a very high, but hidden, human cost. By making such purchases we become an essential and supportive element in the necrophilia of the global economy.

Tellingly this dead matter, money, becomes the so-called "life-blood" of the world's economy, without which the economy "dies," and with it likely many people as well. This "life-blood" artificially created by one section of society gives them control over all others. The workings of the economy are an obscure and arcane area understood by few but the "professionals" leaving the vast majority of people quite helpless in having any direct control over their own lives and fortunes, as demonstrated in earlier chapters. Such overdependence on the mercy of others is unnatural and is opposed to the natural way of life by depending on the living soil directly. Davison Budhoo, Michel Chossudovsky, Naomi Klein and others have demonstrated clearly that the present economy feeds on suffering and death to create jobs and profits, although it could just as well function in a healthy way that supports life, if those who control the budgets were so inclined.

Death is prominent in all aspects of today's society. Take the food industry for example. That which should be the very embodiment of life is managed by death from beginning to end. First with the application of pesticides and herbicides, which deplete the soil, killing it. The food produced from these killing fields is also depleted and lacks the necessary vitamins, nutrients and enzymes necessary to maintain a healthy life. Widespread spraying of pesticides over civilian areas is carried out to control (kill) "pests." In the fall of 2007, 100,000 residents of Monterey County, California were sprayed with chemicals with known health risks, to control the mating habits of less than 750 light brown apple moths, possibly threatening the health and life of the human residents in the process. Likewise in Santa Cruz County, over 100,000 residents were sprayed to control less than 9,000 moths. The motive for this was to protect against $100 million in *possible* agricultural losses, even though there were no recorded losses from this pest prior to this time.[3] A great portion of our food is irradiated in order to kill any lurking pathogens. Another major section of food is produced in castles of death—slaughterhouses—and before these animals are slaughtered and butchered they are raised in "factory farms" a very unnatural and unwholesome environment in which they typically wallow in their own feces, their own dead wastes, another aspect of necrophilia.

If the medium is the message, as Marshall McCluen thought, then what is the message produced by dead electronics? Dead entertainment? Vicarious living as a dismal substitute for the real thing. However much the moving pictures appear to be alive, they are not. They are in fact dead and have no life. They simply project an illusion that we buy into to escape life for a while. And too many of the experiences delivered to us by this medium are also preoccupied with death. "If it bleeds it leads" is the newsman's motto. The "entertainment" that we watch is fascinated with death, and we train our children from very young ages to share in the fascination. The average American child spends 900 hours in school but 1,023 hours in front of a TV every year, and by the age of 18 they have witnessed more than 200,000 acts of violence and 16,000 murders. Children's cartoons that were formerly singing and dancing characters are now dramas filled with anxiety, fear and violence.

Our medical industry is focused not on health and life, but on disease and death. Recovering from disease through the use of complex diagnostic tests, high-tech hospitals and surgery is a highly profitable business dependent upon highly-trained professionals who are seen, literally, as the gate-keepers of death. Maintaining health through exercise, healthy foods and vitamin supplements, is hardly a worthwhile business in comparison. Even still, repeated attempts are being made to pass legislation that will destroy the health-supporting food supplement industry.[4] Patent medicines used to restrict health to only those who can pay the price are another important component of our disease-care systems. Millions of pills are swallowed every day for both physical and mental health to save people from a death-dealing culture that they must somehow survive. Inoculations, an ostensible method for protection from disease, are sometimes contaminated with toxic mercury compounds, and the 20+ vaccinations given to children before they go to school result, not in health, but increasingly neurologic disorders, hyperactivity, learning disabilities, asthma, chronic fatigue syndrome, lupus, rheumatoid arthritis, multiple sclerosis, and seizure disorders, and Autism for more than 1 in 150 children. There is also "sudden infant death syndrome" and other terrible complications for thousands of others.[5]

Every year we pave over thousands of square miles of living nature for dead roads along which tens of thousands of animals and innumerable insects are smashed on car windshields each year. We cut down the living rainforests at an alarming rate to raise cattle for the death menu. Our homes and offices are sprayed with poisonous chemicals to kill insects. Huge flocks of birds once a common sight, have vanished except for relatively small flocks, being brought to death's door by so many poisons, pesticides, man-made diseases, and now from cell phone radiation.

We could go on, but here is the point: our modern society values matter far beyond life. All of the killing mentioned above is done to support our materialistic values. Many will object that we need pesticides and so on, and that may be true in the context of current practices. But there are other ways to live in this world that do not require so much death. The problem is not local, it is systemic. The entire system feeds on and even requires death.

Life comes from spiritual energy and has its characteristics of personality, desire, emotions, love and joy, in an eternal condition of bliss and knowledge. Material energy on the other hand, is temporary, dead, without personality and thus without knowledge, happiness, or emotions. Love of death is called "necrophilous," love life is called "biophilous." Both of these conditions coexist within each individual and within society. What is most important however is which trend is stronger. Those whose necrophilous side is stronger will unconsciously kill the biophilous side. In doing so they harden their hearts and convince themselves that their behavior seems to be the natural response to their circumstances. They are prevented by their consciousness of even seeing another way of behaving. Persons who can become aware of their necrophilous tendencies may change, but those who remain unaware, continually justifying their thinking and actions run the grave risk of becoming totally necrophilous, becoming lost to life with little to no chance of returning.

Regarding the necrophile Fromm writes:

> The necrophilous person loves all that does not grow, all that is mechanical. The necrophilous person is driven by the desire to transform the organic into the inorganic, to approach life mechanically, as if all living persons were things. All living processes, feelings, and thoughts are transformed into things. Memory, rather than experience; having, rather than being, is what counts. The necrophilous person can relate to an object—a flower or a person—only if he possesses it; hence a threat to his possession is a threat to himself; if he loses possession he loses contact with the world. That is why we find the paradoxical reaction that he would rather lose life than possession, even though by losing life he who possesses has ceased to exist. He loves control, and in the act of controlling he kills life. He is deeply afraid of life, because it is disorderly and uncontrollable by its very nature.[6]

A extremely significant characteristic of the necrophile is his attitude toward force, which means the capacity to create a corpse. He is truly enamored by it:

> All force is, in the last analysis, based on the power to kill. I may not kill a person but only deprive him of his freedom; I may want only to humiliate him or to take away his possessions—but whatever I do, behind all these actions stands my capacity to kill and my willingness to kill. The lover of death necessarily loves force. For him the greatest achievement of man is not to give life, but to destroy it; the use of force is not a transitory action forced upon him by circumstances— it is a way of life.[7]

These characteristics of the necrophile do much to explain the behaviors we observe in the world today at the global level and as dealt with in the past two chapters. Judging from the results, the leaders of the world are indeed necrophiles and have arranged the world in such a way to please themselves not considering the implications for you or me or the other 6 billion human beings on the planet, what to speak of the non-human sentient beings. People everywhere are given a way to live, most having little control over the process—they simply do the best they can in the situation in which they find themselves. But because they live in a society oriented toward death they also develop into necrophilous individuals. In Fromm's view this necrophilous orientation is one of evil. It is also the reason that Srila Prabhupada called this a soul-killing civilization.

A Psychology of Evil

American psychologist and well-known author Scott Peck straightforwardly addresses the existence of evil in his book *People of the Lie—The Hope for Healing Human Evil*. Of course many in the psychological profession consider the topic of evil unprofessional because it necessarily mixes the ideas of religion and science, areas generally taken (within scientific circles at least) to be mutually exclusive. Strangely, although all manners of human vice can be studied in scientific ways, to suggest that they are the product of evil, or that there may be a science of evil, is somehow not scientific. Nonetheless Peck takes the multifaceted approach and unapologetically adds a Christian-spiritual perspective to the clinical one which already considers the patient from the biological, the psychological, the psychobiological, the sociological, the socio-biological, the Freudian, the rational-emotive, the behavioral, and the existential points-of-view. Why not also the spiritual? Nonetheless it was a bold undertaking in 1983, considering the limitations to the open mind in science at the time, to state that a psychology of evil must be a religious psychology. But he felt compelled to do so because although evil had been a central topic of religion for ages it was virtually absent in psychology. He was further compelled because in his clinical experience evil human beings are not only not rare, but are instead quite common, and are responsible for creating many social problems desperately needing to be addressed and understood. The word "evil" as we investigate it here does not specifically relate to some mystical "devil" who has the power to challenge God as in the Christian traditions, but rather as a term that refers to the behavior of those who turn away from God.

What are "evil" people like? Perhaps not surprisingly, in his analysis Peck identifies many qualities that accurately match the mentality, attitudes and actions of the suffering-and-death-dealing economic decision makers depicted in our discussion of the economics of ignorance. The evil people he says are: narcissistic, lack empathy, extremely greedy, bald-faced liars; they respect only raw power and do not respond to kindness or gentle persuasion; they create confusion, frustration, angst and futility in their dealings with others, and while often subtle, their destructiveness is remarkably consistent; they seek to avoid incrimination, steadfastly refusing to acknowledge their wrong doing, and instead engage in scape-goating and project their misdeeds onto others; and, he writes "the words 'image,' 'appearance,' and 'outwardly' are crucial to understanding the morality of the evil. While they seem to lack any motivation to be good, they intensely desire to appear good. Their 'goodness' is all on a level of pretense. It is, in effect, a lie. This is why they are the 'people of the Lie.'"[8] Does that sound like the IMF and World Bank?

Malignant Narcissism and "I and mine"

The quality of narcissism is especially important to understand in connection with the consciousness of "I and mine." Narcissism is defined as: "a pattern of traits and behaviors which signify infatuation and obsession with one's self to the exclusion of all others, and the egotistic and ruthless pursuit of one's gratification, dominance and ambition."[9] Fromm defines two categories of narcissism, one benign and the other malignant. Benign narcissism is self-infatuation based on exceptional talents or abilities that a person may have that are far beyond the norm. Knowing his superior talents this person becomes obsessed with himself. The malignant form however is based *only on what a person has*. It may actually be the underlying basis for the obsessive need of unlimitedly increasing wealth beyond any practical use or measure. It also helps to explain how the sense of "I" increases unlimitedly with the sense of "mine." Hence "the more I have" the "more I am," and the reason that billions or even trillions of dollars are never enough if I don't have it *all*. Fromm:

> In the case of malignant narcissism, the object of narcissism is not anything the person does or produces, but *something he has; for instance, his body, his looks, his health, his wealth, etc.* The malignant nature of this type of narcissism lies in the fact that it lacks the corrective element which we find in the benign form. If I am "great" because of some quality I have, and not because of something I achieve, I do not need to be related to anybody or anything; I need not make any effort. In maintaining the picture of my greatness I remove myself more and more from reality and I have to *increase* the narcissistic charge in order to be better protected from the danger that my narcissistically inflated ego might be revealed as the product of my empty imagination.[10]

This statement explains perhaps the atheistic nature of the evil person. If "I do not need to be related to anybody or anything; I need not make any effort"— I am independent and self-sufficient by myself alone, or, I am supreme. I am the enjoyer of all. I am God. Beyond this, malignant narcissism also accounts for cruel behavior and the enjoyment derived from making others suffer. Psychologist Otto Kernberg explains how malignant narcissism can account for the lack of empathy in the IMF, etc. More than just lacking in empathy however, the malignant narcissist takes pleasure in the suffering of others:

This pathological idealization of the self as an aggressive self, clinically is called "malignant narcissism." This is very much connected with evil and with a number of clinical forms that evil takes, such as the pleasure and enjoyment in controlling others, in making them suffer, in destroying them, or the casual pleasure in using others' trust, confidence and love to exploit them and to destroy them.[11]

While the traits of evil people closely match those of the psychopath, Peck specifically does not include them in that category. The difference seems to be that while his evil ones can see and understand their own evil behaviors and vigorously avoid placing fault in themselves, psychopaths have apparently lost the capacity to distinguish between good and evil:

I have said that evil people feel themselves to be perfect. At the same time, however, I think they have an unacknowledged sense of their own evil nature. Indeed, it is this very sense from which they are frantically trying to flee. The essential component of evil is not the absence of a sense of sin or imperfection but the unwillingness to tolerate that sense. At one and the same time, the evil are aware of their evil and are desperately trying to avoid the awareness. Rather than blissfully lacking a sense of morality, like the psychopath, they are continually engaged in sweeping the evidence of their evil under the rug of their own consciousness. The problem is not a defect of conscience but the effort to deny the conscience its due. We become evil by attempting to hide from ourselves. The wickedness of the evil is not committed directly, but indirectly as a part of this cover-up process. Evil originates not in the absence of guilt but in the effort to escape it.

It often happens, then, that the evil may be recognized by its very disguise. The lie can be perceived before the misdeed it is designed to hide—the cover-up before the fact...The disguise is usually impenetrable. But what we can catch are glimpses of the uncanny game of hide-and-seek in the obscurity of the soul, in which it, the single human soul, evades itself, avoids itself, hides from itself.[12]

Peck's evil ones appear to be the first of two types of evil persons distinguished by theologian Martin Buber—those who are in the process of "sliding" into evil. The others are those who have already "fallen victim" to and have been taken over by "radical" evil.[13] If it is the "ordinary" evil ones who are desperately trying to avoid seeing evil in themselves and are in the process of sliding into evil, then it is the psychopaths who have crossed the line and have been taken over by radical evil.

Definition and Use of the word Psychopath

A word must be said to avoid confusion about the meaning of the word *psychopath* since even in the official literature the actual use of the word is unclear. There are also differences in understanding between the American and European schools. In this discussion I follow the convention and explanation of the term psychopath as given by Dr. Hervey Cleckley in his book *Mask of Sanity*. He explains the term and changes in nomenclature as follows:[14]

> Every physician is familiar with the term psychopath, by which these people are most commonly designated. Despite the plain etymologic inference of a sick mind or of mental sickness, this term is ordinarily used to indicate those who are considered free from psychosis and even from psychoneurosis. The definitions of psychopath found in medical dictionaries are not consistent nor do they regularly accord with the ordinary psychiatric use of this word.

> In a 1952 revision of the psychiatric nomenclature the term psychopathic personality was officially replaced by sociopathic personality. Subsequently the informal term, sociopath, was often used along with the older and more familiar psychopath to designate a large group of seriously disabled people, listed with other dissimilar groups under the heading personality disorder. Still another change in the official terminology was made in 1968 when the designation sociopathic personality was replaced by personality disorder, antisocial type.

> The diagnostic category, personality disorder, officially includes a wide variety of maladjusted people who cannot by the criteria of psychiatry be classed with the psychotic, the psychoneurotic, or the mentally defective.

> Until fairly recent years, it was by no means uncommon for the report of a detailed psychiatric examination made on a patient in a state or federal institution to end with this diagnostic conclusion:

1. No nervous or mental disease

2. Psychopathic personality

Political Ponerology—Leadership of the Evil Ones

Political psychologists have widely identified the syndrome of malignant narcissism in corporate and political leaders who threaten political stability and civil society.[15] Perhaps due to the unlimited graft and greed, cronyism, malicious war mongering, disregard for the public welfare, unwarranted usurpation of political liberties, and flagrant disregard for constitutional limitations, some are directly describing our "leaders" as psychopaths.

Susan Rosenthal, M.D. makes that connection in her book *Power and Powerlessness* in which she discusses the grasp on power and control, and the irrational preoccupation of profit at the expense of suffering and death of others that consumes the leaders of corporations and nations. She says that a person perfectly suited to the capitalist system would be a psychopath—someone who is disconnected from emotions, having no empathy and no compassion. Indeed, a study by a team of U.S. scientists, published in the journal Psychological Science contends that psychopaths would make the best financial traders.[32]

Andrzej Lobaczewski, a clinical psychologist in Poland during the Communist era puts it more strongly. He says that many leaders of corporations and government *are* psychopaths. Because psychopaths are absolutely without remorse, and have no compunction about lying or doing any unethical practice in order to get what they want, they can easily climb to the top. Psychopaths, Lobaczewski says, can attach themselves to any ideology and, like a virus, change it from within to something that may eventually be completely alien to its original purpose. At the same time the original workers/followers, continuing to pursue what they believe is the original idea or cause, gradually become mere pawns of a power-hungry, self-serving elite. Although those who have the wherewithal to realize what is taking place often leave such organizations (and countries), the presence of the psychopaths in leadership roles creates disaster in the lives of many people. Compounding the disaster, the psychopaths behind this violence do not understand that their striving for total domination can only lead to the destruction of everyone's interests. They cannot understand the implications of their actions, nor do they care, and neither will they ever stop. [16]

Lobaczewski and his colleagues observed that "an ever-strengthening network of psychopathic and related individuals gradually starts to dominate, overshadowing the others," eventually resulting in a pathocracy—a system wherein a small pathological minority achieves control over various institutions and even over all society. Studying this pathocracy in government, business and other social settings, their conclusions are offered in *Political Ponerology—A Science on the Nature of Evil Adjusted for Political Purposes*. The book's editor does not hesitate to identify America as a pathocracy based on the character and activities of key members of the Bush administration.

Dr. Kevin Barrett, professor at the University of Wisconsin in Madison, challenges that the only conflict that really matters is that of the psychopathic leadership *v.* the rest of humanity. "Civilization, as we know it, is largely the creation of psychopaths. Behind the apparent insanity of contemporary history is the actual insanity of psychopaths fighting to preserve their disproportionate power...Psychopaths have played a disproportionate role in the development of civilization, because they are hard-wired to lie, kill, injure, and generally inflict great suffering on other humans without feeling any remorse." It is urgent, he says, for society to take constructive action to rein-in these out-of-control power mongers before they destroy the world and all of us with it.

> We are witnessing the apotheosis of the over-world—the criminal syndicate or overlapping set of syndicates that lurks above ordinary society and law just as the underworld lurks below it. In 9/11 and the 9/11 wars, we are seeing the power-grab or "endgame" of brutal, cunning gangs of CIA drug-runners and President-killers; money-laundering international bankers and their hit-men, economic and otherwise; corrupt military contractors and gung-ho generals; corporate predators and their political enablers; brainwashers and mind-rapists euphemistically known as psy-ops experts and PR specialists—in short, the whole sick crew of certifiable psychopaths running our so-called civilization.[17]

Twenty years ago when the world scene still seemed somewhat normal, or even improving considering the developments in the USSR and Eastern Europe, Dr. Robert Hare warned about the nature and behavior of psychopaths in what he calls our "camouflage society" which allows these predatory people to blend in and seem as normal as the person next door. In fact they may even be the people next door. He exposed their characteristics and patterns as one of the most frightening, often-hidden social problems affecting people today in his book *Without Conscience*. In 2006, just after we began to hear terms such as predatory capitalism, he updated the warning about psychopaths in the workplace with his newest book *Snakes in Suits: When Psychopaths Go To Work*.

The Nature of the Psychopath

Knowing the symptoms and nature of the psychopath may help us to guard against them in our personal and professional lives, but they are not easy to identify. They often make a very good impression, charming others with the intent of victimizing them. Dr. Robert Hare spent ten years creating a highly reliable and scientifically sound "Psychopathy Checklist" not only for evaluating whether a person is likely to be a psychopath, but also to guard against the danger of improper diagnosis. In *Without Conscience* he explains:

> Given their glibness and the facility with which they lie, it is not surprising that psychopaths successfully cheat, bilk, defraud, con, and manipulate people and have not the slightest compunction about doing so. They are often forthright in describing themselves as con men, hustlers, or fraud artists. Their statements often reveal their belief that the world is made up of 'givers and takers,' predators and prey, and that it would be very foolish not to exploit the weaknesses of others...The hallmark of these often charming—but always deadly—individuals...is a stunning lack of conscience; their game is self-gratification at the other person's expense. Many spend time in prison, but many do not. All take far more than they give.[18]

The stunning lack of conscience exhibited among psychopaths gives us a clue to their spiritual condition. All normal human beings know that conscience is their moral rudder. It is the very element of the human being helping them to do right and avoid doing wrong. If in spite of their conscience they make the wrong choice anyway, as humans so often do, then hounded by feelings of guilt and remorse they seek to make amends and compensate for their errors. This is something that psychopaths cannot understand. "For them, conscience is little more than an intellectual awareness of rules others make up—empty words. The feelings needed to give clout to these rules are missing. The question for them is, why?"

This insight into the psychopathic personality becomes even more significant when we consider that the origin and voice of the conscience is none other than the Supersoul—the Lord in the Heart: "Yet in this body there is another, a transcendental enjoyer, who is the Lord, the supreme proprietor, who exists as the overseer and permitter, and who is known as the Supersoul." (13.23) In other words, those who are not demonic have a connection with the Lord which is called conscience by which He guides us. Those who avoid being conscious of their wrongdoing, as Peck says, are choosing to ignore and deny the guidance of the Supersoul, until finally they can no longer hear the "inner voice." Having no conscience they have no moral compass, no discernment between right from wrong, good or bad, what to do and what not to do. Their standard of behavior is to simply please themselves, to do what they want to do without any thought of anything else. Influenced by *tamo-guna* they continually make the wrong choices and gradually sink further and further down: "Those who are envious and mischievous, who are the lowest among men, I perpetually cast into the ocean of material existence, into various demoniac species of life." (16.19)

"Givers and takers" is the way they see the world—they of course are the takers and the rest of the world is their legitimate prey. Hare repeats the assessment by saying psychopaths "view people as little more than objects to be used for their own gratification. The weak and the vulnerable—whom they mock, rather than pity—are favorite targets." Psychologist Robert Rieber echoes that notion writing: "There is no such thing, in the psychopathic universe, as the merely weak. Whoever is weak is also a sucker; that is, someone who demands to be exploited." Given that understanding, can we look back at the actions of the IMF, World Bank, large corporations and the governments of the world, and make more sense of their actions? With such knowledge we must no longer be surprised that those who are there "to help us" are very often wolves in sheep's clothing.[19]

Psychopaths show no remorse, shame or guilt, and lack any insight into the deficiencies of their own behavior. Not even recognizing that they have done wrong they never seek help or counsel for their behavior. Indeed, if their wrongdoing is pointed out to them they become almost violently angry, denying their fault casting the blame on the victim or the accuser. They misplace the locus of evil in others and then seek to destroy them in name of righteousness.[20]

Their strong will and desire to control others is another striking feature of psychopaths. Kernberg mentions this above and Peck writes "the reader will be struck by the extraordinary willfulness of evil people. They are men and women of obviously strong will, determined to have their own way. There is a remarkable power in the manner in which they attempt to control others."[21] Psychopaths love to have power and control over others and seem unable to believe that other people have valid opinions different from theirs. Hare writes "they have a narcissistic and grossly inflated view of their self-worth and importance, a truly astounding egocentricity and sense of entitlement, and see themselves as the center of the universe, as superior beings who are justified in living according to their own rules. 'It's not that I don't follow the law,' said one of our subjects. 'I follow my own laws.'" Since the narcissistic cannot be wrong and makes his own laws, he therefore attempts to make others be like him, to think like him and act like him, to do things his way. There is little room for individual expression in the world of the narcissist, because the expressions of others that differ from his challenge him or offend him. Acutely sensitive to this fact Fromm broadened the definition of necrophilia to include the desire of certain people to control others—to make them controllable, to foster their dependency, to discourage their capacity to think for themselves, to diminish their unpredictability and originality, to keep them in line.[22]

They have an inflated value of self, are arrogant, cocky, and dominating, loyal only to themselves. Their sexuality is often other than heterosexual and many, especially in white collar situations, are subject to unlimited greed. They are completely cut off from all emotions, they feel nothing, and display emotions only as a show learned by observing others. As Hare tells it there is a "frightful and perplexing theme that runs through the case histories of all psychopaths: a deeply disturbing inability to care about the pain and suffering experienced by others—in short, a complete lack of empathy, the prerequisite for love."

Psychopaths are not mad, according to accepted legal and psychiatric standards. Their acts result "not from a deranged mind, but from a cold, calculating rationality combined with a chilling inability to treat others as thinking, feeling human beings."[23] Although psychopaths are legally competent and responsible, and not insane by clinical standards; they are considered to be a "psychiatric disorder" for lack of a better explanation of their deviant behavior. Making up some 4–6 percent of the population psychopaths are one of the most serious social problems to face modern society. In *The Mask of Sanity* Dr. Cleckley repeatedly states with obvious frustration, that inexplicably this area of pressing need is deliberately ignored by authorities in all fields, including psychiatry, the courts and government. He identifies obfuscation in professional disciplinary understanding of the psychopath and brands it a "conspiracy of evasion." Based on Lobaczewski's writing one may question whether this is because the psychopaths already in charge want to avoid being identified.

Shockingly, Cleckley, Hare and Peck all agree that psychopaths are incurable. As Hare puts it "the behavior of psychopaths is notoriously resistant to change," to a large degree because they don't see anything wrong with themselves and thus feel no need to change, and no need for any "treatment." "Treatment for what?" they may ask. The many well thought out programs designed to help psychopaths in prison or under court-ordered therapy are found to be ineffective. And that only regards treatment for those in custody, completely overlooking the millions of others who are not. Although society has a problem with them they have no problem with themselves and thus no incentive or desire to change. Psychopaths are those who have completely "fallen" by Buber's definition.[24]

It is sometimes difficult for people to accept that psychopaths run many of our corporations, and are highly placed in banking and government. The reason is that good people are rarely suspicious and cannot imagine others doing things they themselves would not do. But the facts are there for everyone to plainly see. The structural adjustment programs that have resulted in starvation, ill-health, ignorance, untold suffering, and death by the hundreds of thousands; the efforts to develop terminator seeds and genetically modified plants that can be patented are efforts to enslave all farmers of the future and hold people captive for their very sustenance. These are not the activities of normal people. The efforts to conceal the cures for and restrict the treatment of terminal illnesses (AIDS, cancer), prohibit safe foods and food supplements; the unlimited capacity to perpetrate and ignore environmental pollution, to perpetuate and encourage gas-guzzling, smog belching cars; the wanton destruction of rain forests; the testing of drugs and diseases on unsuspecting civilian populations, outright lies to garner public support for war; millions of homeless people; commercialized slaughter of billions of animals for food; genocide; unending "wars for peace;" gross dispari-ties in wealth—the list is endless—these acts, a veritable description of the fea-tures of modern society, is also a description of the actions of psychopaths.

People are apt to think that the psychopath is as monstrous in appearance as he is in mind, but that is also as far from the truth as one could well get. Psycho-paths usually look and behave in a more normal manner than actually normal people. "They present a more convincing picture of virtue than virtue presents of itself. Just as the wax rosebud or the plastic peach seemed more perfect to the eye, more what the mind thought a rosebud or a peach should be, than the imper-fect original from which it had been modeled."[25]

Usually people accept the less-dramatic understanding of life as the correct (and safest) one, and let matters rest there. Too often though, the actual manner in which this world functions is so vastly different from what we would like to believe that the truth is unacceptable. It threatens our own false ego, our idea of what this world is and our ability to find shelter in it. Accepting all of this as true—that the demonic run our planet and our lives—leaves us in great fear. Realizing our helplessness the possibilities of future calamities immediately be-come too terrible to contemplate. Better to shut it all out of the mind. Unfortu-nately, but perhaps not, those days are over because reality has come to a neigh-borhood near you, and may in fact be on your own doorstep. At this time when we can see the world poised on the brink of either destruction or slavery or both we must accept the reality before us: some people are not as human as others, and they are too often downright evil. Solving a problem requires that one first accepts that there is one.

The Path to Evil

Accepting this reality immediately begs the question "how do they get to be so?" and "What can we do?" The latter question will be taken up in the next chapter. The first question is extremely important not only to identify the cause for others, but so that we may guard against sliding toward evil ourselves. Peck identifies the unsubmitted will as the essential characteristic of evil people. Everyone who is mentally healthy subordinates themselves to some form of higher authority, be it family elders, employers, God, or their understanding of the truth. Often there is a moral choice to be made in which we must choose right over wrong, that "right" choice being expressed by our conscience or defined by our religious beliefs. We can distinguish between what is true and what we would like to be true, recognizing that our own choices may in fact be faulty or wrong. "Not so the evil, however. In the conflict between their guilt and their will, it is the guilt that must go and the will that must win."[26]

Fromm makes a detailed analysis beginning from the flawed reasoning ability of the narcissist: "The most dangerous result of narcissistic attachment is the distortion of rational judgment. The object of narcissistic attachment is thought to be valuable (good, beautiful, wise, etc.) not on the basis of an objective value-judgment, but because it is me or mine. Narcissistic value-judgment is prejudiced and biased."[27] We note significantly that the narcissist attachment is based on the conception of "I and mine." Fromm saw the genesis of human evil as a developmental process: we are not created evil or forced to be evil, but we become evil slowly over time through a long series of wrong choices willfully ignoring our conscience that tells us the better or proper thing to do, and instead doing what one wills regardless of the consequences. The narcissist thus attempts to preserve his flawed concept of self at the expense of the truth. The result is that after a long succession of such wrong choices one can no longer even recognize the truth, and the ability to free oneself by right action is then lost.[28]

> At the last point of the chain of decisions he is no longer free; at an earlier point he might have been free had he been aware that the real decision was to be made right there and then. The argument for the view that man has no freedom to choose the better as against the worse is to some considerable extent based on the fact that one looks usually at the last decision in a chain of events, and not at the first or second ones. Indeed, at the point of final decision the freedom to choose has usually vanished. But it may still have been there at an earlier point when the person was not yet so deeply caught in his own passions. One might generalize by saying that one of the reasons why most people fail in their lives is precisely because they are not

aware of the point when they are still free to act according to reason, and because they are aware of the choice only at the point when it is too late for them to make a decision.[29]

When the ego desire is so strong that it recognizes only itself and refuses to acknowledge any other authority, especially the authority of God, the Vedas refer to this as *maya*, or being covered by illusion. Srila Prabhupada writes that the *jiva* may even think himself to be God, and as God, can do whatever he likes with impunity. Thus he "falls" into a trap from which he cannot escape. This is the actual fall of the human being, and we are admonished regarding this condition by Sri Krishna in the *Gita* when He states: "I am the only enjoyer and the only object of sacrifice. Those who do not recognize My true transcendental nature fall down." (9.24) We have to recognize our position relative to God and subordinate our will to His just as a child submits to its parents and feels the shelter of their love. Those who refuse to submit to God fall from the transcendental reality to this illusory material world, and as long as we maintain such an attitude of independence we condemn ourselves to stay here, perpetually if need be, rotating in an endless cycle of birth and death. Thus there is only one choice that we continue to be faced with—to acknowledge our position in relationship to God and turn to Him, or to deny Him and turn away from Him. As Peck puts it: "There are only two states of being: submission to God and goodness, or the refusal to submit to anything beyond one's own will—which refusal automatically enslaves one to the forces of evil."[30]

Man's Inherent Nature — Divine or Demonic?

It has long been argued that human nature is one of two basic types. Some say man is inherently evil and requires the devices of religion and social mores to help govern his behavior. Others say that man is basically good, but has weaknesses and sometimes slips from proper behavior. The Vedas say that both positions are correct: there are two kinds of beings in this world—the divine and the demonic. What is it that determines the difference? Are some people permanently evil and others permanently good, or can they change? Or perhaps everyone both divine and demonic at the same time?

As explained above all the living beings in world are parts and parcels of God, qualitatively the same as Him, but vastly different in quantitative potency. Being an aspect of the absolute truth the *jiva* is inherently free from the duality of good and evil. However, when the *jiva* enters this material world he creates the duality that he experiences by his subjective enjoyment of the material energies, and in the process becomes subjected to that same duality. Hence he can turn away from God and become "evil" or demonic, or turn toward God and become "good" or godly. The *jiva* at one end of the spectrum is demonic, but giving up the demonic mentality may move closer to God. Along the path the *jiva* becomes influenced by both good and bad. This is the state of most people in the world—some going in the direction of evil and others going in the direction of good. Finally, when the *jiva* moves close enough to God he can give up his demonic tendencies entirely, and eventually free himself from the material influences and go to the spiritual world becoming free from all duality, misery, birth, death, etc.

The godly are by nature equally disposed to all living beings, but the demonic care only for their own pleasures, usually at the expense of anything and everything else. The struggle between good versus evil is therefore played out continually in this world of duality. It is ever-present and in every culture at every time. It was George Lucas' *Star Wars* that delivered the eternal conflict to the Western world's mind-map a generation ago as a wide-screen saga. Long before that the two great epics of India—*Mahabharata* and *Ramayana*—have thrilled readers with intrigue, drama and suspense between the forces of good and evil for millennia. Because through successive incarnations we have personally participated in this drama we inherently know that this conflict is real. Young boys influenced by such *samskaras*, or soul-memories of previous lives of conflict, are naturally drawn to battle play. By our many lives experience we know that some actions are good and some are bad, that some people are nice or even godly while others are mean, cruel or the very personification of evil. We know that this is true because we see it going on in this world before our very eyes.

The personal qualities of the divine are uplifting to themselves and others include (16.1–3):

> Fearlessness, purification of one's existence, cultivation of spiritual knowledge, charity, self-control, performance of sacrifice, study of the Vedas, austerity and simplicity; nonviolence, truthfulness, freedom from anger; renunciation, tranquility, aversion to faultfinding, compassion and freedom from covetousness; gentleness, modesty and steady determination; vigor, forgiveness, fortitude, cleanliness, freedom from envy and the passion for honor—these transcendental qualities belong to godly men endowed with divine nature.

The demonic however not only lack those qualities but are imbued with their opposites including arrogance, pride, anger, conceit, harshness, ignorance, and more. This description of the demonic personality agrees closely with Peck's evil people, with the malignant narcissist, and with the psychopathic personality.

An entire chapter of the *Bhagavad-gita* is devoted to explanation of the divine and demonic natures. There the demonic nature is explained by Sri Krishna as follows (16.7–24):

> Those who are demoniac do not know what is to be done and what is not to be done. Neither cleanliness nor proper behavior nor truth is found in them. They say that this world is unreal, with no foundation, no God in control. They say it is produced of sex desire and has no cause other than lust. Following such conclusions, the demoniac, who are lost to themselves and who have no intelligence, engage in unbeneficial, horrible works meant to destroy the world. Taking shelter of insatiable lust and absorbed in the conceit of pride and false prestige, the demoniac, thus illusioned, are always sworn to unclean work, attracted by the impermanent. They believe that to gratify the senses is the prime necessity of human civilization. Thus until the end of life their anxiety is immeasurable. Bound by a network of hundreds of thousands of desires and absorbed in lust and anger, they secure money by illegal means for sense gratification.

> The demoniac person thinks: 'So much wealth do I have today, and I will gain more according to my schemes. So much is mine now, and it will increase in the future, more and more. He is my enemy, and I have killed him, and my other enemies will also be killed. I am the lord of everything. I am the enjoyer. I am perfect, powerful and happy. I am the richest man, surrounded by aristocratic relatives. There is none so powerful and happy as I am. I shall perform sacrifices, I shall give some charity, and thus I shall rejoice.' In this way, such persons are deluded by ignorance. Thus perplexed by various anxieties and bound by a network of illusions, they become too strongly attached to sense enjoyment and fall down into hell.

> Self-complacent and always impudent, deluded by wealth and false prestige, they sometimes proudly perform sacrifices in name only, without following any rules or regulations. Bewildered by false ego, strength, pride, lust and anger, the demons become envious of the Supreme Personality of Godhead, who is situated in their own bodies and in the bodies of others, and blaspheme against the real religion.

> Those who are envious and mischievous, who are the lowest among men, I perpetually cast into the ocean of material existence, into various demoniac species of life. Attaining repeated birth amongst

the species of demoniac life, such persons can never approach Me. Gradually they sink down to the most abominable type of existence.

There are three gates leading to hell—lust, anger and greed. Every sane man should give these up, for they lead to the degradation of the soul. The man who has escaped these three gates of hell performs acts conducive to self-realization and thus gradually attains the supreme destination. But he who discards scriptural injunctions and acts according to his own whims attains neither perfection, nor happiness, nor the supreme destination. One should therefore understand what is duty and what is not duty by the regulations of the scriptures. Knowing such rules and regulations, one should act so that he may gradually be elevated.

The Vedas enumerate 8,400,000 species of life, and among these 400,000 are counted as human beings. These divisions are not based simply on a particular bodily form as biologists distinguish species, but are also distinctions of consciousness. These human species are characterized by superior consciousness to animals and specifically by the fact that human beings have free will. They are free to make choices based on understanding and intelligence and are not controlled by instinct as are the animals. A living being is assigned a particular type of body according to his consciousness, and within the human species these can range from divine to demonic. According to the consciousness at the time of death the living being is awarded his next body. Those who have cultivated divine qualities and are situated in the quality of goodness attain the heavenly planets, while those who have developed a demonic mentality take birth in various human species such as *yaksas* and *raksasas,* or even in subhuman species.

Our explanation of the cosmic ages, or *yugas,* indicated that this earth is akin to a multi-purpose room that serves the purposes of the different living beings of this material realm. During *Kali-yuga* the earth is given to the demonic for their purposes, and they have controlled the earth, or portions of it, since before the beginning of the age. At first they did so by the use of the sword—Smith's plunder by raid—but that's a risky business. Therefore methods were later modified to control by belief (religion) with life-threatening methods of conversion—the torture rack and sword for the obstinate. For convincing the undecided nothing was better than publicly burning the recalcitrant alive at the stake. Still that control, although it was more thorough than the sword alone, was yet incomplete. There were many that would not abandon their beliefs even at the peril of life itself. A better system was then devised, and today their control is nearly complete. It is a system from which no person is allowed to escape—the money system—ably backed up by the military's men and guns.

In a strictly spiritual sense the history of the struggle between the divine and the demonic is significant because it offers insightful lessons of the struggle of the individual soul to gain freedom from material consciousness. The demonic are fully invested into the materialistic conception of life, so much so that they deride even the conception of God. They think themselves to be God, that only they are fit to enjoy, and as such are extremely envious of any good fortune of others. Indeed, they become even happier by seeing others suffer. This description of the nature of the psychopaths and their quest for absolute control, does much to explain why today's economy and world functions the way it does, and why, despite centuries of "progress," there are increasing numbers of destitute people.

The Early History of Demonic Control

The demonic desiring to be the Lord of all have always sought to subjugate others. This has been the history since the demonic became manifest. The Bhagavatam relates the ancient history of the rise of the demonic. Diti and Aditi, the co-wives of Kasyapa Muni, spawned the godly and demonic races of human beings respectively. Aditi gave birth first, conceiving her child according to the laws of dharma, at the proper time, in an elevated consciousness. Her descendants became the *devas* or demigods who manage the universal affairs. Diti, being envious of her co-wife approached her husband with strong desire for conception, but at an inauspicious time. Although Kasyapa explained that the auspicious time would be the next *muhurta*, a mere half-hour later, she insisted that she could not wait. Her consciousness was filled with envy, impatience, a competitive spirit determined to do better than Aditi, and with great determination to overcome her husband's reluctance. Diti thus produced twins of the same consciousness, Hiranyaksa and Hiranyakasipu. These two powerful and insolent sons became the scourge of the entire universe, exploiting and enslaving many, and exploiting the resources of the earth to the point when that the earth became imbalanced and fell from its orbit.

To rectify the situation Vishnu assumed the incarnation of Varahadeva who rescued the earth and placed it in its proper orbit. Afterwards Hiranyaksa challenged Varahadeva desiring to kill Him, but in the ensuing match Hiranyaksa was killed.

Eager for revenge of his brother's death at the hands of Vishnu, Hiranyakasipu exhorted his demonic followers to disturb Vishnu as well as His followers (7.2.6–8, 10-15):

> My insignificant enemies the demigods have combined to kill my very dear brother Hiranyaksa. Although the Supreme Lord Vishnu is always equal to both the demigods and the demons, this time being

devoutly worshiped by the demigods He has taken their side and killed Hiranyaksa.

The Supreme Lord Vishnu has given up His natural tendency of equality toward the demons and demigods. Although He is the Supreme Person, He has assumed the form of Varaha to please His devotees, the demigods. I shall therefore sever Lord Vishnu's head from His trunk, and with the profuse blood from His body I shall please my brother Hiranyaksa, who was so fond of sucking blood. Thus shall I too be peaceful.

While I am engaged in the business of killing Lord Vishnu, go down to the planet earth, which is flourishing due to *brahminical* culture and a *ksatriya* government. These people engage in austerity, sacrifice, Vedic study, regulative vows, and charity. Destroy all the people thus engaged! Immediately go wherever there is good protection for the cows and *brahmana* and wherever the Vedas are studied in terms of the *varnashrama* principles. Set fire to those places and cut from the roots the trees there, which are the source of life.

The demons being fond of disastrous activities followed Hiranyakasipu's instructions, and engaged in envious activities directed against all living beings. They set fire to the cities, to the homes of the citizens, the villages, pasturing grounds, cowpens, gardens, agricultural fields and natural forests. They burned the hermitages of the saintly persons, the important mines that produced valuable metals, the residential quarters of the agriculturalists, the mountain villages, and the villages of the cow protectors, the cowherd men. They also burned the government capitals. With digging instruments they broke down bridges, the protective walls and the gates of the cities. Some took axes and cut important trees that produced food.

Although nobody can be equal to or greater than God, under the influence of illusion, *maya*, Hiranyakasipu thought that he could become immortal and defeat Vishnu. With great determination He set out to perform severe austerities with that express intention:

The demoniac king Hiranyakasipu wanted to be unconquerable and free from old age and dwindling of the body. He wanted to gain all the mystic yogic perfections, to be deathless, and to be the ruler of the entire universe. He thought: "By dint of my severe austerities, I shall reverse the results of pious and impious activities. I shall overturn all the established practices within this world. I alone shall assume the supreme position of Brahma."

His austerities, carried out for long, long period of time created disturbances in the universal order. The demigods petitioned Lord Brahma for relief who then went to propitiate Hiranyakasipu. Hiranyakasipu wanted to become immortal, and thinking that he could cheat death he asked for unusual benedictions from Brahma (7.3.35–38):

> O best of the givers of benediction, Brahma, if you will kindly grant me the benediction I desire, please let me not meet death from any of the living entities created by you. Grant me that I not die within any residence or outside any residence, during the daytime or at night, nor on the ground or in the sky. Grant me that my death not be brought by any being other than those created by you, nor by any weapon, nor by any human being or animal.

> Grant me that I not meet death from any entity, living or nonliving. Grant me, further, that I not be killed by any demigod or demon or by any great snake from the lower planets. Grant me the benediction that I may have no rival. Give me sole lordship over all the living entities and presiding deities, and give me all the glories obtained by that position. Furthermore, give me all the mystic powers attained by long austerities and the practice of yoga, for these cannot be lost at any time.

Although such benedictions are rarely attained, Brahma granted them all to Hiranyakasipu.

> The demon Hiranyakasipu, having thus been blessed by Lord Brahma and having acquired a lustrous golden body, continued to remember the death of his brother and remained envious of Lord Vishnu. Hiranyakasipu then conquered the entire universe. Indeed, that great demon conquered all the planets in the three worlds, including the planets of the human beings. He defeated the rulers of all the other planets where there are living entities and brought them all under his control. Conquering the abodes of all, he seized their power and influence. Hiranyakasipu, who possessed all opulence, began residing in heaven, which is enjoyed by the demigods. In fact, he resided in the most opulent palace of Indra, the King of heaven. The palace

was as beautifully made as if the goddess of fortune of the entire universe lived there. (7.4.4–8)

By dint of his personal power, Hiranyakasipu, situated on the throne of King Indra, controlled the inhabitants of all the other planets. In spite of achieving the power to control in all directions and in spite of enjoying every type of sense gratification imaginable, Hiranyakasipu was dissatisfied because instead of controlling his senses he was their servant. He passed a long time being very proud of his opulence and transgressing the laws of the authoritative scriptures. Everyone, including the rulers of the various planets, was extremely distressed because of the severe punishment Hiranyakasipu inflicted on them.

Lounging in their quarters, Hiranyakasipu made the demigods his personal servants who, trembling with fear, endeavored to please him in every way. Attaining such an exalted position, Hiranyakasipu thought himself the supreme enjoyer of the world. He thought that he had become immortal; that he had become God. This consciousness is carried in the blood, and Hiranyakasipu's great-grandson Bali, possessing the same demonic mentality, also attacked the demigods in tumultuous battles, and again defeated them conquering the entire universe.

Hiranyakasipu's and Bali's desires are the same as all demonic people—to take the place of God as the controller and enjoyer, without any rival, and with complete freedom, controlling others with the demonic bent of forcing everyone to their will. However, the demonic can only be temporarily successful the in their bid for total conquest and domination. When the disturbance is too great the Lord Himself steps in to deal with the situation. Hiranyakasipu and Bali were both defeated by the Lord: Hiranyakasipu's "foolproof" plan to cheat death was defeated by the amazing incarnation of Nrisimhadeva who, honoring all of Brahma's benedictions, disemboweled the demon using his sharp fingernails while holding him on His lap in the doorway of a building at dusk. The avatar Vamanadeva begging a small portion of land outwitted Bali regaining the universe without a fight.

These lessons from history are important to understanding the full extent of the demonic nature, which has not changed over all of the eons of time. To this very day the demonic continue to strive for total conquest; the evidence of the previous chapters demonstrating that both their intention as well as their methods are the same as Hiranyakasipu's. While the influences of *Kali*-yuga has reduced their lifespan and power, modern day demons compensate by employing the methods of secrecy, stealth, deception, covert and convoluted ways, cheating, and corruption.

The Demonic Invade the Earth

Since their first days the sons of the goddesses Aditi and Diti, the *adityas* and *daityas* respectively, have had strife between them. The strife continues to the present chapter that began some 6,000 years ago, just prior to the advent of the age of *Kali*. In the heavenly realms the *daityas* were defeated in battle by the *adityas*, and being thrown out of the heavenly planets came to the earth in vast numbers.[31] This battle between the divine and demonic constitutes the epic story of the *Mahabharata*, from which I continue here immediately after the segment quoted in chapter three:

> In this flourishing world of men the *asuras* were born in the land of the kings. For the *daityas* had been defeated in battle by the demigods, and having fallen from their supernal estate, they took birth here on Earth. Wanting to be Gods on Earth, the prideful demons were born, from men and from all manner of creatures that live on earth: from cows, horses, asses, camels, and buffalo, from beasts of prey, elephants and deer. And when they were born and went on being born, the wide Earth could no longer support herself.

> Now some of them were born kings, filled with great strength, sons of Diti and Danu who had now fallen from their world to earth. Powerful, insolent, bearing many shapes, they swarmed over this sea-girt Earth, crushing their enemies. They oppressed the *brahmanas*, the barons, the farmers, even the serfs, and other creatures they oppressed with their power. Sowing fear and slaughtering all the races of creation, they roamed all over earth by the hundreds of thousands, impious, emboldened with power, and insensate with drink they menaced everywhere the great seers in their hermitages.

The calamities created by the *daityas* were so severe that the earth personified petitioned the supreme authority of the cosmos, Brahma, for relief which was promised, culminating in the battle of Kurukshetra, at which place and time Sri Krishna spoke the *Bhagavad-gita* to the valiant warrior Arjuna. In that battle the vast majority of the demonic were eliminated, but the remainder have since reconstituted their numbers and for millennia have ruled the earth. The history of Western civilization is the history of their rule. Naturally then, all history prior to their advent about 5,000 years ago is officially referred to as "pre-history."

Their lust knows no bounds, and they are willing to sacrifice anything to fulfill their desires. On the whole they are extremely intelligent, much more than most people, and for this they have nothing but contempt and disdain for ordinary humans whom they see as non-different from cattle—something useful only for fulfilling their desires. They think themselves as naturally superior to others and as such seek positions of leadership and influence in society. Being charming they win support and acquire such posts. The problem is that they are demonic and hence they make this world a hellish place for everyone. They think that they can not only control the world but improve upon it, conquer it and make it serve their interests. It is this mentality that leads to "unbeneficial horrible works meant to destroy the world."

According to the Vedas the conclusions drawn by Lobaczewski, Barrett, and others are correct. The demonic are real, and judging by the dismal results experienced in almost every quarter they currently rule this world for their self-ish purposes alone. It is becoming increasingly easy to do draw such conclusions as their actions become more bold and transparent. By long and wide experience of endless wars "for peace," predatory economics, vulture capitalism, a "health-care" industry that thrives on continued sickness and death, billions of "throw-away people" who cannot give profit to the overlords, we can recognize that this world is run by the demonic, for them and their pleasure, and not for the happiness, well-being, or even survival of the normal human beings, to say nothing of the animal world, or nature herself.

Now, just to make things perfectly clear, by saying this am I putting forward the notion that all people in government are demonic or psychopaths? Absolutely not. The vast majority of people in the world are decent and moral. But the powers-that-be have their methods of gaining cooperation. Economic Hitman John Perkins relates how offers are made that can't be refused: "In this pocket I have a hundred million dollars for you and your family, Mr. President, if you cooperate with us; and in the other pocket I have a bullet with your name on it in case you don't." "What would you do?" he asks. There are many good people in this world who become powerless being compromised by bribery, coercion and/or threat, and in this way the demonic rule the world.[32]

So what is to be done? Is it our simply our destiny to be the victims of the demonic? Is there nothing we can do to change the situation? Some people upon learning the truths of how this world works want violent revolution—a reaction expected from those also influenced by tamo-guna. But revolution cannot be succeed simply because the powers-that-be are far too strong. They control the governments, they control the military, the banks and money, the media, they control academia—they control just about everything. They are a most formidable adversary, and fighting them on the material plane is a hopeless cause. The only way to save the situation is to conquer the demonic consciousness (which we are all infected by to one degree or another), with the most powerful force in the world—love. We will explain this in more detail in the next chapter.

Chapter Eight

Understanding and Solving the Economic Problem

Completely rejecting all religious activities which are materially motivated, this Bhagavata Purana propounds the highest truth, which is understandable by those who are fully pure in heart. The highest truth is reality distinguished from illusion for the welfare of all. Such truth uproots the threefold miseries. Srimad-Bhagavatam *1.1.2*

Which Way to the Future?

Social commentators and economists have written scores of books during the past several decades analyzing the economic problems and decrying their severity, typically directing the blame at the powerful and wealthy, or at multinational corporations who manipulate national policies to serve their own narrow interests, exclusive of the interests of the rest of world. In their anthology, *The Case Against the Global Economy*, editors Jerry Mander and Edward Goldsmith reveal in an unmistakable way what is going on in the name of so-called free-enterprise:

> It should be clear that the expansion of the global economy directly leads to a corresponding contraction of the local economies that it largely replaces. This inevitably marginalizes and renders obsolete a large segment of the populations of both the industrial and the so-called developing countries. At the same time, it devastates the natural world, homogenizes cultures, and destroys communities, depriving

their members of any semblance of control over their own lives. *This process must be brought to a halt—moreover, it must be reversed—even if, from today's grim perspective, this may seem difficult to achieve.*[1]

Exactly how is the current juggernaut of greed to be stopped? And reversed!? The solution they suggest is:

We must break through this veil of illusion and misrepresentation that is holding us in a self-destructive cultural trance and get on with the work of *re-creating our economic systems in service to people and the living earth*...To effectively rein in these out-of-control economic engines, *we must also strive for fundamental philosophical and structural change*...we have but two choices. We can either stand by and watch an out-of-control economy devour the future, or we can replace it with a system that makes more sense for the long term.

The many contributors to *The Case Against the Global Economy* offer a variety of suggestions for adapting our efforts toward a sustainable future. Significantly many of them, and they are not alone, recognize that changes of our spiritual, moral and cultural ideologies offer the most solid foundation on which to build genuine and lasting change.

Professor of Peace and Global Studies, Dr. Howard Richards also thinks that simply making adjustments to economic policy is insufficient to correct the problems the world now faces:

My thesis is that the solutions to global economic problems are, in the end, cultural rather than economic...Hence, social changes intended to alter the present disastrous course of events *must, if they are going to solve humanity's fundamental problems, change culture.*[2]

In 1992 the Union of Concerned Scientists (UCS), an ad hoc group of scientists dedicated to using their voice to protect the world against abuses from their craft, issued this **Warning to Humanity**:

Human beings and the natural world are on a collision course. Human activities inflict harsh and often irreversible damage on the environment and on critical resources. If not checked, many of our current practices put at serious risk the future that we wish for human society and

the plant and animal kingdoms, and may so alter the living world that it will be unable to sustain life in the manner that we know. Fundamental changes are urgent if we are to avoid the collision our present course will bring about.

WARNING

We the undersigned, senior members of the world's scientific community, hereby warn all humanity of what lies ahead. A great change in our stewardship of the earth and the life on it is required, if vast human misery is to be avoided and our global home on this planet is not to be irretrievably mutilated.

A new ethic is required—a new attitude towards discharging our responsibility for caring for ourselves and for the earth. We must recognize the earth's limited capacity to provide for us. We must recognize its fragility. We must no longer allow it to be ravaged. This ethic must motivate a great movement, convincing reluctant leaders and reluctant governments and reluctant peoples themselves to effect the needed changes.

The scientists issuing this warning hope that our message will reach and affect people everywhere. We need the help of many.

Prompting this alarming statement, signed by some 1500 of the world's leading scientists, are the severe global environmental problems with oceans, air, forests, waterways, soil and resulting extinction of species. Certain environmentalists under the flag of "Deep Ecology" cite the scale of human enterprise as the source of the problem. Why is it that the scale of human enterprise is so gargantuan as to overwhelm nature? It all comes down to economics, as in "economies of scale." Doing things on a very large scale makes more money. But, large scale often means using brute and insensitive forces that ravage nature, passing the costs of increased profits onto her.

It's not that scientists aren't looking for answers to the problems they create; they are. The solutions can often be found—at a price. Too often that price amounts to billions of dollars. $33 billion is the estimated cost of repairing the damage to the Amazon Rain Forest and River Basin. Tens of billions of other dollars would be at stake in removing the threat of endocrine disruptors that threaten the reproductive health of all species on the earth. But when we talk about billions of dollars, politics quickly enters the discussion, because in today's world billions of dollars are only being given to the financial establishment, regardless of the problems of nature or society. While the United States government will find more than a trillion dollars to save the banking system a fraction of this money is not available to save the environment.

The venerable Einstein has given us a hint about finding the solution in his maxim that a problem cannot be solved at the same level of thinking in which it was created. Thomas Kuhn puts it another way. In his seminal book, *The Structure of Scientific Revolutions,* he demonstrates that an old worn-out and failing paradigm will not be replaced by evidence, facts or even the truth, no matter how despairing the truth may be. Rather a new paradigm must be introduced that provides a better understanding of the problems, as well as offering insights into solutions through other ways of thinking. Therefore even the blatant truth in the UCS' warning is insufficient to bring the solution, and they know it! They themselves are calling for a new ethic, a great change in the stewardship of the earth. Where then can such a new ethic be found?

Sut Jhally, a Professor of Communications at the University of Massachusetts at Amherst, asks the same question, and he cites advertising as the cause of the problem. Advertising, he says, has been embraced by the people as a religion because it shows them how to solve the many problems of their lives. But, he says, it is advertising that is creating the consumer culture that is responsible for the environmental calamities. When asked how we can deal with that and catalyze a reformation, he says:

> It's an important question, because I actually believe the survival of the human race is at stake. We're now coming to a stage in human history when that notion of unlimited growth can no longer go unquestioned. The physical limits of the planet are literally bursting at the seams and if we keep producing at this rate, the planet will destroy itself. *What we need now is a vision of society that is not based upon ever increasing numbers of goods.*

The "reformation" will be a questioning of the very nature of economic growth, the health of our society, what we want it to do and how to organize it. The growth ethic is about consumption. It says happiness is connected to the number of things a society produces and the number of things individuals have. But having said that, I don't know how to do it. We can talk and analyze the situation, but when it comes to constructing a new vision, I don't know how to do that...Its not just manipulation and it's not just a question of showing people that they're being fooled. Unfortunately, what we don't have yet is an alternative vision, an alternative way of thinking about ourselves. *I think that for the future of the planet, we need to develop that alternative vision and mobilize people around it.* That's the challenge.[3]

Spiritual Solutions Are Being Called For

While multi-national corporations are easily blamed for the problem, many writers suggest that the actual solutions go beyond the corporate world; they require changes in our cultural, moral and religious, values and understanding.

Lynn White (cited earlier) opines that "since the roots of the ecological crises are so largely religious, the remedy must be essentially religious whether we call it that or not."[4]

British economist E. F. Schumacher, more than thirty years ago, wrote:

The economics of giantism and automation is a left-over of nineteenth century conditions and thinking and it is totally incapable of solving any of the real problems of today. The conventional wisdom of what is now taught as economics by-passes the poor, the very people for whom development is really needed. *An entirely new system of thought is needed, a system based upon attentiveness to people, and not primarily attention to goods...what is needed most today is a revision of the ends which these means are meant to serve. And this implies, above all else, the development of a life-style which accords to material things their proper, legitimate place, which is secondary and not primary.*[5]

Schumacher insists that economics as it is practiced today is derived from dubious, "meta-economic" preconceptions about mankind that disregard his spiritual nature and needs, and that this is what we need to deal with: "What is to take the place of the soul-and life-destroying metaphysics inherited from the nineteenth century? *The task of our generation, I have no doubt, is one of metaphysical reconstruction.*"[6]

The alternative religious renewal that surfaced during the sixties and seventies among disaffected young people (when Hare Krishna devotees were a familiar sight on American streets) were observed by historian and social critic Theodore Roszak as a "profoundly serious sign of the times, a necessary phase of our cultural evolution, and—potentially—a life-enhancing influence of incalculable value"...bringing us to a..."historical vantage point from which we can at last see where the wasteland ends and where a culture of human wholeness and fulfillment begins."[7] In the closing of the book *Where the Wasteland Ends* he writes that politics must reopen the metaphysical issues that science and logic have regarded as closed, and that the next politics must be a religious politics— "not the religion of the churches—(God help us!) but religion born of transcendent knowledge."

Deep ecologist Paul Erlich, is concerned with the scale of human enterprise and its vast destructive power and total dominance over other species to the point of their total annihilation. In a radio interview about the nature of the solution he said:

> I've written in many places, and I've often been beat up for it, that *the ultimate solution to this problem is going to be a quasi-religious transformation,* in the direction of deep ecology, understanding that we are just one of the passengers on this space ship, and I believe we have a substantial responsibility as the dominant passenger to protect the others and see to it that the ship keeps functioning well...You've got to have long range goals that are idealistic.[8]

Multinational corporations concerned only with profits were also identified by David Korten as the primary causative agents for both environmental degradation and the increasing human misery around the globe. He writes that although as an MBA student he believed that global corporations could provide answers to the problems of poverty and human conflict, he concluded that "systemic forces nurturing the growth and dominance of global corporations are at the heart of the current human dilemma."[9] Korten's conclusion is that although mankind has been misdirected by those seeking only to benefit from them financially, the promises that their products offer do little or nothing to fulfill fundamental human needs. He urges therefore that we *"must break free of the illusions of the world of money, rediscover spiritual meaning in our lives,* and root our economic institutions in place and community so that they are integrally connected to people and life."[10]

Roger Terry argues similarly in *Economic Insanity*:

> There is a moral aspect to this question of economics that we must deal with on an individual, rather than a structural level. Implementing a new economic structure with new rules and restrictions would of course reward individuals for behaving in new ways, but some behavioral patterns are quite hard to break—and you can't legislate everything, morality in particular. *Consequently, we must develop a new economic rationale, a moral argument, if you will, to support the types of behavior that must accompany the necessary structural changes.* This moral argument must address two related issues: self-interest and competition.[11]

Ecological economics, a relatively new field of study, has arisen from the growing recognition that there are increasingly destructive anomalies occurring in the world. One of the original concepts was recognizing that Mother Nature has intrinsic values as a whole being (the Gaia hypothesis); as such her gifts should not be seen as piecemeal "resources" to be gobbled up without concern for the "collateral damage" wrought during economic development. Ecological economics identifies the major problems of the world: overpopulation, poverty, inequity, resource depletion, biodiversity loss, ethnic conflicts, environmental degradation, crime and social decay, as interconnected and interdependent. In an introductory paper about ecological economics, Professor Thomas Maxwell pointed out the need for a greater spiritual awareness in order to effectively deal with these problems:

> This widening of our 'circle of understanding and compassion' requires a new mode of perception that transcends the illusion of separateness to discern the unity, the "unbroken wholeness' from which emerges the diverse forms of existence...Although this vision can be elaborated through science, its principal grounding is in spiritual experience...The solution will require an integrated epistemology that embraces both the rational knowledge of scientific empiricism and the inner knowledge of spiritual experience. Ultimately, deep ecological awareness is spiritual or religious awareness...This 'deep ecological awareness' fosters a vision of the cosmos as fundamentally sacred. This paper will describe the contributions of both modern science and contemplative spirituality to this ecological vision, *leading to the conclusion that spiritual awakening promotes a profound sense of earth stewardship that can form the foundation of a new ecological ethic.*[12]

Vaclav Havel, former president of the Czech Republic, is a rather unusual politician, speaking as he does about transcendence as a practical solution to the tough problems of "real" life. In a speech given on July 4, 1994 at the Independence Hall in Philadelphia he said that in this postmodern world where "cultural conflicts are becoming more dangerous than any time in history, *a new model of coexistence is needed, based on man's transcending himself."* He concludes with these words:

> In today's multicultural world, the truly reliable path to coexistence, to peaceful coexistence and creative cooperation, must start from what is at the root of all cultures and what lies infinitely deeper in human hearts and minds than political opinion, convictions, antipathies, or sympathies—it must be rooted in self-transcendence:

> - Transcendence as a hand reached out to those close to us, to foreigners, to the human community, to all living creatures, to nature, to the universe.

> - Transcendence as a deeply and joyously experienced need to be in harmony even with what we ourselves are not, what we do not understand, what seems distant from us in time and space, but with which we are nevertheless mysteriously linked because, together with us, all this constitutes a single world.

> - Transcendence as the only real alternative to extinction.[13]

Fundamental Changes Are Urgent

Since we all live on the same planet the fact is that we all share in these problems whether the hole is in our end of the boat or not. It does no good to ignore the poverty-stricken plight of others as long as your income is (presently) secure. Anybody with two eyes who bothers to look beyond the scope of their own affairs can understand that these problems are very serious. They are not local but systemic. During the social revolution of the 70's in America this challenge was offered to everyone: if you are not a part of the solution you are a part of the problem. Will we wait another three decades until all of the birds, and all of the fish, and the greater part of humanity are dead before we will do our bit as a part of the solution? How bad must it get before we will make the necessary changes in our own lives?

Recall the Union of Concerned Scientists warning: "*Fundamental changes are urgent if we are to avoid the collision our present course will bring about."* As of this writing that plea is sixteen years old. Have we since made any necessary *fundamental* changes? Did this warning make any difference in the manner in which the world has pursued its economic activity? Not by 1997 it didn't. Just prior to the Kyoto conference on global warming, the UCS reiterated their plea:

> ...over four years have passed, and progress has been woefully inaequate. Some of the most serious problems have worsened. Invaluable time has been squandered because so few leaders have risen to the challenge...Leaders must take this first step to protect future generations from dire prospects that would result from failure to meet our responsibilities toward them.

Of course at the Kyoto conference the United States refused to sign the treaty on limiting greenhouse gases, and U.S. president George W. Bush again refused to sign the treaty in 2001. Not to be spurned by a recalcitrant leadership, 100 Nobel Laureates issued another admonishment about the perilous future that we are creating. This time it was not about the environment, but about the great disparity between the haves and have-nots and the possible repercussions. This statement was issued at the Nobel Peace Prize Centennial Symposium in 2001:

> The most profound danger to world peace in the coming years will stem not from the irrational acts of states or individuals but from the legitimate demands of the world's dispossessed. Of these poor and disenfranchised, the majority live a marginal existence in equatorial climates. Global warming, not of their making but originating with the wealthy few, will affect their fragile ecologies most. Their situation will be desperate and manifestly unjust. If then we permit the devastating power of modern weaponry to spread through this combustible human landscape, we invite a conflagration that can engulf both rich and poor. It cannot be expected that in all cases they will be content to await the beneficence of the rich . . . It is time to turn our backs on the unilateral search for security, in which we seek shelter behind walls...*To survive in the world we have transformed, we must learn to think in a new way. As never before, the future of each depends on the good of all.*

Eric Fromm challenges in *The Sane Society* that our entire modern culture is pathological because it is based on a faulty foundation. He states "It is our first task then, to ascertain the nature of man, and what are the needs which stem from this nature. We then must proceed to examine the role of society in the evolution of man and to study its furthering role for the development of men as well as the recurrent conflicts between human nature and society—and the consequences of these conflicts, particularly as far as modern society is concerned."

Fromm further challenges that in our efforts to truly heal society, change in only one area is destructive of all change. The solution must therefore simultaneously include changes in the social, religious, economic, and political spheres. In other words, if we want a healthy society that functions properly on all levels it is not sufficient to deal with the economy alone, or the politics. The entire culture must change.

And to the list of criteria given above I will add one condition of my own: the solution of the economic crisis must effectively deconstruct the pathos of living according to the illusions of modern culture, and establish in their place the reality of the absolute truth as the foundation for a healthy culture. All other "solutions" will simply create more problems.

Finding that Spiritual Vision

Where are we to look for the new vision, the spiritual awakening, the different way of viewing our world, as asked for by these thinkers? Some suggest that worldviews are nothing more than a good story, and that it would be sufficient just to make up something really good; not just any old thing, but a really, really good story with lots of "spiritual" content. Can people rally around such a fictional story like "Trekkies" at a Star Trek convention, each assuming different roles and acting them out? Indeed, we hear about people assuming different identities during online role-playing to the point that it impacts their ability to function in their "other role" in this 3-dimensional world. But no fiction is sufficient to replace a person's heartfelt conviction about why they are in this world, and what the purpose of their life is. Nor is it going to remove the fear of not knowing what lies beyond death's door.

Earlier we saw that the indigenous cultures of the world were guided in their ways of life by their belief structures—their religious truths. Every culture, with the stark exception of our modern, global, materialistic culture, has a complex story about creation: how humans came to be on the earth, who their gods were and how they were to understand their relationships with others in terms of both expectations and responsibilities. Their religious beliefs also provided guidance for how they were to live in this world, how property was to be used, exchanged and shared amongst them. In this way their economic and social systems were defined. Knowing this history we should not be surprised that the above thinkers are calling for us to establish a spiritual foundation on which to base our actions and relationships.

All of these many good people are in earnest in their recognition of the problems and their attempts to find workable and manageable solutions. But while the Nobel laureates suggest that we must think in a new way, where do we find that new system of thought? Where will we find Terry's "new economic rationale, or moral argument?" Where will we find Jhally's "new vision of society," or Thomas Maxwell's "spiritual awakening [that] promotes a profound sense of earth stewardship," Havel's "new model of coexistence," Schumacher's "metaphysical reconstruction," or Mander's "fundamental philosophical and structural change?" How do we achieve the UCS' request for a "great change in our stewardship of the earth," Havel's transcendence, or Erlich's "quasi-religious transformation?" Let me point out the obvious. With all due respect to our would-be saviors who have called for these new ways of thinking, a new morality, a spiritual awakening, none of them—as Sut Jhally frankly admits—know how to do that. While they recognize what we need, they do not tell us how to achieve it. I suggest that they fail to do so because they do not adequately understand the nature of the economic problem.

Let's now return to the questions posed at the beginning of the book: what exactly is the economic problem? Where does it originate? And how can it be solved?

What *is* the Economic Problem?

In answering the question of the economic problem I depart widely from the standard understanding by stating that the foundation of all economic problems is not money, or credit or balance of payments. It is not about derivatives, deficit spending, or capital gain. It is not about any of the things that economists everywhere busy themselves with. All of our behavior, including our economic behavior, is first and foremost determined by our consciousness. The perception of economic problems and their proposed solutions will thus vary according to the consciousness of the individual. According to the consciousness a person has developed through their conditioning by the *gunas* they will see the economic challenge and its solution differently.

For those heavily influenced by the mode of ignorance the economic problem is how to take complete control of, and best plunder the planet and as many people as possible for unlimited gain, without regard to the possible consequences to anybody or anything, either in the present or the future. Overly influenced by *tamo-guna* such persons are unsatisfied with the world the way it is, and thinking that they can improve it, attempt to remake it to suit their own desires. To that end they unnecessarily neglect the actual economic problem and its simple solutions, and create an artificial economy that can be manipulated according to their whim and advantage. What is useful to them is the fact that an artificial economy has many built-in flaws and problems which can be manipulated to influence and control others. Being overly influenced by *tamo-guna* they use destructive methods to achieve their ends. Thus they impose their ways and means on others all the while engaging in "unbeneficial horrible works meant to destroy the world." It is the economics of ignorance that is responsible for the seemingly limitless exploitation of people, animals and the environment.

For those influenced predominantly by *rajo-guna*, the mode of passion, the economic problem in one word is—more—more products, more production, and more sales. *Rajo-guna* is the source of increasing desires and greed, while stress and distress are its results, however pacified we are by increasing varieties of sense enjoyment. Hence there are never enough resources, time, rest or lasting satisfaction. As greed increases focus shifts to profit at the expense of everything else. It is the economics of *rajo-guna* that is condemned by environmentalists as being insane, since production and consumption cannot expand unlimitedly due to the planet's limited carrying capacity. It is economics under the influence of *rajo-guna* that is responsible for increasing demands on the environment, with attendant destruction of habitat and species loss. It is economics under the influence of *rajo-guna* combined with *tamo-guna* that overwhelms the rejuvenating capacity of the earth resulting in the destruction of the environment. And it is *rajo-guna* and *tamo-guna* together that generates and exacerbates impersonalism and alienation (anomie) as the needs and interests of living, sentient human beings are subordinated to the value, production and accumulation of dead material things.

If we ask "what is the economic problem?" from the perspective of the environment—the seas, the rivers and streams, and the forests—the answer is human consciousness conditioned by extreme passion and ignorance. If we ask the question from the perspective of the unemployed, under-employed, and impoverished billions of people, the problem is also human consciousness conditioned by extreme passion and ignorance. If we ask "what is the economic problem?" from the perspective of the other billions of lost souls who are mislead and misusing their valuable human life in unnecessary, wasteful consumption, and senseless, vicarious entertainment, the answer is again human consciousness conditioned by extreme passion and ignorance. If we ask what the economic problem is from the perspective of just about anybody or anything on the planet the answer is the same: crippled human consciousness conditioned by extreme passion and ignorance that cannot go beyond personal sense gratification and limitless possession in an attempt to increase the sense of "I and mine," all the while leaving the person, the soul, unsatisfied and unfulfilled.

The point that must be made explicitly clear is that there is *no* solution to the economic problem for people too heavily influenced by *rajo-guna* and *tamo-guna*. In other words, the economic problems of modern society can *never* be solved once and for all to everyone's satisfaction by the methods of modern society. We cannot find just an economic solution, nor just a socio-political one (deconstructing the corporation), nor a political one. The solution cannot be had by manipulation of various economic, social and political factors or formulae. We cannot have the kingdom of God without God. Neither can we improve on God's already perfect and complete creation. All attempts to do so will only result in the creation of more problems, ending in frustration and failure. If we want to live happily in this world we must live according to the plan and methods already given to us by God.

The Only Solution

There is just one solution to *all* economic problems, and it can only to be found in the consciousness of goodness. *For persons situated in sattva-guna there is no economic problem*. The fundamental economic question of food, clothing, and shelter is easily dealt with on a small amount of land and with resources available within 10 kilometers of one's home. This is born out by experience all over the world and has been the case for millennia.

There are many people who recoil at the thought of such a simple life, conditioned as they are by the modes of passion and ignorance. They prefer instead to attempt to rectify and restore the economic system through various proposed methods such as returning to a more humane and equitable type of capitalism, or through the use of commodity or gold-backed currencies, or the creation of money by governments directly, or even private currencies created by local groups instead of through privately-owned central banks, and so on. But understanding the influence of the *gunas* on the consciousness of human beings we must recognize that a just and equitable economic system cannot be established or maintained without the sufficient influence of *sattva-guna*. If there is not sufficient *sattva-guna* among the populace they will encroach upon the system and subvert it, as has been done throughout the history of Western civilization. If there is not sufficient *sattva-guna* among government officials the system and laws will not be enforced. Those good people, already having some measure of *sattva* who want to make the world a better place for all, must recognize that without sufficient *sattva* amongst the population there can never be a happy and egalitarian society where everyone's needs are properly met. The only way to do this is through the cultivation of the quality of goodness throughout society.

In *sattvic* societies where living is done on a personal scale there are no gargantuan impacts that overwhelm the environment. Societies that live according to *sattva-guna* do not create environmental problems. There was no environmental problem when the entire world lived predominantly in goodness. They developed only after the industrial revolution, when the modes of passion and ignorance became prominent. Hence, if the better part of the world were to return again to the standard of *sattva-guna*, nature could recuperate and all environmental problems would eventually heal. The forests wouldn't need to be clear cut, there would be no habitat loss to pave over yet another parking lot for the gazillionth Walmart, species wouldn't be lost to extinction, the seas wouldn't be depleted of every living thing, nor the waterways fouled with noxious effluents that externalize the costs of manufacturing to nature.

Being naturally happy in *sattva-guna* people do not require increasingly newer, unnecessary, and even useless varieties of sense gratification at low, low prices that justify slave factories and a global economy. If sufficient numbers of people could be elevated to the level of *sattva-guna* all of the problems wrought by the global economy could be eliminated without the need for meetings of the G20, other international conferences, UN decisions, endless politicking over who benefits and who loses, and so on. Thus the *only* economic solution for those who value the world and all of its life is an economy and social arrangement functioning predominantly under the influence of *sattva-guna*. If we are not to progress further down the abyss of predatory economics, at a minimum, the influence of *sattva* must be greatly increased.

There is a fundamental lesson taught by these facts that must not be overlooked: as we artificially increase our needs and wants beyond the minimum established by *sattva-guna*, we *must* increase the dimensions of the economic problem.

Who is Responsible for the Economic Problems?

The global economic crisis that began developing in 2007 has got people rioting around the world. Blaming their leaders for the crisis, some heads of state have been sacked. After all, who else is there to blame? They are running the show, are they not? Factually, only to a degree. There is much more to the story that can be understood through the philosophy of the *Bhagavad-gita*.

Although the government leaders may be the immediate cause, they are not absolute in their ability to control this world. It is always easy blame somebody else for our problems, and it is far more difficult to see how we are also responsible. The fact is that the universe is in perfect order and not a blade of grass blows in the wind without the sanction of the Supreme Lord. As bad as it might sound, everything is as it should be.

The fact is that all the people of the world, including ourselves, share in the responsibility for the economic calamity that is unfolding. How is that? Due to the *karmic* reactions of our activities. Consider that around the world over 55 *billion* animals are unnecessarily slaughtered every year for food. That's more than 100,000 sentient beings killed *every minute* of every day. However much we may think that this is necessary, it is not. Humans can live quite nicely on fruits, grains, vegetables and dairy—foods that are non-violent and do not involve killing sentient beings. Life-long vegetarians have been shown to be healthier and longer-lived than their meat-eating counterparts. We share in the responsibility whether we wield the knife or not—paying the butcher does not absolve us from being participants in the process. It is foolishness to expect peace in our own lives when we are directly or indirectly responsible for so much violence.

Consider further the tens of millions of children that are murdered by abortion each year. All of these children and animals have a right to life just as much as we do. God loves all of His children equally and has arranged this earth as their field of activities, providing all of them with a body. If, in our ignorance, we interfere with their progressive development by killing them, a *karmic* debt is created. This *karmic* debt must be paid—it is the law of God that "as you sow you shall reap." This negative *karma* therefore comes back to us in many ways: as interpersonal conflicts, as health and psychological problems, as weather extremes such as drought or flood, sometimes as mass violent conflicts such as wars, or as economic problems and calamities, and as other aspects of the three-fold miseries of nature. According to the law of *karma*, the difficulties and suffering wrought by the economic calamities are visited upon us as compensation for our debts.

Being influenced by *tamo-guna* we confuse right and wrong and blindly bring about our own destruction. Without proper spiritual guidance we behave as if life were compartmentalized, and that our behavior in one area has nothing to do with events in another. We think that if we lie, cheat, kill, steal in one area of life that that will not impact other aspects of life. Nothing could be further from the truth. As integrated beings, whatever actions we perform in any area of life affect all others.

Who is responsible for our problems, economic and otherwise? We are. Understanding and accepting that fact allows us to change the future by changing our behavior in the present. By giving up our ill-motivated activities and habits we can avoid the stringent reactions of nature. Acting in the mode of goodness will change the entire landscape of life. If the world returned to the standard of *sattva-guna*, everything, including our economic dealings, will automatically be adjusted to be more pleasant, just as it was before the modes of ignorance became so prominent.

In order to solve the economic question once and for all we must increase the measure of *sattva-guna*. But how do we do that in a world addicted to, and conditioned by, the modes of passion and ignorance? We have the answer to that.

Raising Consciousness Through Prayer

The idea of raising consciousness is generally applied to raising a person's awareness of a specific issue, such as women's issues, environmental issues, etc. This is not the manner in which we use the term here. In our use of the term we are concerned with raising a person's consciousness from the lower modes of passion and ignorance to the mode of goodness.

We may first note that throughout history, prayer has been the main activity of religiously-minded people to help them through times of adversity. In recent times scientific studies have shown that prayer produces better results when performed according to specific methods. The most effective methods of prayer have come from ancient cultures according to researcher and author Greg Braden, who teaches that effective prayer acknowledges in the present what we ask for in the future. This is, according to Vedic teachings, but another application of the law of *karma* in action. Greg Braden:

> Much of our conditioning in western traditions for the last one and one half millennia has invited us to 'ask' that specific circumstances in our world change through divine intervention; that our prayers be answered. In our well-intentioned asking, however, we may unknowingly empower the very conditions that we are praying to change. For example, when we ask, 'Dear God, please let there be peace in the world,' in effect we are stating that peace does not exist in the present. Ancient traditions remind us that prayers of asking are one form of prayer, among other forms, that empower us to find peace in our world through the quality of thought, feeling and emotion that we create in our body. Once we allow the qualities of peace in our mind and fuel our prayer through feelings of peace in our body, the fifth mode of prayer states that the outcome has already happened.

> Quantum science now takes this idea one step further, stating that it is precisely such conditions of feeling that creation responds to, by matching the feeling (prayer) of our inner world with like conditions in our outer world. Though the outcome of our prayer may not yet be apparent in our outer world, we are invited to acknowledge our

communion with creation and live as if our prayer has already been answered.

Through the words of another time, the ancients invited us to embrace our lost mode of prayer as a consciousness that we become, rather than a prescribed form of action that we perform upon occasion. In words that are as simple as they are elegant, we are reminded to be 'surrounded' by the answer to our prayers and 'enveloped' by the conditions that we choose to experience. In the modern idiom, this description suggests to us that to effect change in our world, we are invited to first have the feelings of the change having happened.[14]

As we pray to improve the condition of the world we should therefore create in our mind's eye a peaceful and happy world where activities of passion and ignorance are absent and everyone cooperates together, living happily in *sattva-guna*. Acknowledging this as a reality while giving thanks to the Lord for its accomplishment will help to create those conditions as another type of karmic reaction. You may find it helpful while praying to view a picture that reflects the wholesome goodness that you want to bring about.

We can also take some lessons about prayer from the pages of the *Srimad-Bhagavatam* where the *devas,* or demigods finding themselves in an impossible situation in battling against the demonic forces resorted to prayer. In the eighth canto, fifth chapter we read (8.5.15–31, 48, 49):

> When the *raksasas* severely attacked the demigods in a fight, many of the demigods fell and lost their lives, and could not be revived. Lord Indra, Varuna and the other demigods consulted among themselves, but could find no solution. They then went together to the assembly of Lord Brahma, and informed him of all that had taken place. Brahma saw that the demigods were in an awkward position being bereft of all influence and strength and that the three worlds were consequently devoid of auspiciousness. He could further understand that the demons were flourishing. Lord Brahma, who is above all the demigods and who is most powerful, concentrated his mind on the Supreme Personality of Godhead. Thus being encouraged, he became bright-faced and suggested that they go to the Supreme Lord and take shelter of Him.

> Brahma then said: 'For the Supreme Personality of Godhead there is no one to be killed, no one to be protected, no one to be neglected and no one to be worshiped. Nonetheless, for the sake of creation, maintenance and annihilation according to time, He accepts different

forms as incarnations either in the mode of goodness, the mode of passion or the mode of ignorance (Brahma, Visnu, and Shiva).

'Now is the time to invoke the mode of goodness of the living entities who have accepted material bodies. The mode of goodness is meant to establish the Supreme Lord's rule, which will maintain the existence of the creation. Therefore, this is the opportune moment to take shelter of the Supreme Personality of Godhead. Because He is naturally very kind and dear to those who surrender to Him, He will certainly bestow good fortune upon us. No one can overcome the Supreme Lord's illusory energy [*maya*], which is so strong that it bewilders everyone, making one lose the sense to understand the aim of life. That same *maya*, however, is subdued by the Supreme Personality of Godhead, who rules everyone and who is equally disposed toward all living entities. Let us offer our obeisances unto Him.

'Since our bodies are made of *sattva-guna*, we, the demigods, are internally and externally situated in goodness. All the great saints are also situated in that way. Therefore, if even we cannot understand the Supreme Personality of Godhead, what is to be said of those who are most insignificant in their bodily constitutions, being situated in the modes of passion and ignorance? How can they understand the Lord? Let us offer our respectful obeisances unto Him.

'Activities dedicated to the Supreme Personality of Godhead, even if performed in small measure, never go in vain. The Supreme Personality of Godhead, being the supreme father, is naturally very dear and always ready to act for the good of the living entities. When one pours water on the root of a tree, the trunk and branches of the tree are automatically pleased. Similarly, when one endeavors to please Lord Krishna everyone is served, for the Lord is the Supersoul of everyone.'

We note several items of significance in these quotes. First, the demigods decided to invoke the mode of goodness because it is meant to establish the Supreme Lord's rule, which will maintain the existence of the creation. They therefore decide to take shelter of the Supreme Personality of Godhead. This means to not only appeal to the Lord in prayer, but to follow His instructions given as religious principles. The second item of significance is that by pleasing the Lord everyone automatically becomes pleased. One of the best ways to accomplish both tasks is to execute the *yuga-dharma*, or the religion for the age of Kali.

Raising Consciousness to Sattva-guna

Raising consciousness to *sattva-guna* can be accomplished through several methods. The most obvious is to replace activities of the lower modes with those that are *sattvic*—changing from a meat-centered diet to a vegetarian diet, for example. Another would be to abandon consumption of alcohol and other drugs which are *tamasic* in nature. A third would be to give up all forms of illicit sex, including pornography, prostitution, sexual deviancies, and so on. And a fourth would be to give up gambling—including gambling in the stock market. These activities are considered the pillars of sinful life according to the Vedic texts, and all of them increase *tamo-guna*.

As desirable as it might be to make such changes, the reality is that each of these are behaviors that people are conditioned to think of as pleasurable, and don't want to change. Change may be possible given the right circumstances, but very few people have such ideal circumstances in their everyday lives. What to do? There are alternatives that deal with the consciousness directly, causing behavior to change as a result of a changed consciousness.

Beginning as early as 1963 a number of researchers have sought to establish a method for determining consciousness levels as related to the three modes of material nature.[15] In 1971 several researchers created the *"Guna* Inventory" to assess the relative component of the three *gunas* within personality. This inventory was based on the descriptions of the characteristics of the three *gunas* outlined in the *Bhagavad-gita* and *Samkhya Karika*. Later R. C. Das developed the "Gita Inventory of Personality" or GIN,[16] and in 1998 David Wolf developed the "Vedic Personality Inventory" or VPI, in an attempt to establish the connection between the concepts of Vedic personality and the *gunas*.[17] Each of these methods had some degree of success in terms of being able to relatively "categorize" a person at some combination of the *gunas*, which can be used as a quantitative measure of consciousness.

Beyond just measuring the relative content of *gunas*, there have also been tests carried out to determine whether a persons GIN or VPI could be raised. In 2008 researchers of the Vivekananda Swami Yoga Ashrama carried out a study to determine the influence of the practice of hatha yoga on a person's *gunas* and self esteem, using the GIN and other established psychological tests. Their study demonstrated increased *sattva* and decreased *rajas* as a result of hatha yoga practice, along with increased health and self esteem.

In a randomized, controlled study, Wolf examined the changes in a person's VPI as a result of *mantra* meditation. In his test he created a meaningless mantra to be chanted by one group, as well as a control group who did no chanting, while other test subjects chanted the Hare Krishna *maha-mantra*. Results showed that only the *maha-mantra* group increased *sattva* and decreased *tamas*, with no significant change in *rajas* scores. Other test subjects showed no significant changes in their VPI. The study also showed a significant reduction in stress, anxiety, and depression after a month of chanting *maha-mantra*, 20 minutes daily for four weeks.[18]

Both tests demonstrate that significant changes can be obtained in relatively short periods of time by adopting either *sattvic* or spiritual practices. The practice of chanting the *maha-mantra* however, is not only *sattvic*, but it pleases the Lord and lifts the consciousness of others simultaneously.

Chanting of the Lord's Holy Names is the Doubtless and Fearless Way of Success

The great avatar Sri Chaitanya Mahaprabhu appeared in West Bengal during the 15th century. As the *yuga-avatar,* or incarnation for the age, He introduced the *yuga-dharma*—the chanting of the names of God, specifically the chanting of the Hare Krishna *maha-mantra*, the great chanting for deliverance: *Hare Krishna, Hare Krishna, Krishna Krishna, Hare Hare, Hare Rama, Hare Rama, Rama Rama, Hare Hare.* Due to the degraded conditions during *Kali* the process of worship and self-realization is made extremely simple and easy. It requires no qualification, no cooperation with others, no amount of wealth, not even a long life. Anyone can do it at any time or place. All that is required is a simple willingness to do so. The *Brihan-naradiya Purana* confirms that the chanting of the Lord's names is the *yuga-dharma*:

> In this age of quarrel and hypocrisy the only means of deliverance is chanting of the holy name of the Lord. There is no other way. There is no other way. There is no other way.

Referring to this verse Chaitanya Mahaprabhu explains it further in the *Sri Chaitanya-charitamrita* (Adi 17.22–25):

> In this age of *Kali* there is no other religion but the glorification of the Lord by utterance of His holy name, and that is the injunction of all the revealed scriptures. The holy name of the Lord, the Hare Krishna *maha-mantra*, is the incarnation of Lord Krishna. Simply by chanting the holy name, one associates with the Lord directly. Anyone who does this is certainly delivered. This verse repeats the word *eva* [certainly] three times for emphasis, and it also three times repeats *harer nama* [the holy name of the Lord], just to make people understand. The use of the word *kevala* [only] prohibits all other

processes, such as the cultivation of knowledge, practice of mystic yoga, or performance of austerities and fruitive activities. This verse clearly states that anyone who accepts any other path cannot be delivered. This is the reason for the triple repetition 'nothing else, nothing else, nothing else,' which emphasizes the real process of self-realization.

As Sri Chaitanya states, the Lord is non-different from His name. In this material world we have no experience of an absolute truth. Truth here is relative. But the Vedas give us information that there is another world, a spiritual world that has none of the defects of this world. That spiritual world is known as *Vaikuntha*, the place that is free from anxiety. It is the abode of the almighty Personality of Godhead. That world and the Lord Himself are absolute. That is to say that the Lord is non-different from His place, His pastimes or activities, His form, and His holy name. Because He is absolute all of His transcendental potencies are present in His names, which therefore have all of the potencies of His person. Whatever can be affected by Himself personally can be affected by calling on His name.

The *Srimad-Bhagavatam* explains that the means of deliverance offered in *Kali* not only frees us from the qualities of passion and ignorance, but can lift us up to the very highest state of transcendental consciousness (11.5.31–32, 36, 12.3.51–52):

> In *Kali-yuga* the people worship the Supreme Personality of Godhead by the regulations of the revealed scriptures. In the Age of *Kali*, intelligent persons perform congregational chanting to worship the incarnation of Godhead who constantly sings the name of Krishna (Chaitanya Mahaprabhu). He is Krishna Himself accompanied by His associates, servants, weapons and confidential companions. The sinful life of the living beings results from ignorance. To destroy that ignorance, He has brought various weapons, such as His plenary associates, His devotees and the holy names.

> Those who are advanced and highly qualified and are interested in the essence of life know the good qualities of *Kali-yuga*. Such people worship the Age of *Kali* because in this age one can advance in spiritual knowledge and attain life's goal simply by chanting the *maha-mantra*...My dear King, although *Kali-yuga* is full of faults, there is still one good quality about this age. It is that simply by the chanting of *harinama sankirtana*, the transcendental names of God, one can become free from material bondage and be promoted to the transcendental kingdom. Whatever result was obtained in *Satya-yuga*

by meditating on Visnu, in *Treta yuga* by performing sacrifices and in *Dvapara-yuga* by serving the Lord can also be obtained in *Kali-yuga* simply by chanting the Hare Krsna *maha-mantra*.

One should not think that this chanting or mantra is a sectarian affair, thatVisnu or Krishna is the name of a Hindu God, and is not the name of 'our' God. By definition there can only be one God, however He may be known differently through different religions. The name Krishna means "all attractive." The name Rama means "all powerful." Certainly these are attributes of the Supreme Lord. God is the source of everything, including all beauty, strength, knowledge, and wealth. These all spring directly from Him. Whatever knowledge we experience in this world comes from Him. All power comes only from Him. As does all beauty, and pleasure. Sri Krishna is the reservoir of all pleasure, the reservoir of all beauty, of all knowledge, etc.

In the *Padma Purana* (4.25.8–13) the purificatory effect of the *maha-mantra* is explained:

> The way to attain freedom from this world, even for the most wayward sinners, even all those mean men who are destitute of all good ways of behavior, who are of a wicked mind, who are outcaste, who deceive the world, who are intent upon religious hypocrisy, pride, drinking liquor, and wickedness, who are sinful and cruel, who are interested in another man's wealth, wife and sons, become pure if they resort to the lotus-like feet of Vishnu [Krishna]. The name of Vishnu, sure to succeed here, protects those sinful men who transgress even Him who causes divinity, who give salvation to the immobile beings and the mobile beings. A man who has done all kinds of sins is freed if he resorts to Krishna. If a contemptible, wicked biped would commit sin against Krishna, and by chance resorts to His name, he is emancipated due to the power of the name.

One of the *Gaudiya Vaishnava* saints and predecessor *acharyas*, Rupa Gosvami, writes about the potency of the holy name in his *Padyavali* (Text 29):

> The holy name of Lord Krishna is an attractive feature for many saintly, liberal people. It is the annihilator of all sinful reactions and is so powerful it is readily available to everyone, including the man of the meanest character. The holy name of Krishna is the controller of the opulence of liberation, and it is identical with Krishna. Simply by touching the holy name with one's tongue, immediate effects are produced. The results of chanting the holy name do not depend on anything. Neither is it necessary to qualify oneself in any way for

chanting, by initiation, pious activities or strictly following religious principles. The holy name does not wait for all these activities. It is self-sufficient.

When instructing the grandson of Arjuna, King Pariksit, the speaker of the *Srimad-Bhagavatam*, Sri Shukadeva Gosvami glorifies the holy names of the Lord (2.1.11–13): "O King, constant chanting of the holy name of the Lord after the ways of the great authorities is the doubtless and fearless way of success for all, including those who are free from all material desires, those who are desirous of all material enjoyment, and also those who are self-satisfied by dint of transcendental knowledge. What is the value of a prolonged life which is wasted, inexperienced by years in this world? Better a moment of full consciousness, because that gives one a start in searching after his supreme interest."

This chanting of the Hare Krishna *maha-mantra* is the panacea for the ills and problems that we now face. Not only does the chanter receive benefit from this chanting but every living being on earth benefits. Everyone, including all degraded and sinful persons, and all of the demonic, can be elevated in consciousness, even by the chanting of others. Therefore it is considered the highest welfare activity. Thus the chanting of the Hare Krishna *maha-mantra* can raise everyone from the depths of passion and ignorance to the quality of goodness and beyond. It is a song of love, and this love song is what will save the world. If only a small fraction of the people of the world will take up the chanting, even as little as 3-5 percent, that would be sufficient to affect the needed changes. I have practiced this chanting for more than 35 years as my personal meditation and can offer my own testimony to its effectiveness for giving peace of mind and satisfaction. Beyond that I chant the Hare Krishna *maha-mantra* simply because it makes me happy. I therefore advocate the practice for everyone.[19]

Kirtan and *Japa*

There are two basic styles of chanting according to mood and purpose. *Japa* is done as a meditation with the objective of focusing the mind on the sound vibration of the mantra. Typically a practitioners chant a specific number of mantras as a part of their yoga practice. They find that as they continue their meditation that the mind becomes peaceful and attracted to hearing the holy names. The meditation becomes increasingly blissful and brings with it a inner joy and peacefulness.

Devotional chanting in small groups in a temple or one's home, with music accompaniment is called *kirtan*, and congregational chanting in larger gatherings in more public environments is also called *kirtan*, or *sankirtan*. Traditional accompaniment for both is the harmonium, a small hand-pumped organ along with drums and brass cymbals. The Hare Krishna Movement has earned their moniker because of their *kirtan* on the public streets all around the world.

Kirtan is beginning to achieve more universal appeal in other religious spheres. In late 2008 The *New York Times* featured in the Fashion and Style Section an article acknowledging the increasing popularity of *kirtan*, beyond the followers of eastern religions. Rabbi David Ingber commenting online about the article wrote "[*kirtan* is] creating a new form of American spiritual experience where authentic lineages and practices are refracted through the prism of contemporary America experience. This approach appeals to many of us who seek direct experience, unmediated by theology and dogma and are inclined to believe that beneath the important surface/cultural expressions, religions share a deeper, more fundamental structure that is perennial, universal and immediately transformative...A feature of our synagogue is that we regularly chant "*om shanti*" in addition to "shal-om" or "let there be peace."

The increasing popularity of *kirtan* is also reinforced in Steven Rosen's book *The Yoga of Kirtan* which features interviews with twenty-one singers who are leading the *kirtan* revolution in the West, most of them Westerners who have adopted the practice of chanting as their path of spirituality. *Kirtan* has universal appeal, and directly touches the heart. As Srila Prabhupada has stated, "there is no need for understanding the language of the mantra, nor any need for mental speculation, or intellectual adjustment. It springs automatically from the spiritual platform and thus everyone can take part in it, and dance in ecstasy."

The Highest Truth is Reality Distinguished from Illusion for the Welfare of All

The fact is that the solutions asked for can be achieved very quickly and almost effortlessly. While that may appear to be a very bold and rash statement, the fact of the matter is that most of these problems will simply go away *if we stop creating and compounding them*. The first and most fundamental problem is that our modern society is based on a foundation of illusions, the illusion of "I and mine" being the most prominent. We create problems by attempting to live according to the illusions of modern culture. These illusions are the same false assumptions of traditional economic theory: I am the body, a producing/consuming machine, and I will become fulfilled and happy by enjoying and consuming more. These assumptions are patently false. Moreover they lead people to a life of frustration. Apart from the suffering people experience in this life, future karmic consequences lead to an ever-increasing downward spiral of ignorance, ultimately to be born into lower species of life, where eating, sleeping, mating and defending do indeed constitute the complete description of life's purposes.

The masters of Vedic wisdom, speaking to us from the pages of the *Srimad-Bhagavatam*, demonstrate that they had deliberated, solved and disposed of these questions long ago, and have already given us the solution. *All we have to do is pick it up.* Can we do that? Or will we remain anchored in the material conceptions of "I and mine" and be the victims of our own devices? The practical solution is to give up our illusions and live according to the reality of the genuine, non-sectarian spiritual principles of Vedic wisdom.

The Vedic paradigm offers us a scientific method of reframing our perception, giving us the vantage point we need to understand the problems of the world as well as their solution. It is the new level of thinking that Einstein tells us that we need to solve these difficult problems. One may ask, if the Vedic knowledge is ancient, how it can be seen as a "new" way of thinking? The fact is, unencumbered by the three base modes of material nature, Vedic knowledge allows us to see "outside of the box" of modern thought, which we have demonstrated in our analysis of economics according to the *gunas*. Vedic thought offers an entire culture organized around the concept that human life is meant for spiritual emancipation. That culture includes the ways and means of living in this world that is in harmony with the design of the creation, and demonstrates how to easily solve the economic problem as well as all other problems. The Vedic paradigm, as explained and promulgated by Srila Prabhupada is therefore not simply a "religious" solution but a complete cultural solution. It reaches far beyond what traditional religions can begin to explain or achieve. It *is* Terry's "new economic rationale, or moral argument," *it is* Jhally's "new vision of society," *it is* Thomas Maxwell's "spiritual awakening that promotes a profound sense of earth stewardship," *it is* Havel's "new model of coexistence and transcendence," Schumacher's "metaphysical reconstruction," and Mander's "fundamental philosophical and structural change." It is all of these and more. It offers not only the solution to all of the problems, but the means by which everyone can achieve the personal happiness and satisfaction that they so desire.

While none of us has individually created this civilization, or the problems that the world faces today, it is up to each one of us to work toward the solution. It must be obvious by now that such solutions are not going to come from our political or even religious leaders whose thinking is mired in the materialistic paradigm. This can only be a grass-roots effort with each of us making the necessary changes in our own consciousness, and then living our lives accordingly. The leaders of the world continue to sit on their hands doing nothing, or worse, act as the agents of the wealthy and powerful to clear the way for their global predatory economic practices. Will we then just merrily follow them to perdition?

We as individuals have a free will and we can make our own choices. What each of us chooses to do can be the only thing that will make a difference. On which side of the economic ledger do you want to stand? Will we remain a part of the problem, or become a part of the solution?

The way out of the problem—all of the problems—is to understand and act according to the transcendental realities of our existence. We no longer live in a time of ignorance. We have, or can have, understanding, because the truth has been revealed to us in a manner that leaves no room for doubt. We are not the temporary body, but eternal spiritual beings and it is therefore incumbent upon us to act as such. Our happiness and satisfaction are to be found in developing our relationship of eternal love with the One who will give us unconditional, unending love in return. In this way, and only in this way, can we can simultaneously love His entire creation. If we stubbornly desist and cling to outmoded concepts of self we will only be used for the pleasures of those who have manipulated our world to serve their own narrow and selfish interests. If we similarly continue to focus on our own narrow and selfish material interests, falsely identifying with the temporary material things of this world, we will be (or continue to be) the victims of our very own devices. Rise up mortal man! Realize your transcendence and choose the destiny that will free not only yourself, but all of your brothers and sisters who languish in this prison house called the material world. Throw off the chains that bind you. There is nothing, nothing, holding you back except yourself. There is nothing material that can keep you in the darkness of ignorance if you choose enlightenment. Don't be afraid. Live as you were meant to live and act for the highest achievement that human life has to offer—your spiritual emancipation—and at the same time be genuinely happy in this world.

Please join in the ultimate solution for all the problems of material life, by always chanting the *maha-mantra*:

**Hare Krishna, Hare Krishna, Krishna Krishna, Hare Hare,
Hare Rama, Hare Rama, Rama Rama, Hare Hare**

Om Shri Haraye Namah

Please see Appendix A for detailed instructions of mantra meditation

Part 1 completed
15 March 2009 (Month of Vishnu, 522 Gaurabda era)
Mumbai, India

Appendix A

How to chant the Hare Krishna mantra on beads

Chanting on beads is called *japa*. Meditation on the sound of the mantra is called *japa* meditation. It is the *yuga-dharma*, or method of self-realization in this age.

Follow these simple instructions:

1. Hold the beads in your right hand.

2. There's one head bead, a bead that's bigger than all the rest where the two ends are tied together. Grasp the first bead to one side of the head bead with your right thumb and the middle finger of your right hand, as in the illustration. Your index finger doesn't touch the bead.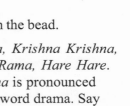

3. Now chant—*Hare Krishna, Hare Krishna, Krishna Krishna, Hare Hare/ Hare Rama, Hare Rama, Rama Rama, Hare Hare*. The word *Hare* is pronounced huh-ray. *Krishna* is pronounced Krish-na. And *Rama* rhymes with the English word drama. Say each syllable of each word as clearly as you can. Concentrate your attention on the sound of each word of the mantra.

4. After you've chanted the complete mantra one time, move your thumb and finger to the next bead and chant the entire mantra again. You may want to roll the bead between your thumb and fingers, or just hold it.

5. Chant on the next bead and then the next, until you have chanted on all 108 beads. You have now reached the other side of the head bead and have completed one full "round."

6. Do not chant on the head bead, and don't cross over it to continue. Instead, turn the whole set of beads around in your hand and chant in the other direction. The last bead of your first round is the first bead for your next round. Chant on this bead, then the next,

and then the next. Stop when you reach the side of the head bead again. Then you'll have completed your second round.

7. While chanting try to focus your mind on the sound of the holy names. This is a meditation. When the mind wanders away patiently bring the focus of attention back to the sound vibration and try to fix it there. After practice it becomes easier. After attaining success in chanting the mind will be spontaneously attracted to the name and will not wander. This is the success that you want to achieve.

8. Continue to reverse directions at the end of each round, and in this way chant your third and fourth rounds, etc. Chant as many rounds as you like, but progress will be quicker if you fix a minimum number of rounds as your daily meditation. You can start with two rounds or even one–but chant regularly, without fail, preferably in the early morning. This regularity of chanting, coupled with a regular program of study of the *Bhagavad-gita*, will enable you to quickly advance along the path to complete spiritual perfection.

9. You can make chanting beads yourself by stringing 108 beads together. Or you may purchase them from a Hare Krishna Temple. Treat your beads respectfully. Don't let them touch the floor, your feet, or any unclean place. Don't take them into the bathroom.

10. You can keep your beads in a bead bag. This holds your beads while you chant, and keeps them clean. When you put your beads away, store them in the bag in a clean place. Don't take your sacred beads into the bathroom, or other unclean places. (If you don't have a bead bag, you can wrap your beads in a clean cloth and keep them in a drawer or on a shelf.)

For further information on chanting the Hare Krishna Mahamantra, please visit my websites: www.spiritual-econ.com/chant and www.dhanesvaradas.com/chant.

Appendix B

The Gitagrad Eco-spiritual Communities

The Gitagrad family of communities are established on the principles that support the development of transcendental consciousness. Modern society is organized for increasing the sense of "I and mine," exactly opposite of pure devotional service. There is a need therefore, to establish refuge from this atheistic materialism where people can live a happy life of Krishna consciousness. This is Gitagrad. At Gitagrad communities the focus of all activity is the satisfaction of the Supreme Lord. Everything is done for His satisfaction without consideration of mundane profit or increasing the consciousness of "mine." Gitagrad communities practice the spiritual economics gift economy, and employ the spiritual relationships of *varnashrama dharma*.

Genuine satisfaction and happiness can be found only by engaging in pure devotional service to the Lord. Following this principal all activity at Gitagrad is performed with the consciousness of giving a specially prepared gift—something that most people only experience at Christmas or birthday celebrations. That gift is first offered to the Lord for His satisfaction, and then, as His *prasadam*, it is distributed to the members of the community and the community's partners (see next appendix). The idea of doing things for the sake of earning money is abandoned, and the residents live as they are meant to live in harmony with God, the earth, and the animals.

Because the focus is removed from producing profit, loving, nurturing, and healing relationships can be established. The earth can be healed from the exploitation of man-made chemicals; the cow can be treated as a family member with love and with affection, and the relationships between the members can be stress free, natural, and mutually supportive. Gitagrad communities thus demonstrate how to heal the world.

Gitagrad communities are organized to be self-sufficient as far as possible, employing the motto "simple living and high thinking." Unnecessary things are eschewed and time thus saved is devoted to spiritual life.

Gitagrad communities are presently forming in E. Europe, but the concepts may be applied anywhere in the world. We invite parties interested in creating a positive future based on spiritual principles to share the developments on our websites at www.gitagrad.org.ua/en, and gitagrad.blogspot.com (English) or www.gitagrad.org.ua (Russian). You may also want to browse www.spiritual-econ.com for additional updates and applications of Spiritual Economics principles to current events. Consider visiting our Gitagrad communities during the summer months on weekends, or stay with us as an intern for a first-hand experience. To do so please contact us through the website.

Appendix C

Partners-for-Life

People Partnering Talents & Resources to Insure a

Healthy and Sustainable Future

The world and the people who live on it are in trouble. Every day more than *one billion* people wake up not knowing where their next meal is going to come from. Every day the industrialized nations of the earth dump more than 2 million tons of pollutants into the air, water and land. Every day both of these statistics are getting worse, and nobody except Srila Prabhupada has offered a genuine and permanent solution to these problems. And Srila Prabhupada's solution is wonderful, because it is not just the solution to these environmental disasters and human despair, *but simultaneously* it is the answer to many more of the world's problems. The solution lies in raising consciousness and working to-gether to establish a *significant alternative* to today's consume and dispose culture. That alternative is established in the Gitagrad communities.

The Gitagrad communities seek to demonstrate the solution to modern man's ills based on a new vision for living. This vision is found in the ancient Vedic scriptures that prescribe a way of life that is in harmony with the other aspects of creation. It provides a place for every living entity based on the premise that the material creation of the Lord is perfect and complete, as enjoined in the *Sri Isopanisad*. It directs people to a God-centered life that allows all of humankind to find their proper place in the creation without conflict or enmity between God and man, man and animal, or man and nature.

Partners–for–Life is a collection of people who feel the need of establishing Gitagrad communities. The Partners are from all over the world, from all walks of life, from all social and cultural strata of society. They are people who can see the severe problems in modern society and want to help change the way the world works. They feel the need for replacing the atheistic, nihilistic and materialistic culture, with a theistic, hope-filled, and spiritual one. Partners–for–Life offers opportunities for everyone to participate according to their own desires and abilities.

The Gift Economy of Spiritual Economics

One of the most significant factors in living according to the precepts of *Bhagavad-gita* is the way in which we practice our economic activity. Lord Krishna very specifically instructs us to do our work in the spirit of devotion and *give* the results to others. Not to sell; not to exchange by barter, but to freely give. Giving of oneself to others creates a joy that is unobtainable in any other way. Giving is the natural function of the soul. Gift economies were formerly found all over the world in *sattvic* cultures. It was done before and it can be done again. Gifting creates a Spiritual Economy that functions for the benefit of all people, and can serve the needs of all people. It is an economy of joy and love. It is an economy which encourages responsibility to the earth, one which eliminates the need or even the desirability of exploitation of others, one which removes the motive for competition, crime, greed, avarice and corruption, one which promotes self-respect and freedom, one which encourages responsibility rather than irresponsible acts, and which demonstrates that we do in fact live in a world of plenty rather than a world of scarcity. The full explanation of Spiritual Economics as a spiritual process and positive alternative to modern predatory economics of tamo-guna is presented in volume two of this work.

In practice Spiritual Economics uses no cash or credit, and no conception of "mine." Spiritual Economics recognizes the Lord's instructions in the Vedic Scriptures that everything in this world is created and therefore owned by the Lord, and that nothing is ours to claim as our own. We come into this world with nothing and we leave with nothing—everything belongs to the creator—the Lord

Himself. As the sons and daughters of the Lord we are all entitled to our quota, a sufficient amount to maintain a simple and healthy life. If we follow this simple guideline there will be enough for every person's need. As Gandhi put it: the Lord provides enough for everyone's need but not for everyone's greed. The results of our work are meant for others, and should be given freely to others. In turn they reciprocate and we accept what we need as their gifts. Thus there is a network of inter-dependence created where we sustain each other through our energies and the gifts of God.

The participants in *daiva-varnashrama* communities are working to establish this Spiritual Economics gift economy to demonstrate how, by living in accordance with the directions of the Lord all mankind can live peacefully and happily. To establish such an economy it is essential that its members produce their life's necessities directly as possible from the land and cow, giving up their consumer status. The consumer culture is finally being recognized in mainstream organizations as the key element destroying the environment. The only way to stop being a consumer is to start being a producer, which is the object of our Gitagrad communities. The participants there do not work for cash income to buy what they need, but produce their needs directly as far as possible.

This method of living generates a number of challenges, the first and foremost being: if one is engaged in a subsistence economy, how can they earn the necessary funds found for those things that they cannot produce? Especially given the limited infrastructure at the beginning? How will the participants get many of the things they need in a world where literally *everything* can only obtained with money? One cannot work for subsistence and for money at the same time.

The problem is solved by people working together to partner their energies and resources to fill the gap. Not everyone who understands the desirability and necessity of Spiritual Economics and the gifting culture will opt out of the cash economy and move to a village. But, understanding the need for establishing the alternative gifting economy they can contribute as they are motivated—with their time and energy, their words, and/or their money. They may make gifts of money, or they may send practical gifts of building materials or other items needed to establish the infrastructure of the community. All of these are needed to achieve the happy, eternally sustainable way of life.

There are three categories of Partners–for–Life: Supporting Partners, Participating Partners, and Practicing Partners.

Supporting Partners

The Supporting Partners participate with their energy in the form of money or their words promoting the establishment of Gitagrad communities. They may offer services in promotion, public relations, and spread the concept of the gift economy as the most practical solution to today's seemingly insoluble economic problems. Supporting partners play a crucial role by providing cash donations greatly needed to establish the self-sufficient infrastructure of the Gitagrad communities. We encourage small contributions of only 1% so as not to create a burden for the Supporting Partners. 1% of a year's income, or of a month's income, or even of a week's income, will be welcomed and appreciated.

All contributions of resources from Supporting Partners will be reciprocated by the Practicing Partners in kind. The Working Partners will gift to the Supporting Partners items which they produce—foodstuffs, woodwork, textiles, and so on. Though they are not producing for the market, they are producing, and will reciprocate as they can with those who have generously assisted them.

Participating Partners

Participating Partners are those who offer their time and energy in lieu of money. This can be done from cities around the world by promoting Spiritual Economics, the gift economy and the Gitagrad communities, and increasing the number of Partners. Or those who live near a Gitagrad community can visit on weekends to lend a hand in planting and harvesting, or in building needed infrastructure.

They may also visit for weekend spiritual retreats that are held several times a year. They can get a taste of simple living while gifting their time and energy, working to establish the community that offers hope for the future.

Practicing Partners

There are many in the world who strongly desire to help establish this vision of a spiritual culture to guide society, and you may be one of them. These people may be seniors who have already given many years of their lives to creating solutions, but still want to do more. And there are many young people who see though the illusions of modern society and its allurements, and are looking for a genuinely alternative way to live.

Wherever they come from, those who are willing to give their life's energy to establishing Gitagrad communities are the Practicing Partners. These people are making a commitment to live a life in which they demonstrate that by living simply and depending on the land and cow, life's demands are minimized making time available for spiritual practices and pursuits. Thus by their practical example they show others how to live a happy life of devotional service.

Whatever your situation, we invite you to join us. Distribute this book in electronic form (www.mediafire.com/spiritualeconomics) or in print (all proceeds from book sales are used to support our Gitagrad communities). Visit our website and download our many lectures, and listen to them to deepen your understanding of the philosophical concepts. Share them with others. Encourage others to become one of our Partners-for-Life.

Creating a cultural alternative is an immense task and it requires the skills, talents and help of many, many people. We invite you to be one of them, and we hope that you will soon visit our Gitagrad community to see firsthand the practice of spiritual economics and *daiva-varnashrama* in action.

You can become one of our Partners by visiting www.gitagrad.org.ua/en and click on the Partners-for-Life link. There you can make your donation in one of two ways:

1. To our Paypal account: gitagrad@gmail.com. To create a Paypal account please go to www.paypal.com. It takes only a few minutes to open an account and it is very convenient for all online transactions.

2. By bank transfer. Please contact us at the above email address for account information.

Appendix D

Further Information About the True Nature of Money & It's Masters

The information presented in these books and videos has nothing to do with conspiracy theories. This information has been well-documented and the serious student can find the primary source material if they so desire. Be warned: because of the nature of money this search can lead to information that will forever change the way that you see the world.

Simple Explanation Videos are posted on my websites:

- www.spiritual-econ.com. Click "Your economic tutorial"
- www.dhanesvaradas.com/econedu

In-Depth Video:

- "The Money Masters" by Bill Still, detailed history of how money has controlled history; can be found on YouTube or ww.themoneymasters.com.

Recommended Economics writers:

- J. W. Smith, Institute for Economic Democracy: www.ied.info
- Ellen Smith, www.webofdebt.com
- Catherine Austin Fitts: http://solari.com
- The recently late Joan Veon: www.womensgroup.org. Google her.

Books:

- Ellen Smith, *The Web of Debt*
- Edward Griffin, *The Creature from Jekyll Island.*
- J.W. Smith, Ph.D., has written very good books explaining an honest money system, free online; more information also, at www.ied.info
- *Billions for the Bankers, Debts for the People* by Sheldon Emry A short, simple, good explanation of how money works, widely available online. i.e., http://www.rense.com/general61/bbil.shtm
- *The Federal Reserve Conspiracy* by Antony C. Sutton
- *Secrets of the Federal Reserve* by Eustace Mullins. This entire book is available free online.

Glossary of Sanskrit Words

Aham mameti—the false conception of "It is Mine"

Ahankara—the false identification of one's self with anything material; false ego

Arjuna—One of the Pandavas, the friend of Lord Krishna and protagonist of the *Bhagavad-gita*; a central figure in the epic history of the Mahabharata

Artha—economic development and/or its results

Asuras—the demonic class of people who do not follow Vedic principles; atheist; one who opposed to the supremacy of the Supreme Personality of Godhead

Atma—the living being, or spirit soul

Atyahara—over collecting of anything, including overeating

Bhagavad-gita—the basic treatise of the spiritual science, or elementary text of Vedic literature explaining God, the living being, time, karma and material nature

Bhaktisiddhanta Saraswati—the spiritual master of A. C. Bhaktivedanta Swami [1874-1937]; a powerful and uncompromising preacher who established the Gaudiya Math, a large spiritual institution to preach the message of Sri Chaitanya Mahaprabhu. He established the principle of yukta-vairagya, the innovative use of material facilities to promote the mission, despite the disapproval of traditionalists who considered them unbefitting of a spiritual renunciate.

Bhaktivinoda Thakura—father of Bhaktisiddhanta Saraswati [1838 1915]. He brought the mission of Lord Chaitanya into the modern age. He was a prolific poet, songwriter and writer who penned dozens of books that are revered by Gaudiya Vaishnavas.

Bhakti-yoga—the yoga of loving devotion to Lord Krishna as taught by the Gaudiya Vaishnavas; the methods of learning and developing love for the Lord.

Bharatvarsa—long ago this was the name of the earth planet. Before the advent of western cultures it referred to India and its surrounding areas. Now refers to India only.

Bhumi—the Earth personified. The personality who is the Earth

Brahma, Lord—one of the three predominating Deities of the material world, in charge of the quality of passion; Brahma is the secondary creator of the material world; he creates after the sum total of ingredients are provided by the Supreme Lord .

Brahmana(s)—the leaders of society; human society is divided into four sections one of which are the brahmanas who are situated in the mode of goodness, and above the modes of passion and ignorance. The natural qualities of the brahmanas are peacefulness, self-control, austerity, purity, tolerance, honesty, knowledge, wisdom and religiousness. Due to these qualities they are able to properly lead and guide the other sections of society.

Chaitanya Charitamrita—the title of the authorized biography of Lord Caitanya Mahaprabhu written in the late sixteenth century and compiled by Srila Krishnadasa Kaviraja Gosvami, presenting the Lord's pastimes and teachings.

Chaitanya Mahaprabhu—The incarnation of Krishna who appeared in Bengal in the fifteenth century to teach yuga-dharma, or the religion of the age, the congregational chanting of Hare Krishna, Hare Krishna, Krishna Krishna, Hare Hare, Hare Rama, Hare Rama, Rama Rama, Hare Hare. He is the most munificent incarnation because he is bestowing freely what no one else has ever given — pure love of God.

Daiva-varnashrama—transcendental varnashrama in which all members act in pure devotional service doing everything for the satisfaction of the Supreme Lord Sri Krishna. daiva-varnashrama is above the gunas and above the principles of varnashrama dharma, but the participants continue to follow the principles of varnashrama dharma for the sake of leading others on the correct path (Bg. 3.25-26)

Dharma—the essential characteristic or nature of anything, but particularly the living being, also called sva-dharma. The Sanskrit term dharma is variously translated as duty, virtue, morality, righteousness, or religion

Gaudiya Vaishnava—any Vaisnava who follows the pure teachings of Lord Caitanya; The name Gaudiya refers to the region of Bengal and Bangladesh. A Vaisnava is a devotee of Visnu or Krishna. Hence, a Gaudiya Vaisnava is a practitioner of the form of Vaisnavism associated with Bengal, as started by Caitanya Mahaprabhu some 500 years ago. See Caitanya Mahaprabhu, Krishna, Vaishnava, Visnu.

Guna(s)—the qualities of material nature, goodness, passion and ignorance, or sattva-guna, rajo-guna and tamo-guna.

Harinam sankirtan—the congregational chanting of the holy names of the Lord, as in the Mahamantra Hare Krishna, Hare Krishna, Krishna Krishna, Hare Hare, Hare Rama, Hare Rama, Rama Rama, Hare Hare.

Jiva—the atma, or spirit soul

Kali-yuga, [the age of Kali]—the age of quarrel and hypocrisy — the last and most degraded age in the progression of ages: Satya, Treta, Dvapara and Kali. It is the present age in which we now live. Through the progression of ages the good qualities of human society are reduced by the tendency of people to engage in sinful activity. Short lives, weak memories, ill-luck, and pervasive disturbances are the qualities of Kali.

Kama—lust

Karma—as used herein: material reaction that accrues specifically because we want the fruits of our action, and consider ourselves to be the doer of activities. The word itself can be understood in four ways: 1. material action performed according to scriptural regulations; 2. action pertaining to the development of the material body; 3. any material action which will incur a subsequent reaction; 4. the material reaction one incurs due to fruitive activities; The law of karma compels a reaction to our activities. For example, if we do good for others we will be blessed with beauty, wealth, education and so on. On the other hand, if we cause pain and suffering to other living beings, we must endure pain and suffering in return; One of the five tattvas, or Vedic ontological truths.

Karma-yoga—activity, or karma, becomes karma yoga when we dovetail our desires and actions to please the Lord, or to serve the purpose of the Lord. The same work when done selflessly for the pleasure of the Lord only is bhakti-yoga, or pure devotional service.

Krishna—the Supreme personality of Godhead; The personality who is God as understood by the Western religious traditions.

Ksatriya(s)—the executive class of the varnashrama social system which divides human society into four social sections Ksatriyas make use of military strength for the purpose of protecting the principles of Vedic culture, the brahmanas, cows, elderly and weak. Their role is to maintain the social order in society by seeing that everyone is properly engaged. These men are influenced predominantly by the mode of passion.

Mahabharata—The epic tale of the history of ancient India. It narrates the struggle between the forces of good and evil, personified by the Pandavas and Kurus respectively.

Maha-mantra—the great chanting for deliverance, the chanting of which is the universal religion for this age of Kali: Hare Krishna, Hare Krishna,

Krishna Krishna, Hare Hare, Hare Rama, Hare Rama, Rama Rama, Hare Hare

Mahaprasadam—the remnants of food offered directly to the Lord according to Vaishnava tradition.

Maya—the illusory energy of the Lord that covers the atma causing him to forget his spiritual identity and identify with his body and possessions.

Modes of (material) nature – see guna(s)

Moksha—liberation into Brahman or Vaikuntha. Traditionally Vedic culture directed human society to find perfection through four stages of development: dharma (religiosity), artha (economic development), kama (sense gratification) and moksha (liberation of the soul from birth and death). This process allowed materially attached people to satisfy their senses in a restricted and religious manner, and finally at the last stage of life to renounce all material things to achieve final liberation. This process has been rendered obsolete by the mercy of Sri Chaitanya Mahaprabhu, who freely bestows love of God directly through sankirtan yajna, the congregational chanting of the holy names of the Lord.

Paramatma—the manifestation of the Lord within the heart of every living being. As the Supersoul he guides the living being to fulfill his previous desires, or to find a bona fide spiritual master when his desire for such arises. As the Supersoul He is the witness to all the activities of the living being.

Paramesvara—Krishna in His feature as the Supreme Controller.

Paratha Sarathi—another name for Sri Krishna, the speaker of *Bhagavad-gita*. This name is given to Him because he is the chariot driver of Paratha (Arjuna).

Prabhupada—the founder-acharya of the International Society of Krishna Consciousness (ISKCON, aka the Hare Krishna Movement). Following the instructions of his guru to preach the philosophy of Sri Chaitanya Mahaprabhu in the English language, he began ISKCON and developed it into a worldwide organization dedicated to delivering the message of Krishna Consciousness.

Praja—dependents

Prasadam—literally: mercy; generally refers to that which is offered to the Lord in sacrifice and afterward accepted by us for our use.

Raja-guna (rajas)—the material quality of passion, the influence of which compels the living beings to fruitive activity.

Raksasa—one of the many human species, they possess superior intelligence and free will, but deny and decry the existence of God. They are considered demonic.

Saktyavesh avatar—an incarnation of the Lord who is empowered for a specific function. Vyasadeva, for example, was empowered to put the Vedic knowledge in writing.

Samsara—the chain of repeated birth and death, sometimes referred to as the wheel of karma, since as a wheel turns any point repeatedly comes again to the same position. Similarly, by the influences of activities in this world a person in a fortunate condition may find themselves degraded to a less pleasant or undesirable position in later births, but again may later find themselves in a favorable or desirable position; or vice versa.

Samskaras—purificatory rites. There are eight samskaras that can be performed for an individual throughout the course of his life. This word also refers to "soul memory" where an individual may faintly remember, or be influenced by, the condition of their previous birth.

Sattva-guna (sattva)—the material quality of goodness which is purifying and elevating.

Satya-yuga—the first of the four ages, aka the Golden Age. During this age there is no influence of ignorance or tamas, all humans are religious, and there is an unbroken reign of peace on the earth.

Shastra—scripture or scriptures. Referring specifically to the Vedic scriptures.

Shiva, Lord—one of the predominating deities of the material world. Shiva is the controller of the mode of ignorance, or tamo-guna.

Shrimatis—those spiritually advanced personalities whom the Lord has blessed to be holders of His wealth.

Shrutis—the spiritually advanced personalities who are fully conversant with the Vedic scriptures and are competent to guide society thereby.

Srimad Bhagavatam—literally, the beautiful story of the personality of Godhead. It is Vyasadeva's commentary on his earlier work, the Vedas, and is considered the essence of all Vedic literature.

Suddha-sattva—pure goodness without any tinge of the qualities of passion or ignorance. The suddha-sattva state is found only in transcendence.

Sudra(s)—one of the four varnas. The sudras are the members of society that do things and get the work done.

Supersoul—see Paramatma

Supreme Personality of Godhead—Krishna as the Supreme personality of all of the manifestation of God in His various incarnations. The Supreme Personality of Godhead is the original manifestation of the Lord and the source of all other manifestations and incarnations.

Tamo-guna (tamas), or the mode of ignorance)—the third quality of the material energy, ignorance. Destruction, ignorance, sloth, madness and illusion are the qualities of tamo-guna.

Vaikuntha—the spiritual realm where there is no influence of time, nor of birth, death, disease or old age. In this transcendental realm the perfected spiritual beings reside in eternal loving union with the Lord.

Vaishnava—a worshiper of Visnu, or Krishna

Vaisya(s)—one of the four varnas, or social orders, of Vedic culture and varnashrama dharma. Vaisyas are those people who are capable of generating valuable and useful artifacts from the natural resources of the earth.

Varnashrama dharma—the social arrangement created by the Lord for the progressive spiritual development of society, organized into four social orders (varnas) and four spiritual orders (ashramas). According to the Vedas, society is not considered human unless the cultural and spiritual principles of varnashrama dharma are followed.

Vedas—the teachings of the Eternal Religion. the Vedas are eternally manifest.

Vishnu, Lord—the Supreme Personality of Godhead. God as understand in the Judeo-Christian traditions.

Vyasadeva—the literary incarnation of the Lord. A Saktyavesh avatar living at the beginning of the age of Kali. He was especially empowered to record Vedic knowledge in writing. He divided the original Veda into four sections—Rig, Yajur, Atarva, and Sama; he later wrote his own commentary on the vast work as the Srimad Bhagavatam. He also wrote the Mahabharata.

Yaksa— one of the many human species, they possess superior intelligence and free will, but deny and decry the existence of God. They are considered demonic.

Yoga—a process by which to connect with and relate to God; literally, union.

Yuga—a great epoch or cycle of time. The material universe passes through four yugas or great ages: Satya, Treta, Dvarpara and Kali. The current age of Kali lasts for 432,000 years of which 5,000 have already passed.

Notes

Preface

[1] E. F. Schumacher, *Small is Beautiful,* Harper Perennial, NY, 1989, p. 79-80.

Introduction

[1] Times Online August 19, 2008, *Credit crunch may take out large US bank warns former IMF chief.* Reference to Prof. Kenneth Rogoff's statement "We're not just going to see mid-sized banks go under in the next few months, we're going to see a whopper, we're going to see a big one — one of the big investment banks or big banks,"

[2] Sept 17, 2008 Reuters News Agency

[3] Mike Shedlock, *Credit Crisis Out of Control- US Government Admission "No One Knows What to Do,'"* MarketOracle.co.uk, Sep 18, 2008

[4] Kevin DeMeritt, "$1.14 Quadrillion in Derivatives – What Goes Up . . . ," Gold-Eagle.com, June 16, 2008. The total GDP of all countries in the world is just $60 trillion. Derivatives are bets, and by leveraging their bets the players have escalated the outstanding liability.

Chapter 1 Understanding Economic Man

[1] Francis Edgeworth, *Mathematical Psychics*

[2] Exactly. Edgeworth's unfounded effort to simplify and mathematically quantify human economic behavior later led to difficult problems after economics gained stature and became the central organizing principle of industrial societies.

[3] Henry George, *Progress and Poverty*, Chapter 26.

[4] Americans like to display their philosophies of life on the bumper of their cars, with an almost endless stream of wit and wisdom (and alas, also vulgarity) for all to see. Some of my other favorites are "Kill Your Television," "Beam me up Scotty, I'm on the wrong planet" and "Eschew Obfuscation."

[5] Amartya Sen, *On Ethics and Economics*, p. 11, Basil Blackwell, New York 1987

[6] Ibid., p. 12

[7] Robert H. Nelson, *Reaching for Heaven on Earth—The Theological Meaning of Economics*, Rowman & Littlefield, Maryland, 1991, p. 6

[8] *Bhagavad-gita As It Is*, 18.22 purport

[9] Understanding according to the gunas is described in the *Bhagavad-gita* texts 18.30-32

[10] www.ndtv.com/convergence/ndtv/story.aspx?id=NEWEN20080041386

[11] Fritjof Capra, *The Web of Life: A New Synthesis of Mind and Matter*, HarperCollins, 1996

279

Chapter 2 Lust, Envy & Greed

[1] From *Essays in Persuasion,* pgs. 371—72, Norton Pub., New York, 1963. Keynes however realized he had misplaced his energies; he later admitted: "I work for a government I despise for ends I think criminal." He did not it seems, have the strength of character to give up his role in that criminal activity.

[2] Conversation June 22, 1976, New Vrindavana

[3] Purport *Srimad Bhagavatam* 2.9.1

[4] A fourth possible voice is the Lord in the heart, or the Supersoul. The subject of the Supersoul is not thoroughly treated in this work and the reader is referred to the *Bhagavad-gita* and *Srimad Bhagavatam.*

[5] By learning that we are the atma, or soul, and by intelligence becoming determined to act in the interests of the soul, one commits himself to following the instructions of a spiritual master. It is the intelligence that directs one to follow the guru's instructions for sense control, while the dictates of the mind encourage sense gratification. If one chooses to follow the instructions of the spiritual master over the mind, then one can learn to bring the mind under the control of the intelligence. The instructions of the spiritual master are the very basis for learning to distinguish between the mind and intelligence. In the case of the *sadhana* (spiritual practices) of bhakti, *japa* meditation gives one regular practice in controlling the restless mind. By this practice the mind can be brought under control, and in that condition, the mind can be the best friend in helping to achieve success in spiritual practice.

[6] The story of the Avanti brahmana from Srimad Bhagavatam Canto 11, chapter 23.

[7] Mount Stuart Elphinstone, *History of India,* 1916 ed.

[8] Anand Parthasarathy, as reported in *The Hindu,* 6-14-2002, and July 2002 in the scientific journal *Sahara.*

[9] Rev. Jabez T. Sunderland, *India in Bondage: Her Right to Freedom,* p. 61

[10] Paul Kennedy, *The Rise and Fall of Great Powers*

[11] Alan Durning, *How Much is Enough?*, World Watch Institute, July 1992, p. 21-22

[12] Thorstein Veblen, *The Theory of the Leisure Class: An Economic Study of Institutions,* Macmillan, New York, 1902, pp. 73, 91.

[13] London's *Financial Times*, February 2001.

[14] Daniel John Zizzo, Oxford University and Andrew Oswald, Warwick University, *Are People Willing to Pay to Reduce Others' Incomes?* January 2000.

[15] Boesky, indicted for insider trading, plea-bargained his way to a rather light sentence of 3.5 years at "Club Fed," a minimal security prison. He was released after only serving two years, and was fined US$100 million, much less than half of the money he made by his illegal activity. Good wages for a two-year stint of relaxation after all that hard work. Milliken, the "Junk Bond King" was indicted on 98 counts of racketeering and fraud in 1989 and given a ten-year sentence, for which only twenty-two months were required. Upon his release, he still had net worth of over $1 billion, despite having paid a total of $900 million in fines and settlements. The message of all this to the public: if you are going to cheat, do it in a BIG way. Crime and greed pay handsomely.

[16] Angus Campbell, *The Sense of Well-being in America: Recent Patterns and Trends* (New York: McGraw-Hill, 1981), cited in Alan Durning's, *How Much Is Enough?*, p. 39; see also Paul Wachtel, *The Poverty of Affluence,* Philadelphia: New Society Publishers, 1989.

[17] *Inside Job*, by Steven Pizzo, Mary Fricker, and Paul Muolo.

[18] A study by petroleum industry analyst Tim Hamilton showed, for example, that from January 17th to April 18th 2005 gasoline prices jumped 65 cents per gallon while refiner profits rose by 61 cents per gallon. From a study released by the Foundation for Taxpayer and Consumer Rights California September 1, 2005

[19] The original statement was made in a phone conversation between David Freeman (Chairman of the California Power Authority) and Kenneth Lay (CEO of Enron) in 2000, according to the statements made by Freeman to the Senate Subcommittee on Consumer Affairs, Foreign Commerce and Tourism in April and May 2002.

[20] *Congestion Manipulation "DeathStar,"* McCullough Research. See www.mresearch.com/pdfs/19.pdf (June 5, 2002).

[21] Letter from David Fabian to Senator Boxer, February 13, 2002, p.1, quoted in Congestion Manipulation "DeathStar," McCullough Research (June 5, 2002) at p.4.

[22] In an interview with *The Los Angeles Times* published 18 May 01.

[23] *Houston Firm Indicted For Role In Energy Crisis: Reliant Energy Accused of Forcing Up Electricity Prices,* by Bob Egelko and Mark Martin; The San Francisco Chronicle, 9 April 2004.

[24] www.frec.gov/industries/electric/indus-act/wec/enron/summary-findings.pdf/

Chapter 3 The Economics of Goodness

[1] Mahabharata, Adi Parva, Chapter 25, translation by Hridayananda Goswami, from http://www.philosophy.ru/library/asiatica/indica/itihasa/mahabharata/eng/01_adi.html

[2] Coblentz, Stanton, *Avarice*, Public Affairs Press, Washington D.C. 1965, p. 5-9

[3] Margaret Mead, *Coming of Age in Samoa*, New York, 1928.

[4] Evan-Prichard, Edward, *The Nuer, A Description of the Modes of Livlihood and Political Institutions of a Nilotic People*, Oxford, 1940. Quoted in Avarice

[5] Sahlins, Marshall, *Stone Age Economics*, Aldine-Atherton, Inc., Chicago 1972

[6] W. H. R. Rivers, *Social Organization*, New York, 1924

[7] Ruth Benedict, *Patterns of Culture*, Boston, 1934. Quoted in *Avarice*

[8] Robert H. Lowie, *Primitive Society*, New York, 1947. Quoted in *Avarice*

[9] Coblentz, Stanton, *ibid.*, pgs. 10-11

[10] Bengal is now politically divided into West Bengal, a state of India; and Bangladesh, East Bengal, an independent nation. The culture of the Gaudiya Vaishnavas in Bangladesh and West Bengal is practically identical. But while Gaudiya Vaishnavism is the predominating culture of Bangladeshi Hindus, in West Bengal the same culture is prominent but not predominating.

[11] Bhakti Vikasa Swami, *Glimpses of Traditional Indian Life*, Bhakti Vikasa Books, Jahangirpura, Gujarat, India, 2004, pgs. 23-25.

[12] While the market in and of itself may function in a sattvic manner, in today's world it is infused with *rajo* and *tamo-guna*, because its chief purpose is to increase wealth. I should add that there are many levels on which the market functions, from the individual shopkeeper to international business now including such organizations as the WTO and IMF. When I say that the market is increasingly influenced by *tamo-guna*, I principally mean that in relationship to global business. The distinctions should become more apparent as the reader progresses through the following chapters.

[13] Karl Polanyi, *The Great Transformation*, Beacon Press, 2001, Chapter 4

[14] Helena Norberg-Hodge, *The Pressure to Modernize and Globalize*, from *Case Against the Global Economy*, p. 41

[15] Ibid.

Chapter 4 The Economics of Passion

[1] Max Weber, *Essays in Sociology*, XII The Protestant Sects and the Spirit of Capitalism, 1906

[2] Weber, ibid., p. 211

[3] R.H. Tawney, *Religion and the Rise of Capitalism,* Peter Smith Publisher, January 1950

[4] R. H. Tawney, ibid. p. 195

[5] Max Weber, *Essays In Sociology*, XII, The Protestant Sects and the Spirit of Capitalism, p. 206.

[6] Max Weber, ibid., p. 206

[7] Max Weber, ibid., p. 206

[8] Max Weber, ibid., p. 211

[9] The rights of commoners in England were established in "Halsbury's Laws"

[10] Peter (Pyotr) Alexeyevich Kropotkin, Chapter 7, *Mutual Aid—A Factor of Evolution*, 1902. From The Project Gutenberg, online.

[11] Neeson, *Commoners: Common Right, Enclosure and Social Change in England, 1700-1820* Cambridge University Press, Cambridge, 1996. This book challenges the view that England had no peasantry or that it had disappeared before industrialization. It documents 18th century debate on the enclosure laws from original sources, and shows that parliamentary enclosure changed social relations, created antagonisms and a pervasive sense of loss on the popular culture. All 18th century commentators saw a relationship between the survival and decline of common right and the nature of social relations in England. Both sides of the published debate agreed that enclosures would end independence, the only argument was whether to welcome or disapprove of the change.

[12] Dr. R.E. Search, *Lincoln: Money Martyred*, Omni Publications, Palmdale, CA

[13] Gustavus Myers, *History of the Great American Fortunes*

[14] Eric Fromm, *The Sane Society*, Holt, Rinehart and Winston, New York, 1955, p. 92

[15] Lev Tolstoy, *What Shall We Do?* 1891

[16] In modern society the concepts of possession and ownership are established in legal terms. Interestingly they are not even mentioned in any of the dozen or more college level economics textbooks that I examined, even though they form the very bedrock of all economic practice. And that is why they are not discussed, for to consider any alternatives would be to undo the very fabric of society in the manner in which the rulers have decided. This omission indicates that the matter is considered to be decisively settled with no further need, or even room, for discussion. It cannot be discussed.

[17] Kropotkin, Mutual Aid, Chapter 7

[18] Thomas R. Berger, *Village Journey – The Report of the Alaska Native Review Commission,* Hill and Wang Publishers, NY 1985. Berger, a Canadian, was hired by The Inuit Circumpolar Conference, an international organization of Eskimos from Alaska, Canada, and Greenland, to investigate the results of the United States Congress' Alaska Native Claims Settlement Act. The World Council of Indigenous Peoples, an international organization of Native peoples co-sponsored his work. Both of the sponsors are affiliated with the United Nations and represent indigenous peoples at meetings of international bodies. His working group was called The Alaska Native Review Commission (ANRC), hence the title of the book.

[19] Unlawful in the sense that it is not provided for in the *Manu Samhita*, the law book for mankind. Manu (from whose name the word "man" is derived) is the demigod who gives the laws for human society.

[20] See J.W. Smith's *Economic Democracy*, especially chapters 2, 4 and 5. Online at www.ied.com.

[21] Karl Polanyi, Henri Pirenne, Eli F. Heckscher, Immanuel Wallerstein, cited by J.W. Smith, *Economic Democracy*, The Institute for Economic Democracy, www.ied.com; from the chapter From Plunder by Raids to Plunder By Trade

[22] Smith, ibid.

[23] Adam Smith, *Wealth of Nations*, Book I, VIII The Wages of Labour. There are so many editions of this classic work that it is almost fruitless to cite page numbers. I have used The Harvard Classics online edition at www.bartleby.com.

[24] Peter Alexeyevich Kropotkin, ibid., Chapter 7

[25] Adam Smith, *ibid*.

[26] from Nehru's *Discovery of India*; quoted in Noam Chomsky, *The Prosperous Few and the Restless Many,* Odonian Press, Berkeley 1993, p. 56;

[27] Lewis Mumford, *Technics and Civilization,* Harcourt Brace Jovanovich, New York 1963, p. 184-85

[28] Hartman and Boyce, *Needless Hunger*, pp. 10, 12

[29] Lynn Townsend White, Jr, The Historical Roots of Our Ecological Crisis, Science, Vol 155 (Number 3767), March 10, 1967, pp 1203-1207. This essay is widely available on the internet.

30 Keith Helmuth, *Earth Process and the Wish for Human Exemption*, p 14-15 Earth Light Magazine Issue #25, Spring 1997

[31] Jeremy Seabrook, Preface, *What Went Wrong? Why Hasn't Having More Made People Happier?* Pantheon Books, NY, 1978

[32] Tawney, R. H., ibid.

Chapter 5 The Economics of Ignorance

[1] *A Simple Example Of Communal Decline - A Letter From South Africa* by Jim Peron, September 1998 http://www.ourcivilisation.com/die.htm

[2] Central Intelligence Agency, "Russia," from *World Factbook 2007*, www.cia.gov

[3] Sabrina Tavernise, *Farms as Business in Russia*, New York Times, 6 November 2001

[4] *Russia has More Than 715,000 Homeless Children*, RIA Novosti - Russian News Agency, 23 February 2006, http://rian.ru; also Carel De Rooy, Children in the Russian Federation, UNICEF, 16 November 2004, www.unicef.org. For the interested reader there are dozens of books that explain the looting of Russia. See for example, *The Godfather of the Kremlin* by Paul Klebnikov.

[5] Joseph Kay, Enron Executives Looted Company Prior To Its Bankruptcy, wsws.org 22 June 2002

[6] David Brinkerhoff reporting for Reuters News Service, 17 June 2002

[7] World's richest 1% own 40% of all wealth, UN report discovers, The Guardian, 6 December 2006.

[8] Ferdinand Lundberg, *The Rich and the Superrich: A Study of Money and Power and Who Really Owns America*, Lyle Stuart Inc., Secaucus, NJ, 1988 p. 15; citing Professor Robert J. Lampman, The Share of Top Wealth-Holders in National Wealth, 1922-1956. A study for the National Bureau of Economic Research, Princeton University Press, Princeton, NJ, 1962.

[9] The World Institute for Development Economics Research of the United Nations, global study, as of the year 2000. From *The Guardian* 6 September 2006.

[10] Lundberg, ibid., p. 206

[11] Report by Northern Illinois University and the Center for Tax and Budget Accountability in Chicago. Online at http://ctba.inspidered.com/home/home.html.

[12] from The Nation, 1 May 2006; citing economist Jared Bernstein of the Economic Policy Institute

[13] www.anitaroddick.com, article posted June 7, 2002

[14] Quoted in *Power & Powerlessness*, Susan Rosenthal, Trafford Publishing, Victoria, BC Canada, p. 9

[15] Phyllis Kilbourn and Marjorie McDermid, *Sexually Exploited Children: Working to Protect and Heal*, MARC, Monrovia, CA 1998, p. 9

[16] Barbara Starr, *Former Soviet Union a Playground for Organized Crime: A Gangster's Paradise*, ABC News, 14 September 1998.

[17] Bill Wallace & Benjamin Pimental, San Jose Women Held After Raid in Sex Slave Cases, San Francisco Chronicle, 13 September 1997

[18] Associated Press article November 14, 2006

[19] Michel Chossudovsky, *America's "War on Terrorism,"* 2nd edition, Global Research, Quebec, 2005

[20] Stephen Lendman, *Reviewing Michel Chossudovsky's 'America's War On Terrorism'*, online at http://www.globalresearch.ca/index.php?context=va&aid=6014

[21] Ibid.

[22] quoted from Jeff Wells, *Yellow Cake and Black Shirts*, in *Rigorous Intuition*, 18 August 2004; http://rigorousintuition.blogspot.com/2004/08/yellow-cake-and-black-shirts.html

[23] "Michael Ledeen," *Disinfopedia*, http://www.sourcewatch.org/wiki.phtml?title=Michael_Ledeen

[24] John Perkins, *Confessions of an Economic Hit Man*, Penguin Books, NY, 2004. Quotation from interview with Amy Goodman's television show *Democracy Now*, 9 November 2004, available online.

[25] *House of Graft: Tracing the Bhutto Millions*, New York Times, Jan 9, 1998

[26] Dr. J. W. Smith explains this process thoroughly in his books available online: www.ied.com.

[27] Davison L. Budhoo, *Enough Is Enough: Dear Mr. Camdessus.. Open Letter of Resignation to the Managing Director of the International Monetary Fund*, New Horizons Press, New York 1990

[28] Davison Budhoo, *IMF/World Bank Wreak Havoc on Third World*, from *50 Years Is Enough: The Case Against the World Bank and the International Monetary Fund*, South End Press, Boston, MA 1994, pgs. 20-24

[29] *New York Times*, March 28, 1999

[30] Susan Meeker-Lowry, Mr. Budhoo's Bombshell: A people's alternative to Structural Adjustment, from Earth Island Journal, September 1995

[31] Michel Chossudovsky, *The Globalization of Poverty and the New World Order*, 2nd ed., Global Research – Center for Research on Globalization, Quebec, Canada, 2003, p. 20

[32] ibid., p. 20

[33] ibid., p. 21

[34] ibid., p. 59

[35] ibid., p. xxi

[36] Michel Chossudovsky, ibid., p. xxii

[37] Michel Chossudovsky, *The Globalization of Poverty*, p. 10, 11

[38] *Joseph Stiglitz, What I learned at the world economic crisis. The Insider, The New Republic April 17, 2000*

[39] Joseph Stiglitz, *Globalization and Its Discontents*, W. W. Norton, N.Y., 2003, p. 206

[40] Joseph Stiglitz, *ibid.*, p. 15

[41] Greg Palast, *The Globalizer Who Came In From the Cold*, The London Observer; 10 October 2001

[42] Milton Friedman, *Capitalism and Freedom*, 2nd edition, Univ. of Chicago Press, Chicago, IL, 1982, p. ix

[43] Robert Harvey, *Chile's Counter-Revolution: The Fight Goes On*, The Economist, 2 February 1980.

[44] A Senate investigation in 1975 into U.S. intervention in Chile disclosed that the CIA had provided training to Pinochet's military for "controlling subversion"; from Covert Action in Chile 1963-1973, U.S. Government Printing Office, December 18, 1975; cited by Klein, p. 92. Kubark Counterintelligence Interrogation, Central Intelligence Agency, July 1963. Excerpts from this manual are available from the National Security Archives at http://www.gwu.edu/~nsarchiv/NSAEBB/ NSAEBB27/01-01.htm

[45] Davison Budhoo, *Enough is Enough*, p. 17-19

[46] Linda McQuaig, *Shooting from the Hippo*; cited by Klein pgs. 257-8.

[47] Davison Budhoo, *Enough Is Enough: Dear Mr. Camdessus . . . Open Letter of Resignation to the Managing Director of the International Monetary Fund*, New Horizons Press, New York, 1990.

[48] Antony Sutton, *Wall Street and the Bolshevik Revolution*, Preface. Published by Buccaneer Books, 1993. The entire book is available online. I have used the online edition which indicates a publishing date of March 1974. The electronic version has no page numbers to refer to, but a simple word search will retrieve the quotes.

[49] Arsene De Goulevitch, *Czarism and the Revolution,* Omni Publications, Hawthorne, California, 1962

[50] Hermann Hagedorn's biography *The Magnate: William Boyce Thompson and His Time (1869-1930)* reproduces a photograph of a cablegram from J.P. Morgan in New York to W. B. Thompson, "Care American Red Cross, Hotel Europe, Petrograd." The cable is date-stamped, showing it was received at Petrograd "8-Dek 1917" (8 December 1917), and reads: "New York Y757/5 24W5 Nil — Your cable second received. We have paid National City Bank one million dollars as instructed — Morgan." Cited in *Wall Street and the Bolshevik Revolution*, Chapter 4.

[51] Knickerbocker Column of the *New York Journal American*, February 3, 1949

[52] Pgs. 1018-19.

[53] Published in 1931, Vol. 1, (p. 371-376). This State Department Report was compiled years later under the Hoover administration after the Bolshevik Revolution had become an accomplished fact. It later disappeared from active circulation, but reproductions of salient passages are presented in Elizabeth Dilling's *The Jewish Religion: Its Influence Today.*

[54] Antony Sutton, *Wall Street and the Bolshevik Revolution*, Chapter XI. Cited in this passage by Sutton: Voline (V.M. Eichenbaum), *Nineteen-Seventeen: The Russian Revolution Betrayed* (New York: Libertarian Book Club, n.d.).

[55] U.S., Senate, Russian Propaganda, hearings before a subcommittee of the Committee on Foreign Relations, 66th Congress, 2d session, 1920, p. 71. Cited in Sutton's *Capitalists and Bolsheviks*, Chapter 9.

[56] Antony Sutton, *Wall Sreet and the Bolshevik Revolution*, Chapter 4.

[57] *Economic Review of the Soviet Union*, April-December 1930, cited in Frank Allan Southard, American Industry in Europe, Ayer Publishing, 1976, p. 204

[58] U.5. State Dept. Decimal File, 861.659 Du Pont de Nemours & Co/5, Du Pont to Secretary of State Stimson, Feb. 19, 1932.

[59] UPI release dated July 17, 1973

[60] *The War Against the Peasantry, 1927–1930 The Tragedy of the Soviet Countryside*, edited by Lynne Viola, et. al., Yale University Press, New Haven, CT, 2005, p. 58

[61] Ibid., p. 13-14

[62] *The Journal of Historical Review*, Summer 1986 (Vol. 6, No. 2), pages 207 - 220.

[63] from the Original Electronic Text at the web site of Revelations from the Russian Archives (Library of Congress).

[64] See J.W. Smith, *Why?*, available online at www.ied.com, and *The Money Masters* video by Bill Still (Appendix D).

Chapter 6 The Economics of Atheism

[1] Herbert A. Simon, *Models of Bounded Rationality*, vol. 2, p. 477, MIT Press, Cambridge, Mass. 1982

[2] Robert Nelson, *Reaching for heaven on earth—the theological meaning of economics*, Rowman & Littlefield Publishers, Lanhans, Maryland, p. 6-7

[3] Robert Nelson, *Economics as religion: from Samuelson to Chicago and Beyond*, Pennsylvania State University Press, University Park, PA 2001

[4] Robert Nelson, *Reaching for heaven on earth—the theological meaning of economics*, p. 7.

His definitions and logic are fatally flawed according to the Vedic worldview. As we have seen in Chap. 1 there are many varieties of rationality according to one's conditioning by the *gunas*. Nelson assumes that his is the only valid understanding, and only his definition of what is rational is actually rational. I quote him here with pertinent sections italicized:

"*Despite the fact that economists often disagree in practice on what is rational, almost all are convinced that the same rationality must apply to all people in all places.Since rationality is the basic term of ethical approval, the whole world therefore is subject to a common moral standard.* As economic truth is spread to all nations, the world can become a single harmonious community bound together by this common rationality and morality.

"*The belief that there is one rationality*, and that all human beings are ultimately guided by the same rational laws, has yet another consequence of fundamental significance: All humanity throughout the world must be created equal. There are none who are so enveloped in darkness that rational behavior is beyond their capacity. In practice, pervasive irrationality may be found in the world, but to behave rationally is potentially within the reach of all mankind."

[5] Ibid., p. 8

[6] *Quest for Enlightenment,* Bhaktivedanta Book Trust, Los Angeles, CA

[7] *Wealth of Nations*, Book IV Chapter II. Of Restraints Upon the Importation from Foreign Countries of Such Goods as Can Be Produced at Home, Adam Smith, 1776.

[8] *Wealth of Nations*, Book IV Chapter II

[9] Svetasvatara Upanisad

[10] Thom Hartmann, To Restore Democracy First Abolish Corporate Personhood,

www.thomhartmann.com, excerpted from his book *Unequal Protection: The Rise of Corporate Dominance and the Theft of Human Rights*, Rodale Books, 2002. He notes in the article that he had found a handwritten note in the J.C. Bancroft Davis collection in the Library of Congress, from Chief Justice Waite to reporter Davis, explicitly stating, "we did not meet the constitutional issues in the case."

[11] Ferdinand Lundberg, op. cit., p.113-114

[12] Russell Mokhiber, *Top 100 Corporate Criminals of the Decade*, 25 June 2007, www.commoncouragepress.com/corporate.html

[13] Anthony Cherniawski, *Global Stock Market Crash Warning and Loss of American Financial Privacy*, 20 June 2008, www. MarketOracle.co.uk

[14] www.cathybuckle.com, 29 June 2008

[15] *Money—Funny, Scary, Paper Money*, Douglas Herman, http://www.strike-the-root.com

[16] in a speech on November 3, 1827, in Philadelphia, PA

[17] John Kenneth Galbraith from *Money: Whence It Came, Where It Went,* Houghton Mifflin, 1975, p.5

[18] Henry Ford, Sr. quoted in *The Federal Reserve Hoax*, Wickliffe B. Vennard, Sr., privately published, 1962.

[19] Joan Veon, *Who Runs The World And Controls The Value Of Assets?* From her website, www.womensgroup.org, 29Jan07.

[20] The Creature from Jekyll Island: A Lecture on the Federal Reserve, http://www.flash.net/~jaybanks/real/g_edward_griffin_-_the_creature_from_jekyll_island.rm

[21] Quoted in *Someone Has to Print the Nation's Money . . . So Why Not Our Government?*, *Monetary Reform Online*, reprinted from *Victoria Times Colonist* October 16, 1996.

[22] Casimir Frank Gierut, *Repeal the Federal Reserve Banks*, p.31

[23] Eustice Mullins, *Secrets of the Federal Reserve*, entire book available online. See especially the Addendum, p. 178. http://www.apfn.org/apfn/Doc/RESERVE.doc.

[24] See for example: private enterprise money: http://www.mind-trek.com/treatise/ecr-pem/index.htm; The Global Village Bank: http://www.gvb.org/; LETS: http://www.u-net.com/gmlets; DigiCash: http://www.digicash.com; grail dollars: http://www.northlink.com/~derekb/; and the book New Money for Healthy Communities, full text online: http://www.well.com/user/cmty/market/money/;

[25] A Ponzi scheme is a n investment swindle in which early investors are paid off with funds raised from later ones.

[26] Milton Friedman, *A Monetary History of the United States*, 1963

[27] Quoted in James Wesley, *Derivatives – The Mystery Man Who'll Break the Global Bank at Monte Carlo*, SurvivalBlog.com; September 2006

[28] Ellen Brown, September 18, 2008, www.webofdebt.com/articles/its_the_derivatives.php

[29] Stan Jonas, *Derivatives Strategy*, April, 1998, p.19

[30] Peter Gowan, *The Global Gamble: Washington's Faustian Bid for World Dominance,* Verso, New York 1999, pg. 96, see also 95-138.

[31] Harry Rositzke, *The CIA's Secret Operations: Espionage, Counterespionage, and Covert Action,* Westview Press, Boulder, Colorado, 1988, p.162.

[32] Robert McChesney, *Communication Revolution - Critical Junctures and the Future of Media*, New Press, 2008

[33] Noam Chomsky, *The Common Good, Odonian Press, 1998*

[34] Edward Herman and Noam Chomsky, *Manufacturing Consent: The Political Economy of the Mass Media*, Pantheon Books, New York, 1988

[35] E.O. Wilson, *Sociobiology: The New Synthesis*, Harvard University Press 1975; as quoted by Lewontin p. 91

[36] Richard Lewontin, *Biology as Ideology*, Harper Perennial, NY, 1993, p. 103

[37] David Korten, *Rights of Money versus Rights of Living Persons*, People-Centered Development Forum, May 1997

Chapter   7 Divine & Demonic Consciousness

[1] C.G. Jung, *The Archetypes and The Collective Unconscious*

[2] Erich Fromm, *The Heart of Man – It's Genius for Good and Evil*, Harper & Rowe, NY, 1964, p. 37

[3] Thousands Exposed to Poison by Government's Aerial Spraying; www.NewsTarget.com/022434.html

[4] See www.lef.org for information regarding CODEX which would harmonize regulations between countries banning dietary supplements and "unapproved" alternative health care regimens. In the United States this effort failed due to vigorous objection from concerned consumers. The Food and Drug Administration whose ostensible purpose is to promote health, has become the agent of the pharmaceutical business and has taken another approach. Their current (2007) plan is to interfere with business and intentionally eliminate dietary supplement companies and increase the price of supplements. Under the guise of a final rule for dietary supplement good manufacturing practices "140 very small [less than 20 employees] and 32 small dietary supplement manufacturers [less than 500 employees] will be at risk of going out of business.... costs per establishment are proportionally higher for very small than for large establishments....The regulatory costs of this final rule will also discourage new small businesses from entering the industry." This FDA rule will directly raise the price of dietary supplements for all consumers. The FDA acknowledges this and says "We expect that the majority of these costs will be borne by consumers of dietary supplements, who will likely respond to the increase in prices by reducing consumption."

[5] See for example http://www.gulfwarvets.com/vexing.htm, and http://www.whale.to/c/cantwell_alan.html

[6] Eric Fromm, *The Heart of Man*, p. 41

[7] Fromm, ibid., p. 40

[8] Scott Peck, ibid., pgs. 68-79, 165

[9] Sam Vaknin, *Malignant Self Love: Narcissism Revisited*, Narcissus Publications, Prague, 2001, p. 10

[10] Fromm, Ibid, pgs. 73-77; quote p. 77

[11] Susan Bridle, *The Seeds of the Self: An Interview with Otto Kernberg*, in the magazine "What Is Enlightenment?", issue 17; http://www.wie.org/j17/kern.asp.

[12] Scott Peck, ibid., p. 76

[13] Martin Buber, *Good and Evil – Two Interpretations*, Chas. Scribner's Sons, NY, 1953, pgs. 139-140

[14] Hervey Cleckley, *The Mask of Sanity – An Attempt to Clarify Some Issues About the So-called Psychopathic Personality*, Published by Emily Cleckley, Augusta, GA 1988, pgs. 10-11

[15] Aubrey Immelman, *Malignant Leadership*, Unit for the Study of Personality in Politics September 17, 2001; http://www.cshsjn.edu/uspp/Research/Malignantleadership.html.

[16] Andrzej Lobaczewski, *Political Ponerology – A Science on the Nature of Evil Adjusted for Political Purposes*, 2nd ed. Red Pill Press, 2007. Quotes are from pgs. 192-193.

[17] Kevin Barrett, *Twilight of the Psychopaths,* The Canadian, online edition: http://www.agoracosmopolitan.com/home/Frontpage/2008/01/02/02073.html

[18] Robert Hare, *Without Conscience: The Disturbing World of the Psychopaths Among Us*, Pocket Books (Simon & Schuster), NY 1988, p. 49, 1.

[19] Robert Hare, ibid., p. 44; quote from Robert Rieber, *The Psychopathy of Everyday Life and the Institutionalization of Distress*. New York: Basic Books. See also Aubrey Immelman, *Inside the Mind of Milosovic*, Unit for the Study of Personality in Politics, 1999; online at www.csbsju.eduluspp/Milosevic/Milosevic.html

[20] Scott Peck, ibid., pgs. 74, 260

[21] Scott Peck, ibid., p. 78

[22] This definition necrophilia from Fromm, ibid., p. 39. For control of others pgs. Fromm 37-60; quote from Hare, ibid., p. 38.

[23] Robert Hare, this and preceding paragraph, pgs. 41, 6, 5; For the characteristics of psychopaths also see Cleckley, especially pgs. 337-364, 387-390.

[24] See Hare pgs. 201-203

[25] William March, *The Bad Seed*, quoted in Hare, ibid.

[26] Scott Peck, ibid., p. 78

[27] Erich Fromm, ibid., p. 73

[28] Erich Fromm, ibid., pgs. 78, 135-139

[29] Erich Fromm, ibid., p.135

[30] Scott Peck, ibid., p. 83

[31] Some will find here striking parallels to the Biblical story of Lucifer and the "fallen angels."

[32] "Confessions of an Economic Hitman," Part 2; http://www.youtube.com/watch?v=GAqG51uwzMI

Chapter 8 Understanding and Solving the Economic Problem

[1] Jerry Mander, and Edward Goldsmith, *The Case Against the Global Economy,* p 391.
[2] From his website at: http://howardrichards.org
[3] This interview appeared in Vol. 2 No. 3 of *Adbusters Quarterly* magazine
[4] American PBS Show "New Dimensions radio for the Deep Ecology"
[5] E. F. Schumacher, *Small is Beautiful*, p. 79, p. 315
[6] Ibid., p. 106
[7] Theodore Roszak, *Where the Wasteland Ends*, p. xxii
[8] American PBS Radio Show "New Dimensions radio for the Deep Ecology"
[9] David Korten, When Corporations Rule the World, p. 9
[10] Ibid., p. 7
[11] Roger Terry, Economic Insanity, p. 142
[12] Integral Spirituality, Deep Science and Ecological Awareness, University of Maryland Ecological Economics website, http://iee.umces.edu/tom/maxwell.html/
[13] His speech was entitled: "The Need for Transcendence in the Postmodern World"
[15] Lakhwinder Raj, *Personality Inventories Based on Trigunas*, http://multani-lakhwinder.blogspot.com/2009/03/personality-inventories-based-on.html
[16] Das, R.C. *Standardization of the Gita Inventory of Personality*; Journal of Indian Psychology, 9 (1&2), 47-54, 1991.
[17] Wolf, D.B., *The Vedic Personality Inventory: A Study of Gunas*; Journal of Indian Psychology, 16 (1), 26-43; 1998.
[18] Dhira Govinda Dasa, *Effects of the Hare Krsna Maha Mantra on Stress, Depression, and the Three Gunas*; http://www.vnn.org/usa/US9907/US10-4267.html, 1999. For the complete study see: www.yedaveda.com.
[19] Even still it is not necessary to chant the name Krishna, but whatever name of God as understood by the worshipper will be fully efficacious and give relief from the miseries resulting from life in the modes of passion and ignorance. If you feel that the names of Krishna and Rama are sectarian then you may chant any other bona fide name of God: Allah, or Jesus for example.

About the Author

Dhanesvara Das is a devotee of Sri Krishna, an American yogi, spiritual teacher/guru, social healer, and social economist. He teaches the gift economy of Spiritual Economics as a way life, to solve the economic and spiritual problem for everyone. He holds a MS degree and formerly worked as a securities broker and licensed securities principal, at which time the concepts of Spiritual Economics were born. Dhanesvara lives at large as a global citizen, traveling, writing, teaching, and building communities in N. America, Europe, the former Soviet Union and India. The primary focus of his activity is the creation of a New Spiritual World Order based on the transcendental Vedic culture. He is the founder and spiritual guide of the "Gitagrad" family of eco-spiritual communities, that function on the basis of *Bhagavad-gita* and Spiritual Economics, and is also the founder of Partners-for-Life, an association of people working together to create a New Spiritual World Order.

Index

Made in the USA
Charleston, SC
24 April 2012